THE LAW AND ECONOMICS OF TAKEOVERS

This book studies takeovers from the acquirer's perspective. More precisely, the book focuses on the legal and regulatory treatment of the risks faced by the acquiring company shareholders in takeovers. The identified risks are categorised into two main groups: first, risks generated by managerial choices and secondly, regulatory or external risks. The analysis considers the legal context but also draws on the economic literature, seeking to map the area under consideration and to suggest measures to improve the present position from the perspectives of both law and economics.

More specifically, the book examines various methods of protecting the acquiring shareholders against value-decreasing or self-interested acquisitions, such as the class transaction rules, fiduciary duties, the acquiring directors' responsibilities under the Takeover Code, the court scheme procedure, the role of institutional shareholders and reward strategies, and methods of making the acquiring directors more exposed to the discipline of the market. The effects of the choice of the medium of payment are also covered.

In addition, it covers the Takeover Code's position with regard to auction situations and seeks to identify ways of addressing the acquiring shareholders' interests in auctions, including auctions where buyout teams or White Knights are involved. Moreover, it identifies situations where deviations from horizontal equality rules, which increase takeover premia, are or should be recognised. To that end the Code's rules on mandatory bids, the determination of the price and the form of payment offered, partial offers and squeeze outs are considered.

The analysis covers both hostile and friendly situations. In relation to hostile takeovers, the legal and regulatory framework of toehold strategies is analysed (the Takeover Code's requirements, the Disclosure Rules and Companies Act disclosure requirements, etc). Market Abuse issues in relation to stake-building are also highlighted. In relation to friendly takeovers the operation of lock-up agreements and break fees (the Takeover Code's requirements, fiduciary law, financial assistance and other contract law concerns), are also explored. Finally, the Takeover Panel's position on adverse changes, pre-conditions and conditions which the offer can be subject to, and the bidder's exposure to Material Adverse Change risk are assessed.

The book discusses developments in the area under consideration including the Takeover Code regime after the implementation of the Takeovers Directive and the Companies Act 2006.

CONTEMPORARY STUDIES IN CORPORATE LAW

Corporate law scholarship has a relatively recent history despite the fact that corporations have existed and been subject to legal regulation for three centuries. The modern flourishing of corporate law scholarship has been matched by some broadening of the field of study to embrace insolvency, corporate finance, corporate governance and regulation of the financial markets. At the same time the intersection between other branches of law such as, for example, labour, contract, criminal law, competition and intellectual property law, and the introduction of new inter-disciplinary methodologies, affords new possibilities for studying the corporation. This series seeks to foster intellectually diverse approaches to thinking about the law and its role, scope and effectiveness in the context of corporate activity. In so doing, the series aims to publish works of high intellectual content and theoretical rigour.

Titles in this series

Working Within Two Kinds of Capitalism: Corporate Governance and Employee Stakeholding: US and EC Perspectives
Irene Lynch Fannon

Contracting with Companies
Andrew Griffiths

The Jurisprudence of the Takeover Panel
Tunde Ogowewo

The Law and Economics of Takeovers

An Acquirer's Perspective

Athanasios Kouloridas

·HART·
PUBLISHING

OXFORD AND PORTLAND, OREGON
2008

Published in North America (US and Canada) by
Hart Publishing
c/o International Specialized Book Services
920 NE 58th Avenue, Suite 300
Portland, OR 97213-3786
USA
Tel: +1 503 287 3093 or toll-free: (1) 800 944 6190
Fax: +1 503 280 8832
E-mail: orders@isbs.com
Website: http://www.isbs.com

Hart Publishing, 16C Worcester Place, OX1 2JW
Telephone: +44 (0)1865 517530 Fax: +44 (0)1865 510710
E-mail: mail@hartpub.co.uk
Website: http://www.hartpub.co.uk

British Library Cataloguing in Publication Data
Data Available

ISBN: 978-1–84113–664–6

Typeset by Hope Services, Abingdon
Printed and bound in Great Britain by
TJ International Ltd, Padstow, Cornwall

Foreword

One of the central curiosities of takeover rules across jurisdictions is that they say virtually nothing about the position of the shareholders of the bidding company or companies. Their focus is on the shareholders of the target company, in relation to both the bidder(s) and the management of the target company. It is well recognised that target company shareholders may incur agency costs in relation to their own company's management and face coordination problems when dealing with the bidder which wishes to acquire their shares – though the answers to the questions of what should be done about these issues are controversial. The lack of attention paid to the agency and other problems of the bidding company's shareholders is surprising, for, as is well known, the empirical data suggests that target company shareholders do well out of takeover bids, whereas the successful bidder (and its shareholders) are much less likely to be financially better off in consequence.

The traditional answer to the point just made is that the agency and other problems of the bidding company's shareholders can be dealt with through the general mechanisms of corporate governance applicable to all major decisions taken by company managements, whether involving a takeover bid or not. One of the several merits of this book is that it subjects that proposition to a wide-ranging appraisal: what are these general mechanisms and how precisely and how well do they function in the case of a decision by a company's management to launch a takeover bid? A second great merit of the book is that it takes the point that it is wholly unrealistic to treat the regulation of the target shareholders' agency and coordination problems as without impact on the issues facing the bidding company's shareholders. Protecting the interests of the target company shareholders may have an adverse impact on the interests of the bidding company's shareholders (for example, by reducing the bidder's freedom of manoeuvre) or, conceivably but less likely, may promote those interests (for example, by discouraging potential bidders from launching an offer). A second main area for study in this book is thus the impact of takeover rules, ostensibly aimed at target shareholder protection, on the interests of the bidder's shareholders, an approach which sheds new light on the operation of those rules.

Third, but certainly not the least among the book's merits, is its conceptual and methodological approach to the above topics. Firmly grounded in the 'law and economics' school of legal analysis, the book uses the insights from that approach to generate novel perspectives on the legal rules in this area – but without losing the lawyer's respect for the legal rules as important things in themselves. The bringing together of the legal literature on control shifts with the writing from the social sciences more broadly is something which the book achieves with sophistication and thoroughness. I am sure that this work of Athanasios Kouloridas will prove a milestone in the takeover literature and I commend it to readers with great enthusiasm.

Paul L Davies
Cassel Professor of Commercial Law at
the London School of Economics and Political Science.

Acknowledgements

I am very grateful to my supervisor, Professor P L Davies, for his invaluable direction and near-inexhaustible patience throughout my research and writing at London School of Economics. I also owe a particular debt to the Hellenic Observatory of the European Institute of London School of Economics and Political Science without which it would not have been possible to have access to up-to-date information in order to transform my dissertation to this book. I am also most grateful to my viva examiners Professors Eva Lomnicka and Eilis Ferran for their invaluable comments and their appreciation of my work in their report that permitted this thesis to be published as a book.

None of the above is, of course, responsible for the defects in this work.

I am thankful to my publisher for his hard work in publishing this book. I also owe an enormous debt to my fiancée Despina for her tolerance, support, encouragement and active assistance in completing this work and to my parents, Stefanos and Despina Kouloridas. I can only express my gratitude to them by the token of dedicating this first book to them.

Athanasios Kouloridas
London, 2007

Table of Contents

List of Figures and Tables

Tables

Figures

Table of Cases

Takeover Panel Adjudications

Table of Statutes and Statutory Instruments

UK Statutes

National Legislation

Austria

Germany

Italy

Switzerland

United States

EC Legislation

Table of Rules of the Takeover Code

Table of FSA Rules

1

Introduction

I THE PARADOX OF CORPORATE ACQUISITIONS AND THE NEED TO SHIFT ATTENTION TO ACQUIRERS

CORPORATE ACQUISITIONS HAVE been, without any doubt, an important, if not dominant, strategy for corporate growth. Despite their popularity though, many acquisitions do not eventually produce the benefits expected or desired for the acquiring firm. More precisely, many empirical studies, both in the United States and the United Kingdom, indicate that while the shareholders of the target company receive on average huge premiums over the market price of their shares, the acquiring firm's market price usually under-performs, not only after failed bids but also after successful takeover offers.

Generally two types of studies exist. First, 'event studies', being the most common in the finance literature, which measure the acquisition's effect on the acquirer, by looking at the acquirer's stock price in the months preceding and following the announcement and the completion of the acquisition.[1] Secondly, there are studies that measure the productivity of the combined firm following the acquisition.[2]

[1] Despite their popularity, event studies can be subject to a number of qualifications. The choice of benchmark and the 'window' or amount of time before and after the acquisition announcement used for computing the acquirer's returns has a great effect on the results. See BS Black, 'Bidder Overpayment' (1989) 41 *Stanford Law Review* 597. For an analytical review of the different forms of benchmarks used by different studies and their effects see A Gregory, 'An Examination of the Long Run Performance of UK Acquiring Firms' (1997) 24(7) and (8) *Journal of Business Finance and Accounting* 971. See also A Agrawal, JF Jaffe and GN Mandelker, 'The Post-Merger Performance of Acquiring Firms; a Re-Examination of an Anomaly' (1992) 47 *Journal of Finance* 1605, E Dimson and P Marsh, 'Event Study Methodologies and the Size Effect' (1986) 17 *Journal of Financial Economics* 113, EF Fama and FK R, 'Multifactor Explanations of Asset Pricing Anomalies' (1996) 50 *Journal of Finance* 131, A Gregory, J Matatko and L Luther, 'Ethical Unit Trust Financial Performance: Small Company Effects and Fund Size Effects' (1997) 24(5) *Journal of Business Finance and Accounting* 703. In addition, it is in the first place difficult to measure the acquirer's gains. See MC Jensen and RS Ruback, 'The Market for Corporate Control' (1983) 11 *Journal of Financial Economics* 5, at 18; R Romano, 'A Guide to Takeovers' in KJ Hopt and E Wymeersch (eds), *European Takeovers: Law and Practice* (London, Butterworths, 1992). What is striking, however, is that no matter what benchmark is used or how the acquirer's profits are calculated, a considerable number of studies seems consistently to report on average negative or at least zero returns for the acquirer's shareholders both in the UK and the US.

[2] The results of those studies are at best inconclusive. The most famous of those studies in the US was written by Caves, who concluded that mergers and acquisitions did not produce

One major study by Gregory,[3] which used a comprehensive list of all successful UK domestic takeovers with a bid value of over £10m for the period 1984–92 as a data set, showed that the post-takeover performance of UK companies undertaking large domestic acquisitions is, on average, negative in the long term, irrespective of the benchmark used. Previous studies also confirm these findings (see table 1).

In the United States, the findings of cumulative studies suggest that acquirers earn, at best, zero abnormal returns.[4] Other individual studies during the 1980s calculate even less favourable returns for the acquirer (see table 2).

Table 1: Acquirers' returns in the UK

Study	*Sample period*	*Sample size*	*Event window*	*Average acquirer CAR*	*Benchmark used*
Firth (1980)[5]	1969–75	434	Announcement month	–6.30%	market model
			+1, +36	0%	market model
Franks and Haris (1989)[6]	1955–85	1048	0, +24 months	–12.60%	market model
				4.50%	CAPM

the expected gains following the completion of the transaction: RE Caves, 'Mergers, Takeovers and Economic Efficiency' (1989) 7 *International Journal of Industrial Organization* 151; Business Week also reported that in a study they conducted with Mercer Consulting of 150 deals valued at $500 m. or more and completed between 1990 and 1995, of the deals analysed, 50% resulted in shareholder losses to the acquirer, judged in relation to Standard & Poor's industrial indexes: 'The Case against Mergers' (1995) (October) *Business Week* 123; Agrawal, Jaffe and Mandelker also found in a sample of 937 mergers and 227 tender offers that market-wide or economy-wide adjustments result in negative returns: Agrawal, Jaffe and Mandelker, 'The Post-Merger Performance of Acquiring Firms; a Re-Examination of an Anomaly' (n 1 above); On the contrary, Healy, Palepu and Ruback found that industry-adjusted post-merger performance was positive: PM Healy, KG Palepu and RS Ruback, 'Does Corporate Performance Improve after Mergers?' (1992) 31 *Journal of Financial Economics* 135; In the UK, both Meeks and Kumar found that over 3 years after merger there was a significant decline in the profitability of the merging firms: GMeeks, *Disappointing Marriage: A Study of the Gains from Mergers* (Cambridge, Cambridge University Press, 1977); M Kumar, *Growth, Acquisitions and Investment* (Cambridge, Cambridge University Press, 1984); On the contrary Cosh et al reported a significant improvement on average in the profitability of their sample over three and five years after merger: A Cosh, A Hughes and A Singh, 'The Causes and Effects of Mergers: An Empirical Investigation for the UK at the Microeconomic Level' in DC Mueller (ed), *The Determinants and Effects of Mergers*, (Cambridge, MA, Oelshlager, Gunn & Hain, 1980).

[3] A Gregory, 'An Examination of the Long Run Performance of UK Acquiring Firms' (1997) 24(7) and(8) *Journal of Business Finance and Accounting* 971.

[4] BS Black, 'Bidder Overpayment' (see n 1 above); WG Schwert, 'Markup Pricing in Mergers and Acquisitions' (1996) 41 *Journal of Financial Economics* 153

[5] M Firth, 'Takeovers, Shareholders' Return and the Theory of the Firm' (1990) (March) *Quarterly Journal of Economics* 225.

[6] JR Franks and RS Harris, 'Shareholder Wealth Effects of Corporate Takeovers: The UK Experience 1955–1985' (1989) 23 *Journal of Financial Economics* 81.

Study	*Sample period*	*Sample size*	*Event window*	*Average acquirer CAR*	*Benchmark used*
Limmack (1991)[7]	1977–86	448	Announcement month	–0.20%	LBS beta market model
			0, +24 months	–4.67%	LBS beta market model
			0, +24 months	–7.43%	zero-one model
			0, +24 months	–14.96%	market model
Sudarsanam, Holl & Salami (1996)[8]	1980–90	429	(–20, +40) days	–4.04%	market model
Gregory, (1997)[9]	1984–92	All successful UK acquisitions over £10 millions	0, +24 months	from –11.82% to –18.01%	6 different models used
Cosh (2001)[10]	1985–96	58 hostile acquisitions	Announcement period	–0,2%	median abnormal returns reported
			0, +4 years	–4,0%	
			Announcement and post takeover period	–7,4%	
		123 friendly takeovers	Announcement period	1.1%	
			0, +4 years	–22.%	
			Announcement and post takeover period	–16.6%	

More astonishingly, even in cases where acquisitions produce positive returns on a combined basis, the results are not positive for the bidder. Weston and Johnson,[11] after having studied a sample of 364 transactions that accounted for almost half of the total M&A values between 1992–98,

[7] RJ Limmack, 'Corporate Mergers and Shareholder Wealth Effects: 1977–1986' (1991) (Summer) *Accounting and Business Research* 239.

[8] PS Sudarsanam, P Holl and A Salami, 'Shareholder Wealth Gains in Mergers: Effect of Synergy and Ownership Structure' (1996) 23(5) and (6) *Journal of Business Finance and Accounting* 673.

[9] Gregory, 'An Examination of the Long Run Performance of UK Acquiring Firms' (n 3 above).

[10] A Cosh, 'The Long-Run Performance of Hostile Takeovers: UK Evidence' (2001) *ESRC Centre for Business Research, University of Cambridge Working Paper No 215.*

[11] JF Weston and BA Johnson, 'What It Takes for a Deal to Win Stock Market Approval' (1999) 34 *Mergers and Acquisitions* 43.

Table 2: Acquirers' returns in the US

Study	*Sample period*	*Sample size*	*Event window*	*Average acquirer CAR*	*Positive acquirer CARs—%*
Asquith, Bruner & Mullins (1987)[12]	1973–83	343	(–1, 0)	–0.85%	41%
Banerjee & Owers (1992)[13]	1978–87	57	(–1, 0)	–3.30%	21%
Bradley, Desai & Kim (1988)[14]	1981–84	52	(–5, +5)	–2.90%	35%
Byrd & Hickman (1993)[15]	1980–87	128	(–1, 0)	–1.20%	33%
Jennings & Mazzeo (1991)[16]	1979–85	352	0 day	–0.80%	37%
Morck, Shleifer & Vishny (1990)[17]	1980–87	172	(–1, +1)	na	37%
Servaes (1991)[18]	1981–87	366	0 to closing	–3.35%	na
Varaiya & Ferris (1987)[19]	1974–83	96	(–1, 0)	–2.15%	na
You, Caves, Smith & Henry (1986)[20]	1975–84	133	(–1, +1)	–1.50%	33%

Source: Part of the table from Gilson and Black, The Law and Finance of Corporate Acquisitions, 2nd edn (1995) 301.

found that, although about two-thirds of the deals had positive returns for the total sample on a combined basis, 51.1 per cent of the deals had negative returns for the buyer, while only 10.7 per cent had negative returns for the target.[21] Moreover, at the same time, the premiums paid over the

[12] P Asquith, R Bruner and D Mullins, *Merger Returns and the Form of Financing* (Boston, Harvard Business School, 1987).

[13] A Banerjee and J Owers, 'Wealth Reduction in White Knight Bids' (1992) *Financial Management* 48.

[14] M Bradley, A Desai and EH Kim, 'Synergistic Gains from Corporate Acquisitions and Their Division between the Stockholders of Target and Acquiring Firms' (1988) 21 *Journal of Financial Economics* 3.

[15] J Byrd and K Hickman, 'Do Outside Directors Monitor Managers?: Evidence from Tender Offer Bids' (1992) 32 *Journal of Financial Economics* 195.

[16] R Jennings and M Mazzeo, 'Stock Price Movements around Acquisition Announcements and Management's Response' (1991) 64 *Journal of Business* 139.

[17] R Morck, A Shleifer and R Vishny, 'Do Managerial Objectives Drive Bad Acquisitions' (1990) 45 *Journal of Finance* 31.

[18] H Servaes, 'Tobin's Q and the Gains from Takeovers' (1991) 46 *Journal of Finance* 409.

[19] N Varaiya and K Ferris, 'Overpayment in Corporate Takeovers: The Winner's Curse' (1987) (May–June) *Financial Analysts' Journal* 64.

[20] V You, RE Caves, M Smith and J Henry, 'Mergers and Bidders' Wealth: Managerial and Strategic Factors' in LG Thomas (ed), *The Economics of Strategic Planning: Essays in Honor of Joel Dean* (Lexington, Lexington Books, 1986).

[21] JF Weston, JA Siu and BA Johnson, *Takeovers, Restructuring & Corporate Governance*, 3rd edn (London, Prentice Hall, 2001) 216.

target's market price ranged from 33 per cent to 44 per cent.[22] Previous studies also report similar findings.[23] Similarly, a study (2003)[24] of the wealth effects of large intra-European takeover bids reports large announcement effects of nine per cent for target firms and a cumulative abnormal return of 23 per cent for the target's shareholders. In contrast, the share price of bidding firms reacts positively with a statistically significant announcement effect of only 0.7 per cent. Moreover, the higher the market-to-book ratio of the target companies the more negative the price reaction of the acquiring firms.[25]

Even in unsuccessful takeovers, the weighted average abnormal returns to shareholders of target firms have been reported to be substantially positive (35.2 per cent),[26] while in other studies, unsuccessful acquirers suffer losses of eight per cent in their market price by the end of 180 trading days after the announcement date.[27]

II SCOPE AND STRUCTURE OF THE THESIS

In view of the above, a substantial number of studies, irrespective of the 'window' period or the benchmark used, or the market they cover, report that target shareholders earn, almost always, significant returns, while acquirers most commonly suffer losses or at best earn, on average, zero or insignificant returns. These results could be attributed to four axiomatic explanations that need to be further explored:

1. Takeovers are not value maximising events for the acquirer and they are pursued for other reasons ('Agency explanation').
2. Takeovers are intended to maximise the value of the acquirer but most of the time, the acquirer's managers tend to overpay and, thus, it is the target shareholders that benefit from the transaction ('Business explanation').
3. Takeovers are intended to maximise the value of the acquirer, but the acquiring company's shareholders can be adversely affected by the financial structure of the acquisition and the choice of the medium of payment ('Financial explanation').

22 *Ibid*, 215.

23 Jensen and Ruback, 'The Market for Corporate Control' (n 1 above) 10; Weston, Siu and Johnson, *Takeovers, Restructuring & Corporate Governance* (n 21 above) 200.

24 M Goergen and L Renneboog, 'Shareholder Wealth Effects of European Domestic and Cross-Border Takeover Bids' (2003) *ECGI Working Paper Series in Finance, Working Paper No 08/2003*.

25 *Ibid*.

26 Jensen and Ruback 'The Market for Corporate Control' (n 1 above) 14.

27 M Bradley, A Desai and EH Kim, 'Synergistic Gains from Corporate Acquisitions and Their Division between the Stockholders of Target and Acquiring Firms' (1988) 21(3) *Journal of Financial Economics*.

4. Takeovers are intended to maximise the combined value of the two firms. However, due to reasons external to the acquirer and, especially, due to regulatory intervention, it is the target shareholders that secure the benefits of the acquisition ('Regulatory explanation').

In other words, looking at the same problem from a different perspective, the bidder's shareholders are exposed to four different risks: first, agency risks; secondly, risks associated with poor managerial choices; thirdly, financial risks; and finally, risks related to regulatory intervention.

The first four chapters of the thesis deal with risks that relate to the first three of the above explanations: agency, business, and financial risks. The common denominator of all those risks is that they are all generated by managerial choices, whether they materialise as acquisitions driven by managerial self-interest, overpayment, dilution or high leverage. Chapter two provides an in-depth analysis of those risks, while chapters three to five focus on the available or potential responses. As those risks are generated by managerial choices, the responses could not logically do other than focus on monitoring and limiting managerial discretion. Accordingly, chapter three reviews the limitations of market-based responses, such as diversification or the operation of the market of corporate control. Chapter four focuses on traditional legal remedies, such as directors' fiduciary duties and other forms of judicial review of the transaction. Chapter five examines corporate governance strategies that seek to increase shareholders' voice in relation to takeovers, either formally (approval rights) or informally (pressure from institutional investors or reward strategies).

Chapters six to nine deal with the fourth set of risks identified above, namely, regulatory or 'external' risks. Since such risks fall outside the control sphere of the acquirer's management, they cannot be effectively addressed by the market and corporate governance strategies, discussed in the previous chapters. Any intervention must be made at a regulatory level and involve a considerable investigation of efficiency and policy issues. Accordingly, this part of the thesis examines how regulation reconciles, or could reconcile, the interests of the shareholders of the target company, on the one hand, and those of the shareholders of the acquiring company, on the other hand.

More precisely, chapters six and seven examine the effects that auctions have on the acquirer and the probability that the latter might lose the target, and identify the available or potential remedies in three different cases: friendly takeovers, hostile takeovers and in cases of Management Buyouts (MBOs) and 'white knights'. Chapter six examines the auction rules of the City Code, the equal information principle among competitive bidders, and the legal and regulatory treatment of stake-building. Chapter seven reviews the legal and regulatory treatment of non-financial and financial exclusivity undertakings given by the target board or major target shareholders.

Chapter eight addresses the risk that the equality rules of the City Code increase takeover premia and result in wealth transfers from the acquirer's shareholders to target shareholders. Chapter eight also seeks to identify situations where deviations from the equality rules of the Takeover Code are necessary to protect the interests of the bidder's shareholders.

Finally, chapter nine deals with cases where the value of the target decreases, after the offer is announced. In such cases, the main problem that arises is who bears the risk of such adverse changes, the acquiring or the target's shareholders (adverse change risk). Hence, the chapter examines the ability of the bidder to make the offer subject to the occurrence or not of certain conditions, such as market adverse change ('MAC') conditions.

2

The Acquiring Shareholders' Internal Risks

I INTRODUCTION

WHILE THERE HAS been much of a controversy[1] over the position of the shareholders in a company,[2] it is not questioned that the relation of managers and shareholders is subject to a number of conflicts of interest[3] (or 'agency costs',[4] as they are commonly named in the economic literature), especially in public companies, due to the high dispersion of the voting capital. Such conflicts of interest can also appear, as it will be argued, within the context of a takeover. The risk faced

[1] J Kay and A Silbestron, 'Corporate Governance' in F Patfield (ed), *National Institute Economic Review*, vol 1995 (London/The Hague/Boston, Kluwer Law International, 1995); P Ireland, I Grigg-Spall and D Kelly, 'The Conceptual Foundations of Moden Company Law' (1987) 14(1) *Journal of Law and Society* 149; P Ireland, 'Company Law and the Myth of Shareholder Ownership' (1999) 62 *Modern Law Review* 32; JE Parkinson, *Corporate Power and Responsibility: Issues in the Theory of Company Law* (Oxford, Clarendon Press, 1993).

[2] Historically, the constitutional position of the shareholders, and a widespread assumption of many corporate governance specialists and practitioners has been that the shareholders are the owners of the company. The shareholder/ownership model was the basis for Berle and Means' research on the separation of ownership and control; see AA Berle and GC Means, *The Modern Corporation and Private Property (Revised Edition)* (New York, Harcourt, Brace & World Inc, 1968); see E Ferran, *Company Law and Corporate Finance* (New York, Oxford University Press, 1999) 25. This assumption continues to command support in practice. The Cadbury report in dealing with the accountability of the board to shareholders, states that the shareholders as owners of the company elect the directors to run the business on their behalf and hold them accountable for their progress. Cadbury Committee 1992 *The Financial Aspects of Corporate Governance (Report of the Cadbury Committee)* para 6.1.

[3] The issue appeared for the first time in the essay of Berle and Means, *The Modern Corporation and Private Property (Revised Edition)* (n 2 above), and then it has been carried forward by different scholars.

[4] From an economic perspective, whenever an individual depends upon another, an agency relationship arises. An agent as self-interested actor will always be tempted to put his own interests ahead of those of his principal. When he in fact does so, he imposes agency costs on the principal. These are composed of the value of the output, lost from the agent's self-serving conduct, together with the costs the principal incurs in attempting to regulate such behaviour. The economic theory of agency costs must be distinguished from the legal concept of agency. Under English law corporate managers are not agents of the shareholders. B Cheffins, *Company Law: Theory, Structure, and Operation* (Oxford/New York, Oxford University Press, 1997) 45 and MC Jensen and WH Meckling, 'Theory of the Firm: Managerial Behavior, Agency Costs and Ownership Structure' (1976) 3 *Journal of Financial Economics* 305.

by shareholders in such situations is called agency risk and represents a loss of value to the shareholders.

In addition, the fact that the shareholders are the ultimate beneficiaries of the decisions that the managers take means that there may be circumstances where, although managers seek to increase their shareholders' wealth, their decisions are not sound, in business terms. As a result, the acquirer's shareholders bear the risk that a potential acquisition will not produce the synergies that their managers expect (synergy risk), or that their managers will pay more than they should, resulting in a wealth transfer to the target shareholders (overpayment risk). It will be further examined below under what circumstances each of those risks arises.

Finally, shareholders may be affected by the financial structure of the acquisition. The choice of the medium of payment and the financial structure of the acquisition affects the financial exposure of the bidder and the distribution of the acquisition profits and consequently the value of the bidder's shares.

II AGENCY RISK

The thesis that takeovers involve significant conflicts of interest between the acquirer's managers and shareholders is not unquestionable. Some commentators argue that the decision to implement an acquisition policy involves no more of a conflict between the interests of shareholders and managers than any other business decision.[5] However, two important things differentiate corporate acquisitions from other less acute types of investments: their size and the ability to concentrate the effect of a time-consuming internal growth strategy on a small amount of time. Both these characteristics cause more acute problems to the acquirer's shareholders than any other incremental types of business decisions.

An internal growth strategy, due to the time involved, can show some weaknesses that can serve as alert devices for shareholders. Furthermore, in internal growth strategies, cash outflows are spread over time, leaving an opportunity for the acquirer to forego future expenditures if, at an early stage, things go wrong. Moreover, both the size and the short time-scale of a takeover may demand heavy and abnormal issuance of debt or equity. On the other hand, internal growth projects can be more easily financed through internally-generated cash flows. Finally, managers who tend to make bad or self-interested corporate acquisitions will not be disciplined

[5] DR Fischel, 'Efficient Capital Market Theory, the Market of Corporate Control and the Regulation of Cash Tender Offers.' (1978) 57 *Texas Law Review* 43. Bradley on the other hand argues in favour of the existence of significant agency costs related to corporate acquisitions. See C Bradley, 'Corporate Control: Markets and Rules' (1990) 53 *Modern Law Review* 170.

by the market of corporate control if they put themselves beyond its reach by increasing the size or the debt of the firm and thus making it more difficult to be acquired.[6]

There are a number of explanations why managers may pursue an acquisition that is not profitable for their shareholders. However, the underlying rationales for such an acquisition can be classified into two main categories:

Incentives for return maximisation, either in the form of compensation or in the form of prestige or visibility.

Incentives for risk reduction and increase in managers' job security.

A Incentives for Return Maximisation

(i) *Empire Building*

It is documented that managers may seek to maximise growth of the firm's size, even at the expense of their shareholders' welfare.[7] This means that corporate acquisitions may be motivated by managerial desire to increase the size of the firm.[8] Such behaviour is usually described as 'empire-building' syndrome.[9] There are a number of reasons why managers may engage in such an activity:

— First, by increasing the size of their company, managers enjoy corresponding increases in prestige and compensation,[10] either because executive compensation tends to be a fraction of the firm's size (eg in

[6] See below.

[7] W Baumol, *Business Behavior, Value and Growth* (New York, Harcourt, Brace and World, 1967); JK Galbraith, *The New Industrial State* (James Madison Library in American Politics, 1967); O Williamson, *Corporate Control and Business Behavior: An Inquiry into the Effects of Organization Form on Enterprise Behavior* (Englewood Cliffs, NJ, Prentice Hall, 1970); O Williamson, *The Economics of Discretionary Behavior: Managerial Objectives in a Theory of the Firm*; R Maris, *The Economic Theory of Managerial Capitalism*; R Maris and DC Mueller, 'The Corporation Competition and the Invisible Hand' (1980) 18 *Economic Literature* 32.

[8] For a comprehensive statement of this thesis see all of the above (n 7). See also RJ Gilson and BS Black, *The Law and Finance of Corporate Acquisitions*, 2nd edn (Westbury, New York, The foundation Press Inc, 1995) 354; PS Sudarsanam, *The Essence of Mergers and Acquisitions* (London, Prentice Hall, 1995) 16; GW Dent, 'Unprofitable Mergers: Toward a Market-Based Legal Response' (1986) 80 *Northwestern University Law Review* 777 at 781; MP Hechler, 'Towards a More Balanced Treatment of Bidder and Target Shareholders' (1997) 2 and 3 *Columbia Business Law Review* 319 at 320; and JC Coffee, 'Regulating the Market for Corporate Control: A Critical Assessment of the Tender Offer's Role in Corporate Governance' (1984) 84 *Columbia Law Review* 1145.

[9] The term was first used by Gordon: RA Gordon, *Business Leadership in the Large Corporation* (Washington DC, Brookings Institution, 1945) 305–12.

[10] Large acquisitions tend to be followed by an increase in the cash compensation of the acquirer's CEO. See A Khorana and M Zenner, (1998) Executive Compensation of Large Acquirors in the 1980s, 4 *Journal of Corporate Finance* 209; Gilson and Black, *The Law and Finance of Corporate Acquisitions* (n 8 above).

terms of assets or sales),[11] or due to the greater complexity of larger firms.[12]

— Moreover, acquisitions, especially when they are financed by share issues, dilute the shareholdings of large investors. This means less control over managers' decisions and thus, greater managerial autonomy.
— Managers may also seek growth through acquisitions in order to expand their opportunities for promotion inside the firm.[13]
— Finally, corporate acquisitions justify the continuous employment of those who are acquisition specialists.

(ii) *Free Cash Flows*

The 'empire-building' syndrome is not the only explanation for acquisitions driven by managers' incentives to maximise their returns. 'Free cash flow' theory provides a similar explanation. According to Jensen,

> free cash flow is cash flow in excess of that required to fund all projects that have positive net present values when discounted at the relevant cost of capital.[14]

In other words, free cash flow is the operating cash flow after the firm has met its tax liabilities and after it has financed all currently available investment opportunities.[15] In this case, the management of a firm should distribute those profits to shareholders through dividend payments or by buying back equity capital. However, self-motivated managers who, as seen above, prefer growth to profits, have strong incentives to invest that cash or any form of excess borrowing capacity in less than optimal acquisitions. For the acquiring shareholders, such an activity constitutes, at minimum, an asset substitution, but it may also be accompanied with negative market price reactions.

The theory continues that, because the bidder is using funds that could not be used for projects with positive returns, it overpays by definition for the acquisition and thereby transfers most or even all of the gains to target

[11] MC Jensen, 'Agency Costs of Free Cash Flow, Corporate Finance and Takeovers' (1986) 76 *The American Economic Review* (Papers and Proceedings of the Ninety-Eighth Annual Meeting of the American Economic Association) 323; K Murphy, 'Corporate Performance and Managerial Remuneration: An Empirical Analysis' (1985) 7 *Journal of Accounting and Economics* 11.

[12] Sudarsanam, *The Essence of Mergers and Acquisitions* (n 8 above) 16.

[13] That is further magnified by the tendency of certain firms to reward middle range managers through promotion rather than yearly bonuses. Jensen, 'Agency Costs of Free Cash Flow, Corporate Finance and Takeovers' (n 11 above) 323; G Baker, *Incentives in Hierarchies: Promotions, Bonuses and Monitoring* (Boston, MA, Harvard Business School, 1987).

[14] Jensen, 'Agency Costs of Free Cash Flow, Corporate Finance and Takeovers' (n 11 above).

[15] Jensen, 'Agency Costs of Free Cash Flow, Corporate Finance and Takeovers' (n 11 above); MC Jensen, 'The Takeover Controversy: Analysis and Evidence' in JC Coffee, L Lowenstein and S Rose-Ackerman (eds), *Knights Raiders & Targets: The Impact of the Hostile Takeover* (Oxford, Oxford University Press, 1988).

shareholders. Since free cash flows describe a situation where no value-adding projects are present, they cannot by definition be used for synergistic value-adding acquisitions in the same market in which the acquirer trades. Accordingly, in order to use such cash flows, self-motivated managers are more likely to pursue diversifying acquisitions.[16] Free cash flows are more likely to occur in mature industries with large cash flows, such as the oil, tobacco, or broadcasting industries. These predictions have been validated by some empirical evidence.[17] Overall, the problem for the acquirer's shareholders is how to motivate managers to

> disgorge the excess cash rather than invest it at below the cost of capital or waste it on organisational inefficiencies.[18]

This suggests that it is not a free cash flow, but the improper use of free cash flows that constitutes a manifestation of the conflict of interest between managers and shareholders.

B Incentives for Risk Reduction

(i) *Diversification*

Diversification can reduce the fluctuations in a firm's earning stream. The inclusion of diversification, as a motive for acquisitions, among agency costs implies two different claims: first, that diversification at a firm level does not benefit the acquirer's shareholders; and secondly, that managers have reasons to prefer diversification at a firm level.[19]

The crux of the first claim is whether the firm can diversify more cheaply than its shareholders.[20] If this is the case, then diversification at a firm level can benefit the acquirer's shareholders because it minimises transaction

[16] See below.

[17] In the 1960s, many firms in tobacco, food, oil and other mature industries diversified into unrelated businesses with poor subsequent financial performance and value decline for their shareholders. (Sudarsanam, *The Essence of Mergers and Acquisitions* (n 8 above); Jensen, 'The Takeover Controversy: Analysis and Evidence' (n 15 above)). Palepu also finds strong evidence consistent with the free cash flow theory of corporate acquisitions: KG Palepu, 'Predicting Takeover Targets: A Methodological and Empirical Analysis.' (1986) 8 *Journal of Accounting and Economics* 3. Romano also supports that several studies provide evidence consistent with the free cash flow explanation. (R Romano, 'A Guide to Takeovers' in KJ Hopt and E Wymeersch (eds), *European Takeovers: Law and Practice* (London, Butterworths, 1992)). See for example H Servaes, 'Tobin's Q and the Gains from Takeovers' (1991) 46 *Journal of Finance* 409; L Lang, R Stulz and RA Walking, 'Managerial Performance, Tobin's Q and the Gains from Successful Tender Offers.' (1989) 24 *Journal of Financial Economics* 137). ML Mitchell and K Lehn, 'Do Bad Bidders Become Good Targets?' (1990) 98(2) *Journal of Political Economy* 372.

[18] Jensen 'Agency Costs of Free Cash Flow, Corporate Finance and Takeovers' (n 11 above).

[19] See the analysis that follows.

[20] Gilson and Black, *The Law and Finance of Corporate Acquisitions* (n 8 above) 317.

costs. However, it seems likely that the transaction costs of diversification are lower for shareholders than for firms, since differences in commission for owning a diversified portfolio, instead of buying a bundle of shares in one firm, are small. In addition, small investors can diversify by buying a mutual fund at the cost of paying the fund's fees. For large institutional investors the transaction costs of diversification are even smaller. If one takes into consideration the 'market impact' of block purchases, large institutional investors have even less transaction costs when diversifying than when buying a block of shares in a single firm. Contrary to diversification at an individual level, a corporate acquisition typically involves substantial transaction costs and takes place at a substantial premium over the target's market price.

A more promising argument for firm-level diversification is not that corporate acquisitions involve less transaction costs, but that managers can pick better investments than individual shareholders.[21] However, there is no apparent reason why managers take better diversifying decisions than shareholders. Managers of firms that operate in a specific market do not necessarily have better information over different markets, while conglomerate managers lack the specialised knowledge of specific markets from which shareholders could benefit. In that sense, diversification at a firm level does not minimise information asymmetries and accordingly, it cannot be argued that it results in better investment decisions. Moreover, what conglomerate managers can probably do, according to the above argument, is already achieved by mutual funds and insurance managers. Finally, diversification does not necessarily involve a highly sophisticated and informed choice based on inside information. Passive diversification can perform equally or even better than an active one. It is argued that a portfolio based on just the five biggest firms of the FTSE index may produce equal or better returns than a highly sophisticated portfolio, which may reflect personal aptitudes towards risk or preferences for certain markets or firms.[22]

The fallacy of the argument that capital allocation decisions within the firm are better than that of external markets, is also revealed by a number of empirical studies that unanimously prove the failure of the 'US conglomerate experiment' during the merger waive of the '60s.[23] Not only did

[21] See O Williamson, 'The Modern Corporation: Origins, Evolution, Attributes' (1981) 19 *Journal of Economic Literature* 1537; M Salter and W Weinhold, *Diversification through Acquisition* (New York, The Free Press (Macmillan Inc 1979) 65–78.

[22] See RH Mason and M Goudzwaard, 'Performance of Conglomerate Firms: A Portfolio Approach'(1976) 31 *Journal of Finance* 39. Their results indicate that randomly selected portfolios offered superior earnings performance and shareholder returns than did the conglomerates in their sample. The statistical tests indicated that the portfolios outperformed the conglomerates in terms of both rates of return on assets and accumulated stockholder wealth over the 1962 to 1967 period.

[23] For a comprehensive review of those studies see Gilson and Black, *The Law and Finance of Corporate Acquisitions* (n 8 above) 339.

the conglomerate firms under-perform relatively to the prior target's performance,[24] but also, after a short period of time, many of the conglomerate acquisitions were followed by divestitures.[25] In addition, other studies find significantly higher returns for bidders in cases where there is a relationship between the acquirer's and the target's businesses, than in cases of conglomerate mergers, where the returns appear to be negative.[26]

In view of the above, it is clear that diversifying acquisitions do not benefit the acquirer's shareholders. However, managers value diversification at a firm level. The risk preferences of managers and shareholders differ.[27] While shareholders can diversify their investment across firms, managers' wealth is tied up to their firm and they cannot diversify. Managers over-invest in their firms mainly for three reasons: first, they depend on their firm for their income; secondly, they may have developed firm-specific human capital that is not valued at the same level outside the firm; and finally, they may have increased investment in their firm in cases they receive compensation in the form of equity.[28] Hence, managers are subject to firm-specific 'employment' risk.[29] Since financial distress or firm failure may have greater impact on the firm's managers than the shareholders, the former have more incentive to attempt diversification at a firm level. There is empirical evidence to support the argument that diversifying acquisitions can involve agency costs.[30]

[24] See D Ravenscraft and FM Scherer, *Mergers, Sell-Offs & Economic Efficiency* (Washington DC, Brookings Institution, 1987).

[25] *Ibid*; M Porter, 'From Competitive Advantage to Corporate Strategy' (1987) *Harvard Business Review* 43, (74% of unrelated units bought by sample of 33 active acquirers between 1950 and 1980 had been sold off by 1986); S Kaplan and M Weisbach, 'The Success of Acquisitions: Evidence from Divestitures' (1992) 47 *Journal of Finance* 107, (60% of unrelated large acquisitions between 1971 and 1982 had been divested by 1989).

[26] For the UK see A Gregory, 'An Examination of the Long Run Performance of UK Acquiring Firms' (1997) 24(7) and (8) *Journal of Business Finance and Accounting* 971 at 996. For intra-European takeovers see M Goergen and L Renneboog, 'Shareholder Wealth Effects of European Domestic and Cross-Border Takeover Bids' (2003) *ECGI Working Paper Series in Finance, Working Paper No 08/2003*. For the US, K Scanlon, J Trifts and R Pettway, 'Impacts of Relative Size and Industrial Relatedness on Returns to Shareholders of Acquiring Firms' (1989) 12 *Journal of Financial Research* 103; N Sicherman and R Pettway, 'Acquisitions of Divested Assets and Shareholders' Wealth' (1987) 42 *Journal of Finance* 1261; BE Eckbo, 'Mergers and the Market Concentration Doctrine: Evidence from the Capital Market' (1985) 58 *Journal of Business* 325.

[27] Romano, 'A Guide to Takeovers' (n 17 above).

[28] Sudarsanam, *The Essence of Mergers and Acquisitions* (n 8 above).

[29] Y Amihud and B Lev, 'Risk Reduction as a Managerial Motive for Conglomerate Mergers' (1981) 12 *Bell Journal of Economics* 605.

[30] *Ibid*. Lloyd, Hand and Modani confirm Amihud and Lev's findings—namely, that manager-controlled firms make more diversifying acquisitions, controlling for firm size. W Lloyd, J Hand and N Modani, 'The Effect of the Degree of Ownership Control on Firm Diversification, Market Value and Merger Activity' (1987) 15 *Journal of Business Research* 303. Davis, Diekmann and Tinsley also find a significant negative correlation between ownership concentration and frequency of unrelated acquisitions. G Davis, K Diekmann and C Tinsley, 'The Decline and Fall of the Conglomerate Firm in the 1980s: The Deinstitutionalization of an Organizational Form' (1994) 59(4) *American Sociological Review* 547.

(ii) *Takeover Deterrence*

In addition to diversification, another motivation for self-interested acquisitions is the managers' desire to secure their jobs by protecting their company from being target in the future. Overall, acquisitions to increase firm size are consistent with managerial defensive motives. Increased firm size makes a potential takeover more expensive and complicated, and increases the likelihood of antitrust or other regulatory obstacles.[31] Defence motives are also consistent with the free cash flow theory: managers can repel potential bidders by replacing excess cash or borrowing capacity with debt. Despite the confinements of the City Code on Takeovers and Mergers ('the Takeover Code'),[32] and especially the application of rule 21, which asks for the previous approval of the shareholders before any frustrating action can be taken by their managers,[33] it is very difficult to identify precisely a defensive acquisition, since takeover deterrence motives may be well hidden at the time of the announcement of the takeover.

Overall, much empirical data suggests that self-motivated acquisitions occur frequently, and the above analysis suggests that considerable conflicts of interest exist not only between the target's managers and their shareholders but also between the shareholders of the acquiring company and their managers.

III FINANCIAL RISK

Irrespective of the motives or the business merits of an acquisition, its financial structure may have a considerable impact on the acquiring shareholders. Both debt and equity can carry advantages and disadvantages. The acquiring shareholders' main concerns are dilution risk for share exchange offers and high leverage for debt-financed acquisitions.

[31] Dent, 'Unprofitable Mergers: Toward a Market-Based Legal Response' (n 8 above) 781.

[32] See old Principle 3 of the Takeover Code, effective from the transposition of the Directive on Takeover Bids (2004/25/EC), new Principle 3 and restated r 21.1.

[33] Rule 21.1 of the Takeover Code, 8th edn (London, Panel on Takeovers and Mergers, May 2006). Especially after the implementation of the Takeover Directive, r 21.1 was widened to cover the wording of Art 9 of the Directive, which is wider than r 21 before the implementation. Art 9 requires the consent of target company shareholders for any frustrating action, whereas r 21.1 contained a list of specific actions in respect of which shareholders' consent was required. Rule 21.1 has now been widened to require shareholders' consent in general meeting for 'any action which may result in any offer or bona fide possible offer being frustrated or in shareholders being denied the opportunity to decide on its merits' and the list of particular actions that requires shareholders' consent is now included by way of a non-exhaustive list of examples.

A Debt-financed Acquisitions and Financial Leverage

Debt-financed acquisitions increase the bidder's financial leverage. Financial leverage is the level of debt in relation to equity in a firm's capital structure. The more long-term debt the firm has, the greater the financial leverage is.[34]

Leverage is a double-edge sword for the acquiring company shareholders. On the one hand, in good days, debt is less expensive than equity, since, due to the seniority of debt over equity, creditors can settle with a lower return. On the other hand, contrary to equity, debt has servicing costs that are not contingent on the profitability of the acquisition. This makes debt a higher-risk source of financing for the bidder.

This trade-off between a risk increase and higher expected earnings in debt-financed takeovers is called, in the finance literature, 'EPS (earnings per share) variability'.[35] In other words, a leveraged cash offer increases the variance of post acquisition earnings. This can be graphically presented[36] as follows:

Figure 1: Variance of post acquisition earnings

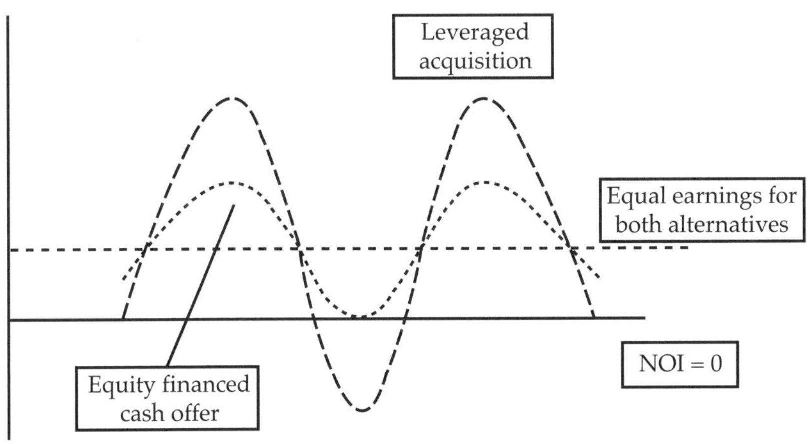

The above EPS variability may make the acquirer more vulnerable to liquidity or operating and market risks, but when not extremely volatile it can be addressed by proper planning, evergreen facilities,[37] the securing

[34] J Downes and JE Goodman, *Barron's Dictionary of Finance and Investment Terms*, 5th edn (New York, Barron's Educational Series, 1998) 322.

[35] H Levy and M Sarnat, *Capital Investment and Financial Decisions* (London, Prentice Hall, 1990) 373.

[36] *Ibid*, 378.

[37] Short-term loans that can be continuously renewed rather than repaid.

of mezzanine finance, or interest cap rates. In addition, since the acquiring company shareholders can diversify their investment in the bidder, they may prefer a higher earning but also a higher risk deal than to share the risk and the gains with the target shareholders. Finally, debt can also operate as a mechanism to control the quality of the proposed acquisition. Debt financing is accompanied with a thorough examination of the viability of the proposed business plan and many post-acquisition performance covenants. The fact that, in the long term, monitoring the performance of the bidder is necessary for the creditors to secure the repayment of their loans, makes it very likely that the acquirer's shareholders will also benefit from free riding on the control that the creditors provide.[38]

However, some acquisitions and acquisition plans are accompanied with extremely high levels of debt that alter the internal structure of the company and affect dividend payments and the risk of the shareholders' investment. In the past, many such acquisition programs eventually collapsed causing substantial losses to shareholders, despite the fact that they were based on business plans and operating cash flows projections which were thoroughly examined by the financiers, and their financing was accompanied with a considerable number of sophisticated safeguards. The end of the 1980s witnessed a number of such failures after an epic growth in high-yield bond financing or 'junk bonds', as they have been more commonly known.[39] Examples not associated with the use of the notorious junk bonds can be found even today in the telecommunications market, none more notable than that of NTL, a couple of years ago, whose leveraged acquisition program ended in tears for its shareholders, leaving their investment at zero value. Such leveraged acquisitions may impose substantial risks to the acquiring company shareholders' returns. This is especially the case in a modern corporation, where shareholders' returns are not regarded as the only mandate that managers have to serve.

B Equity Financed Acquisitions—Dilution Risk and Market Volatility

Contrary to debt financing, equity financed acquisitions carry a different type of risk. Any new issue of securities inherently carries a dilution risk for the present owners of the same class. The bigger the size of a shareholder's participation in the acquirer, the greater the risk of dilution. In corporate acquisitions this problem is further magnified by a number of reasons.

[38] This is one of the main arguments in Jensen's free cash flow theory, where he argues that free cash flows may be a solution to agency risk, on the grounds that the substitution of cash with debt increases the creditors' control over the management of the bidder. See Jensen, 'Agency Costs of Free Cash Flow, Corporate Finance and Takeovers' (n 11 above).

[39] See BJ Baskin and JPJ Miranti, *A History of Corporate Finance*, 1st edn (New York, Cambridge University Press, 1997) 293 and RA Brealey and SC Myers, *Principles of Corporate Finance*, 6th edn (London, McGraw-Hill, 1999) 538.

First, as will be further analysed in chapter four, in the case of share exchange offers, unlike other increases in share capital, the present shareholders in the acquirer are not typically awarded any pre-emptive rights.[40] Secondly, dilution may be magnified by management's overpayment, in which case the overbidding premium is translated into a bigger portion of the combined entity being transferred to the target shareholders.[41] The form, also, of the share exchange offer can affect the acquiring shareholders' exposure to volatility and, as a result, to dilution.

There are mainly two ways in which the acquirer can structure a share exchange offer having either a fixed number of shares offered or a fixed value. In the first case, the bidder agrees to exchange the target's shares for a fixed number of shares in the bidder. Accordingly, the number of shares needed to complete the acquisition, depending on acceptances of course, is known and fixed. In the second case, however, the bidder agrees to exchange the target shares not on a number-by-number basis but on the basis of the value that the target's and the bidder's shares have at the closing date of the offer. As a result, the proportional ownership in the combined company is left in doubt until the closing date. Both deals produce dilution risk for the acquiring company shareholders with one difference. In a fixed-value share offer the dilution risk is double: if the acquirer's market price decreases during the period of the offer the bidder is obliged to offer more shares to reach the offer price.

As many commentators argue, the volatility and dilution effect is also aggravated by the signals that share offers send to the market. The inherent difficulties in appreciating the intrinsic value of a share offer as compared with cash, and information asymmetries make markets more reluctant to accept positively share exchange offers. A number of commentators have identified the risk that the market will assess that the reason why the bidder is offering shares could be, among others, that the market price of the bidder's securities is higher than the acquiring managers' assessment of their intrinsic value. The argument continues that, since the market cannot have the same information about the acquirer as its managers have, market participants will appreciate share offers as incentives to offer overvalued equity, and as a result, they will revise their estimate of the value of the bidder.[42]

[40] See however about the Pre-emption Guidelines in ch 5.

[41] See below under 'Overpayment Risk'. This is not the same as 'synergy risk', in which case the risk is divided between the acquiring and target shareholders. See below.

[42] RG Hansen, 'A Theory for the Choice of Exchange Medium in Mergers and Acquisitions' (1987) 60(1) *Journal of Business* 75; JW Wansley, WR Lane and HC Yang, 'Gains to Bidder Firms in Cash and Securities Transactions' (1987) 22 *The Financial Review* 403; JR Franks, RS Harrisand C Mayer, 'Means of Payment in Takeovers: Results for the United Kingdom and the United States' in AJ Auerbach (ed), *Corporate Takeovers: Causes and Consequences* (Chicago/London, University of Chicago Press, 1988); BE Eckbo, RM Giammarino and RL Heinkel, 'Asymmetric Information and the Medium of Exchange in Takeovers: Theory and Tests' (1990) 3(4)*Review of Financial Studies* 651; CW Smith, 'Raising

Other commentators argue that market psychology is negatively affected by the risk-sharing effect of share offers. It is true that in share offers the acquiring shareholders share with their target counterparts not only the benefits of the acquisition but also the risks.[43] However, this may be appreciated by the market as a lack of confidence for the value of the acquisition.[44] One way to mitigate the above market distrust and increase the confidence of the market in the bidder is to offer higher premia. However, this leads to overpayment, further dilution and subsequently further decline in the bidder's market price.

Apart from market psychology, risk-sharing through equity-financed acquisitions, contrary to leverage, imposes its own costs, in that the enlarged shareholder base can lead to a decline in the bidder's EPS,[45] resulting in further discounts in the bidder's market price. In addition, risk sharing is not always beneficial to the acquiring shareholders in liquid markets, since they can protect themselves against increased business risk in a less expensive way by diversifying their portfolio.[46] A considerable number of empirical studies consistently show that market reaction to share offers is more negative than to cash offers.[47] This by itself is a major concern for the acquiring shareholders.

Capital: Theory and Evidence' in JM Stern and DH Chew (eds), *The Revolution of Corporate Finance*, 3rd edn (Oxford, Blackwell Publishers, 1997).

[43] For an illustrative example of such risk sharing see below under 'Synergy Risk'.

[44] Franks, Harris and Mayer 'Means of Payment in Takeovers: Results for the United Kingdom and the United States' (n 42 above); MJ Fishman, 'Pre-emptive Bidding and the Role of the Medium of Exchange in Acquisitions' (1989) 44(1) *Journal of Finance* 41 who argues that cash is associated with high value bids.

[45] Earnings per Share ratio.

[46] See above the discussion about diversification at a firm level.

[47] Gregory finds that the 24-month API (abnormal price index) is not significantly different from zero for cash offers, but significantly negative for share offers (–11.57%): Gregory, 'An Examination of the Long Run Performance of UK Acquiring Firms' (n 26 above). Travlos also reports similar findings, for a shorter however 'window': NG Travlos, 'Corporate Takeover Bids, Methods of Payment, and Bidding Firms' Stock Returns' (1987) 42(4) *Journal of Finance* 943. See also P Asquith, and D Mullins 1986 'Equity Issues and Offering Dilution', *Journal of Financial Economics* 15; R Masulis and A N Korwar 1986 'Seasoned Equity Offerings: An Empirical Investigation' *Journal of Financial Economics* 15 and WH Mikkelson and MM Partch, 'The Valuation Effects of Security Offerings and the Issuance Process' (1986) 15 *Journal of Financial Economics*, have all found that the market value of existing equity drops on the announcement of a new issue of common stock; MA Hitt, JS Harrison and RD Ireland, *Mergers and Acquisitions, a Guide to Creating Value for Shareholders* (Oxford, Oxford University Press, 2001) 36; Wansley, Lane and Yang, 'Gains to Bidder Firms in Cash and Securities Transactions' (n 42 above). A study by P Asquith, R Bruner and D Mullins (Asquith, Bruner and Mullins, *Merger Returns and the Form of Financing* (Boston, Harvard Business School, 1987)) focused directly on the impact of the form of financing on merger returns. Using a sample of 343 US mergers over the years 1975–83, the authors found that equity offers were associated with significantly smaller returns to both bidders and targets than were cash offers. For targets the month 0 results for the United Kingdom, for example, indicate targets with all-cash offers earned a 30.2% bid premium, which was significantly higher than the 15.1% premium in all-equity offers. The differences in the United States are even more dramatic, with the month 0 premium of 11.1% in all-equity offers being less than half the all-cash figure of 25.4%. In all-cash offers the bidders earned significantly positive gains of 2% in

IV BUSINESS RISK

As mentioned at the beginning of this chapter, the separation of ownership and control and the diffused corporate ownership of public companies do not necessarily lead only to loyalty problems. There are cases where managers' decisions are just not sound in business terms. There are plenty of reasons for the poor analysis of a decision to acquire a target, like exuberance of the synergetic value of the deal or enthusiasm built up during the excitement of negotiations or just simply because the acquirer's managers pay too much for the acquisition. More precisely, the acquirer's shareholders bear the risk that a potential acquisition will not produce the synergies that their managers expect (synergy risk), or that their managers will pay more than they should, resulting in wealth transfer towards the target shareholders (overpayment risk).

A Synergy Risk

Ex ante, the true value of a potential target in a takeover, especially a hostile one, is usually unknown. A bidder has to make an initial estimate of the target's value, relying, in the case of hostile bids, only on information available in the market. However, assessing the current value of the target is not the only problem that the acquirer faces. Value is not, by any means, a static figure. Since a firm's value includes future cash flows and expectations, the value of the target is different in the hands of the acquirer, due to the synergies associated with the combination of the two firms (economies of scope, economies of scale, etc). So, an additional problem for the bidder is to assess the synergies expected and their probability of being materialised. Synergy value is the main reason why the acquiring company pays a premium over the target's market price, for it anticipates that it can put the target assets to a better use. The profit for the combined entities, after the acquisition premium, is called synergy value added,[48] and the risk whether this will materialise or not, is called synergy risk.

month 0. In contrast, in all-equity offers they experienced a significant loss of 0.9%; Franks, Harris and Mayer, 'Means of Payment in Takeovers: Results for the United Kingdom and the United States' (n 42 above) 223, report significant losses to bidder shareholders in equity acquisitions.

Other research also demonstrates that target firm shareholders earn larger returns when receiving cash payments rather than when shares are offered. See Y Huang and RA Walking, 'Target Abnormal Returns Associated with Acquisition Announcements: Payment, Acquisition Form and Managerial Resistance' (1987) 19 *Journal of Financial Economics* 329; KJ Martin, 'The Method of Payment in Corporate Acquisitions, Investment Opportunities, and Management Ownership' (1996) 51(4) *Journal of Finance* 1227.

48 A Rappaport and ML Sirower, 'Stock or Cash? The Trade-Offs for Buyers and Sellers in Mergers and Acquisitions' *Harvard Business Review on Mergers and Acquisitions* (Boston, Harvard Business School Press, 2001).

The magnitude of the synergy risk to the acquirer's shareholders is subject to the size of the acquisition premium offered and the relative size of the target to the acquirer.[49] In other words, as Rappaport argues, the relative magnitude of synergy risk to the acquiring shareholders' wealth is the premium percentage multiplied by the relative size of the seller to the buyer.[50] This index is also called shareholder value at risk ('SVAR').[51] For example, in an acquisition, where the premium paid is 30 percent over the market price and the target is half the size of the bidder, 15 percent of the acquiring shareholder's wealth is at risk.

However, the portion of the synergy risk that the acquirer's shareholders bear is also subject to the medium of payment. While in cash transactions, the acquiring shareholders bear the entire risk, in stock transactions the synergy risk is shared between the acquiring and target shareholders, in proportion to the percentage that each will own in the combined company.[52] Thus in the previous example, when target shareholders own 30 percent of the combined company, the SVAR for the acquirer's shareholders reduces from 15 to 10 percent.[53] This means that, if no synergies materialise, the acquiring company shareholders will lose 15 percent of their shares' value in a cash offer, while in a share offer only 10 percent is at risk. Overall, the synergy risk that the acquiring shareholders face is subject to three parameters: the synergy premium, the relative value of the target and the medium of payment used.

B Overpayment Risk

Central to the above analysis was the assumption that the premium paid reflects the synergistic value that the target carries for the acquirer. However, it may be the case that the premium paid is too big to be compensated by the synergies expected. In such cases, the synergy value added will be negative. The offer price then appears to have another component: a premium over the synergy value of the target, which is an overpayment premium.

There are a number of reasons why the acquirer's managers may overpay. Error is one of those reasons; conflicts of interest can be another.[54] In the case of a contested bid, for example, managers may stay in the bidding too long just because they perceive dropping out as a failure. It has also

[49] *Ibid*, 94.

[50] A Rappaport and ML Sirower, 'Stock or Cash?' (n 48 above) 93.

[51] A Rappaport and ML Sirower, 'Stock or Cash?' (n 48 above).

[52] A Rappaport and ML Sirower, 'Stock or Cash?' (n 48 above) 92.

[53] In any case it should be noted that SVAR is a rather conservative measure of risk and it assumes that the value of the target is safe and only the premium is at risk. A Rappaport and ML Sirower, 'Stock or Cash? (n 48 above) 96.

[54] See above.

been argued that overpayment would incur even if conflicts of interest or negligence did not exist, just because of managers' optimism. The bidder may overestimate its assessment of the attainable level of operating income, the target's future growth rate or even its integration skills. A relatively small error in any of these estimates can lead to a substantial overestimate of the target's value.

'Winners' curse', a situation inherent in any auction, is another reason for overpayment. The bidder, even if he accurately estimates value on average, is more likely to win the bidding when he overestimates an asset's true value, and thus tends to overpay on average.[55] There is no need for the existence of an actual competitive bidder. It is enough that there are potential bidders, waiting to free ride on the acquirer's identification of the target and make a higher offer if the first bid is too low.[56] In this context, overpayment serves as a deterrence mechanism for potential contesters.[57]

Exaggerated defence documents and profit forecasts issued by the target may also induce the bidder to offer a higher price. This could lead to a situation where the bidder, once acquiring control, realises that the documents published were deceitful or, at least, negligently prepared. The problem is further amplified by the fact that the normal answer to this problem, namely suing the target, is not a practical option since now the target is a wholly-owned subsidiary of the bidder.

Overpayment harms the acquirer's shareholders, who bear exclusively the whole risk irrespective of the medium of payment used. In cash offers, overpayment takes the form of a cash outflow that equals the difference between the premium paid and the synergy value added. Even in share offers when the acquisition premium has already covered all synergy gains, overpayment will result to a transfer of wealth to target shareholders, which equals the percentage of ownership in the acquirer that the overpayment premium reflects. This can be illustrated through the following example:

The acquirer, A, has a current market value of £60m. The target company, T, has a current market value of £40m. As independent companies, they value £100m together, while the synergies of the combination increase the total value to £120m. The acquirer decides to make a share offer of £50m for the target. Accordingly, target shareholders receive a premium of 20 percent in the form of shares in the acquirer, and end up with almost 42 percent of the combined entity.[58] Assume now that the acquirer

[55] BS Black, 'Bidder Overpayment' (1989) 41 *Stanford Law Review* 597.

[56] *Ibid*; Gilson and Black, *The Law and Finance of Corporate Acquisitions* (n 8 above).

[57] MJ Fishman, 'A Theory of Preemptive Takeover Bidding' (1988) 19 *Rand Journal of Economics* 88; Fishman 'Pre-emptive Bidding and the Role of the Medium of Exchange in Acquisitions' (n 44 above) 41; B Chowdhry and V Nanda, 'The Strategic Role of Debt in Takeover Contests' (1993) 48(2) *The Journal of FinanceEuropean Financial Management* 423.

[58] $X = 50 \div 120 \times 100 = 41.6$.

makes a share offer of £60m for the target. The T shareholders will own now the 50 percent of the combined company. Moreover, since the synergy gains of the combination are valued at £20m the acquirer's shareholders do not receive any of the synergy gains.

Things are even worse if the acquirer's managers make an offer for £65m. Since the synergy gains are valued at £20m and the premium paid is £25m, the acquirer overpays £5m. The fact that the total value of A and T is £120m means that £5m are deducted from the acquirer's value, in the form of transfer of an ownership percentage that reflects those £5m of overpayment. The acquiring shareholders will now own less than 50 percent of the combined entity. In addition, the intrinsic value of the acquirer in the combined entity reduces from £60m to £55m, and under the efficient market hypothesis, it translates to a decline in the market price of the acquirer of 8.3 percent.[59]

Overall, overpayment represents a wealth transfer from the acquiring shareholders to the target shareholders, either in the form of an initial cash outflow or in the form of an additional percentage in the combined entity. In addition, assuming that the market is efficient, it penalises the bidder who overpays. Hence, overpayment is accompanied with decreases in the acquirer's market price. The relation between synergy and overpayment risk is illustrated graphically in Figure 2.

V CONCLUSION

This chapter identified three types of internal risks for the acquiring company shareholders: agency, financial and business risks. First of all, the chapter submitted the view that corporate acquisitions, as more acute types of business decisions, involve significant conflicts of interest, and classified the rationales behind managers' intentions to pursue acquisitions that are not profitable to their shareholders into two main categories: incentives for return maximisation, either in the form of compensation or in the form of prestige or visibility; and incentives for risk reduction and increase in managers' job security. The first set of incentives includes 'empire building' and misuse of 'free cash flow' situations. The second set of incentives comprises allocations of corporate wealth to acquisitions that seek either to diversify at a firm level or deter potential bidders. The analysis is consistent with many empirical studies considered above.

Secondly, the acquiring company shareholders were found exposed to risks associated with the financial structure of the takeover. High leverage affects the profitability and the insolvency risk of the shareholders' investment in the bidder and completely alters the capital structure of the

[59] $X = 5 \times (100 \div 60) = 8.33$.

Figure 2: Synergy and overpayment risk in cash and share offers

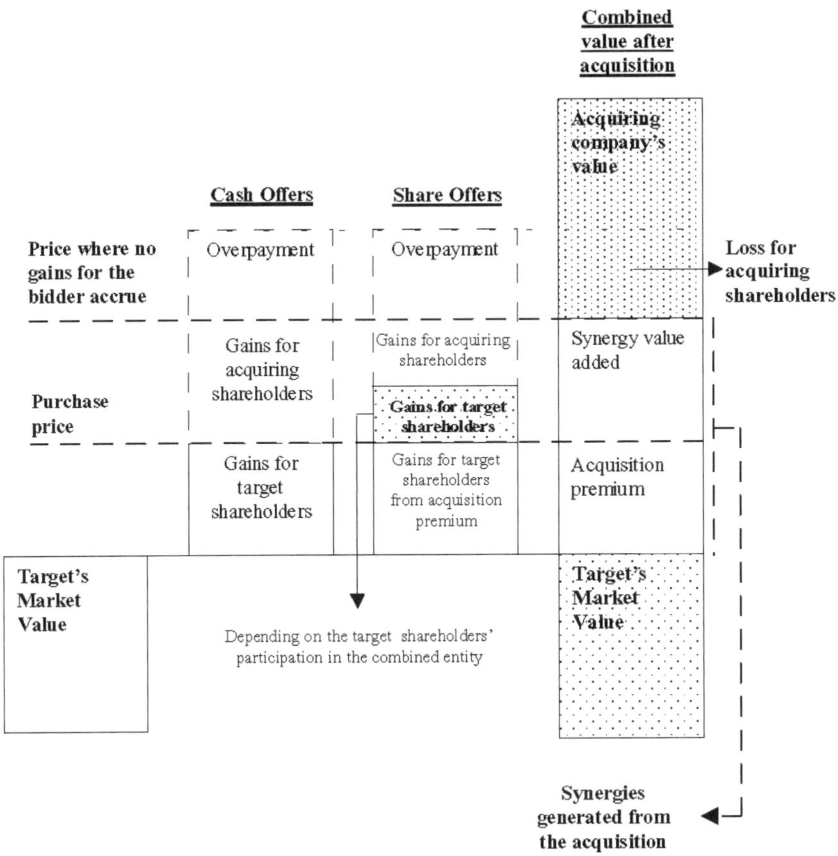

acquiring company, while share offers make shareholders vulnerable to dilution and market volatility. Finally, the acquiring company's shareholders face the risk that a potential acquisition will not produce the synergies their managers expect (synergy risk), or that their managers will pay more than they should (overpayment risk). While synergy risk is relative to the type of the offer—share offers minimise synergy risk—, overpayment risk is a risk borne exclusively by the acquirer's shareholders regardless of the type of the offer.

The above findings are consistent with the first three explanations provided in the introduction in an attempt to explain why the acquiring company shareholders receive, on average, negative returns. The existence of the above risks also justifies an enquiry into the protective mechanisms available to the acquiring company shareholders. Therefore, chapter three will focus on the protection that the market affords to the acquiring company shareholders, while chapter four will examine the effectiveness of traditional legal remedies. Finally, shareholders' rights and especially the role of institutional shareholders will be the subject of chapter five. The following table provides a preview of the mechanisms that will be considered in the next three chapters.

Table 3: Legal and regulatory responses to the internal risks faced by the shareholders of the acquiring company

Chapter 3: Market control	*Chapter 4: Legal and regulatory review of the transaction*	*Chapter 5: shareholders' voice and reward strategies*
1. The operation of capital markets:	1. Ex ante judicial review: the case of court schemes	1. Shareholders' rights:
— Exit	2. Ex post judicial review:	— Authorisation rights
— Diversification	— The duty to act bona fide for the best interests of the company	— Pre-emptive rights
— Risk arbitrage	— The proper purpose doctrine	— Approval rights
— The market price's role	— The no-conflict rule	2. Institutional investors
2. The market of corporate control	— The directors' duty of care and the diligence requirements of the Takeover Code.	— The treat of ex post discipline
3. The market for managerial services	3. Information requirements in the context of takeovers	— Ex ante intervention
	— Ex ante quality controls	3. Reward Strategies
	— Directors' liabilities	

3

Market Control

I INTRODUCTION

A COMMON CHARACTERISTIC of the risks faced by the acquiring shareholders is that they do not represent a 'final period problem'. This is an extremely important difference between the position of the acquiring company and the target company shareholders.

The economics of 'final period' suggest that when a transaction is the last or only one (final period), the incentive to cheat increases, because the party that cheats cannot be penalised.[1] In this context, the target managers have every incentive to cheat because they leave the market after the acquisition and are replaced by the acquirer's managers. For them, the acquisition is a final period transaction. However, this is not the case for the acquirer's managers. After the acquisition the acquirer's managers will continue to run the company, while their performance remains under the scrutiny of the market: if the acquisition is poor or not in the interests of the shareholders, it is predicted that the market should penalise their poor management. This creates a substantial incentive not to make such acquisitions. As a result, the question that arises is whether markets can effectively exercise such a function and protect the acquirer's shareholders in practice. Three types of markets are identified: the capital market, the market of corporate control, and the market for managerial services.

II THE FUNCTIONS OF THE CAPITAL MARKET

A Exit Rights

The existence of formal markets, where public companies are listed, promotes the free transfer of their shares and makes them highly marketable

[1] RJ Gilson and BS Black, *The Law and Finance of Corporate Acquisitions*, 2nd edn (Westbury, New York, The Foundation Press Inc, 1995) 720, who use the same argument to support the need for shareholder's voting rights in the target company and additional legal mechanisms like the 'de facto merger' doctrine.

commodities.[2] Traditionally, regulators seek to enhance the liquidity of their markets. The FSA is no exception and strongly opposes restrictions on the free transferability of the shares listed to regulated markets in the United Kingdom.

As a result, the acquirer's shareholders, who do not agree with their manager's decision to acquire the target and believe that the acquisition will decrease the value of their investment, can just exit the firm by selling their shares. However, this is not an all-gain situation. First of all, the ability of a shareholder to exit the firm without incurring a loss depends on the liquidity of the market. Secondly, since market prices reflect additional information about the value of listed companies,[3] the market price of the acquirer's shares will decrease if the terms of an announced takeover indicate that the acquisition will not be to the benefit of the acquiring shareholders. Accordingly, a 'beat the market' problem arises for the acquirer's shareholders. On the one hand, due to the insider-dealing provisions, an acquiring shareholder who is in possession of inside information that a takeover offer is about to be announced cannot trade his securities before any such information becomes public.[4] On the other hand, once the supposedly value-decreasing acquisition is announced, the market will discount the bidder's price to reflect the negative returns it expects from the acquisition.[5] Hence, the acquiring shareholder will not be able to avail himself of a market price that does not reflect the negative effects of the takeover announcement. Accordingly, he will bear all or part of the losses, regardless of whether he exits the firm or not.

B Diversification

The existence of a liquid market also provides shareholders in listed companies with another more sophisticated alternative, namely the ability to diversify their investment. Diversification is the process whereby an investor can reduce the risks involved in investing in one company by constructing a portfolio in which risky investments are balanced by other low-risk, low-yield investments.[6] By holding shares in more than one

[2] Limited liability makes the wealth of other investors irrelevant and shares of the same class are traded at one price in liquid markets regardless of who holds them. See, eg FH Easterbrook and DR Fischel, *The Economic Structure of Corporate Law*, 4th edn (Cambridge, MA, Harvard University Press, 1998).

[3] Financial economists have characterised this pattern in a formal fashion by way of the Efficient Capital Market Hypothesis ('ECMH'). See, eg RA Brealey and SC Myers, *Principles of Corporate Finance*, 6th edn (London, McGraw-Hill, 1999).

[4] For further analysis see below.

[5] See below under D The Market Price Function.

[6] In a regime of unlimited liability, diversification would have the exact opposite effect of increasing the risk of the portfolio, since every time an investor added a new share to his portfolio that would expose him to the risk of being personally liable for all the new company's debt: see Easterbrook and Fischel, *The Economic Structure of Corporate Law* (n 2 above) 43.

company, an individual shareholder can reduce his exposure to the firm-specific risks that each share carries. Diversification is available at remarkably low cost. In its most passive form—by which an investor does not investigate or pick the securities he invests in but just randomly chooses some from one of the financial indexes—a diversified portfolio is even cheaper than a non-diversified one, because it allows investors to avoid investigating and monitoring costs.[7]

However, portfolio diversification does not eliminate systemic risk.[8] This raises the question whether the internal risks identified above are firm-specific or systemic. Traditionally, there have been strong statements in the relevant literature that those risks can be diversified.[9] Such an approach stems from the assumption that risks associated with conflict of interests or bad management are firm-specific risks. This may be partly true, in the sense that the acquiring shareholder can minimise the impact of the aforementioned risks on his portfolio, either by investing in firms that do not have acquisition programs or by investing in other takeovers and hoping that not all of them will be driven by wrong incentives or wrong predictions.

Nevertheless, such a view fails to take into account that the same internal risks may appear in any firm and in any deal, regardless of the fact that their actual materialisation depends on the specific circumstances that surround each acquisition. Unless there are mechanisms to minimise managerial discretion or to provide the right incentives there is always the chance that management may pursue acquisitions for the wrong reasons or under wrong business assumptions; and this is a risk against which an acquiring shareholder cannot totally insulate himself, even if he holds a diversified portfolio. The more such a possibility exists, the more investigating and monitoring costs the acquiring shareholder has to undergo. However, this minimises the desirability of diversification, since the main advantage of diversifying lies in its ability to allow investors to avoid any investigating and monitoring expenses.

C Risk Arbitrage

Risk arbitrage is the practice of purchasing shares in the target company for short-term resale at a higher price[10] to the bidder who offers the higher

[7] Easterbrook and Fischel, *The Economic Structure of Corporate Law* (n 2 above) 122.

[8] This is the risk of variability in returns of an investment due to macro-economic developments like changes in tax regimes, exchange rates etc.

[9] For example, Easterbrook explicitly states that 'risks associated with corporate control transactions are diversifiable': Easterbrook and Fischel, *The Economic Structure of Corporate Law* (n 2 above) 122.

[10] JF Weston, JA Siu and BA Johnson, *Takeovers, Restructuring & Corporate Governance*, 3rd edn (London, Prentice Hall, 2001) 13.

premium. In other words, risk arbitrage allows the acquiring shareholder to take an offsetting position in the target.

An investor holding shares in both the acquirer and the target is mainly concerned about the total gains of the transactions and not with how the gains will be divided between the acquiring and the target shareholders. An example will better illustrate the above: Company A, the bidder, trading at 90p per share, places a bid for company T, the target, trading at 50p per share. The bidder is offering 70p per share (a premium of 40 percent). After the announcement of the bid, the acquiring shareholder can hedge his position by changing his portfolio so as to hold more shares in the target than in the bidder. This can be done by selling some of the acquirer's shares and investing in the target. Now, let us assume that the market appreciates that the bidder overpays and that the premium offered is too high, and accordingly the acquirer's price falls. Let us also assume that the acquiring shareholder buys shares in the target at the price of 55p per share (the price of the target goes up after the announcement of the bid) and sells some of the shares he holds in the bidder at the price of 85p per share. If the acquisition does eventually go through, even if the acquirer's price falls, the shareholder will tender his shares to the bidder, realising a 15p premium for every share he holds in T. If the bid fails, the shareholder can still realise his investment either by selling in the market or by tendering his shares to another bidder that may have entered the scene.[11]

Easterbrook and Fischel put a lot of emphasis on the above practice. They argue that the acquirer's shareholders, as rational actors, are expected to hold shares in both companies. Those investors, they continue, would see any expense in allocating the gain between the two firms as a pure loss.[12] Hence, the acquirer's managers should be primarily concerned with the total outcome of the transaction and not with the effect of the acquisition on the acquirer's shareholders.[13] Finally, they conclude that any legal or regulatory intervention in corporate control transactions, in the name of protecting investors in the bidder that choose not to invest in the target, penalises other investors who do so and thus reduce their risk, and reduces the number of value-maximising corporate transactions.[14]

It is true that risk arbitrage is a technique that permits the acquirer's shareholders to offset some of the losses they may suffer due to an announcement of a deal that is not greatly appreciated by the market. However, it does not provide a solution to the actual risks identified above, but merely a short-term relief from some of their symptoms. This is

[11] See below under Auction Risk (chs 6 and 7).

[12] Easterbrook and Fischel, *The Economic Structure of Corporate Law* (n 2 above) 122. Although they refer to the operation of holding shares in both companies as diversification, there is no doubt that they describe the operation of risk arbitrage.

[13] Easterbrook and Fischel, *The Economic Structure of Corporate Law* (n 2 above).

[14] Easterbrook and Fischel, *The Economic Structure of Corporate Law* (n 2 above).

because it does not provide the right incentives to the acquiring managers or minimise their discretion so as not to proceed with a value-decreasing acquisition in the first place. Risk arbitrage does not differentiate between bad and good acquisitions. As long as the acquirer's shareholders have a long position in the target, they will tender their shares even though the acquisition is not sound or is made for managerial profits.

In addition, risk arbitrage may actually be a problem instead of a solution for the acquiring shareholders, since it can increase market volatility and amplify downward pressures on the bidder's market price. In practice, risk arbitrage is associated with a common market practice called short-selling. The risk arbitrageur realises profits by going short on the bidder and long on the target. In other words, he sells today shares of the bidder that he is going to buy tomorrow, betting that the shares will fall in price, and buys today shares in the target that he is going to sell tomorrow, betting that the shares will increase in value. However, this activity by itself, due to its volume, puts the bidder's market price under pressure and drives upwards the price of the target's shares.

Risk arbitrage is one of the most common practices associated with takeovers.[15] Numerous studies reveal that the increased trading volume after takeover announcements is, in large part, associated with arbitrage activities,[16] not only by individual investors but especially by risk arbitrage funds. It has been found that in many takeovers the risk arbitrage community came in control of more than 30 to 40 percent of the target's stock.[17] Price pressures in this volume inevitably affect the efficiency of the market price function, which is going to be considered below, and the operation of the market of corporate control, which also relies heavily upon the assumption that prices reflect the market's impartial view of the quality of the announced deal.

D The Market Price Function

Although the above market mechanisms, available to the acquirer's shareholders at an individual level, provide a limited protection against the symptoms of the shareholders' risks, they fail to produce the necessary incentives to align the acquiring managers' interests with those of their

[15] Risk arbitrage used to be a very inconspicuous activity, but in mid 1970s the emergence of Ivan Boesky and the increase in takeover activity made it more visible. See F Cornelli and DD Li, *Risk Arbitrage in Takeovers* (Philadelphia, The Rodney L White Center for Financial Research, 1999); C Welles, 'Inside the Arbitrage Game' (1981) (August) *Institutional Investor* 41. The success of risk arbitrage during those early years is evident by the fact that Ivan Boesky's arbitrage fund was started in 1975 with an initial investment of US$700.000 which grew to over US$1 billion by November 1986, for a compound annual growth rate of 93.6%.

[16] See Cornelli and Li, *Risk Arbitrage in Takeovers* (n 15 above) 1 and note 1, where numerous case studies are referred.

[17] Cornelli and Li, *Risk Arbitrage in Takeovers* (n 15 above) 1.

shareholders and to minimise their discretion. However, there is another more 'collective' function of the market: that of the disciplinary role of the market price.

This operation of the capital markets stems from the fact that not only can shares of the same class be traded at the same price, but also their price accurately reflects all publicly-available information about the company. That means that, in the case that an acquisition is not highly regarded by the market, the latter will penalise the bidder by decreasing the market price of its shares. In that sense, capital markets provide an important 'warning signal' about the quality of the deal proposed. Their disciplinary role depends upon the function of other protective mechanisms, such as the market of corporate control or the exercise of shareholders' rights. A decrease in the market price of the bidder during or after an acquisition either makes it a possible target or generates concerns on the part of institutional shareholders who hold considerable blocks of shares in the acquirer. Leaving aside those other mechanisms, the capital market by itself operates as a constraint only to the extent that the diminution in the acquirer's market price increases the cost of new capital in circumstances where the bidder cannot finance the acquisition through retained earnings or debt.[18]

A notable example of the market's reaction to announced bids is that of the supermarket chain Morrison's bid for Safeway. Many analysts confirmed the potential synergies that the deal could generate. Among three other rivals, Morrison's offer faced the least antitrust burdens and outstripped rivals on just about every measure, including return on capital, sales densities and margins. However, shortly after the announcement of its offer, Morrison Supermarkets' shares dropped to their lowest level since summer 2000, decreasing its value from £2.9bn, when announced, to £2.2bn.[19] This was because the market doubted the ability of the Morrison's management to realise the full potential expected to be generated by the deal.

No matter how important the function of capital markets is, it is not unproblematic. First of all, a negative market reaction constitutes an immediate loss for the acquiring shareholders. Hardly can this be called an effective protection. In addition, the ability of the market to present accurately the company's value is not unquestionable. It is argued that the stock market fails to price adequately corporate acquisition announcements, because of persistent biases by uninformed traders (noise trading).[20] Noise trading distorts share prices by introducing pressures that

[18] Gilson and Black, *The Law and Finance of Corporate Acquisitions* (n 1 above) 369.

[19] P Smith and L Saigol, 'Share Drop Cuts Morrison Offer to £2.2bn' *Financial Times* (1 February 2003).

[20] R Kraakman,'Taking Discounts Seriously: The Implications of "Discounted" Share Prices as an Acquisition Motive' (1988) 88 *Columbia Law Review* 891.

have little or nothing to do with the valuation of the announced acquisition.[21] One such type of trading is risk arbitrage, which consistently puts pressure on the acquirer's market price.

Even if one assumes the credibility of the efficient capital market hypothesis, there are still circumstances where share prices diverge from the actual or 'true' value of the corporation and result in a discounted price.[22] Under the discount hypothesis the share price of the acquirer may represent a market's discount based on a rational belief that the managers of the bidder will mis-invest future cash flows.[23] In that sense, if the market believes that the bidder's managers are incompetent it has already discounted the bidder's market price, even before the takeover offer is announced. If the announced deal is even worse than expected, the acquirer's market price further decreases. However, if the particular acquisition, although unsound in general terms, constitutes a better than expected investment for the bidder, the price of the bidder is expected to rise, despite the fact that still the acquisition carries long-term negative effects for the bidder's shareholders. The above constitutes a situation where the capital market cannot discipline the bidder's managers.

The market discount hypothesis can also be associated with another characteristic of modern capital markets, that of short-termism, to create yet another inefficiency. Overall, there is regular criticism that investors, driven mostly by liquidity concerns, prefer short-term profits to the prospect of potentially larger profits in the longer term (the 'jam today' argument).[24] The above short-term orientation has as a result that long-term future cash flows are heavily discounted at a 'rate that is unnecessarily high given the time period and the risks involved'.[25]

[21] 'There is a growing theoretical literature on "mispricing" behaviour which argues that uninformed traders may introduce persistent biases or cumulative noise into share prices, or that speculative trading might lead to positive or negative price bubbles. Large scale noise trading arising from misconceived strategies, erroneous valuation assumptions, fashions and fads, or simple pleasure in trading- might distort share prices and generate discounts or premia through the sheer pressure of trading' (*Ibid*, 899–900).

[22] R Kraakman,'Taking Discounts Seriously: The Implications of "Discounted" Share Prices as an Acquisition Motive' (n 20 above).

[23] R Kraakman,'Taking Discounts Seriously: The Implications of "Discounted" Share Prices as an Acquisition Motive' (n 20 above).

[24] For a thorough and analytical account of the issues see E Ferran, *Company Law and Corporate Finance* (New York, Oxford University Press, 1999) 76–80, who provides many references to further texts that support the short-termism argument. For relevant empirical studies see, among others, D Miles, 'Testing for Short-Termism in the UK Stock Market' (1995) 103 *Economic Journal* 1379.

[25] Ferran, *Company Law and Corporate Finance* (n 24 above) 76; Miles, 'Testing for Short-Termism in the UK Stock Market' (n 24 above). The transitory nature of public share ownership is also associated with short-termism. Their relationship is more of a chicken–egg dilemma. Is short-termism a sociological aspect of the nature of the modern investor? Or is it the market environment, the diversification opportunities and the failure of control under the traditional legal model that guide investors towards new patterns of economic behaviour? In any case, what is essential here is that short-termism is not only a regular criticism for small investors, but also a behaviour strongly manifested by institutional

In view of the above, it is very likely that the negative returns that bidders experience after takeover announcements may constitute market discounts, which are irrelevant to the quality of the acquisition announced. Hence, in this sort of trading activity, one can hardly distinguish between disciplinary discounts in the acquirer's market price and diminutions in share prices that reflect the market's short-term orientation. Actually, the fact that empirical studies consistently report negative returns for the acquiring company after the announcement of a takeover offer[26] only serves to corroborate the above argument, since it is very unlikely that all announced takeovers are value-decreasing.

Information asymmetries may also be responsible for market biases towards specific forms of acquisitions and financial choices. It has already been considered that share offers are usually accompanied with negative responses by the market.[27] Such a biased reaction has been attributed to information asymmetries, and more specifically to the market's appreciation that the acquiring managers would offer shares mostly in cases where the bidder's shares are overpriced. On the basis of such an assumption, the market adjusts its valuation of the acquirer's shares by diminishing their price.[28] In that sense, the market can be a source of problems rather than a solution for the acquiring shareholders.

III THE MARKET FOR MANAGERIAL SERVICES

Little can the market for managerial services do, either, to protect the acquirer's shareholders. It is very unlikely that the market for managerial services will constrain self-dealing.[29] As Gilson argues, the buyers of managers for public corporations are other managers and there is no reason to believe that 'an efficient manager's penchant for high pay or perquisites will be negatively viewed'.[30] On the other hand, while the market of managerial services can constrain managerial inefficiency, at the same time, it creates the exact opposite incentives. Once the intention to make a takeover offer is announced, the pressure of the market of managerial services on the shoulders of the acquirer's management increases. Accordingly, it is more difficult for them to drop out or accept defeat,

shareholders. The issue is even more important when examining the role that the institutional shareholders can play in protecting the acquirer shareholders' rights. Can short-termism affect their role?

[26] See Introduction, above.

[27] See above.

[28] See above.

[29] RJ Gilson, 'A Structural Approach to Corporations: The Case against Defensive Tactics in Tender Offers' (1981) 33 *Stanford Law Review* 819, reprinted in Gilson and Black, *The Law and Finance of Corporate Acquisitions* (n 1 above) 369.

[30] Gilson and Black, *The Law and Finance of Corporate Acquisitions* (n 1 above) 369.

especially in contested takeovers. As Mario Monti, EU Competition Commissioner revealed, he knows more CEOs 'regretting discreetly that their deals had been authorised than regretting that their deals had not been authorised'.[31] However, such behaviour, as seen above, may result in overpayment and wealth transfers from the acquirer's shareholders.[32] Moreover, managerial prestige and compensation is, as seen above, usually relative to the size of the firm.[33] This further creates incentives for self-motivated acquisitions. Finally, the market for managerial services is more likely to impose constrains to junior managers than to senior executives, who eventually decide whether to pursue a corporate acquisition or not.

IV THE MARKET OF CORPORATE CONTROL

A Theory, Examples and Empirical Data

Since Henry Manne first unveiled his theory about the role of the 'market of corporate control',[34] it has been considered as the primary market mechanism to constrain managerial discretion. The operation of the market of corporate control stems from the same principles as the capital market price function: the acquirer's management self-dealing or incompetence, materialised through the announcement of a value-decreasing takeover offer, is penalised by the market through discounting the price of the acquirer's stock. That creates an opportunity for another bidder to purchase control of the company, displace the self-dealing or inefficient management, and put the company's assets to a more profitable use. In other words, the above hypothesis suggests that bidders who strike unprofitable deals for their shareholders are likely to be subsequently taken over.[35]

There is a number of US empirical studies that examine the probability of an 'unsuccessful acquirer' being subsequently taken over. The majority of those studies focus on the divestures of huge conglomerates that took place in the 80s, either through voluntary sell offs or through hostile bust-up takeovers. As seen above, diversifying acquisitions or 'empire building' is an operation that does not create value for the acquirer's shareholders. As the theory predicts, the empirical data reveals that

[31] 'Observer in Davos', *Financial Times* (27 January 2003) 20.

[32] See above about overpayment.

[33] See above about empire building.

[34] H Manne, 'Mergers and the Market for Corporate Control' (1965) 73 *Journal of Political Economy* 110.

[35] This hypothesis has been developed by Jensen, who argued that many takeovers discipline managers who use free cash flows to make value-reducing acquisitions: MC Jensen, 'Agency Costs of Free Cash Flow, Corporate Finance and Takeovers' (1986) 76 *The American Economic Review* (Papers and Proceedings of the Ninety-Eighth Annual Meeting of the American Economic Association) 323.

conglomerates are under the scrutiny of the market of corporate control. For example, Davis, Diekmann & Tinsley report a positive correlation between the level of diversification of a company and its likelihood of being acquired.[36]

A number of studies also report that the more value destruction that diversified acquisitions cause, the more likely it is for the conglomerate to be a target of a bust-up takeover. Berger and Ofek report that the main value effect of diversification for diversified targets which are broken up is –21 percent to –37 percent, contrary to only –five percent for those that are not subsequently broken up.[37]

There are also more general empirical studies. In a study of 1158 public companies in 51 industries, Mitchel and Lehn found evidence that, although in aggregate the returns to acquiring firms are approximately zero, the market does discriminate between good bidders, which are less likely to become targets (non-targets), and bad bidders, which are more likely to become targets of disciplinary takeover (targets). More precisely, significant differences exist between the average stock price effect associated with acquisitions made by non-targets, and the corresponding effect attributed to acquisitions made by subsequent targets. While the stock price of non-targets increases after the announcement of acquisitions (0.82 percent and 3.32 percent depending on the window), the market price of targets declines significantly (–1.27 percent and –3.38 percent, respectively).[38] Moreover, for the entire sample of acquisitions, the average stock price effect associated with acquisitions that are subsequently divested is significantly lower (–1.53 percent and –4.01 percent, respectively) than that of acquisitions that are not subsequently divested (0.56 and 1.89).[39] The difference is even more striking for bidders that become targets of hostile divestitures. In that situation the average stock price return of the initial acquisition is –2.07 and –7.04 respectively.[40]

A notable British example of the role of the market of corporate control in disciplining 'bad' bidders is the unsuccessful bid of NatWest Bank for Legal and General Insurance and its successive acquisition by its rival

[36] For example, firms at the 75% percentile in degree of diversification were 2.3 times as likely as industry-focused firms to be acquired during the decade, after controlling for the firm size. G Davis, K Diekmann and C Tinsley, 'The Decline and Fall of the Conglomerate Firm in the 1980s: The Deinstitutionalization of an Organizational Form' (1994) 59(4) *American Sociological Review* 547. See also S Kaplan and M Weisbach, 'The Success of Acquisitions: Evidence from Divestitures' (1992) 47 *Journal of Finance* 107; S Bhagat, A Shleifer and R Vishny, 'Hostile Takeovers in the 1980s: The Return to Corporate Specialization', *Brookings Papers on Economic Activity* (1990) 1; M Porter, 'From Competitive Advantage to Corporate Strategy' (1987) *Harvard Business Review* 43.

[37] PG Berger and E Ofek, 'Bust-up Takeovers of Value-Destroying Diversified Firms' (1996) 51(4) *The Journal of Finance* 1175.

[38] ML Mitchell and K Lehn, 'Do Bad Bidders Become Good Targets?' (1990) 98(2) *Journal of Political Economy* 372 at 375.

[39] *Ibid*.

[40] ML Mitchell and K Lehn, 'Do Bad Bidders Become Good Targets?' (n 38 above) 375.

Royal Bank of Scotland. More precisely, NatWest launched a friendly takeover for Legal and General, the announcement of which was badly received by the market on the basis that NatWest overvalued the target and was overpaying. NatWest shares fell nine percent on the announcement day and 26 percent after two weeks! As a result, two rival banks, the Bank of Scotland and the smaller in size Royal Bank of Scotland (RBS), launched surprise bids for NatWest. Initially, NatWest defended both bids but eventually after its institutional investors' intervention,[41] it accepted and recommended the RBS bid.

What really epitomises the dynamic of the market's intervention is the statement of one spokesman of PDFM, one of NatWest's major shareholders: 'The market has clearly decided that NatWest should lose its independence'. While NatWest traded at 1211p before the announcement of its bid for Legal and General, its shareholders received an offer of around 1440p per share, or in other words a 19 percent premium. In addition, they kept the control of the combined company by owning 62 percent of the combined group.

However, empirical studies report results that are not in keeping with the above example. As far as divestments are concerned, empirical studies suggest that hostile takeovers are associated with significant asset disposals.[42] Nevertheless, there is no proof of negative correlation between the probability of assets disposals and the pre-takeover performance of the target.[43]

Other empirical studies also seem to suggest that takeovers do not perform the expected disciplinary role.[44] Cosh, in a study of 320 hostile acquisitions completed between 1985 and 1996 in the United Kingdom, found no evidence that post-takeover profit performance of the combined firm is negatively related to the pre-takeover profit performance of the target, as the disciplinary hypothesis would predict, and concluded that the evidence 'provides little support for the view that hostile takeovers perform an important disciplinary function in the UK stock market'.[45] Franks and

[41] See about the role of institutional investors later on, under ch 5.

[42] A Cosh, 'The Long-Run Performance of Hostile Takeovers: UK Evidence' (2001) *ESRC Centre for Business Research, University of Cambridge Working Paper No 215.*

[43] *Ibid.*

[44] For an analytical account of US studies, see Gilson, 'A Structural Approach to Corporations: The Case against Defensive Tactics in Tender Offers' (n 29 above); JC Coffee, 'Regulating the Market for Corporate Control: A Critical Assessment of the Tender Offer's Role in Corporate Governance' (1984) 84 *Columbia Law Review* 1145; S Deakin and G Slinger, 'Hostile Takeovers, Corporate Law and the Theory of the Firm' in S Deakin and A Hughes (eds), *Enterprise and Community: New Directions in Corporate Governance* (Oxford, Blackwell Publishers, 1997); see also R Powell,'Modelling Takeover Likelihood' (1997) 24(7) and (8) *Journal of Business Finance and Accounting* 1010. Some theoretical commentators also question the effectiveness of the market of corporation control. See among others, Coffee; also C Bradley, 'Corporate Control: Markets and Rules' (1990) 53 *Modern Law Review* 170.

[45] Cosh, 'The Long-Run Performance of Hostile Takeovers: UK Evidence' (n 42 above).

Mayer[46] also find little support for the disciplinary role of the market for corporate control, since hostile bids do not appear to be directed to poorly performing companies, while other studies identify leverage or firm size as the only determinants of hostile acquisitions.[47]

Finally, significant negative returns for the acquiring shareholders (reported by many studies cited in the introduction of this paper) do not sit easily with the market of corporate control hypothesis. This is because the acquirers' post-acquisition performance under the disciplinary hypothesis is expected to improve, since assets are supposed to be transferred from bad management to the control of better management.

B Limitations

Regardless of the results reported by the above studies, there are a number of diseconomies that limit the role of the market of corporate control in protecting the acquirer's shareholders. First, since the operation of the market of corporate control stems from the same principles under which the capital market functions, it is inevitable that it is subject to the same inefficiencies.[48]

Secondly, the main problem with the operation of takeovers as a protection against unprofitable takeovers derives from the fact that the takeover is both the problem and the solution.[49] Seeking protection in a takeover mechanism conflicts with the fact that the same mechanism failed in the very first place. Had the market of corporate control worked in the very first place, there would be no need for a second takeover as a corrective action. For example, the fact that a divestiture is needed to increase the wealth of the conglomerate shareholders by offering them a premium means that the conglomerate failed to increase their wealth at the very first place.

The above casts doubts over the efficiency of the market of corporate control in two ways. First, there is no assurance that this time it is the market that monitors the unsuccessful acquirer, or just an individual bidder who is prone to the same mistakes or is carried by the same self-interests as the initial bidder. Secondly, corporate acquisitions involve considerable

[46] JR Franks and C Mayer, 'Hostile Takeovers and the Correction of Managerial Failure' (1996) 40 *Journal of Financial Economics* 163.

[47] KM Holland and L Hodgkinson, 'The Pre-Announcement Share Price Behaviour of Uk Takeover Targets' (1994) 21(4) *Journal of Business Finance and Accounting* 467; P Levive and S Aaronovitch, 'The Financial Characteristics of Firms and Theories of Merger Activity'(1981) 30 *The Journal of Industrial Economics* 149. See, however, VA Kennedy and RJ Limmack, 'Takeover Activity, Ceo Turnover, and the Market for Corporate Control' (1996) 23(2) *Journal of Business Finance and Accounting* 267.

[48] See above.

[49] Jensen, 'Agency Costs of Free Cash Flow, Corporate Finance and Takeovers' (n 35 above).

costs and there is no guarantee that the premium offered will restore the total loss caused by the unprofitable acquisition. Due to these costs, an internal monitoring mechanism that could prevent the unprofitable acquisition from happening in the very first place could be more preferable.

Moreover, a hostile takeover may be a sub-optimal corrective mechanism due to the imperfect correlation between the value destroyed by an unprofitable acquisition and the value gained from a corrective hostile takeover. First, the market of corporate control seems to fail to deal adequately with the problem of risk.[50] Highly leveraged acquirers are less likely to be taken over due to the increased insolvency risk. Secondly, empirical findings suggest that there is a negative correlation between the size of the firm and the probability of being taken over.[51] Finally, not all unsuccessful bidders are subject to the same threat of being taken over. Empirical findings suggest that only firms with intermediate asset specificity face a credible takeover threat.[52] High asset specificity increases integration costs and minimises synergies, while low asset specificity means very marketable assets, which can be easily obtained cheaper through product markets than through the market of corporate control.

Furthermore, the threat of the market of corporate control fuels managerial incentives for self-interested acquisitions. As seen above, where the acquirer shareholders' risks were considered, managers may engage in 'empire building' in an attempt to go beyond the threat of the market of corporate control. They may also attempt a defensive takeover. In other words, the threat of the market of corporate control makes 'last period' incentives appear earlier in time. There is no need for bad managers to wait to become targets. The threat of them being displaced is enough to make them act in the same way they would have acted if they were really displaced. This means that either they resort to self-interested acquisitions—manifestations of the agency risk discussed above—or they try to protect themselves from bust-ups by attempting a management buy-out.

V CONCLUSION: REGULATORY ENHANCEMENTS

This chapter examined the role of market mechanisms in protecting the acquirer's shareholders. The ability of the acquirer's shareholders to exit the bidder does not compensate them against the losses that an announcement of a bad acquisition produces, since their exit price is not guaranteed. Although diversification minimises the effects that the aforementioned

[50] Coffee, 'Regulating the Market for Corporate Control: A Critical Assessment of The Tender Offer's Role in Corporate Governance' (n 44 above).

[51] See above ch 2.

[52] AWA Boot, 'Why Hang on Losers? Divestitures and Takeovers' (1992) 47 *The Journal of Finance* 1401 at 1417.

risks have on the acquiring shareholders' portfolios, it fails to insulate them completely against those risks. It neither provides the right incentives, nor minimises the discretion of the acquirer's management over corporate control transactions. Finally, risk arbitrage does protect the acquirer's shareholders against overpayment, but fails to differentiate between good and bad acquisitions; it creates inverted agency problems and, in the long term, affects the efficiency of the market of corporate control and increases market risk.

The price function performed by capital markets can provide an important 'warning signal' against the quality of the deal proposed and it is an underlying prerequisite for the operation of the market of corporate control. However, the market price function suffers from its own limitations, such as noise trading (especially the operation or risk arbitrage funds), discounted prices, short-termism and information asymmetries. It has also been suggested that capital markets by themselves cannot really provide any substantial sanctions to value-reducing bidders unless they are accompanied by other mechanisms, such as the market of corporate control or the active role of institutional investors. It was also argued that the market of executive services fails to create the necessary incentives.

The above analysis also indicated that although empirical studies provide very little evidence on the disciplinary role of the market of corporate control in self-interested or unsuccessful acquisitions in the United Kingdom, there are some high profile examples where bad acquirers were eventually disciplined by the market. However, the market of corporate control does carry some inherent limitations. First, it carries the same inefficiencies that accompany the operation of capital markets. Secondly, takeovers appear to be both the solution and the problem at the same time. Finally, the costs associated with takeovers, the imperfect correlation between the value destroyed from the 'bad' acquisition and the value gained from the corrective takeover, the pre-materialisation of the last period incentives, and the negative externalities produced, negatively affect the role of the market of corporate control in disciplining 'bad' bidders and, hence, in protecting the acquirer's shareholders.

Overall, a number of prerequisites must be ensured in order for the market to protect effectively the acquiring shareholders. To this extent, regulatory intervention can play an important role:

First, the market must be liquid to permit shareholders to exit or diversify and make 'bad' acquirers more susceptible to the market of corporate control. To this extent, the provisions of the Listing and the Stock Exchange Rules that seek to enhance liquidity are very important.

Secondly, high-quality information is an underlying assumption of the effective operation of all market mechanisms. Disclosure requirements and provisions that seek to ensure a high standard of published information, included in both the City Code on Takeovers and Mergers ('the

Takeover Code') and the Listing Rules, minimise market biases and help towards an accurate market valuation of the announced offer increasing the effectiveness of the market of corporate control. Such rules will be examined later on this book.

Also, in order for the acquirer's price to reflect accurately the market's appreciation of the acquisition, noise trading should be minimised. Since risk arbitrage accounts for most of noise trading in takeovers, one way to address this issue is by limiting the operation of short-selling during takeovers. This could decrease market volatility and relieve the acquirer from some of the downward price pressures that it experiences once the offer is announced. However, a consultation process initiated by the FSA in 2002 revealed that neither the FSA nor market participants preferred the introduction of restrictive measures.[53] Accordingly, since short-selling requires the borrowing of shares from institutions that hold them, in order for delivery of the shares to be made to the buyer, it falls upon the institutional shareholders to control such operations, when the acquirer's price is depressed. The revised version of the Takeover Code now includes provisions regarding the disclosure of any short positions in the offeree company where disclosure of dealings is required for associates or other persons under the Code.[54] Such requirement is extended to short positions in the bidder's shares where, however, the offeror's shares are used as a medium of payment.[55] While such rules do not regulate short-selling in a takeover situation they could help identify the extent of short-selling impact on Takeovers and its effects. However, the confinement of disclosure of short positions in the bidder only in share-for-share exchange offers is not justified by the above analysis.

Finally, in order to address some of the price pressures of short-termism and the reaction that share exchange offers receive from the market, the bidder could be permitted to use some of the price-stabilising techniques that are allowed in initial public issues for cash. Accordingly, the operation of some of the Price Stabilising Rules[56] could be extended, in the case of takeovers, to share exchange offers, subject to the approval and monitoring of the Panel. Currently, the rules create a defence, or 'safe harbour', against the offences of market abuse and insider dealing,[57] and allow lead

[53] Financial Services Authority, *FSA Discussion Paper No 17: Short Selling* (October 2002); Financial Services Authority, *Feedback on DP17* (April 2003).

[54] See The Takeover Code, 8th edn (London, Panel on Takeovers and Mergers, May 2006) note 5 on r 8.

[55] See note 2 on r 8 of the Takeover Code.

[56] The price stabilising rules are issued on the basis of Commission Regulation (EC) of 22 December 2003, implementing the Market Abuse Directive as regards exemptions for buy-back programmes and stabilisation of financial instruments (No 2273/2003) and s 144 of the Financial Services and Markets Act 2000 and form a chapter (MAR 2) of the Market Conduct Sourcebook in the FSA's Handbook of Rules and Guidance.

[57] See ss 118A, 397(4) or (5)(b) of the FSMA 2000 and para 5(1) of Schedule 1 of the Criminal Justice Act 1993.

managers to support the price of new issues of equities and bonds—and some secondary offers—for a limited period time, by buying them on the secondary market.

4

Legal and Regulatory Review of the Transaction

I FIDUCIARY DUTIES

TRADITIONALLY, COMPANY LAW deals with managerial opportunism through the imposition of fiduciary[1] duties on corporate directors.[2] One of the most significant and controversial changes brought about by the Companies Act 2006 ('CA 2006') is the codification of these fiduciary duties. The Act introduces a statutory statement of duties that replaces many existing common law and equitable rules.[3] While wording is not the same the Act provides that regard is to be made to common law duties in interpreting and applying the statutory duties.[4] In addition, section 178 of CA 2006 provides that the civil consequences of breach (or threatened breach) of the statutory duties are the same as would apply if the corresponding common law rule or equitable principle applied. It also makes clear that the statutory duties are to be regarded as fiduciary, with the exception of the duty to exercise reasonable care skill and diligence which is not under the present law regarded as a fiduciary duty.

However, the main changes focus on directors' duty to act in good faith, first, because of the introduction of the duty to promote the 'success' of the company and second because of the introduction of the so-called principle

[1] 'A fiduciary is someone who undertakes to act for or on behalf of someone else in circumstances which give rise to a relationship of trust and confidence between the parties'. See E Ferran, 'Creditors' Interests and "Core" Company Law' 20(10) *Company Lawyer* 314; *Bristol and West Building Society v Mothew* [1998] Ch 1 (CA) 18 (Millett LJ).

[2] More precisely, fiduciary duties have been traditionally imposed on corporate directors. However, in the case of modern large public companies the company's management is usually delegated to high rank employees, the senior managers who may not be directors of the company. Although less litigated than director's fiduciary duties, the fiduciary position of senior managers has been recognised in a number of cases (*Canadian Aero Services Ltd v O'Malley* (1973) 40 DLR 371 (SC Can); *Freen v Bestobell Industries Pty Ltd* (1982) 1 ACLC 1 (WA SC); and *Sybron Corporation v Rochem* [1984] Ch 112 (CA) 127 (Stephenson LJ)).

[3] Section 170(3) of the Companies Act 2006.

[4] Section 170(4) of the Companies Act 2006. Section 170(4) also provides that when interpreting and applying the statutory duties, regard should be had to the common law rules and equitable principles which the statutory duties replace; thus developments in the law of trusts and agency should be reflected in the interpretation and application of the duties.

of 'enlightened shareholder value' in determining the list of factors that the directors are required to have regard at in discharging their duty to the company.[5] The question that arises is whether fiduciary duties can provide an effective protection against managerial opportunism, in the context of corporate acquisitions. To that extent the analysis that follows mainly focuses on the common law interpretation of fiduciary duties, and covers their statutory restatement where it is likely to lead in the future to different interpretations or deviations from the established case law.

The term fiduciary duties, traditionally, includes the following duties:

— the duty to act in good faith in the interests of the company, or the duty to promote the success of the company, as restated in section 172 of CA 2006;
— the duty to exercise directors' powers for the proper purposes, or the duty to act within powers, as restated in section 171 of CA 2006;
— the directors' duty not to fetter their own discretion, or the duty to exercise independent judgement, as restated in section 173 of CA 2006;
— the directors' duty not to place themselves in a position in which there is conflict between their duties to the company and their personal interests.[6] A conflict of interest may, in particular, arise when a director makes personal use of information, property or opportunities belonging to the company or when a director enters into a contract with his company. Conflicts of interest may also arise whenever a director makes a profit in the course of being a director, in the matter of his directorship, without the knowledge and consent of his company. This duty is codified in section 175 of CA 2006. Instances of the 'no-conflict' duty are also found in the rule prohibiting the exploitation of the position of director for personal benefit, such as the acceptance of benefits (including bribes). This is now codified in section 176 of CA 2006 and in the equitable rule that directors may not have interests in transactions with the company unless the interests have been authorised by the members, which is replaced by the statutory duty to disclose any interest, direct or indirect, that a director has in relation to a proposed transaction or arrangement with the company (section 177 of CA 2006).

The rationale behind the application of the general law of fiduciary duties in the case of corporate acquisitions and especially from the acquirer's perspective is simple: if a corporate acquisition with the characteristics described in chapter two, namely a corporate acquisition made

— to increase manager's returns, or
— to diversify at a firm level, or

[5] See also below.

[6] The latter case includes situations where directors misappropriate corporate property or misuse corporate information or opportunities for their own interests.

— to dilute shareholders' control, or
— to waste free cash flows or, finally,
— to deter a potential bidder,

can be characterised, in legal terms, as

— being made in bad faith against the interests of the company, or
— being made for improper purposes, or
— being made in breach of the no-conflict rule,

then the acquirer's directors are in breach of their fiduciary duties or of their general duties under the Act.

A The Duty to Act in Good Faith in the Interests of the Company (Section 172—Duty to Promote the Success of the Company)

Under this duty, directors must exercise their discretion 'bona fide in what they consider—not what a court may consider—is in the interests of the company'.[7] The statutory duty of section 172 codifies the current law and enshrines in statute what is commonly referred to as the principle of 'enlightened shareholder value'. The duty requires a director to act in the way he or she considers, in good faith, would be most likely to promote the success of the company for the benefit of its members as a whole and, in doing so, to have regard to the factors non-exhaustively listed in the section.

The duty demands directors to display 'subjective good faith'.[8] This means that the court cannot find the directors to be in breach of their duty just because it disagrees with their assessment of what is in the interest of the company. The existence of an economic or commercial justification of the directors' actions proves their honesty.[9] A breach of duty can only be based on a tangible proof of a completely unreasonable action, or such extravagant conduct, on the basis of which the court is able to conclude that the directors did not act 'in the genuine belief'[10] that their actions were in the company's interests. From the acquirer's perspective, this means that just the mere fact that a takeover was made in order to increase the size of the firm, or to diversify at a firm level, or to use excess cash flows, does not suffice in order for a director to be found in breach of his duty to act in good faith.

[7] *Re Smith and Fawcett Ltd* [1942] Ch. 304 (CA) 306 (Lord Greene MR).

[8] PL Davies, *Gower's Principles of Modern Company Law*, 6th edn (London, Sweet & Maxwell, 1997).

[9] See *Regentcrest Plc (In Liquidation) v Jeffrey Saul Cohen* [2001] BCLC 80 (HC).

[10] The term 'genuine belief' has been used by Lord Oliver in *Brady v Brady* [1989] AC 755 (HL). For a further analysis of the different meanings of the terms genuineness, honesty and good faith see E Ferran, *Company Law and Corporate Finance* (New York, Oxford University Press, 1999) 158.

It is also well established that directors owe their duties to the company as a separate legal personality.[11] This is also stated in section 170(1) which makes it clear that, as in the existing law, the general duties are owed by a director to the company. It is established, though, as part of the interpretation of the common law position, that in acting for its economic benefit, the directors are not expected to disregard the interests of the company's shareholders.[12] However, the expected benefits for the company, as viewed by the directors, do not need to materialise fully and immediately in dividend payments or increases in share value. A diversifying acquisition may not be to the immediate benefit of the shareholders, but in the longer term it may be beneficial for the company because it decreases the business risk under which the company operates. An exchange offer may be more expensive for shareholders, but may be less burdensome for the realisation of the post-acquisition business plan. This is more clearly restated in the statutory codification of the duty that adopts the principle of 'enlightened shareholder value', which requires directors to take into account, in making their decisions, other parameters and factors than simply shareholders' value. Such factors that the directors may need to consider are, among others, the interests of the company's employees,[13] the need to foster the company's business relationships with suppliers, customers and others, the impact of the company's operations on the community and the environment, or the desirability of the company maintaining a reputation for high standards of business conduct.[14]

Directors are also not bound to any particular time frame within which to promote the shareholders' interests.[15] Since the directors' duty to act bona fide is a subjective one, it is the directors' appreciation of the balance between short-term and long-term objectives that matters and not that of the court.[16] Thus, it is up to the directors to decide whether, in their view, the shareholders' interests are best promoted by a long-term strategy, implemented in the form of a corporate acquisition, rather than by distributing some profits in the short-term. In addition, section 172(1) now clearly provides that the directors, in taking their decision, must take into account the likely consequences of any decision in the long term.[17]

Under the above circumstances, it will be difficult for the acquirer's shareholders to show that their directors' decision to make a takeover offer stands as a breach of their duty to promote the success of the company. The principle of 'enlightened shareholder value' embodied in

[11] *Percival v Wright* [1902] 2 Ch 421 (Ch).

[12] Davies, *Gower's Principles of Modern Company Law* (n 8 above); Ferran, *Company Law and Corporate Finance* (n 10 above).

[13] See also the old s 309(1) of the Companies Act 1985.

[14] See s 172(1) cases (b) to (e) of the Companies Act 2006.

[15] Davies, *Gower's Principles of Modern Company Law* (n 8 above) 604.

[16] Davies, *Gower's Principles of Modern Company Law* (n 8 above) 604.

[17] See s 172(1) case (a) of the Companies Act 2006.

statute is more likely to operate in corporate acquisitions, due to their inherent uncertainty and complexity, as a statutory defence for directors rather than a crystallised duty.

B The Directors' Duty to Exercise their Powers for Proper Purposes (Section 171—Duty to Act within Powers)

The main difference between the duty to act in good faith and the proper purpose doctrine is that the latter provides an objective test of the directors' behaviour,[18] as opposed to the subjective nature of the former. Directors are in breach of their duty if they exercise a power conferred to them by law or by the articles of association, for a purpose different from that for which the powers were bestowed on them. The answer to the question whether the powers were exercised for the proper purposes is a matter of law,[19] and the honest belief of the directors, although given credit, does not prevent the purpose from being improper.[20] In other words, the issue is not whether the directors act in good faith, but whether, in the first place, they have the authority to act in such a way and on the basis of the purposes of their powers. This means that, even if, for example, the acquiring company's directors believe that entrenching their position within the company is in the best interests of the company, thereby meeting the good faith test, under the proper purpose test their actions are reviewed objectively and independently of their honesty and integrity, on the basis of whether they were allowed, in the first place, to use their powers in that way. What also enhances the effectiveness of the 'proper purpose' test over the 'subjective bona fide' test is that, once the court prima facie identifies an impropriety in the exercise of the directors' decision, the burden of proof shifts from the shareholders to the directors to prove the propriety of their decision.[21] The proper purpose test also differs from the duty of care, in that it is one thing to act improperly and another to act within the boundaries of one's power but carelessly. In other words, under the proper purpose doctrine the court does not review the

[18] *Rolled Steel Products (Holdings) Ltd v British Steel Corporation* [1986] Ch 246 at 297 (Slade LJ), and 307 (Browne-Wilkinson LJ); *Bishopsgate Investment Management Ltd. (in liquidation) v Maxwell (No 2)* [1994] 1 All ER 261 (CA) at 265 (Hoffmann LJ). See also RC Nolan, 'The Proper Purpose Doctrine and Company Directors' in BA Rider (ed), *The Realm of Company Law* (London, Kluwer Law International, 1997).

[19] Ferran, *Company Law and Corporate Finance*(n 10 above) 163: in the words of a leading authority when 'a dispute rises whether directors . . . made a particular decision for one purpose or another . . . the court is entitled to look at the situation objectively' (Lord Wilberforce, in *Howard Smith Ltd v Ampol Petroleum Ltd* [1974] AC 821 (PC) at 832).

[20] *Hogg v Cramphorn Limited* [1967] Ch 254 [1966] 3 All ER 420; *Cayne v Global Natural Resources Plc* (12 August 1982, unreported) (Sir Robert Megarry VC).

[21] See the wording in Hoffmann LJ's statement above; *Bishopsgate Investment Management Ltd (in liquidation) v Maxwell (No 2)* [1994] 1 All ER 261 (CA) 265.

manner in which power is exercised, but it controls the ends for which such power is exercised.[22]

When the board of the acquiring company decides to acquire a target, it is logical to assume that the expected test of review by the courts would include questions as to whether the directors reached their decision in good faith, properly informed and with due care. However, there could still be room for the application of the proper purpose doctrine in certain circumstances. An underlying assumption of the operation of the proper purpose doctrine is that an improper exercise of a power bestowed on the board occurs when such exercise interferes with the shareholders' constitutional rights[23] or legitimate expectations, or when it directly affects the shareholders, and not simply in consequence of its effect on the company's economic performance.[24] This caused some literature to argue that the operation of the doctrine weakens in the case of powers that relate to internal functions of a company compared to external ones.[25]

In the case of internal powers the improper purpose doctrine seems to be less effective,[26] since on the one hand, such a power is conferred on the board by statute[27]—subject of course to any limitations that may be included in the articles of association and in the Companies Act—and on the other hand, business decisions are very unlikely to interfere with the shareholders' constitutional rights.[28] However, there may be circumstances where the exercise of the board's power to make a takeover offer is accompanied by or directly affects other internal functions in the bidder. Three cases can be identified:

— First, when the proposed acquisition is accompanied by a heavy issue of shares, which can alter the majority shareholding in the bidder (altering the majority in the bidder).

[22] 1 All ER 261 (CA) 265 (Hoffmann LJ).

[23] The underlying assumption behind the court's decision in the *Criterion Properties* case was that the majority shareholders were deprived of their constitutional rights to remove their directors at any time, since by doing so they would expose the company to a 'a serious and wholly gratuitous liability'. (*Criterion Properties Plc v Stratford UK Properties LLC* [2002] 2 BCLC 151 (CA)). See also L Sealy, *Cases & Materials on Company Law*, 6th edn (London, Butterworths, 1996) 319.

[24] RC Nolan, 'The Proper Purpose Doctrine and Company Directors' in BA Rider (ed), *The Realm of Company Law* (London, Kluwer Law International, 1997).

[25] *Ibid.*

[26] *Ibid.*

[27] Article 70 of Table A of the Companies Act 1985: For the majority of companies limited by shares on the register at the date that the Companies Act 2006 comes into force, the 'default' model articles will continue to be the Companies Act 1985 Table A ('Table A'). Subject to the provisions of the Act, the memorandum and the articles of association, and any directions given by special resolution, the business of the company shall be managed by the directors, who may exercise all the powers of the company'

[28] Unless, of course, such decision rights are conferred on the general meeting by special provisions in the articles of association.

— Secondly, when the acquisition entrenches the board against potential bidders (defensive acquisition: interfering with the shareholders' right to change control, or their right to discharge their investment in favourable terms).
— Thirdly, when the acquisition represents a misuse of free cash flows (as strictly defined above), which could otherwise have been distributed to the bidder's shareholders (interfering with the shareholders' expectation, as residual claimants, to receive profits that cannot be reinvested in profitable ways—free cash flows).

It is now well established that English cases concerning the directors' power to allot shares confirm that the exercise of such a power is reviewable by the courts, on objective grounds, and independently of the directors' personal beliefs.[29] From the acquirer's perspective, this means that there is little doubt that when the acquirer's directors make a takeover accompanied by a heavy issuance of new shares in order to diminish internal control by further diluting the shareholdings within the company, such capital raising can be found to go beyond the directors' powers. Of course, the benefits of the operation of the doctrine, in this respect, are reduced by the operation of the Companies Act pre-emptive rights[30] and the Pre-emption Guidelines applicable to all listed companies.[31]

In the case of *Criterion Properties v Stratford UK Properties LLC*,[32] it was also found that entering into a 'poison pill' agreement with the sole purpose of protecting the company against a possible takeover and change of management constituted, under the specific circumstances surrounding the agreement, an improper use of the board's power. The court arrived at its judgment, because of the range of events which could trigger the buy-out clause of the poison pill arrangement, including any takeover—hostile or beneficial—or the departure of the chairman or the managing director for reasons unrelated to the particular threat faced by the company at the time. Even if the purpose of deterring a specific predator and the power of directors to use a contingent transfer of assets to achieve it were accepted as lawful, it would be difficult to see how the agreement could be justified as a reasonable exercise of that power in the company's interests.[33] The logic of the court was that the effect of the exercise of the agreement on the company would have been more damaging than the acquisition by a

[29] *Howard Smith Ltd v Ampol Petroleum Limited* [1974] AC 821 (HL) 834–6; *Re Smith and Fawcett Ltd* [1942] Ch 304 (the action did not succeed, though); *Hogg v Cramphorn Limited* [1967] Ch 254, [1966] 3 All ER 420 (Ch).

[30] Section 89 of CA 1985, now s 561 of the Companies Act 2006.

[31] Especially since the latter also apply to vendor placings. See below.

[32] *Criterion Properties Plc v Stratford UK Properties LLC* [2002] EWHC 496, [2002] 2 BCLC 151 (Ch); on appeal [2003] 1 WLR 2108 (CA).

[33] *Ibid.*

potential bidder.[34] In other words, the poison pill agreement was caught by the proper purpose test because it went further than was necessary to just deter an unwanted takeover, which leaves room for doubt as to whether the criterion is quantitative or qualitative.

Applying this 'quantitative' test in the case of defensive acquisitions (case two of the three cases identified at the outset), the impropriety of directors could lie in the fact that the acquisition is made to entrench the directors' position *without any commercial justification*, resulting not only in a loss for the bidder, but also depriving the shareholders of a possible offer. Similarly, an improper use of free cash flows, which by definition cannot be put to value-maximising use,[35] deprives the acquiring shareholders of a dividend distribution (case three).

The ability of the improper purpose doctrine to work in such cases is subject to a number of limitations. First of all, when directors make an acquisition or raise capital to finance it they do something which is prima facie for the benefit of the company as an economic unit. If the acquisition simply fails to produce subsequently the expected benefits, there is no room for the application of the proper purpose doctrine. Accordingly, there clearly has to be a wide-ranging investigation of all the facts and circumstances to assess whether the exercise of the power to transact or the capital raising power was in fact motivated, when considered objectively, by an improper desire to deprive an existing majority of shareholders of their position as such, or to deprive shareholders of a potential offer, or the distribution of profits.[36]

A more substantial problem derives from the fact that, in many situations, the directors' action in question may be found to have been taken for more than one purpose, some proper and others improper. *Mills v Mills*[37] shows that when the main purpose of the directors' resolution is to benefit the company, it matters not that it incidentally benefits a director as well. In the case of the acquiring shareholders, this means that under this primary purpose test,[38] once it can be shown that there are benefits for the company, it is extremely difficult to argue that the interests of the company are not the predominant purpose of the acquisition. And if no benefits for the company accrue, then it is easier for the plaintiffs—as it will be argued below—to base their case on a breach of the directors' duty of care, in the light of the stricter relevant requirements imposed by the Code.

[34] *Criterion Properties Plc v Stratford UK Properties LLC* [2002] EWHC 496, [2002] 2 BCLC 151 (Ch) para 22 and [2003] EWCA Civ 1783, [2003] 1 WLR 2108 (CA) para 18.

[35] See above about the definition of free cash flows in ch 2 above.

[36] *Criterion Properties Plc v Stratford UK Properties LLC* [2002] EWHC 496, [2002] 2 BCLC 151 (Ch).

[37] *Mills v Mills* (1938) 60 CLR 150 (HCA).

[38] See *Howard Smith Ltd v Ampol Petroleum Ltd* [1974] AC 821 (PC).

Moreover, the position of the case law has been, until recently, that even if one assumed the impropriety of a takeover offer that had already been accepted by the target shareholders, this did not automatically make it void or unenforceable. This required a certain level of knowledge of the impropriety by the target shareholders.[39] No matter what level of knowledge were required—whether actual or constructive, dishonesty or unconcionability[40]—it would be impossible for it to be the case in a hostile takeover, since all target shareholders could not be in possession of such knowledge. As for friendly takeover agreements it would require a consideration of all actions and knowledge of both the acquiring and the target's board as a whole in the context of their relationship.[41] However, in the recent case of *Criterion Properties Plc v Stratford UK Properties LLC*,[42] the House of Lords held that the conscionability or otherwise of a party seeking to enforce an agreement which has been entered into for improper purposes by the other party is irrelevant. In contrast, for the House of Lords the issue was whether those signing on behalf of the parties had actual or ostensible authority to do so. In other words for the House of Lords the case turned primarily on agency law, rendering the proper purpose test a question of authority. This is where the restatement of the duty in statute (section 171 of the CA 2006) seems to be heading as well.

Having, however, authority in the first place is something different to how authority is exercised. Are the agent's motivations relevant to his authority? Or are such motivations examined on equitable constraints grounds? The former is what the House of Lords in the *Criterion Properties* case seems to suggest.[43] However, if this is the case how is abuse of directors' powers regulated? This would mean that the only way is to seek protection in the 'non-conflict' rule. Nevertheless, not every abusive exercise of director's powers gives rise to a conflict of interest situation.

In any case even if one assumes that the target shareholders or the target directors—in a hostile offer or a friendly merger agreement respectively—cannot rely on the ostensible authority of the acquiring directors to make the offer in question, the acquiring shareholders need to show that their directors did not have the authority to make a takeover offer in these

[39] For a well-known summary of the relevant authorities see Slade LJ in *Rolled Steel Products (Holdings) Ltd v British Steel Corporation*[1986] Ch 246 (CA).

[40] See about the different tests among others *BCCI v Akindele* [2001] Ch 437 (CA); *Manchester Trust v Furness* [1895] 2 QB 539 (CA); *Eagle Trust plc v SBC Securities* [1993] 1 WLR 484 (ChD) 497); *Re Montagu's Settlement* [1987] Ch 264 (Ch); *Belmont (No 2)* [1980] 1 All ER 393 (CA).

[41] *Criterion Properties Plc v Stratford UK Properties LLC* [2003] EWCA Civ 1783, [2003] 1 WLR 2108 (CA).

[42] *Criterion Properties Plc v Stratford UK Properties LLC* [2004] UKHL 28, [2004] 1 WLR 1846.

[43] See, however, *AL Underwood Ltd v Bank of Liverpool & Martins* [1924] 1 KB 775 (CA); and *Reckitt v Barnett, Pembroke & Slater Ltd* [1928] 2 KB 244 (HL). See also P Watts, 'Case Comment, Authority and Mismotivation' (2005) 121 *Law Quarterly Review* 4.

terms and under the specific circumstances. This, by any means, is not an easy burden to discharge for the reasons already discussed above.

In addition, as it will be argued in chapter nine, the Panel is very unlikely to accept a withdrawal of an offer in such cases, and it is very likely that the acquiring directors will be in breach of rule 2.5 of the City Code on Takeovers and Mergers ('the Takeover Code').[44] This inevitably means that is very difficult for an offer, once posted, to be withdrawn on the basis that the offer was made for improper purposes. Hence, even in cases where the acquisition is found to have been made for improper purposes, enforcement must come very quickly if it is to be effective.

The area which the proper purpose doctrine covers, whether it is subsumed in the issue of authority or extends to providing constraints in such authority, is closely related to the no conflict rule examined below, since equitable constraints of authority are also imposed by a no-conflict rule. To that effect the proper purpose doctrine and the no-conflict rule touch on common ground in this case.

Finally, on the basis of the aforementioned analysis, one could conclude that even if the proper purpose doctrine can, theoretically, provide (on the basis of such wide interpretation) a means of protection against self-interested acquisitions, such an approach exceeds the current strict judicial interpretation of the doctrine. It can only work in extreme cases, expressed through the grounds of review of such actions like 'Wednesbury unreasonableness' or 'capriciousness', 'utter unreasonableness', or 'amiable lunacy'.[45] However, such cases are very unlikely to escape the discipline of the market.

C The No-Conflict Rule (Sections 175 and 177 of CA 2006)

This part does not seek to cover the general operation and mechanics of the common law disability or the statutory duties related to conflicts of duties and interests for company directors. Under the no-conflict rule, directors should not place themselves in a position where their personal interests or duties to other persons are liable to conflict with their duties to the company.[46] The typology of conflicts of interest includes situations when a director makes personal use of information, property or opportu-

[44] The Takeover Code, 8th edn (London, Panel on Takeovers and Mergers, May 2006). See ch 9 below and part III of this chapter.

[45] Nolan, 'The Proper Purpose Doctrine and Company Directors' (n 18 above) 21; *Mills v Mills* (1938) 60 CLR 150 (HCA) 163 (Latham CJ); *Leon v York-O-Matic* [1966] 1 WLR 1450 (Court); *Re Manisty's Settlement Trust* [1973] 2 All ER 1203 (ChD); *Hutton v West Cork Ry Co* (1883) 23 Ch D 654; Re a Company (No 00370 of 1987) [1988] 1 WLR 1068 (Ch). See also L Sealy, 'Bona Fides and Proper Purposes in Corporate Decisions' (1989) 15 *Monash University Law Review* 265.

[46] *Aberdeen Rly v Blaikie Bros* (1854) 1 Macq 461 (HL).

nities belonging to the company or when a director enters into a contract with his company. Conflicts of interest may also arise whenever a director makes a profit in the course of being a director, in the matter of his directorship, without the knowledge and consent of his company. This latter case has been developed almost as a separate no-profit rule.[47] The prohibition of conflict of interest is not an absolute prohibition rule. It is well accepted that conflicts of interest which could otherwise give rise to breaches of the common law no-conflict or no-profit rule can be authorised by the shareholders, despite the difference in the severity and scrutiny shown by various courts in determining the existence of such conflicts.[48] In other words, common law has developed certain disabilities rather than duties (absolute prohibitions).[49]

Under the Companies Act 2006, section 175 establishes a duty that replaces the no-conflict rule applying to directors. This duty covers all conflicts, actual and potential, between the interests of the director and the interests of the company. This includes conflicts relating to the exploitation of the company's property, information or opportunity for personal purposes. The only conflicts not covered by this duty are those relating to transactions or arrangements with the company (interests in transactions or arrangements with the company must be declared under section 177 in the case of proposed transactions or under section 182 in the case of existing transactions, unless an exception applies under those sections). Section 180 preserves the ability of the members of a company to authorise conflicts that would otherwise be a breach of this duty, and allows for such an authorisation by the independent directors if the constitution of a public company permits this explicitly. Finally, under section 180 of the CA 2006 the duty is not infringed in situations that cannot reasonably be regarded as likely to give rise to a conflict of interest.

Section 177 of the CA 2006 requires a director to disclose any interest, direct or indirect, that he has in relation to a proposed transaction or arrangement with the company. The director does not need to be a party to the transaction for the duty to apply. An interest of another person in a contract with the company may require the director to make a disclosure under this duty if that other person's interest amounts to a direct or indirect interest on the part of the director. While in the case of conflicts of interests, under section 175 of the CA 2006 shareholders' authorisation is required, shareholder approval for the transaction is not a requirement of the statutory duty under section 177. The duty requires directors to disclose their interest in any transaction before the company enters into the transaction.[50]

47 For a discussion on this issue see Ferran, *Company Law and Corporate Finance* (n 10 above) 189.

48 See, eg *Regal (Hastings) Ltd v Gulliver* [1942] 1 All ER 378, [1967] 2 AC 134n (HL). See also *Henderson v Merrett Syndicates* [1995] 2 AC 145 (HL).

49 *Movitex Ltd v Bulfield* [1988] BCLC 104 (ChD).

50 Section 177(4).

The director must declare the nature and extent of his interest to the other directors. Disclosure to the members is not sufficient. It is also not enough for the director to merely state that he has an interest. No declaration of interest is required if the director's interest in the transaction cannot reasonably be regarded as likely to give rise to a conflict of interest.[51]

Nevertheless, it should be noted that disclosure in itself will not validate a transaction where it is entered into by a director either in breach of his duty to act bona fide in the interests of the company as a whole, or for improper purposes.[52]

On the basis of the above typology, in the case of self-interested acquisitions one could identify mainly three instances of the no-conflict rule. One should bear in mind that for the purpose of the analysis, one assumes that the director has neither a direct or indirect relation with the target company nor receives any gift or benefit pursuant to the transaction by the target company. The typology of self-interested acquisitions has been already covered in chapter three. There the view was submitted that corporate acquisitions, as more acute types of business decisions, involve significant conflicts of interests. The rationales behind manager's intentions to pursue acquisitions that are not profitable to their shareholders were there classified into two main categories: incentives for return maximisation—either in the form of compensation or in the form of prestige or visibility—and incentives for risk reduction and increase in managers' job security. The first set of incentives was found to include 'empire building' and misuse of 'free cash flow' situations. The second set of incentives comprises allocations of corporate wealth to acquisitions that seek either to diversify at a firm level or deter potential bidders.

On the basis of the analysis submitted there, it is unlikely that acquisitions proposed on the basis of the aforementioned incentives will give rise to situations where the acquiring directors have a direct or indirect interest in the bid under the meaning of section 177 of CA 2006. This is because under such a statement one needs to prove that a director or a third party with whom the director is connected is a party to the transaction. However, this is not a case covered by the aforementioned classification of self-motivated acquisitions. Any indirect benefits the director may have, according to the abovementioned classification of self-interested acquisitions, will not constitute an interest within the meaning of section 177. If there is a breach of the Companies Act it is more likely to be a conflict under section 175 of CA 2006.

In addition, there is great difficulty arguing that the increased visibility or job-security received by a director pursuant to a self-motivated acquisition is a 'secret profit' covered by section 175 of CA 2006. Even in cases where the acquisition results in an increase in the director's remuneration

[51] Section 177(6)(a). Previously Reg 85 of Table A imposed a materiality test.
[52] *Neptune Ltd v Fitzgerald (No 2)* [1995] BCC 1000 (ChD).

due to the increased 'size' of the company pursuant to the acquisition, this is more likely to be considered a result of the operation of an already approved reward policy, rather than a 'secret profit' from the acquisition. Such types of acquisitions may, of course, be caught under section 172 of CA 2006 as already analysed, but from a policy perspective they are more likely to be effectively caught by rules related to directors' remuneration or more effective performance-based reward strategies.[53]

The final question that arises is as to what extent a self-interested acquisition could amount to misappropriation of corporate property (namely, the purchase price). Misappropriation of corporate property broadly falls within the typology of conflicts covered by section 175. In addition, under common law, if the director is found to have disposed of corporate property (the purchase price) in breach of trust, or in breach of his duty to act in good faith for the best interests of his company, then such an action (in contrast to other instances of the no-conflict rule) is not ratifiable. Nevertheless, this distinction is not carried forward in the Companies Act 2006, which treats all instances of conflicts of interests, save for interests in a company's contracts, in the same way. In any case any takeover offer that will amount to a misappropriation of corporate property is more likely to be caught, as implied already, by the duty to act in good faith for the interests of the company, or the restated statutory duty of section 172 of the CA 2006 that directors should promote the success of the company. In addition, the same argument provided in the case of the application of the proper purpose doctrine, equally applies in the case of the no-conflict rule. Once it can be shown that there are benefits for the company from the proposed bid, it is extremely difficult to argue that the bid constitutes a misappropriation of corporate property to the benefit of the director. And if no benefits for the company accrue then it is easier for the plaintiffs, as it will be argued below, to base their case on a breach of the directors' duty of care, in the light of the stricter relevant requirements imposed by the Code.

An additional limitation of the operation of the no-conflict rule in takeovers is the type of remedies that the company has. It is well established that where directors place themselves in a position where their duties and their personal interests conflict, any contract involved is voidable at the instance of the company. It is not necessary for a conflict to actually materialise. A real possibility of conflict will suffice to set aside the contract.[54] This would mean that, if a bid were established to have been launched on the basis of an undisclosed interest of one of the acquiring directors or were found to be a misappropriation of corporate property, the acquiring company would have the right to retract the offer. Such

[53] See ch 5 below.

[54] *Boulting v Association of Cinematograph Television and Allied Technicians* [1963] 2 QB 606 (CA).

result, however, is in direct conflict with the position established in the Code, which now also has a statutory footing. In addition, it is very likely that the interests of the target shareholders will be found to intervene as bona fide third parties' rights.[55]

Overall it should be noted that while it seems reasonable that a no-conflict duty is the obvious remedy to address possible self-interested acquisitions falling into the typology described above, it is not necessarily a solution with any material practical benefits. This is because the types of 'profits' that directors receive in self interested acquisition are not so obvious for a clear cut application of the rule, and if they are so obvious according to the specificities of each case other duties may also apply, to which reliance may be easier. In addition such cases are very unlikely to escape the discipline of the market. Finally, disclosure at a regulatory level seems to be an easier way to regulate such conflicts.[56]

II SHAREHOLDERS SUITS AND LIMITATIONS OF EX POST JUDICIAL REVIEW

The application of directors' duties, as an effective mechanism to protect the acquirer's shareholders, is hampered by a number of limitations and procedural burdens. Since fiduciary duties are owed to the company and not to individual shareholders, any action against the directors must be taken, under normal circumstances, by the board[57] on the company's behalf, which means that if the board is not willing to do so the shareholders need to remove it.

This means, first of all, that the acquiring shareholders are not in the position to pursue a personal action since directors owe no fiduciary duties to individual shareholders except in special circumstances where they take upon themselves to offer advice to their shareholders.[58] In addition, the mere diminution in the share value of the acquiring firm cannot be considered a personal loss of its shareholders but a reflection of the loss suffered by the bidder. Accordingly, permitting shareholders to have a personal action against the acquirer's directors would result in double recovery.[59]

[55] *Hely-Hutchinson v Brayhead Ltd* [1968] 1 QB 549, [1967] 3 All ER 98 (HL).

[56] See below.

[57] Also the liquidator, or some times the general meeting.

[58] *Gething v Kilner* [1972] 1 All ER 1166 (ChD).

[59] *Prudential Assurance Co Ltd v Newman Industries Ltd* [1982] Ch 204; *Johnson v Gore Wood* [2001] 1 All ER 481, on both of which there is now an extensive subsequent case law. However, the acquiring shareholders may have a case where their directors owe them fiduciary duties for their advice. This may happen when the acquirer's directors advise the shareholders to agree not to exercise their pre-emptive rights in relation to a share issue, in order for these shares to be used as a consideration offered to target shareholders. In that situation, the acquirer's shareholders suffer a personal loss, namely, that of the dilution of their shareholdings, since they waive their personal pre-emptive rights.

The situation does not change, even in circumstances where the shareholders' approval is required for the acquisition in question and the shareholders are misguided, either fraudulently or negligently, to approve a value-decreasing acquisition. This is because, regardless of the nature of the subsequent loss, which would be a discount in the market price, the acquiring shareholders, in approving the transaction, act collectively as an organ of the company—the general meeting—and they do not exercise a personal right. Their personal rights are limited to voting in the general meeting. It is the resolution of the general meeting that approves the transaction or not. However, shareholders can be compensated for the costs incurred for attending the meeting.[60] An example where a shareholder may have a personal action is when he is induced to exercise prematurely an option in otherwise unfavourable terms in order to support the acquisition in the meeting approving the transaction.[61] Overall, the issue will be further considered later in this chapter, where the directors' liabilities for published information in the context of a takeover will be analysed. This is an area where the possibility of personal actions seems, at least theoretically, more viable.

A petition under section 994 of the CA 2006 (which reinstated section 459 of the Companies Act 1985), on the grounds that the shareholders have been unfairly prejudiced by their directors' decision to launch a specific takeover offer, will not afford much assistance to the acquiring shareholders either, since the application of section 459 in public companies has been very limited. A statistical survey covering the period between 1988 and 1997 showed that 97 per cent of the petitions filed under section 459 at the High Court in London related to private companies, and 93 per cent to companies with ten or fewer members.[62] The reason behind this is that there must be a breach of the articles of association or of another shareholders' agreement in order for the petition to be accepted.[63] However, such agreements are very unlikely to take place in public companies, due to dispersed share ownership, and section 994 of the CA 2006 does not introduce anything new that could change the current approach.

The above limitations leave as a single viable option that of derivative action. The derivative action, as it has been formulated in common law, as well as the 'Majority Rule' and 'Proper Plaintiff' principles rationalised as 'the rule in *Foss v Harbottle*',[64] impose a number of restrictions in terms of a derivative action to remedy wrongdoing by one or some of the company's directors. Under the common law rule, if an individual shareholder

[60] *Prudential Assurance Co Ltd v Newman Industries Ltd* (n 59 above).

[61] For a further analysis of directors' liabilities to individual shareholders see below under directors' liabilities.

[62] Law Commission, *Shareholder Remedies: A Consultation Paper* (1996).

[63] *Re Blue Arrow* (1987) 3 BCC 618; [1987] BCLC 585 (ChD). *O'Neill v Phillips* [1999] 1 WLR 1092 (HL).

[64] *Foss v Harbottle* (1843) 2 Hare 461 (CA).

wants to pursue an action on the company's behalf, he has to prove that the acquisition in question amounts to a fraud on the minority, in order for a derivative action to be permitted[65]—although if he proves it the company has to pay the costs.[66] A self-motivated acquisition rarely involves an actual misappropriation of corporate property,[67] and negligence on the part of the directors about the value of the target is not enough by itself to constitute fraud on the minority.[68] In general, as the law stands now, the obscurity and the complexity of the law relating to the ability of a shareholder to bring proceedings on behalf of the company makes the derivative action an ineffective means of protection for the acquirer's shareholders.[69]

Section 260 of the CA 2006 introduces a new statutory derivative procedure with different criteria for to whether a shareholder can pursue an action on behalf of the company. In line with the recommendations of the Law Commission,[70] the derivative claim is available for breach of the duty to exercise reasonable care, skill and diligence, even if the director has not benefited personally, including, therefore, misjudgement as a permitted basis for the action to be brought forward. It is also not necessary for the applicant to show that the wrongdoing directors control the majority of the company's shares.

Sections 261 to 264 of the CA 2006 introduce a two-stage procedure for permission to continue a derivative claim. At the first stage the applicant will be required to make a prima facie case for permission to continue a derivative claim and the court will be required to consider the issue on the basis of the evidence filed by the applicant only, without requiring evidence from the defendant. The courts must dismiss the application if the applicant cannot establish a prima facie case. At the second stage—but before the substantive action begins—the court may require evidence to be provided by the company. The sections set out a list of the matters which the court must take into account in considering whether to give permission and the circumstances in which the court is bound to refuse permission.

Some of the problems could be alleviated through the proposed statutory derivative action, but the above procedural problems that arise in the case of an ex-post judicial review, namely who and under what circum-

[65] The exception was set in *Foss v Harbottle* (n 64 above) and was further explained in *Prudential Assurance Co Ltd v Newman Industries Ltd* [1982] Ch 204 (CA).

[66] Civil Procedure Rules.

[67] C Bradley 'Corporate Control: Markets and Rules' (1990) 53 *Modern Law Review* 170; see also *Burland v Earle* [1902] AC 83 (PC) 93.

[68] See *Pavlides v Jensen* [1956] Ch 565 (Ch).

[69] A new statutory derivative action governed by rules of court, which will replace the main exception to the rule in *Foss v Harbottle*, may alleviate some of the problems associated with the application of derivative action.

[70] The Company Law Review Steering Group, *Modern Company Law for a Competitive Economy: Final Report* (2001).

stances and procedures can bring an action to the court are not the only problems associated with the application of fiduciary duties. An additional problem derives from the fact that the court has hindsight of the transaction contrary to the managers' foresight. In other words, courts review the transaction under question ex post. In that sense, it is difficult for the court to know whether an acquisition with a bad outcome for the acquirer's shareholders is a product of disloyalty or just poor management or whether it can be attributed to many other factors that affect markets and businesses.

III DUE DILIGENCE AND THE DUTY OF CARE AND SKILL

It is well established that acquisitions are complex transactions that require substantial due diligence processes. Such processes involve valuing the target, investigating its business history and legal structure, analysing its financial resources, the synergies expected, the costs associated (such as purchase costs, costs of capital, post-acquisition and integration costs), examining customer and marketing related issues, market characteristics, major processes in the target, its human resources and many other aspects of the target and the transaction. A proper due diligence minimises overpayment and synergy risk.

It is also well established that directors' owe a duty of care to their company. Accordingly, an initial logical conclusion that one can arrive at is that, if an acquisition proves to be under-performing and negligence can be identified during the pre-acquisition due diligence process, then the company could be compensated—and thus the shareholders—by claiming damages for breach of duty of care and skill from the directors.[71]

The duty of care, although now also stated in statute, traditionally can be based on equity, tort,[72] or even contract, where an employment contract exists between the company and the director. The latter is more likely to be the case with directors in big public companies, which are the subject of this analysis. The practical consequence of such a distinction is that contractually-drafted duties of care and skill may be structured as stricter than the equitable or tortious duty, provided, though, that relevant clauses are included in the employment contract.

Traditionally, English courts have been reluctant to intervene in the business decisions of corporate directors.[73] According to a famous and often repeated dictum of Lord Eldon LC in *Carlen v Drury*,[74] courts are not

[71] Whether the directors can pay or not is another issue.

[72] The two overlap and, as Ferran states, there is evidence that the equitable and tortious duty of care may be the same: Ferran, *Company Law and Corporate Finance* (n 10 above).

[73] *Howard Smith v Ampol Petroleum* [1974] AC 821 (PC) 835 (Lord Wilberforce); *Harlowe's Nominees Pty Ltd v Woodside (Lake Entrance) Oil Co NL* (1968) 121 CLR 483 (H Ct of Aust) 492.

[74] *Carlen v Drury* (1812) 1 Ves & B 154 (HL).

required 'on every occasion to take the management of every Playhouse and Brewhouse in the Kingdom'. The reluctance of courts to review matters of business management is also largely noticed and reported in the relevant literature.[75] This unwillingness of English courts to intervene in business judgements does not extend to the lengths of the US 'business judgement rule', which forms a procedural barrier to claims for negligent management against company directors. However, courts seem to favour examining a case on the basis of whether the directors were acting in honesty for the best interests of their company, rather than judging the quality of the transaction on the basis of whether it was a management mistake or not. As Lord Wilberforce stated in *Howard Smith Ltd v Ampol Petroleum Ltd*,

> [t]here is no appeal on merits from management decisions to courts of law nor will courts of law assume to act as a kind of supervisory board over decisions within the powers of management honestly arrived at.[76]

Until recently, even when courts have intervened, the subjective nature of the 'reasonable layman test' applied by the courts has made the application of the common law duty of care extremely difficult. This has been because, as Ferran argues, incompetence has been its own defence.[77] However, recent cases accept, as an accurate expression of the common law duty, the test contained in section 214(4) of the Insolvency Act 1986 in relation to wrongful trading, which provides an objective standard for directors' behaviour.[78] It is also that section on which new section 174 of the CA 2006—in codifying the director's duty to exercise reasonable, care, skill and diligence—is modelled, including an objective assessment of the director's conduct. The section provides that a director owes a duty to his company to exercise the same standard of care, skill and diligence that would be exercised by a reasonably diligent person with:

(a) the general knowledge, skill and experience that may reasonably be expected of a person carrying out the same functions as the director in relation to that company (an objective test); and
(b) the general knowledge, skill and experience that the director actually has (a subjective test).

The reluctance of courts to intervene in business decisions is also manifested through the degree of mismanagement that has to be established for

[75] Davies, *Gower's Principles of Modern Company Law* (n 8 above); Ferran, *Company Law and Corporate Finance* (n 10 above); Nolan, 'The Proper Purpose Doctrine and Company Directors' supra; L Sealy, 'Bona Fides and Proper Purposes in Corporate Decisions' (1989) 15 *Monash University Law Review* 265, B Cheffins, *Company Law: Theory, Structure, and Operation*, (Oxford/New York, Oxford University Press, 1997) 309–21.

[76] *Howard Smith Ltd v Ampol Petroleum Ltd* [1974] AC 821 (PC) 835.

[77] Ferran, *Company Law and Corporate Finance* (n 10 above) 213.

[78] *Norman v Theodore Goddard* [1991] BCLC 1027; *Re D'Jan of London Ltd* [1994] 1 BCLC 561 (ChD); *Cohen v Selby* [2001] 1 BCLC 176 (CA) 183.

a director to be found liable for a breach of his duty. Even recent cases applying an objective test seem to require conduct which amounts to more than a mere mismanagement and has been given the characterisation of 'gross negligence', although the term does not seem to have a fixed meaning.[79] For example, in *Dorchester Finance Co Ltd v Stebbing*[80] the non-executive directors were signing blank cheques; in *Re D'Jan of London Ltd*[81] the director signed an insurance proposal form without reading it; while in *Cohen v Selby*[82] the director abjectly surrendered his director's duties to another person, who effectively acted as the manager of the company.

Another limitation on the application of the duty of care, in the case of takeovers, is that the conduct of the offer is usually delegated to some of the company's directors and that the bidder's board usually relies on valuations and reports produced by senior employees, professional experts and even the target.[83] Hence, directors cannot guarantee that all the information analyses, on which the decision to acquire the target is based, are accurate.

However, in contrast to other business decisions, the Takeover Code specifies, to a very technical extent, the level of due diligence and care required by the acquiring directors in takeovers. In that respect, the application of a uniform and objective duty of care for corporate directors can serve as a 'blank rule', permitting the diligence requirements of the Takeover Code to provide significant substance to the new Companies Act objective test for corporate directors and to address some of the aforementioned inefficiencies of the application of the common law duty of care.

According to new rule 2.5, which has been amended pursuant to the implementation of the Takeovers Directive (2004/25/EC) to incorporate the old General Principle 3, an offeror should only announce an offer after the most careful and responsible consideration. Although it can be argued that rule 2.5 seeks to protect the reasonable expectations of the market and the target shareholders that an announced takeover will materialise into an actual offer and no false market will be created,[84] it cannot be denied that, at the same time, the same requirements can have an added value in determining the acquiring directors' duty of care towards their own shareholders, under the Act.

According to the Panel, General Principle 3 (now rule 2.5) requires that the offeror's directors make an offer on a fully-informed basis. The more important the information to the decision of the offeror, the greater are the steps that should be taken by the acquiring directors and their advisers

[79] Ferran, *Company Law and Corporate Finance* (n 10 above) 213.
[80] *Dorchester Finance Co Ltd v Stebbing* [1989] BCLC 498.
[81] *Re D' Jan of London Ltd* [1994] 1 BCLC 561 (ChD).
[82] *Cohen v Selby* [2001] 1 BCLC 176 (CA) 183.
[83] Especially for the last issue see the last part of this chapter.
[84] See ch 9 below.

before the offer is announced.[85] The required due diligence depends on the type of the offer.[86] In friendly takeovers, the bidder is able to put pressure on the target for additional information, while in hostile offers it can only rely on information available to the market and on its own estimates. Similarly, in the case of an offer by a very large company for a very small one, purely to obtain a particular product, the target's profitability or future borrowings might be irrelevant to the bidder and therefore be ignored. On the other hand, in a merger of companies of similar size, such information could be crucial.[87] In the case of Wm Low's offer for the supermarket Budgens plc, the Panel held that relying on a computer model was not enough for the offeror to discharge its duty of care under the Code. For that, it would require the acquiring directors and their advisers to seek specific estimates about Budgens' future borrowings and ascertain which part of future capital expenditure should be committed.[88]

Moreover, according to Appendix 3 of the Takeover Code, in cases where the board of directors delegates the conduct of the offer or the preparation of the takeover documents to individual directors or a committee of directors, the board, as a whole, must ensure that proper arrangements are in place to enable it to monitor that conduct so that each director may fulfil his responsibilities under the Code. Responsibility thus lies collectively on all the acquirer's directors, regardless of whether responsibility for specific conduct has been delegated to a part of the acquirer's board.

In addition, the full board must be kept fully informed of any details associated with the takeover, for example, details about dealings in relevant securities, agreements, undertakings, guarantees, or expenditure, including fees or any other obligations entered into by their company in the context of the offer. All directors must also be promptly furnished with copies of all documents and announcements issued on behalf of their company that bear on the offer.[89] Furthermore, the directors to whom the responsibility for the offer has been delegated should be in a position to justify their actions and proposed courses of action.[90] Moreover, the opinions of the advisers must be available to the board, where appropriate.[91] To the same end, regular meetings must be held during the offer period for all the directors to be kept informed about any actions taken. Finally, a director that has a question concerning the propriety of any action, as far as the Code is concerned, should ensure that the Panel is consulted.[92]

[85] Proposed Offer of Wm Low and Co plc for Budgens plc, Panel Statement 1989/14 (August 1989).
[86] *Ibid.*
[87] Panel Statement 1989/14 (n 85 above).
[88] Panel Statement 1989/14 (n 85 above).
[89] Appendix 3, 1(a) of the Takeover Code.
[90] Appendix 3, 1(b) of the Takeover Code.
[91] Appendix 3, 1(c) of the Takeover Code.
[92] Appendix 3, 1 of the Takeover Code.

In view of the above, the Takeover Code imposes an enhanced and collective duty on the board of the acquiring company: to make a takeover decision on a fully-informed basis and after the most careful consideration—which extends, under certain circumstances, to the requirement of actively seeking additional information; to be kept fully informed and actively participate in the monitoring of the takeover during the offer period, regardless of any delegation of responsibility to specific persons in the board; and finally, to disclose any concerns to and closely communicate with the Panel. These requirements may be useful in determining the directors' common law and statutory duties of care and skill in a takeover situation.

Non-executive directors must also comply with the above requirements and thus are obliged to monitor more actively an acquisition process. Whereas previously non-executive directors could argue that they did not possess the skills to monitor and raise any concerns during a takeover, now they are expected to meet the standard of care required by the Code.[93]

Finally, the Takeover Code's duty of care is further defined in the Code's information provision requirements. In fact, as directors who are found liable for negligence may not have sufficiently 'deep pockets' for their company to be compensated, the ability of the shareholders to be able to make a fully-informed judgement of their own about the prospects of the acquisition may be even more important. For that purpose, the prompt and effective dissemination of high quality information is essential.

IV INFORMATION PROVISION IN THE CONTEXT OF TAKEOVERS, AND THE ACQUIRING DIRECTORS' LIABILITIES

Information provision serves three functions in the context of a takeover. First, it facilitates the decision making of the acquirer's shareholders, when it is up to them to approve a takeover. In that context, information provision is an underlying assumption of shareholders' approval rights or of other manifestations of shareholders' voice and internal control.[94] Secondly, information provision facilitates the operation of capital markets. As discussed above, high quality information increases market confidence in the acquisition and plays an important role in the operation of capital markets.[95]

Finally, information provision in the context of a takeover externalises the acquiring directors' duty of care. The strict standards of care required during the preparation of the takeover documents or the listing particulars, where necessary, not only constitute an early alert mechanism for any

[93] See below.
[94] See ch 5 below.
[95] See ch 3 above.

of the acquiring directors' misjudgements but they also, as seen above,[96] serve as an objective account of the directors' care and diligence in takeovers.

In addition, the information provision requirements of the Takeover Code and the Listing Rules represent not only an answer to directors' negligence, but also a response to self-interested acquisitions. The need to publicise a number of critical details about the acquisition means that directors who want to pursue an acquisition for their own benefit have to openly lie or, at least, exaggerate the potential benefits of the transaction in question. In that sense, there can be an indirect form of control over self-interested acquisitions through controlling the quality of the information that the directors have to produce in relation to a takeover. Accordingly, an internal company issue indirectly becomes a public policy concern.

However, in order for the information provision requirements to serve the above functions, a number of prerequisites must be met. First, the content and type of information published must be of use to the acquiring shareholders, irrespective of whether it is directly addressed to them or not. Secondly, there must be sufficient ex ante quality controls, and thirdly, breaches of the relevant requirements should be accompanied by sanctions and liabilities that can discipline the acquiring directors.

A The Content of Takeover-related Information

(i) *The UK Listing Authority Rules*

The detail of information produced by the acquirer, in accordance with the UK Listing Authority ('UKLA') Rules, depends upon the size of the transaction and the consideration offered. In the case of acquisitions whose value does not exceed 5 per cent of the value of the acquirer[97] (class 3 transactions),[98] no announcement is required unless the consideration includes the issue of securities for which listing will be sought.[99] In that case, a very basic notification is required—which is not of great use to the acquiring shareholders—including the amount of the securities being issued and brief details about the parties involved and either the value of the transaction or the value of the net assets acquired, whichever is greater. If for any other reason the bidder is required to make a public announcement, any information that the company releases to the market must also be notified to a Regulatory Information Service.[100] The notifica-

[96] See above the analysis about the duty of care.
[97] See below under Approval Rights, ch 5, for how the comparison of the size is made.
[98] LR 10.2.2(1) of the Listing Rules.
[99] LR 10.3.1 of the Listing Rules.
[100] LR 10.3.2 of the Listing Rules.

tion must include the particulars of the transaction and either the value of the consideration offered and how it is being satisfied, or the net assets acquired or disposed.

When the value of the consideration offered or the target is more than five per cent but less than 25 per cent of the value of the bidder (class 2 transaction), the bidder has to notify a Regulatory Information Service without delay after the terms of the transaction are agreed. The notification must include more detailed information than class 3 transactions, including, among other things, some more substantial pieces of information, such as how the consideration offered is satisfied, the value of the net assets of the target, the profits attributable to the target, the effect of the transaction on the bidder (including any benefits which are expected to accrue to the bidder) and details of any service contracts of proposed directors of the bidder.[101] The Financial Services Authority ('FSA') must also be advised and a supplementary notification shall be made if, at any time after the initial notification, there has been a significant change affecting any matter contained in the earlier notification, or a significant new matter has arisen which needs to be disclosed.[102]

In the case where the takeover is classified as class 1 transaction,[103] information requirements become more substantial. The bidder has to comply with the information requirements for class 2 transactions. In addition, an explanatory circular must be dispatched to the acquirer's shareholders in order for the company to seek the shareholders' approval.[104] The class 1 circular must comply with the general requirements relating to circulars set out in rule 13 of the UKLA Listing Rules, and must be normally submitted to the FSA for approval prior to its publication.[105] Moreover, it must comply with rule LR 13.5 of the Listing Rules in respect of the financial information included in the circular, and it must include a statement of the effect of the acquisition on the assets or earnings and liabilities of the group,[106] and a declaration of full responsibility for the information contained in the document by the acquiring directors.[107]

Among other things, the circular must also contain any major interests in shares, material contracts, significant changes, the working capital, any directors' interests in shares or in the transactions, or any changes in the directors' service contracts, the group prospects, as well as a report by a competent professional on any profit forecast included. The Listing Rules also include a number of additional requirements as well as the content and the basis on which the information required to be included must be

[101] LR 10.4.1 of the Listing Rules.
[102] LR 10.4.2 of the Listing Rules.
[103] See ch 5 below.
[104] LR 10.5.1 of the Listing Rules.
[105] LR 13.2.1 of the Listing Rules.
[106] LR 13.4.1(5) of the Listing Rules.
[107] LR 13.4.1(4) of the Listing Rules.

presented[108]. The analysis of these requirements goes beyond the scope of the present work and for that, readers are referred to rules LR 13.4 to LR 13.8, the annex to rule 13 and rule 6 of the Listing Rules.

In the case where the takeover is classified as a transaction with a related party, LR 11.1 of the Listing Rules stipulates that a circular has to be dispatched to the bidder's shareholders containing the information required by LR 13.3 and LR 13.6. If the transaction also falls within class 1, the information required to be included in a class 1 circular must be included in a related party transaction circular as well.[109] In any other case, information requirements focus on the particulars of the related party transaction, directors' interests and directors' service contracts.[110] Moreover, a statement by the directors must be included (other than any director who is, or of whom an associate is a related party, or who is a director of a related party, in respect of the transaction) to the effect that the transaction is fair and reasonable, as far as the shareholders of the company are concerned, and that the directors have been so advised by an independent adviser acceptable to the FSA.[111] Where applicable, a statement that the related party will abstain—and has undertaken to take all reasonable steps to ensure that its associates will abstain—from voting at the meeting, must also be included.[112]

In cases where securities in the offeror are being offered as consideration, or used to finance the acquisition, both a circular to shareholders of the offeror and a prospectus or a document containing information which is regarded by the FSA as being equivalent to that of the prospectus will be required in connection to a takeover.[113] It should be noted that the acquirer's shareholders are not the normal addressees of the prospectus or the equivalent document, except in the case where the securities issue is made for cash and the acquirer's shareholders are given the opportunity to participate in it or in the case of reverse takeovers. In normal circumstances and in cases of share-for-share exchanges, a prospectus or the

[108] Chapter 13 (LR 13) of the Listing Rules.

[109] LR 13.6.1(7) of the Listing Rules.

[110] LR 13.6 of the Listing Rules.

[111] LR 13.6.1(5) of the Listing Rules.

[112] LR 13.6.1(6) of the Listing Rules.

[113] Under the Prospectus Rules, the bidder will be exempt from the prospectus requirements for public offers or the admission of securities to trading in connection with takeovers and mergers if it produces a document containing information which is regarded by the FSA as being equivalent to that of the prospectus. Since a prospectus needs to be approved by the FSA, the FSA has made it clear that it will apply a full vetting process in order to decide whether a document is equivalent to a prospectus (Issue No 10, List!, June 2005). Alternatively, listing particulars must be prepared and published where a prospectus is not required under the new prospectus regime. Listing particulars will therefore be required where the listed company has applied for the admission of securities specified in Schedule 11A to the FSMA (other than securities specified in paras 2, 4 or 9 of that Schedule) or any other specialist securities for which a prospectus is not required under the Prospectus Directive (LR 4.1.1, Listing Rules).

equivalent document will accompany the offer document. However, since the information required to be included in a circular would otherwise duplicate much of the information included in the prospectus or the equivalent document, it is common practice for the acquirer, when a circular must be sent to its shareholders, to satisfy that requirement by dispatching a short circular accompanied by the actual prospectus or offer document.[114]

(ii) *The Takeover Code*

Probably the most important document required by the Takeover Code is the offer document itself. This contains the formal offer to shareholders of the target and, in compliance with General Principle 2 and rule 23 of the Takeover Code, its content is designed to address the concerns of the target shareholders and inform them, as effectively as possible, about the value of the offer and its prospects.

The offer document is not addressed to the acquiring shareholders. Nevertheless, the detail of information included in it and the scrutiny and standard of care required during its preparation, function as a quality-control mechanism of the offer itself. In addition, it is standard practice for the bidder to discharge its obligation to send a circular to its shareholders, when such an obligation arises, by sending the actual offer document accompanied by a short circular convening an EGM for the purposes of approving the offer. Among other information that must be included in the offer document, the pieces of information that matter more to the acquirer's shareholders are:

— the actual terms of the offer;
— the bidder's intentions concerning the future business of the target company and itself[115];
— the bidder's strategic plans for the target company and itself, and their likely repercussions on employment and the location of the target company's and the bidder's places of business[116];
— the bidder's intentions regarding any redeployment of the fixed assets[117];
— the long-term commercial justification of the proposed offer[118];
— detailed information of the offeror's financial standing[119];
— detailed description of how the offer is to be financed[120];

[114] See G Stedman, *Takeovers* (London, Longman, 1993) 391.
[115] Rule 24.1(a) of the Takeover Code.
[116] Rule 24.1(b) of the Takeover Code
[117] Rule 24.1(c) of the Takeover Code
[118] Rule 24.1(d) of the Takeover Code.
[119] Rule 24.2 of the Takeover Code.
[120] Rule 24.2(f) of the Takeover Code.

— in the case of a securities exchange offer, the effect of full acceptance of the offer on the offeror's assets, profits and business[121];
— detailed account of at least the already published information about the offeree company and its business and financial standing[122];
— detailed account of any shareholdings and dealings of the offeror in the target or vice versa, or of the directors of the offeror and any persons acting in concert[123];
— the offer document must state (in the case of a securities exchange offer only) whether and in what manner the emoluments of the offeror directors will be affected by the acquisition of the offeree company or by any other associated transaction. If there will be no effect this must be stated.

Apart from the offer document, there are a number of voluntary documents that the bidder is likely to publish in the context of a takeover, with the purpose to support its offer. Such documents or statements are more likely to include softer but, at the same time, more critical and specific information on the value, prospects and benefits of the takeover. According to the Takeover Code any advertisements issued during the offer period by the offeror (and the offeree company) in respect of the offer are governed by rule 19.4 and are essentially prohibited, unless they are confined to statements of fact or the Panel consents.[124] The purpose of the present analysis is not to cover the whole regulatory framework of voluntary documents during a takeover offer but to focus on aspects that may be relevant to the acquiring shareholders.

Profit forecasts and asset valuations are two types of voluntary documents that can be used by either the offeror or the target to support their arguments. Those documents seek to demonstrate or attack, depending on who publishes them, the attractiveness of the offer. Profit forecasts may be used in cases where the attractiveness of the transaction lies into the potential synergies of the business combination, while asset valuations are likely to be used when the value of the target lies in its assets rather than its profits, or in cases where the target's assets are undervalued.

Because information included in those documents is soft and considerably subjective, problems arise in relation to its objectivity and verifiability. The Takeover Code attempts to address those problems both by requiring a high standard of care and by a number of verification processes during the documents' preparation and by regulating the type of information included in such documents. In relation to the latter, the

[121] Rule 24.2(d)(ix) of the Takeover Code.
[122] Rule 24.2(e) of the Takeover Code.
[123] Rule 24.3 of the Takeover Code.
[124] Rule 19.4(x) of the Takeover Code. See especially r 19.4(iii) and Stedman, *Takeovers* (n 114 above) 238.

Code defines what can constitute a profit forecast[125] and demands that any assumptions—including commercial assumptions—on which such forecasts are based[126] or any reports verifying the forecasts' calculations or accounting policies[127] be included in the published document.

Notes 1 and 2 on rule 28.2 give detailed guidance on how the assumptions on which a profit forecast is based should be prepared and presented. Among others, the assumptions must be able to indicate the reasonableness and the reliability of the forecast,[128] highlight and, if possible, quantify any uncertain factors that may materially disturb the outcome of the forecast,[129] indicate any limitations to the accuracy of the forecast and specify any major hazards in forecasting profits.[130] Assumptions must also be specific and definite rather than general and vague.[131] Even the most specific assumption may still be dismissed on the grounds that it leaves shareholders in doubt as to its implications. Profit forecasts must also be accompanied by reports on the accounting policies and calculations by the auditors or the consultant accountants of the bidder—or the target. Any financial advisers mentioned in the document must also report on the forecasts.[132] Even in circumstances where the requirements of the Panel cannot be met for reasons of an exceptional nature, a full explanation must be included in the forecast of why the requirements of the Takeover Code were not capable of being met.[133] Similarly, asset valuations should clearly state the basis of the valuation[134] and be accompanied by the report and consent letter of an independent and qualified valuer, depending on the type of the asset, as the Code stipulates.[135]

In the case of share offers the Takeover Code also regulates the content of any merger benefit statements issued by the bidder. Such a statement may be, for example, that the bidder expects from the offeree company to contribute an additional £x million of profit post-acquisition.[136] According to the Code, such statements must be followed by the publication of the bases of the belief (including sources of information) supporting the statement, bases of figures for any comparison, reports by financial advisers and accountants that the statement has been made with due care and consideration, and sufficient analysis and explanation to enable shareholders

[125] Rule 28.6 of the Takeover Code.
[126] Rule 28.2 of the Takeover Code.
[127] Rule 28.3 of the Takeover Code.
[128] Note 1(a) on r 28.2 of the Takeover Code.
[129] Note 1(a) on r 28.2 of the Takeover Code.
[130] Note 1(b) on r 28.2 of the Takeover Code.
[131] Note 2(a)(ii) on r 28.2 of the Takeover Code.
[132] Rule 28.3(b) of the Takeover Code.
[133] Rule 28.4(d) of the Takeover Code.
[134] Rule 29.2 of the Takeover Code.
[135] Rule 29.1(a) and (b) of the Takeover Code.
[136] Note 8 on r 19.1 of the Takeover Code.

to understand the relative importance of the constituent elements of the statement.[137]

The importance of such merger benefit statements for the acquirer's shareholders arises especially in cases of statements that the acquisition will enhance an offeror's earnings per share, where such enhancement depends in whole or in part on material merger benefits. In such cases the Code extends the applicability of the above requirements to also cover such statements.

The above analysis does not seek to provide an exhaustive account of the Code's information-related requirements. It only attempts to indicate that a considerable amount of information is published in the context of a takeover. Such information requirements alert the acquiring shareholders about the business merits of the transaction and provide an initial obstacle to directors who may wish to 'spice up' the prospects of an otherwise self-interested or value-decreasing acquisition. This, coupled with high standards of care, liability rules and quality controls can provide the right incentives to the acquirer's directors to refrain from questionable self-interested or value-decreasing acquisitions and increase the attention paid to the business merits and prospects of a potential acquisition.

B Standard of Care and Directors' Responsibility—Non-executive Directors.

The Takeover Code places considerable importance on the standard of care required for the preparation of the takeover documents. Rule 19.1, as amended to incorporate old General Principle 5 pursuant to the implementation of the Takeovers Directive, stipulates that each document or advertisement issued, or statement made, during the course of an offer must be prepared with the highest standards of accuracy and the information given must be adequately and fairly presented. This applies whether it is issued by the company board or by any adviser on its behalf. Even in the case of profit forecasts, although the Code recognises that there are obvious hazards attached to the forecasting of profits, this by itself, in the eyes of the Panel, is not enough to detract from the necessity of maintaining the highest standards of accuracy and fair presentation in all communications to shareholders in an offer.[138]

The Panel regards that the directors of the offeror are primarily responsible for any document issued to shareholders and for any advertisement published. Even in the case of profit forecasts, which are usually prepared by the financial advisers of the bidder, the directors are considered by the Code as being solely responsible for their compilation, while financial

[137] Note 8 on r 19.1 of the Takeover Code.
[138] Rule 28.1 of the Takeover Code.

advisers must satisfy themselves that the forecast has been prepared in the highest standards by the directors. Rule 19.2 requires that the acquiring directors include a relevant statement of responsibility in all takeover documents. Responsibility lies with all directors in the bidder collectively. If it is proposed that any director should be excluded from such a statement, the Panel's consent is required.[139] Such consent is given only in exceptional circumstances, and in such cases the omission and the reasons for it must be stated in the document or advertisement.[140]

In addition, if detailed supervision of any document or advertisement has been delegated to a committee of the board, each of the remaining directors of the company must reasonably believe that the persons to whom supervision has been delegated are competent to carry it out, and must have disclosed to the committee all relevant facts directly relating to himself or known to him.[141] This does not, however, override the requirements of the UKLA Rules relating to the acceptance of responsibility for a prospectus or equivalent document, where applicable.[142]

As with the Takeover Code, the UKLA Rules require that the directors of the issuer assume responsibility for all the information provided in the prospectus or the equivalent document.[143] Responsibility covers all parts of the prospectus. The exemption provided under the regime prior to the implementation of the Prospectus Directive, which permitted split responsibility where the directors of the target, in the case of recommended offers presumably, accepted responsibility for the information provided to the bidder, was incompatible with the Prospectus Directive (2003/71/EC).[144] Under the previous regime the bidder's directors were only responsible for the rest of the information included in the prospectus. A similar responsibility statement must also accompany class transaction circulars.[145] As in the case of takeover documents, responsibility for the prospectus lies with all directors in the bidder collectively. This, as in the case of takeover documents, lessens the distinction between executive and non-executive directors for the purposes of the duties of care and skill. Hence, a greater degree of diligence may be expected from non-executive directors than would be the case for other corporate matters. According to PR 5.5.6 of the Prospectus Rules, a director can escape responsibility only if the prospectus is published without his knowledge or consent and if, on becoming aware of its publication, he gives reasonable public notice as soon as is practicable that it was published without his knowledge or consent. Overall the bidder directors' responsibility with regards to

139 Rule 19.2(b) of the Takeover Code. See also note 5 on r 19.2.
140 Rule 19.2(b) of the Takeover Code.
141 Note 1 on r 19.2 of the Takeover Code.
142 *Ibid.*
143 Prospectus Rules, PR 5.5.4.
144 See old LR 5.3(b) of the Listing Rules.
145 LR 13.4.1 of the Listing Rules.

information disclosed in the context of a takeover offer is part of a broader, currently open, debate on responsibility for disclosures regarding whether the Transparency Directive (2004/109/EC) liability regime, governing disclosures deriving from the Transparency Directive requirements, should be extended to other disclosures. The issue will be reviewed below where directors' responsibility for information disclosed in the context of a takeover will be examined.

C Ex Ante Quality Controls

Until now, it has been argued that the Code's standard of care requirements and the information produced and published in respect of a takeover can assist in the determination of the corporate directors' duty of care under common law. What remains to be analysed is what quality controls and additional liability remedies exist in order to ensure that the acquiring shareholders are safeguarded against negligent conduct by the offeror's directors (namely, negligent misstatements in the offer documents or fraudulent attempts to disguise self-interested or value-decreasing acquisitions).

The Financial Services and Markets Act 2000, the UKLA Rules and the Takeover Code include a number of ex ante quality controls of the information included in takeover documents, circulars or prospectuses, where applicable. Three different types can be identified:

- notification and approval by a competent authority or the supervisory body;
- report by an independent professional;
- confirmation by a competent and authorised—but not independent—professional.

(i) *Notification and Approval by a Competent Authority or the Supervisory Body.*

According to the UKLA Listing Rules, in cases where the acquisition falls into the definition of class 1 transaction, drafts of the required circulars must be submitted to the FSA for approval.[146] Similar requirements exist with regards to prospectuses where they need to be issued.[147] In addition, while approval of an equivalent to a prospectus document is not required, a person who wishes the FSA to vet an equivalent document must submit the relevant document for vetting.[148] In contrast, the Takeover Code does

[146] LR 13.2.1 of the Listing Rules.
[147] Prospectus Rules, PR 3.1.1.
[148] Prospectus Rules, PR 3.1.14.

not require the prior approval by the Panel or the Executive, of the offer document or any other voluntary takeover documents such as profit forecasts. However, according to rule 19.7, before an offer document is made public a copy must be lodged with the Panel. This requirement has been added to the Code as part of the Code amendments to implement the Takeovers Directive. The Code Committee has confirmed that it considers the current practice of dispatching the offer document under the direction of a financial adviser to the Panel at the same time as it is posted to shareholders to be acceptable in order to comply with rule 19.7 as amended. In addition, the Panel must be consulted in cases that the bidder wishes to depart from the requirements of the Code. In such cases departure is only permitted when the Panel approves the content of the information sought to be published.

(ii) *Report by an Independent Professional.*

There are circumstances where both the UKLA Rules and the Takeover Code require that the acquirer receive a report from an independent competent professional as regards to some aspects of the transaction or the information needing to be published. One such case is asset valuations. According to rule 29.1 of the Takeover Code, when a valuation of assets is given in connection with an offer, it should be supported by the opinion of a named 'independent valuer'.[149] This rule applies not only to land or buildings but also to other assets, such as stocks and individual parts of a business.[150] In addition, the financial information table of a class 1 circular must be accompanied by an accountant's opinion, which must be given by an independent accountant who is qualified to act as an auditor.[151]

What is also of considerable importance to the acquirer's shareholders is that the Takeover Code stipulates in rule 3.2 that the board of the offeror must obtain competent independent advice on any offer when the directors are faced with a conflict of interest or when the offer being made is a reverse takeover. The substance of such advice must be made known to its shareholders.[152] Such advice should be as to whether or not the making of the offer is in the interests of the company's shareholders.[153] Similar requirements are imposed by the UKLA Listing Rules in cases where a takeover falls within the definition of a related-parties transaction.[154] The Code identifies, though non-exhaustively, a number of cases where conflicts of interests may arise, such as where there are significant cross-shareholdings between an offeror and the offeree company, where there

[149] See the Takeover Code, r 29.1(b) and Practice Statement 5 of the Manual.
[150] Rule 29.1(a) of the Takeover Code.
[151] LR 13.5.23 of the Listing Rules.
[152] Rule 3.2 of the Takeover Code.
[153] Note 1 on r 3.2 of the Takeover Code.
[154] See above and chapter 11 (LR 11) of the Listing Rules.

are a number of directors common to both companies, or when a person has a substantial interest in both companies.[155] The board is required to seek independent advice before announcing the offer or any revised offer and shareholders must be given sufficient time to consider the advice prior to any general meeting held to implement the proposed offer.[156]

(iii) *Confirmation by a Competent and Authorised Professional*

While the role of an independent report is restricted to specific circumstances, confirmation of the validity of the published information by the offeror's financial adviser is required in respect of almost any document produced in the context of a takeover. Both the FSA and the Takeover Panel put considerable emphasis on the role of the issuer's / offeror's financial advisers. LR 8.2.1 of the Listing Rules prescribes that a company with, or applying for, a primary listing of its equity securities must appoint a sponsor on each occasion that it makes an application for admission of equity securities which requires the production of a prospectus; or is accompanied by a certificate of approval from another competent authority; or when is required to produce a class 1 circular. In other words in all public offers accompanied by a prospectus, or a certificate of approval from another competent authority, or a class 1 circular, a sponsor of such an offer must be appointed. However, while financial advisers were included as persons responsible for the content of a prospectus under the previous regime,[157] under the new UKLA Prospectus Rules they will only be deemed responsible if they have accepted responsibility for the prospectus or part of it, or authorised its contents, or acted as guarantor of the issue.[158] A considerable departure from the previous regime is the inclusion, in PR 5.5.9 of the UKLA Prospectus Rules, of the disclaimer clause that

> nothing in the rules in this section is to be construed as making a person responsible for any prospectus by reason only of the person giving advice about its contents in a professional capacity.

More importantly though, takeover offer documents fall within the definition of financial promotions and, accordingly, need to be issued or approved by an authorised person, usually the offeror's merchant bank, stockbroker or financial adviser.[159] Moreover, the Takeover Code emphasises that the Panel regards financial advisers as being responsible to the

[155] Note 3 on r 3.2 of the Takeover Code, see also above about approval of related parties transactions.

[156] Note 1 on r 3.2 of the Takeover Code.

[157] See s 152(1)(d) and (e) of the Financial Services Act 1986 and reg 13 in terms of public offers of unlisted securities.

[158] See PR 5.5.3 and PR 5.5.4 of the Prospectus Rules.

[159] See s 21 of the FSMA 2000.

Panel for guiding their clients with regard to any information released during the course of an offer.[160] According to the Code, advisers must ensure at an early stage that directors and officials of companies are warned that they must consider carefully the Code's requirements.[161]

Special importance is given by both the FSA and the Takeover Panel to the role of financial advisers and other authorised professionals in respect of less factual information, such as profit forecasts, which are likely to be especially influential to unsophisticated investors. The UKLA Listing Rules require that the company's auditors and reporting accountants confirm that they are satisfied that the forecast was compiled after due and careful inquiry by the issuer and on the basis of the assumptions stated in the forecast.[162] Similarly, although the Takeover Code recognises that a forecast and the assumptions on which it is based are the sole responsibility of the directors, a duty is also placed on the financial advisers to satisfy themselves that the forecast has been made with due care and consideration.[163] Auditors or consultant accountants must also satisfy themselves that the forecast, as far as the accounting policies and calculations are concerned, has been properly compiled on the basis of the assumptions made.[164] The Code continues that the financial advisers and accountants obviously have substantial influence on the information about assumptions to be given in a circular; and that they should neither allow an assumption which appears to be unrealistic to be published, nor should they allow one which appears to be important to be omitted, without commenting appropriately in their reports.[165] The above reports should accompany the publication of the relevant forecasts.[166]

D Directors' Liabilities

Statutory law, regulation and common law provide a number of ex post liability remedies in cases where the company's directors negligently or fraudulently omit information or provide inaccurate information in takeover documents. Such remedies may provide for compensation to people who suffer losses because of omissions or inaccuracies—civil liability—or impose criminal sanctions on the issuers or other persons responsible for the content of the documents published. As a systematic analysis of the various remedies goes beyond the scope of the present work, what this part will concentrate on is to identify when compensation

160 Note 1 on r 19.1 of the Takeover Code.
161 *Ibid.*
162 See chapter 13 (LR 13) of the UKLA Listing Rules.
163 Rule 28.1 of the Takeover Code.
164 Note 1(c) on r 28.2 of the Takeover Code.
165 Note 1(c) on r 28.2 of the Takeover Code.
166 Unless the offer is solely for cash. See r 28.3(a) and (b) of the Takeover Code.

rights are awarded to the acquiring shareholders, and whether criminal sanctions are effective in protecting them.

(i) *Criminal and Administrative Sanctions*

A claim has been made in the introduction of this part that the rules governing the dissemination of information in takeovers transform an internal corporate governance issue, namely how to prevent the acquirer's directors from pursuing value-decreasing or self-interested acquisitions, into a public policy concern. It should be noted though, that it is not argued that this is the only or primary function of those rules. However, as seen above, there is an inevitable causation between the quality of information published and the quality of the underlying acquisition.

When the acquiring directors decide to knowingly publish misleading or selective information, they may face—depending on the circumstances—criminal sanctions. Although such sanctions are designed to address situations of market manipulation, or attempts to defraud or deceive, they also indirectly penalise the underlying purpose of such conduct, which can be, in the case of takeovers, a self-interested or a value-decreasing acquisition that cannot be openly justified without tampering with the information that needs to be published.

The bidder's directors may be found guilty of the common law crime of conspiracy to defraud[167] and the statutory offences of 'misleading statements and practices' under section 397(1) and (2) of the FSMA 2000. According to the offence, any statement, promise or forecast which induces or is likely to induce a shareholder to sell or refrain from selling shares, irrespective of whether the shareholder is the addressee of the statement, could constitute an offence if the person making the statement knew or was reckless as to whether it was misleading, false or deceptive or dishonestly concealed any material facts.

In addition, section 953 of the Companies Act 2006 contains a new criminal offence of non-compliance with the contents requirements of the offer document rules under the Code. The offence can be committed by the 'person making the bid' as well as by any director, officer or member of the bidder who caused the offer document to be published. The offence covers both wilful and reckless non-compliance and is punishable by a fine. The criminal offence only applies in relation to transactions to which the Takeovers Directive applies, that would include takeovers of companies admitted to the London Stock Exchange but not takeovers of companies whose shares are traded on AIM.

Although the FSA or the Panel has the power to prosecute the aforementioned statutory offences, the main limitation of relying on criminal

[167] *R v de Berenger* (1814) 105 ER 536; *Scott v Brown, Doering, McNab & Co.* [1892] 2 QB 724 (CA).

sanctions has been the burden of proving the elements of these crimes 'beyond reasonable doubt'. The above difficulty inevitably means that only in very few cases have the persons responsible been successfully prosecuted.

To that effect administrative sanctions can constitute a more effective deterrence mechanism. In the past, section 143 of the Financial Services and Markets Act 2000 ('the FSMA'), by endorsing the Takeover Code, provided a mechanism for the Financial Services Authority to bring disciplinary and enforcement action against authorised persons for misconduct in relation to the Code.[168] The Panel's previous sanctions regime, which was set out in the Introduction to the Takeover Code, provided for private and public statements of censure of persons in breach of the Code. It was also possible for the Panel to issue 'cold-shouldering' statements in appropriate cases, namely statements obliging authorised persons in certain circumstances not to act for a person named in such a statement. The introduction of the new statutory regime, which confers on the Panel the power to make rules for imposing sanctions[169] for breach of its rules or directions given under section 946 of the Companies Act, has not altered much. The Panel's current sanctions regime, which is set out in the Introduction to the Takeover Code, remained in place under the Act, meaning that the Panel will not impose fines for breaches of the Code, but it will ask FSA to exercise such power.

Contrary to the Panel's sanction rules, section 91 of the FSMA provides a power for the FSA to fine listed companies for breach of the Listing Rules. The FSA may impose a penalty of such amount as it considers appropriate. If the FSA considers that a director of the listed company was knowingly concerned in the breach of the Listing Rules, it may also impose a penalty on the director.

The FSA's policy on financial penalties for breach of the Listing Rules is contained in the Enforcement Manual. The policy contains that the FSA will consider all relevant circumstances of a contravention when it determines whether to impose a sanction. The size of the fine is particularly important since economic analysis and agency theory predict that the effect of a sanction on the incentives of the offender depends on whether the size of the penalty, multiplied by the probability of the offender being successfully prosecuted, exceeds the size of the benefit achieved through the offence.[170]

[168] Given that the Takeover Code is replaced by rules which have legal force as a consequence of the Companies Act 2006, s 964 of the Act repeals s 143 of the FSMA 2000.

[169] Section 952 of the Companies Act 2006.

[170] In 2004, the FSA imposed the highest fine ever imposed by a UK financial regulator (£17 million) on the Shell Group of companies for both breach of the former Listing Rules and market abuse for misstatements of its proved reserves. However, the fine was based on the FSA's findings of market abuse and no additional penalty was imposed for the breaches of the Listing Rules.

(ii) *Civil Liability and Compensation Rights*

Probably, the most important limitation to the effectiveness of any of the civil remedies that could be used by the acquiring shareholders against negligent or fraudulent misstatements by their directors, is that English law traditionally holds that, when the loss of the shareholders is restricted to a diminution in the company's share price, such a loss simply reflects the loss of the company.[171]

In order for the acquirer's shareholders to be granted personal rights of compensation, they need to suffer a loss other than just the diminution in the value of the shares they hold. This is likely in three cases: first, when new or existing shareholders are induced to subscribe in a share offer, when such an offer is made to finance the acquisition. Second, in cases of after-market purchases or sales of shares in the acquirer by new or existing shareholders, on the basis of information included in takeover documents. Thirdly, in the case of major shareholders in the acquirer entering into an agreement with their directors to finance or support the acquisition. Such agreements may include private placings, or in case of share exchange offers, undertakings not to dispose one's shares for a specific period of time, after the offer closes. This is to consolidate the share exchange and ensure an orderly aftermarket.[172]

The acquirer's shareholders, depending on the circumstances, may base a personal action against the directors of the company on the remedy of section 90 of the FSMA and on the general law of negligent misstatement under common law and the Misrepresentation Act.

Section 90 of the FSMA provides that any person responsible for the prospectus, as such persons are defined in the Prospectus Rules issued by the FSA are liable to pay compensation to any person, who has acquired any of the securities to which the prospectus relates and suffered a loss, as a result of any untrue or misleading statement in the particulars,[173] or as a result of any omission to publish any such information.[174] Despite the apparent advantages of these remedies—reversed onus of proof, no need to prove reliance, and applicability to aftermarket purchases—, the provisions of section 90 of the FSMA apply only to information included in the prospectus and not to any other investment advertisements accompanying the actual prospectus. However, since the prospectus is not likely to include any substantial information about the subsequent offer, it is highly unlikely that section 90 will afford much assistance to the acquiring shareholders. The same applies since the exemptions in Prospectus Rules PR 1.2.2R and 1.2.3R for securities offered in connection with takeovers and

[171] See above under shareholders suits.
[172] Stedman, *Takeovers* (n 114 above) 174.
[173] Section 90(1)(b)(ii) of the FSMA 2000.
[174] See s 90(3) of the FSMA 2000.

mergers which require for the publication of a document considered by the FSA to be equivalent to a prospectus means that in most circumstances no prospectus will be published in the case of takeovers, and section 90 statutory liability does not cover equivalent documents to a prospectus.

New sections 90A and 90B could also be relevant. Section 1270 of the Companies Act 2006 inserted sections 90A and 90B into the FSMA. This established a regime for civil liability to third parties by issuers admitted to trading on a regulated market in respect of disclosures made public in response to provisions implementing obligations imposed by the Transparency Directive. The essential features of this new regime and their potential impact on takeovers as well as its limitations can be summarised as follows:

— The issuer (and no one else) should have liability to investors for mistakes or omissions from the reports. This means that the issuer's directors contrary to the prospectus liability regime cannot be found directly liable.

— That liability should only arise if the investor, having acquired securities relied on the information published and suffered a loss as a result of any untrue or misleading statement in, or omission from, such information and a manager of the issuer knew that the information contained the untrue or misleading statement or omission or was reckless as to whether it did. These limitations depart form the prospectus liability regime of section 90 but they are close to the common law regime for negligent misstatements.

— The statutory regime of sections 90A and B is confined to untrue or misleading statements, or omissions, in information published pursuant to Transparency Directive. This means that it will primarily include annual and half yearly financial statements and management reports, the sign-off by directors or other responsible parties, as well as interim management statements. However, a UK-listed acquirer is also subject to other disclosure requirements, for example, under the Listing Rules class tests (class circulars), which are also swept into the disclosure regime under the Transparency Directive as a result of being within the definition of 'regulated information'. This is because the Listing Rules are part of the regulations adopted under Article 3(1) of the Transparency Directive. This is not the case however with regards to the Takeover Code. However, subsection (1)(a) of the new section 90A provides that the civil liability regime set out in section 90A applies to those reports and statements required by provisions implementing Articles 4 to 6 of the Transparency Directive, and not additional requirements to those laid down in the Takeovers Directive, such as class transactions circulars. Nevertheless information that origins from management reports or interim management statements may also be repeated in class circulars, or takeover documents.

— Issuers are not liable for any liability other than that provided for by sections 90A and 90B and any person who is not the issuer is not liable, other than to the issuer. To that effect, managers and directors can only be found liable against the company, which mean that the acquiring shareholders must rely on the mechanics of derivative action described above.

Nevertheless, the enactment of a special statutory liability regime for certain disclosures required by the Transparency Directive, no matter how close it is to the common law position for negligent misstatements, does not sit well with the common law origin of such liability in the United Kingdom, and could lead to different results especially, in the light of the absence of a proximity test in the statutory regime, which is substituted by a higher standard of proof. Similarly, the new statutory regime is different from the one related to prospectus related information and statements. Although a detailed analysis goes beyond the scope of the present book it suffices to be said in this part that new sections 90A and B of the FSMA and the uncertainty related to their application are part of a considerable ongoing debate[175] as to extending the regime for other disclosures, which obviously requires at least a consideration of all information within the scope of the Transparency Directive definition of regulated information. To that effect, subsection (1) of new section 90B establishes a power to make further provision about liability for published information.

In situations not covered by the statutory liability regimes of the FSMA, the acquiring shareholders have to rely on the general law of misrepresentation, namely the common law remedy of fraudulent or negligent misrepresentation and the statutory remedies of negligent and innocent misstatements of the Misrepresentation Act 1967.

Statutory and common law remedies offer little protection to existing or potential shareholders, who, based on information included in mandatory or voluntary documents in the context of a takeover, decide to further invest in the bidder or the target by acquiring shares in the market. Although the statutory remedy of negligent misstatement under section 2(1) of the Misrepresentation Act 1967 is a generalisation of the statutory provisions related to prospectus liability, and thus, could be used in cases that the misstatement is included in other takeover documents, it applies only in cases that the misstatement is made by a party to a subsequent contract.

Moreover, in relation to liabilities for fraudulent and negligent misrepresentation under common law, apart from the obvious difficulties associated with the burden of proof, an important implication arises in respect

[175] Davies's Review is expected to clarify some of the main issues in the area of liability for disclosures, and answer as to the necessity of extending the current statutory liability regime. However, other than minimising liability exposure, a question that arises is how on policy grounds this statutory regime is different form the prospectus liability regime.

of the purpose of the documents where the misstatement was included. The purpose of the document defines the proximity of the claimant to the director and thus, determines whether the director owed a duty of care to the claimant.[176] The restrictive approach of the House of Lords in *Caparo v Dickman*,[177] namely that the purpose of the annual accounts is not to offer investment advice, has been also confirmed in relation to documents and announcements put out by directors and their advisers, according to the requirements of the Listing Rules and the Takeover Code.[178] This means that documents prepared in the context of a takeover and addressed to target shareholders have as a purpose only to help them exercise their right to accept or reject the offer.[179]

Even in the Court of Appeal decision in *Morgan Crucible Co Plc v Hill Samuel & Co Ltd*,[180] where the court, reversing the High Court's decision, assumed, under the specific circumstances of the case, a wider purpose of the defence documents,[181] one cannot assume that the purpose of takeover documents is to induce purchases or sales in the aftermarket. In addition, later judgments also confined the impact of the *Morgan Crucible* case.[182] As Leveson J stated in *Partco v Wragg*,

> although I recognise that duties are cast on the individual directors (on the basis of the takeover code and the listing rules), I do not accept that these provisions necessarily say anything about personal assumption of responsibility in tort.[183]

As with takeover documents, which have as a sole purpose to help target shareholders to exercise their right to accept or reject the offer, class 1 circulars only intend to inform the acquiring shareholders so as to exercise their right to vote in a general meeting approving the acquisition. None of those documents has as a purpose to encourage purchases in the aftermarket and thus, cannot usually form the basis of a claim for losses incurred in aftermarket.[184]

[176] See *Caparo plc v Dickman* [1990] 2 AC 605 (HL) and subsequent case law.

[177] *Ibid*.

[178] *Partco Group Ltd v Wragg* [2002] EWCA Civ 594, [2002] 2 BCLC 323. Similarly, in *Al-Nakib Investments (Jersey) Limited v Longcroft* [1990] BCC 517, the court held that whilst directors owed a duty of care to those who subscribed for shares under the rights issue in reliance on the prospectus, they did not owe a duty of care to a shareholder or anyone else who relied on the prospectus for the purpose of deciding whether to purchase shares through the stock market and the relationship between the directors and the shareholders was not sufficiently proximate for a duty of care to arise.

[179] *Morgan Crucible Co Plc v Hill Samuel Bank & Co Ltd* [1991] Ch 295, [1990] 3 All ER 330; reversed by *Morgan Crucible Co Plc v Hill Samuel Bank Ltd* [1991] Ch 295, [1991] 2 WLR 655 (CA); *Partco Group Ltd v Wragg* (n 178 above).

[180] *Morgan Crucible Co Plc v Hill Samuel & Co Ltd* [1991] Ch 295, [1991] 2 WLR 655 (CA).

[181] See below.

[182] *Williams v Natural Life Health Foods Ltd* [1998] 1 WLR 830 (HL); *Partco Group Ltd v Wragg* (n 178 above).

[183] *Partco v Wragg* [2002] 2 BCLC 323 at 335 (Leveson J), accepted by the Court of Appeal [2002] 2 BCLC 323 at 361 (Potter LJ).

[184] For a general account see A Alcock, '*Partco v Wragg*: Liability for Misrepresentation Affecting Secondary Market Dealings' (2003) (September) *Journal of Business Law* 515.

There is a theoretical argument that, although the directors have not assumed personal responsibility, the acquirer as a company, in whose name documents or announcements were issued or the agreements were made, may have.[185] However, this is of little help in the above cases, where the shareholders would only be suing their own company. Especially in cases that no specific representations were made, this could lead to the very unattractive proposition that statements made to all shareholders could be used by some to make claims against the company.[186]

However, the issue becomes slightly different, when an acquiring shareholder acts, or refrains from acting, on the basis of an agreement with his directors. In such a case, the shareholder is more likely to have been provided with specific representations by the directors. However, is the mere fact that such representations were made adequate to establish the necessary proximity for a duty of care to arise? As the law stands now, the answer can be positive provided that the specificities of each case are examined.[187] The strict approach of the court in *Partco v Wragg* requires the examination of whether the directors assumed or not, explicitly or implicitly, responsibility for the accuracy of the provided information.[188] In that respect, clauses that attempt to exclude directors' responsibility are relevant indications in the view of the court.[189]

On top of the liability regimes described above, financial redress rules and restitution procedures may be relevant, subject however to a number of considerable limitations. Section 954 of the Companies Act 2006 confers on the Panel the power to make rules providing for financial redress (together with interest (including compound interest)) in consequence of a breach of rules which require monetary payments to be made.[190] However, such rules are unlikely to provide any compensation rights to the acquiring shareholders for negligent misstatements in takeover documents. In exercising such power the Takeover Code limits the application of such compensation rights to breaches of Rules 6, 9, 11, 14, 15, 16 or 35.3 of the Code and to the target shareholders only.

Some comfort may be provided through the restitution procedures of sections 383 and 384 of the FSMA 2000 in extreme cases where misstatements in the published takeover documents are found to amount to market abuse under section 118 of the FSMA. According to section 383, the FSA may apply to the court to order persons who engaged in market abuse

185 *Ibid.* See also *Williams v Natural Life Health Foods Ltd* (n 182 above).

186 *Ibid.*

187 *Morgan Crucible Co Plc v Hill Samuel Bank Ltd* (n 180 above).

188 *Partco Group Ltd v Wragg* (n 183 above); *Williams v Natural Life Health Foods Ltd* (n 182 above).

189 *Partco Group Ltd v Wragg* (n 183 above).

190 For instance, a payment by the bidder to shareholders of any difference between the price actually paid and any higher price for shares that the bidder should have paid under the rules.

to pay to the FSA such sum as appears to the court to be just, having regard to the profits that the persons accrued from the action found to be a market abuse, or/and to the extent of the loss suffered by others.[191] Any amount paid to the authority, in pursuance of the above order, must be paid or distributed by it to any persons identified by the court as having suffered a loss. Similarly, section 384 confers to the FSA similar power to that of the court, but only in respect of authorised persons engaging in market abuse.[192] The latter mainly concerns the financial advisers of the bidder, since it partially reduces the barriers of claiming compensation from professionals raised by common law in the *Caparo v Dickman* case.[193] In both cases, the directors or the advisers have to satisfy the court or the authority that they took all reasonable precautions and exercised all due diligence to avoid engaging in a market abuse.[194]

However, not all misleading statements constitute market abuse. Pursuant to the implementation of the Market Abuse Directive, section 118 of the FSMA 2000 provides for seven categories of behaviour that may constitute market abuse instead of three that existed under the previous regime. The types of behaviour that could be relevant in case of statements made in documents normally published in case of takeovers are 'misleading dissemination',[195] where false or misleading information is knowingly or negligently disseminated to the market, or 'misleading behaviour',[196] where behaviour could be regarded by a regular market user who is aware of the behaviour, as a failure on the part of the person responsible to observe the standards, which could be reasonably expected of a person in his position, as well as 'misuse of information' in cases of behaviour (in this case a misstatement) which relates to unpublished information, which, if available to a regular market user, would be likely to be regarded by him as relevant, or likely to give him a false or misleading impression, or finally, likely, in his view to distort the market.[197] Overall, it should be noted that while the Takeover Code does not any longer provide a safe harbour for market abuse, it can be derived from the Code of Market Conduct that failure by the bidder to meet the disclosure requirements imposed by the Code and the standards of care required thereof, could expose the bidder to the possibility of its behaviour being caught under the market abuse regime, since conformity with such

[191] See s 383(1) and (4) of the FSMA 2000.

[192] See s 384 of the FSMA 2000. For the definition of authorised persons see s 31 and Part IV of the FSMA.

[193] See above.

[194] Sections 383(3) and 384(4) of the FSMA 2000.

[195] Section 118(7) of the FSMA 2000.

[196] Section 118(8) of the FSMA 2000.

[197] Section 118(4). The regular user test does not appear in the Market Abuse Directive and is therefore retained only for those categories of abusive behaviour that are not drawn from the Directive.

Provisions of the Takeover Code will not, of itself, amount to market abuse.[198]

(iii) *The Case of the Target Directors' Representations*

It has already been mentioned, when overpayment risk was discussed, that exaggerated profit forecasts and defence documents by the target directors may induce the bidder to increase his offer price, resulting in paying substantially over the real value of the target. Can, therefore, the bidder claim the damages it suffered as a result of such misstatements? The courts have been faced with the above question in a number of cases, where bidders after increasing their bids as a response to defence statements, won control of the company and then, maintained that the statements made by the directors and advisers of the target were at least negligent.

In *Morgan Crucible Co Plc v Hill Samuel & Co Ltd*[199] the Court of Appeal considered that during the conduct of a contested takeover, once an identified bidder had emerged, directors and financial advisers of a target company, in choosing to make express representations with a view to influencing the conduct of the bidder, owed a duty to the bidder not negligently to mislead. On the facts pleaded, the bidder, in deciding whether to make an increased bid, was found to have relied on representations made by the target directors, and the target directors were found to have intended, when making the representations, that the plaintiff would rely on them. This was enough for the court to ascertain that there was a relationship of proximity sufficient to give rise to a duty of care.[200] However, it has been emphasised that

> (The City Code) does not explicitly envisage that persons concerned in preparing defence documents will owe a duty of care to potential or actual bidders. (Neither . . . does it impose any obligations on such persons to volunteer profit forecasts).[201]

The impact of the above case has been confined, as mentioned above, by the Court of Appeal decision in *Partco v Wragg*.[202] The case involved a friendly takeover that included the target directors staying in their position after the offer was consummated. The proceedings arose after the bidder maintained that during the critical period prior to the takeover offer being made unconditional, the target's directors had failed to disclose a

198 The Code of Market Conduct, MAR 1.10.4C.

199 *Morgan Crucible Co Plc v Hill Samuel & Co Ltd* (n 180 above).

200 *Ibid.* See also M Stallworthy, 'Company Law: Negligence: Directors' and Financial Advisers' Representations - Statements Influencing Conduct of Bidder' (1991) 6 (3) *Journal of International Banking Law* 50.

201 *Morgan Crucible Co Plc v Hill Samuel Bank Ltd* [1991] Ch 295 at 320 (Hoffman, J).

202 *Partco Group Ltd v Wragg* (n 183 above).

serious deterioration in the trading position and profitability of the company. In respect of the issue whether a duty of care arises, the court held, contrary to *Morgan Crucible*, that the mere supply of information by directors in the course of a takeover, in the absence of any additional indication of any assumption of personal responsibility for the supply of information, could not be regarded as sufficient to found a liability in negligence.[203] It also seems that, if it had not been a friendly takeover, Leveson J, at first instance, would have been prepared to strike out the negligent misstatement claim, to which approach the court of appeal agreed as well.[204] The court concluded, as seen already, that whether such an assumption of personal responsibility had in fact taken place depended upon the existence of personal assurances. The uncertainty of the current common law position on this issue can be epitomised in the wordings of Potter LJ that

> the potential liability of directors in a situation of this kind has still to be regarded as a developing jurisprudence or at least one which is uncertain in its application.[205]

Overall, it could be stated that in the light of the developments in *Partco v Wragg*[206] and earlier in *Williams v Natural Life Health Foods Ltd*[207] the target's directors will be extremely unlikely to be found liable for negligence against the bidder in hostile takeovers, unless for deceit.[208] In friendly takeovers, the specific particulars of the agreement and the representations need to be examined. However as identified in *Parcto*, disclaimers of responsibility, notwithstanding their reasonableness under section 2(2) of the Unfair Contract Terms Act 1977, provide evidence that no such responsibility was assumed. Accordingly, it is necessary for the bidder to avoid such clauses and receive explicit personal assurances from the target's directors about the validity of the provided information and the non-existence of other material undisclosed information.

V EX ANTE JUDICIAL REVIEW—THE CASE OF COURT SCHEMES

Many of the inefficiencies and costs involved in the case of an ex post judicial review of a corporate transaction, which has been a characteristic of most of the legal remedies examined by now, could be partly mitigated by moving the point of judicial intervention earlier in time. Under such a rule, the court's review of the fairness of the acquisition not only pre-exists the

203 *Partco Group Ltd v Wragg* (n 183 above).
204 *Partco Group Ltd v Wragg* (n 183 above)at 358.
205 *Partco Group Ltd v Wragg* (n 183 above)at 363.
206 *Partco Group Ltd v Wragg* (n 183 above).
207 *Williams v Natural Life Health Foods Ltd* (n 182 above).
208 See *Morgan Crucible Co Plc v Hill Samuel Bank Ltd* (n 180 above).

completion of the transaction, but also is a condition for its completion. In that way, the court's decision is not biased by any ex post events that alter the outcome of the transaction and could not have been considered by the acquirer's management when the transaction took place. Many procedural matters can also be solved in this way, since there is no need for the shareholders to prove any impropriety or unfair prejudice on behalf of their management, or the existence of a specific duty of care, or an assumption of responsibility by their directors, in order to seek judicial intervention. English law recognises such kind of ex ante judicial review of the fairness of an acquisition in the case of court schemes.

The statutory framework of the schemes of arrangement is to be found in new Parts 26 and 27 (section 895 onward) of the Companies Act 2006, which restated sections 425 to 427 and section 427A of the Companies Act 1985. A court scheme represents an alternative to a takeover offer as a method of acquiring control of a public company. Under section 895 onward of CA 2006, the target company can enter into a compromise or arrangement between itself and its members, provided that it is agreed to by a 75 per cent majority of its shareholders and is sanctioned by the court.[209] The court has a discretion at two distinct stages of the procedure: first, as to whether to order a meeting of shareholders to approve the scheme[210] (procedural function) and secondly, as to whether to sanction the scheme following its approval by the statutory majority (substantive function).[211] In doing so, the court has to decide in its discretion whether the arrangement is fair. At this point, the question that arises is whether the acquiring shareholders can be effectively protected against their management's disloyalty when a court scheme procedure rather than a typical takeover offer is implemented. To answer the above question, it is necessary to examine the two different functions that the court has in the proceedings.

As far as the first function is concerned and as the law stood under the Companies Act 1985 (and now under the Companies Act 2006 since Part 26 simply restated the old regime), it is unlikely that the court will order different classes of the acquiring shareholders to approve the transaction, when the scheme is carried out by means of transfer of shares. This is because, under such circumstances, a court scheme is an arrangement between the target company and its members. Thus, the acquirer's shareholders do not get to vote and the acquirer can only participate in the proceedings as a bound party in the transaction, by appearing by counsel at the hearing of the petition and giving the appropriate undertakings. Thus, under normal circumstances, since most schemes are carried out in the

[209] Section 899 of the CA 2006.
[210] Section 896 of the CA 2006.
[211] Section 899 of the CA 2006 onward.

United Kingdom by means of transfer of shares,[212] no special class is formed for the acquirer's shareholders who do not participate in the proceedings.

However, this is not the case when Part 27 (section 902) of the CA 2006 applies, namely when the scheme involves public companies and it is carried out by means of transfer of undertakings. More precisely, according to section 902, where a scheme is proposed to be carried out by means of transfer of undertakings and the consideration offered to the shareholders of the transferor company is to be shares in the transferee company with or without any cash payment, the court may, on relevant application, order a meeting of the members of the *transferee* company or creditors or any class of them.[213] Accordingly, any of the acquiring shareholders can ask the court to order such a meeting. This permits the court to exercise its discretion to sanction the scheme under section 899 of the CA 2006 for the benefit of the acquiring shareholders, since, if the court after such a meeting is not satisfied with the fairness of the transaction in respect of the acquirer's shareholders, it has the discretion not to sanction the scheme or modify its terms.[214] The problem, though, is that the acquiring directors may easily circumvent the application of section 938 by forming a separate company vehicle to carry out the scheme.

In view of the above, the question shifts to the second function of the court, namely its discretion to grant or withhold its approval of the scheme on the merits of reasonableness and fairness. In exercising its second function, what the court has to see is

> whether the proposal is such that an intelligent and honest man, a member of the class concerned and acting in respect of his interest, might reasonably approve.[215]

However, in practice, in doing so, the court places a great deal of reliance on the approval of the statutory majority of shareholders and on the fact that the financial advisers have recommended shareholders to approve the scheme.[216] The above reasoning makes the latter substantial function of the court a duplication of its procedural function and minimises its

212 One reason being to circumvent the more stringent requirements of s 427A CA 1985.

213 Section 938 of the CA 2006.

214 For the court's discretion to modify the scheme as a condition of its sanction see *Re Canning Jarrah Timber Company (Western Australia) Ltd* [1900] 1 Ch 708.

215 *In Re Dorman Long & Co* [1934] Ch 365.

216 'If creditors and members are acting on sufficient information and with time to consider what they are about, and are acting honestly they are much better judges of what is to their commercial advantage than the court can be'. *Re English, Scottish & Australian Bank* [1893] 3 Ch 385 (CA) (Lindley LJ). See also MA Weinberg and MV Blank, *Takeovers and Mergers*, 2nd edn (London, Sweet & Maxwell, 1989) 2051; Stedman, *Takeovers* (n 114 above) 45; opposite, Davies in Davies, *Gower's Principles of Modern Company Law* (n 8 above) 765, who finds greater evidence of courts' reluctance to rely as heavily on the above assumption.

practical importance,[217] since the court just carries out a check of whether the necessary resolutions have been passed by the statutory majority after having consulted an independent adviser. Even in circumstances where the courts do not seem to be satisfied with the terms of the arrangement, they tend to base their disagreement on procedural shortcomings, rather than on their discretionary power to sanction or the scheme or otherwise.[218]

Moreover, the courts' considerable reliance on the majority approval of the scheme removes from their role the function of protecting the shareholders as a class against self-interested managerial actions—which is the question here—and renders it merely a tool to protect minority shareholders[219] and opposing creditors. This reveals a central problem of the judicial review of corporate acquisitions, whether ex post or ex ante. This has already been discussed above: when the courts get to review and evaluate a business decision, they find it an extremely difficult task to discharge and they show great reluctance to get into the substance of the transaction.

VI CONCLUSION

This chapter focused on the legal and regulatory review of the directors' decision to acquire a company. The following areas of law and regulation were discussed:

- the law of fiduciary duties of corporate directors and the limitations of shareholders' suits;
- the common law and statutory duties of care of corporate directors and the standard of care requirements of the Takeover Code;
- the role of the information provision requirements of the Takeover Code and the UKLA Listing, Prospectus and Disclosure and Transparency Rules and the ex ante quality controls of the information produced in the context of takeovers;
- the statutory and common law liabilities for fraudulent and negligent misstatements; and
- the court scheme procedure of Parts 26 and 27 of the Companies Act 2006.

[217] See also Weinberg and Blank, *Takeovers and Mergers* (n 216 above) 2050.

[218] Davies, *Gower's Principles of Modern Company Law* (n 8 above) 765.

[219] See, eg *Carruth v ICI* [1937] AC 707 (HL), where it was demonstrated that the majority voted in favour of the scheme because of their interests as shareholders of another class, or *Re National Bank Ltd* [1966] 1 WLR 819 and *Re Hellenic & General Trust Ltd* [1975] 3 All ER 382 (ChD) where the question was whether the court will sanction the scheme where the relevant procedures are used to achieve what could not be achieved under the compulsory acquisition provisions of s 429 CA 1985.

On the one hand, ex post judicial review, in the form of directors' fiduciary duties, was considered to be broadly ineffective in countering self-interested acquisitions. The subjective nature of the duty to act in good faith for the best interests of the company, together with the limitations of the 'improper purpose' doctrine in respect of business decisions, the limitations of the 'predominant purpose' test in respect of mixed-purpose transactions, the difficulties associated with the operation of the 'no conflict' rule and the procedural limitations of shareholders' suits leave little room for an effective and timely judicial intervention. The new statutory derivative action provides more flexibility and addresses some of the limitations of the common law regime, but it remains to be seen how it will operate in practice. Similarly, ex ante judicial intervention—currently limited only to cases of court schemes—addresses some of the procedural burdens and limitations of the ex post judicial review, but, unfortunately, it is currently limited to dealing with mainly procedural issues.

Common law and statutory developments towards an objective duty of care help to form uniform standards for directors' care and skill. For takeovers, the application of a uniform standard can serve as a 'blank rule', permitting an effective enforcement of the diligence requirements of the Takeover Code and the UKLA Listing Rules, which, in this way, can provide significant substance not only to the executive directors' duties, but also to those of non-executive directors, during a takeover. An enhanced duty of care can, thus, arise in the context of takeovers, which collectively requires the entire board of the acquiring company to operate on a fully informed basis—which may extend to seeking additional information—to continually monitor the acquisition process and immediately to raise any disagreement or disclose any concerns to the Panel. To that extent the Prospectus Rules' requirement that a director, in order to escape responsibility, must, as soon as practicable, give reasonable public notice that the prospectus was published without his knowledge or consent, could also be helpful in the case of takeover documents.

Information provision in the case of takeovers was also found to serve the acquirer's shareholders in three ways: first, it is an underlying assumption of any approval requirements when it is up to the acquiring shareholders to approve a takeover; secondly, it facilitates the operation of the capital market and the market of corporate control in penalising a 'bad' bidder; and finally, it further defines and externalises the acquiring directors' duty of care in the context of a takeover, and creates additional obstacles, which the acquiring directors have to surmount to publicly justify a self-motivated or a value-decreasing acquisition. In that way, ex ante quality controls of the information published and criminal and administrative sanctions, although designed to ensure the proper operation of financial markets, can also minimise the occurrence of value-decreasing or self-interested acquisitions. In this context the statutory footing of the

Takeover Panel provides certain advantages. However, the minimum changes have been made to retain the regime that was in place prior to the implementation of the Directive. Providing the Panel with the power to fine for breaches of the Code, extending the Panel's power to provide financial redress in cases of breaches of takeover rules that relate to published information during a takeover, or introducing a restitution procedure for misstatements made in takeover documents (including defence documents) could also be helpful.

Finally, in relation to the ability of the acquiring shareholders to claim damages for losses suffered due to misstatements included in takeover documents, it has been identified that directors in the acquiring company will be found liable for individual losses suffered by their shareholders—other than when they have acted fraudulently—only when a specific agreement exists between them and their shareholders and they have assumed such responsibility. The same applies to the ability of the acquirer to claim damages for misstatements made in defence documents by the target directors. In this context, and in the light of the ongoing debate regarding the need for a statutory liability regime for disclosures, the statutory liability regime for statements and omissions contained in prospectus could be a useful starting point.

5

Shareholders' Voice and Reward Strategies

I INTRODUCTION

MOST OF THE legal remedies described in the previous chapter have a compensatory element and they operate ex post. Ex ante judicial review, as is the case where the transaction is effected using the court scheme procedure and regulatory review of the information published could address some of the problems associated with the ex post examination of the transaction in question. However, the above mechanisms are not designed to examine the validity of business judgements. There is a simpler way to address this issue, namely by allowing the acquirer's shareholders to intervene in the decision process of the acquisition, either directly by being awarded special decision rights or indirectly by other mechanisms of internally controlling managers' incentives.

II AUTHORISATION RIGHTS

Traditionally, approval rights have been associated, in company law, with share issues. According to section 551 of the Companies Act 2006 ('CA 2006'), directors cannot exercise any power to allot either shares in the company or rights to subscribe for shares in the company, unless they are authorised by the shareholders by virtue of an ordinary resolution.[1] Any such authority is accompanied by restrictions on quantity and timing, as it must state the maximum number of securities that can be issued and the date by which the authority can be exercised. That date must not be later than five years from the date of the ordinary resolution conferring such authority to the directors, although it can be renewed through an ordinary resolution for successive periods, not exceeding five years.[2]

The above means that, as long as the acquirer's directors do not have the authority to allot shares and want to finance an acquisition by using the

[1] Or by the company's articles of association: see the Companies Act 2006 s 551.
[2] Section 551(5) of the CA 2006.

company's shares, they need their shareholders' approval. Accordingly, the protection provided is limited to share exchange offers or cash offers where cash is to be raised through a share issue. Also, the above protection can only be incidental, to the extent that the acquiring shareholders are afforded approval rights as long as they had not provided such an authority to the directors in the past. It should also be noted that other than the limitation of the five-year period, the Companies Act 2006 does not provide any limitation as to the amount of shares in respect of which the authority is given. However, guidelines adopted by the Investment Committee of the Association of British Insurers ('ABI') and the National Association of Pension Funds ('NAPF') indicate that the number of shares that the directors are authorised to issue should not exceed the one-third of the issued ordinary share capital. [3]

While the sanction of an ordinary resolution is enough to permit the directors to proceed with a new share issue of the same class, shares of a new class may need to have their rights established, by amending the offeror's articles of association. For that purpose, a special resolution is required.[4] However, section 551(8) of the CA 2006 makes it clear that an ordinary resolution of the company's members will suffice for the purposes of giving authority to the directors, even where the effect of the resolution is to alter the company's articles of association (which would normally require a special resolution). In addition, the articles of association may permit the directors to issue any class of shares they find necessary, without the need for a special resolution. Where a company's capital consists of more than one class of shares, rights attached to any class of shares can only change with the consent of the class. As a result, depending on the shares that the bidder intends to issue and the articles of association, an ordinary resolution may not suffice, and the consent of a specified majority of a specific class may be required.[5]

Authorisation by the acquirer's shareholders may also be required where borrowing restrictions in the bidder's articles of association prohibit the directors from raising the necessary funds to finance the takeover. In some cases, it may be provided by the articles of association that the borrowing limits can be overridden with the sanction of an ordinary resolution. In other cases, the bidder's articles of association may have to be amended, which will require a special resolution.

[3] See the Association of British Insurers' Guidelines on Directors' Power to Allot Shares (May 1995).

[4] Section 9 of CA 2006. See also G Stedman, *Takeovers* (London, Longman, 1993) 105; E Ferran, *Company Law and Corporate Finance* (New York, Oxford University Press, 1999) 331.

[5] For the latter to be required the proposal must affect a specific class of shares and amount to a variation of class rights. For further information, see Ferran, *Company Law and Corporate Finance* (n 4 above) 337–54.

III PRE-EMPTIVE RIGHTS

The protection of the acquiring shareholders is carried one stage further in cases where they are afforded pre-emptive rights. In that way, the acquirer's shareholders are able to protect the proportion of their shareholdings and thus entrench themselves against the dilution risk that share offers carry. This is very important to the acquiring shareholders, since it is very likely that large issues of shares, made either to serve as a medium of payment or with the purpose to raise cash for the acquisition, are likely to be at some sort of discount to induce investors to subscribe or the target shareholders to accept the offer.

Pre-emptive rights are directly related to the form of consideration received by the bidder in exchange for its shares. The application of the pre-emption rule only extends to issues of shares for cash.[6] This clearly means that, while the acquirer's shareholders are afforded pre-emptive rights in the case where their company uses its own shares to raise cash for the actual offer, they are deprived of the pre-emption rule protection when shares are issued to individuals through vendor placings, or in share exchange offers. This is because, in the latter cases, the acquirer's shares are issued for a consideration other than for cash, namely in exchange for the target's assets or shares.

Even in circumstances where the acquirer's shareholders are entitled to a pre-emptive offering, as Davies argues,

> statutory pre-emptive rights can be disapplied with relative ease and afford an individual equity shareholder precious little assurance that his existing pre-emptive rights will be preserved, unless his shares carry sufficient votes to block the passing of a special resolution.[7]

The new Companies Act 2006 has not changed much in this area, since section 570 of CA 2006, restating section 95 of the CA 1985, provides that the general meeting may confer, by virtue of a special resolution, the power to the directors to exclude or modify pre-emptive rights for shares whose allotment has been authorised.[8] When the directors have general authority to allot shares under section 551 of the CA 2006 pre-emption rights can also be excluded or modified by the articles of association.[9]

Until relatively recently, LR 9.20 of the Listing Rules provided that authority to disapply pre-emption rights could last no longer than 15 months from the date of the relevant special resolution.[10] The time limit

[6] Section 561 of the CA 2006. See also ss 89(4) and 94 of the CA 1985.

[7] PL Davies, *Gower's Principles of Modern Company Law*, 6th edn (London, Sweet & Maxwell, 1997) 310.

[8] See s 570(1) of the CA 2006.

[9] *Ibid* and LR 9.3.12 of the Listing Rules.

[10] See also PL Davies, 'Institutional Investors in the United Kingdom' in T Baums, RM Buxbaum and KJ Hopt (eds), *Institutional Investors and Corporate Governance* (Walter de

has been dropped in the current version of LR 9.3.12, which simply provides that pre-emption rights can be disapplied in accordance with section 95 of CA 1985 (now section 570 of CA 2006).

However, more substance is given to the pre-emption rule through pressure exercised by institutional shareholders. Guidelines drawn up by the Pre-Emption Group set limits to the size of share issues not involving pre-emption rights that will be approved by institutional shareholders when voting on a resolution under section 570 of the CA 2006, and regulate the price at which such an issue can be made.[11] In that way, institutional shareholders commit themselves to vote in favour of a disapplication proposal, as long as the number of the shares to be issued on a non-preemptive basis is limited to five per cent of the issued capital in any one year and to 7.5 per cent in any rolling period of three years. As regards to the price of an issue to non-shareholders, the Pre-emption Guidelines provide that any discount should not exceed five per cent of the market price.[12] Requests for disapplication with the above characteristics are classified as routine disapplications. Non-routine requests for disapplication, namely disapplications which exceed the aforementioned thresholds, require a number of additional considerations to be observed on a case-by-case basis.[13] The above guidelines, in contrast with section 570 of the CA 2006, do not only apply to public offers but to vendor placings as well.

The Investment Committee's guidelines on shareholders' pre-emption rights[14] also address the issue of the lack of pre-emption rights in share exchange offers, but only in cases where a cash alternative is offered at the same time. In such circumstances, when the consideration is to include an option for target shareholders to elect for either shares or cash, the latter is usually provided by an underwriter, who agrees to purchase the shares that target shareholders reject over cash. In that case, the Guidelines insist on an arrangement known as open offer or 'claw-back'. Under such an arrangement, the acquirer's shareholders enjoy priority over the underwriter in purchasing the shares that the target shareholders decline in order to receive cash. Shares are available to the acquirer's shareholders at the same agreed price and on a pro rata basis. Any shares that are not acquired by the acquirer's shareholders are offered for a private placing

Gruyter & Co, 1994) 274; M Button and S Bolton, *A Practitioner's Guide to the Stock Exchange Yellow Book* (London, City and Financial Publishing, 1997) 146.

[11] The Pre-emption Group, *Displaying Pre-emption Rights—A Statement of Principles* (May 2006).

[12] *Ibid*, para 11. Davies, 'Institutional Investors in the United Kingdom' (n 10 above) 275; G McCormack, 'Institutional Shareholders and the Promotion of Good Corporate Governance' in BA Rider (ed), *The Realm of Company Law* (London, Kluwer Law International, 1997) 155.

[13] See above n 11.

[14] See The Investment Committee, *Shareholders' Pre-emption Rights and Vendor Placings* (August 1993).

or end up in the hands of the underwriters who provided the cash alternative.

IV APPROVAL RIGHTS AND LISTING RULES

While the above protection is confined to acquisitions that involve a share issue, the UK Listing Authority ('UKLA') Listing Rules provide a more direct approach to approval rights in cases of takeover offers, regardless of the medium of payment or the financial structure used. Chapter 10 of the UKLA Listing Rules is principally concerned with disposals and acquisitions (including takeovers) made by listed companies, while Chapter 11 deals with transactions with related parties. Although many of the provisions of Chapters 10 and 11 are designed to ensure that the shareholders are kept informed of significant acquisitions, there are cases where the transaction in question is subject to shareholders' approval.

There are three cases where a takeover offer may be subject to the acquiring shareholders' approval: first, when the takeover offer is classified as a class 1 transaction according to Chapter 10 of the Listing Rules; secondly, when a takeover is considered to be a transaction with a 'related party'; and finally, when the takeover has the characteristics of a reverse takeover as defined in LR 10.2.2 of the Listing Rules.

A A Takeover as a Class 1 Transaction

According to the Listing Rules, a transaction (in this case a takeover) is classified by assessing its size relative to that of the listed company proposing to make it.[15] Takeovers that require the shareholders' approval are those that generate a percentage ratio of 25 per cent or more (Classification: Class 1) after comparing the target's gross assets, profits or gross capital to those of the bidder, or alternatively, comparing the consideration offered to the value of the ordinary share capital of the bidder.[16]

In circumstances where any of the above calculations produce an anomalous result or where the calculations are inappropriate to the sphere of activity of the listed company, the UK Listing Authority may disregard the calculation and may substitute other relevant indicators of size, including industry-specific tests.[17]

The approval of the acquirer's shareholders can either be obtained prior to the transaction being entered to—ie at the announcement of the offer or even after—but in any event, prior to the completion of the transaction, by

[15] LR 10.2 of the Listing Rules.
[16] LR 10, Annex 1 of the Rules.
[17] See LR 10, Annex 1, para 10G of the Listing Rules.

the time that the offer is declared wholly unconditional as to acceptances. In the latter case, any agreement affecting the transaction must be conditional upon such approval being obtained.[18] The City Code on Takeovers and Mergers ('the Takeover Code') permits a class 1 approval condition to be attached to a voluntary offer.[19] It prohibits, though, the offeror from putting itself in a position that it has to make a mandatory offer.[20]

Allowing for the general meeting to take place after the acquisition is announced provides shareholders with cheap and instantaneous access to additional information about the value of the acquisition, merely by assessing the drop or rise in the market price as a result of the announcement of the offer: if the bidder's price falls, its shareholders have the option not to approve the acquisition, expecting that the rejection of the transaction will restore the discount in their share value effected by an adverse market reaction to the announcement of the acquisition.

B A Takeover as a Related-Parties Transaction

According to LR 11.1 of the Listing Rules, a transaction with a related party means:

— a transaction (other than a transaction of a revenue nature in the ordinary course of business) between a listed company and a related party; or

— an arrangement pursuant to which a listed company and a related party each invests in, or provides finance to, another undertaking or asset; or

— any other similar transaction or arrangement (other than a transaction of a revenue nature in the ordinary course of business) between a listed company and any other person the purpose and effect of which is to benefit a related party.[21]

A related party can be a 'substantial shareholder', a director or a shadow director, a person that has been a director within 12 months preceding the date of the transaction, either of the acquiring company or any company of the same group,[22] a 50/50 joint venture partner, or a person exercising significant influence other than a 50/50 joint venture partner.[23] A substantial shareholder is defined as any person (excluding a bare trustee) who is, or was within the 12 months preceding the date of the transaction,

[18] See LR 10.5.1 of the Listing Rules.
[19] See the analysis in ch 9 below.
[20] Rule 9.3(b) of the Takeover Code, 8th edn (London, Panel on Takeovers and Mergers, May 2006).
[21] LR 11.1.5 of the Listing Rules.
[22] Such as any company that is or has been a subsidiary of the acquiring company, or the parent, or a fellow subsidiary of the parent or an associate or a related party of the above.
[23] LR 11.1.4 of the Listing Rules.

entitled to exercise or to control the exercise of 10 per cent or more of the votes able to be cast on all, or substantially all matters at general meetings of the company.[24]

The acquisition by the bidder of its subsidiary or any other company that the former holds shares of 10 per cent or more does not fall by itself within the Listing Rules' definition of a related parties transaction, so as to require the approval of the acquirer's shareholders, since the target is not a 'related party' as defined in the Listing Rules. In contrast, a takeover offer will constitute a related party transaction in the case of cross-holdings that exceed 10 per cent or when just the target owns a portion of the acquirer's ordinary shares that carries votes that count for 10 per cent or more of the total voting rights. Also, in cases where any of the directors or the substantial shareholders of the bidder own shares in the target, the transaction falls under the definition of a related party transaction. However, in this case, it is not the whole takeover offer that needs approval, but only the acquisition of the specific shares held by the persons in question.

LR 11, Annex 1 of the Listing Rules allows for a considerable number of exceptions to the requirements for shareholders' approval. A de minimis exception applies where the value of the transaction is equal to or less than 0.25 per cent of the value[25] of the acquirer.[26] This is more likely to be an issue when substantial shareholders or directors in the acquirer hold shares in the target. If the value of those shares does not exceed the 0.25 per cent threshold neither approval nor any other of the usual requirements set out in LR 11.1.7 is required.

In addition, in circumstances where the transaction would have otherwise been qualified as a related party transaction, but the value of the transaction does not exceed the five per cent threshold in any of the tests described in LR 10, Annex 1 of the Listing Rules, no approval by the shareholders is necessary.[27] In contrast,[28] the acquirer has to provide the Financial Services Authority ('FSA') with written confirmation by an adviser that the terms of the proposed transaction with the related party are fair and reasonable, as far as the shareholders of the company are concerned.

Another exception, relevant in takeover situations, applies when the related party is such only by virtue of being a substantial shareholder of

[24] Or any other company which is its subsidiary undertaking or parent undertaking or is a fellow subsidiary undertaking of its parent undertaking. See the Glossary of Definitions of the Listing Rules.

[25] See above about the calculation used to define the value of the target compared to the bidder.

[26] LR 11, Annex 1.1.1 of the Listing Rules.

[27] See LR 11.1.10 of the Listing Rules.

[28] And provided of course that the transaction exceeds the 0.25 per cent threshold in one or more of the tests described in LR 10, Annex 1 of the Listing Rules.

an 'insignificant subsidiary'.[29] The latter is a subsidiary which contributed less than 10 per cent of the turnover and profits, and which represented less than 10 per cent of the assets of the listed company, in each of the three years preceding the date of the transaction.[30] The exception is of practical importance in the case of takeovers where the target is a substantial shareholder in one of the acquirer's subsidiaries that fits the definition of an insignificant subsidiary. It should be noted that the exception will not apply where the subsidiary is itself a party to the transaction or where securities in the subsidiary or its assets are used to finance the acquisition and the ratio of the consideration to the market capitalisation of the issuer is 10 per cent or more.[31]

In practical terms, the acquiring shareholders are afforded approval rights in takeovers that do not constitute class 1 transactions, mainly in two instances. The first case is when the target is a related party to the bidder. This practically means when the target owns shares in the bidder of more than 10 per cent of the bidder's capital, and the value of the takeover offer represents—by any of the calculation methods set out in the Listing Rules—five per cent or more of the bidder's value. In this case, the acquiring company shareholders should approve the whole takeover. The second case is when the directors of the bidder or any substantial shareholder[32] own shares in the target whose value exceeds five per cent of the value of the bidder. In this case, the acquiring shareholders must approve only the specific transaction, namely the acquisition of those shares and not the whole takeover. If, in any of the above two instances, the value of the transaction represents—by any of the calculation methods set out in the Listing Rules—less than 5 per cent of the bidder's value, but more than 0.25 per cent, the requirement for approval is replaced by an independent valuation report confirming that the terms of the transaction are fair, as far as the acquiring company's shareholders are concerned.

C Reverse Takeovers

The Listing Rules define a reverse takeover as an acquisition by a listed company of a business, or an unlisted company, or assets, where any of the calculation methods set out in LR 10, Annex 1 result in a percentage ratio of 100 per cent or more, or which would result in a fundamental change in the business, the board, or the voting control of the listed company. Further analysis of the mechanics of a reverse takeover transaction goes

[29] As defined in LR 11, Annex 1.1.9 of the Listing Rules.
[30] *Ibid.*
[31] See above.
[32] As defined in the Listing Rules, any person holding more than 10 per cent of the company's shares (see above).

beyond the scope of the present work. What suffices to be said is that, as far as the approval requirement is concerned, reverse takeover transactions need to meet the class 1 transaction requirements.[33] In addition, when a listed company completes a reverse takeover the FSA will generally cancel the listing of its securities[34] and the company will be required to re-apply for the listing of the securities and satisfy the relevant requirements for listing.[35]

However, a number of exceptions limit the occasions when the above cancellation of listing is required. A reverse takeover will be only treated as a class 1 transaction as long as the following conditions are met[36]:

— none of the percentage ratios resulting from the calculations under each of the class tests in LR 10, Annex 1 exceed 125 per cent;
— the subject of the acquisition is in a similar line of business to that of the acquiring company;
— the undertaking which is the subject of the acquisition complies with the conditions for listing set out in Chapter 6 of the Listing Rules; and
— there will be no change of board or voting control.

If one of the above conditions applies, no suspension of listing is required and the general meeting for the shareholder's approval can be scheduled for a later date, after the takeover offer is announced and posted. Overall, the approval requirements of the Listing Rules for all three cases are summarised in Table 4 on page 100.

D Characteristics of Approval Rights

In connection to the formulation of an approval procedure, two main questions instantly arise: first, how many votes are required for a transaction to be approved?; and secondly, who gets to vote?

Currently, the approval requirement of the Listing Rules is satisfied with an ordinary resolution. The rationale behind this is that business decisions are, under normal circumstances, a competence awarded to the board and not to the general meeting. In the absence of the Listing Rules approval requirement and in order to stop an unwanted acquisition, the shareholders should have changed the company's directors, for which an ordinary resolution is required. It should also be noted that the added benefit of the Listing Rules' approval requirement is that the offer may be contingent upon the approval of the acquirer's shareholders. In contrast,

33 LR 10.6.1 of the Listing Rules.
34 LR 5.2.3G of the Listing Rules.
35 Except that LR 6.1.3R(1)(b) of the Listing Rules will not apply in relation to the listed company's accounts.
36 LR 10.2.3R of the Listing Rules.

Table 4: Shareholders' approval requirements under the Listing Rules

*Value of the takeover in comparison to the bidder**	*Approval requirement*
> 25%	All takeovers (class 1 transactions).
< 25% but > 5%	Only related party takeovers: namely when the target owns more than 10% of the shares of the bidder (the whole takeover needs approval); or when the bidder's directors or substantial shareholders own shares in the target (only the acquisition of those shares needs approval as long as it falls within the 525% threshold).
< 5% but > 0.25%	Independent report of the fairness of the terms replaces approval requirement. Only for related-party takeovers, see above.
< 0.25%	De minimis exception.
No threshold required	Reverse takeovers.

* Calculated on the basis of the tests in LR 10, Annex 1 of the Listing Rules

even if the acquiring shareholders change their directors, this does not mandate that they can withdraw an offer that has already been posted.[37]

However, one could argue that a 'supermajority' rule is better designed to protect minority interests. Nevertheless, it is a fact that the UK market is characterised by dispersed shareholdings, and listed companies with majority shareholdings are not a common phenomenon. In a company with dispersed shareholdings, an ordinary resolution can effectively address conflicts of interests between directors and shareholders.

Even if there were a more widespread concern about minority protection in the United Kingdom, the implementation of a supermajority rule is not by itself entirely justifiable in the cases of corporate acquisition transactions. First, other than in the case of related parties transactions, there seems to be no apparent reason why the minority shareholders would lose from an announced takeover, while at the same time the majority owners would benefit. If it is just a distribution issue, then company law traditionally has based minority treatment on the grounds of fairness rather than equality. Moreover, as it will be argued later on, the Takeover Code's equality rules indirectly address some of the acquiring minority shareholders' concerns.[38] Even in the case of reverse takeovers, where there seems to be a minority concern that needs to be protected—on the grounds that the acquirer actually becomes the target of the transaction and the

[37] See ch 9 below.
[38] See ch 8 below.

acquirer shareholders lose control of their company—the Takeover Code addresses the problem by extending its protection to cover such situations.

Instead of a supermajority rule, addressing the issue of who gets to vote is even more important to minority shareholders. In the case of related party transactions, where the most acute problem for minority shareholders arises, the Listing Rules require that a substantial shareholder who is a related party should abstain from voting for the approval of the transaction.[39] Such a rule protects more effectively minority interests than a supermajority rule, since it leaves the approval of the transaction entirely in the hands of minority shareholders.

E Limitations

Although approval rights can address conflicts of interests between directors and shareholders, and between majority owners and minority interests in the acquirer, they cannot be considered a panacea. The main concern about approval rights is how to provide voting rights to bidder shareholders in an inexpensive fashion. The quantity of information that has to be produced in relation to a related party or class 1 transaction, and the standard of care required, have been considered by the market as considerable costs for the bidder. This has been the main concern of many respondents in a discussion paper published by the Financial Services Authority in 2003 concerning the review of the Listing Rules.[40]

Although there was very strong support for shareholders' rights provisions, it was noted that the requirement for shareholder approval could, in a competitive bidding situation, put a UK-listed company at a disadvantage to an overseas company not subject to same requirements.[41] Many respondents also noted that the United Kingdom is the only European jurisdiction that imposes this kind of requirement and that significant costs (namely, the preparation rather than the communication costs) are involved in producing circulars.[42] To that extent, electronic communication methods, although helpful, were not considered significantly effective in reducing the costs of production.[43] A few respondents also felt that some minor changes could be made to the class tests, for example raising the threshold at which the class test is applied for smaller companies.[44] Finally, it should be noted that the Company Law Review by the Steering

[39] See LR 11.1.7 of the Listing Rules.

[40] Financial Services Authority, *FS14: Review of The Listing Regime; Feedback on DP14* (January 2003).

[41] *Ibid*, para 3.18.

[42] *Ibid*, para 3.19.

[43] *Ibid*, para 3.20.

[44] *Ibid*, para 3.19.

Group revealed a strong preference against incorporating the shareholder approval requirements of major transactions into statute.[45]

The argument that approval rights are associated with substantial costs is not entirely justifiable. Much of the information included in circulars that need to be prepared in class 1 transactions, for which concerns have been raised, considerably overlaps with information contained in documents that must be prepared by the bidder, under the Takeover Code, regardless of whether approval is required by the acquiring shareholders or not.[46] Actually, it is standard practice for the bidder to discharge its duty to prepare a circular by just sending a copy of the offer document and any listing particulars marked 'for information only', together with a short circular, which just incorporates a notice convening the Extraordinary General Meeting (EGM) for the purposes of approving the offer.[47]

However, there is a viable concern in relation to competitive bids, especially when the rival bidder is not subject to the same requirements. If the shareholders approve a takeover offer at a specific price and a rival offeror emerges, then the initial bidder has to issue and send new circulars and seek again the approval of its shareholders. The same procedure should be followed every time an increase is made in the offer price or a change is made in the consideration or the mixture of the considerations offered. Accordingly, a problem of 'multiple resolicitation'[48] arises, which imposes a number of burdens—both in terms of costs and time—on a bidder who is required to obtain shareholders' approval. In practice, the bidder can secure the shareholders' approval and at the same time obtain the authority to revise the offer if a counter offer emerges. However, such a practice defeats one of the purposes of shareholders' approval, namely the protection against overpayment. A transaction may be attractive at a specific price but it may be unjustifiable at a higher price. A solution to this problem is for the shareholders to set a ceiling that the directors cannot exceed without requiring additional approval. Yet, this solution signals to the market that the bidder is willing to offer a higher price and may induce target shareholders to require a higher offer before tendering their shares.[49]

Limitations may also arise in relation to the objectivity of the information produced and the communication of different views. The information produced by the directors may be biased. Shareholders may be presented with one aspect of the transaction. What is needed for an informed decision is free and inexpensive communication among shareholders. But, even if the necessary channels exist for easy communication among share-

[45] The Company Law Review Steering Group, *Modern Company Law for a Competitive Economy: Final Report*(January 2001) 113 (5.61).

[46] See under Information Requirements, ch 4 above.

[47] Stedman, *Takeovers* (n 4 above) 237.

[48] JC Coffee, 'Regulating the Market for Corporate Control: A Critical Assessment of The Tender Offer's Role in Corporate Governance'(1984) 84 *Columbia Law Review* 1145 at 1270.

[49] *Ibid.*

holders, this does not solve the problem of the quality of the information communicated. A first alternative is for shareholders to rely on the market's reaction to the announced acquisition. If the price of the bidder falls considerably after the announcement of the takeover offer the acquirer's shareholders will not approve the acquisition. However, the market price function is subject to a number of inefficiencies and biases, as already discussed above.

As a result, the production and communication of views different from that of the company's management depends on the shareholders' activism and determination to circulate their views on the transaction. Towards that end, the responsibility inevitably lies with the institutional shareholders, who have the resources and the sophistication to carry out such a task.

There are also a number of other practical limitations associated with the approval procedure of the Listing Rules. As already emphasised, the size of modern listed companies and the dispersion of their shareholdings mean that many shareholders cast their votes by proxies, even before the EGM takes place. Dispersed ownership also means that many shareholders do not have either the interest or the resources to vote at all. As seen above, many commentators also accuse investors of being passive. Such passivity increases the chances of the transaction being approved. Again, this is an area where the commitment of institutional investors is necessary for an approval mechanism to operate in an effective way. In that sense, self-regulation in respect of institutional voting and communication is, in the end, what provides practical substance to the approval requirements of the Listing Rules.

V THE ROLE OF INSTITUTIONAL SHAREHOLDERS AND SHAREHOLDERS' ACTIVISM

Although institutional shareholders have been portrayed by many commentators as a highly regarded disciplinary mechanism, at the same time, there has been considerable recognition of the disparities between the potential active role of institutional investors and economic reality. The role of institutions has been hampered by a number of allegations of short-termism and passivity.[50] Nevertheless, the Myners Review on

[50] For a thorough analysis of the role of institutional shareholders in the United Kingdom see among others PL Davies 'Institutional Investors in the United Kingdom' (n 10 above); McCormack, 'Institutional Shareholders and the Promotion of Good Corporate Governance' (n 12 above). For the United States, see JC Coffee, 'Liquidity Versus Control: The Institutional Investor as Corporate Monitor' (1991) 91 *Columbia Law Review* 1277; JN Gordon, 'Institutions as Relational Investors: A New Look at Cumulative Voting' (1994) 94 *Columbia Law Review* 124; R Romano, 'Public Pension Fund Activism in Corporate Governance Reconsidered' (1993) 93 *Columbia Law Review* 795.

Institutional Investment brought forward, once more, the issue of institutional investors' activism and prompted revisions of statements and guidelines of the professional associations of institutional investors[51] and the Financial Reporting Council's Combined Code on Corporate Governance ('the Combined Code'). Those documents recognise the importance of institutional activism or engagement as defined in the new version of Statement of Principles issued by the Institutional Shareholders' Committee ('ISC')[52] and set out, amongst other things, the institutions' duties and responsibilities in voting, monitoring the performance of the investee companies and assessing the circumstances for intervention, when necessary.[53] Empirical findings also indicate that institutional shareownership is negatively correlated to the probability of takeovers being structured as share-for-share exchange offers,[54] and that institutional control is positively correlated to more value-creating takeovers.[55] The above recent developments and the relevant empirical data provide an indication, at least, that institutional shareholders can play a vital role in the decision process during a takeover. This is supported by two recent surveys conducted by the Institute of Management Accountants ('IMA') and the National Association of Pension Funds ('NAPF'). The IMA's survey covered 34 fund managers representing 55 per cent (£552 billion) of all UK equities managed within the United Kingdom. The NAPF's survey covered 66 pension funds, including all 50 of the biggest funds, with assets of approximately £350 billion, which is approximately half the total assets of all UK pension funds. The findings support that there has been a general increase in the level of engagement with investee companies.[56]

[51] Institutional Shareholders' Committee, *The Responsibilities of Institutional Shareholders and Agents—Statement of Principles* (2002) 1; Investment Management Association, *The Terms for Discretionary Fund Management* (2001) 1; Association of Unit Trusts and Investment Funds, *Code of Good Practice; Institutional Investors and Corporate Governance* (2001) 1.

[52] Institutional Shareholders' Committee, *The Responsibilities of Institutional Shareholders and Agents—Statement of Principles* (updated June 2007).

[53] Institutional Shareholders' Committee, *The Responsibilities of Institutional Shareholders and Agents—Statement of Principles* (October 2002) 1.

[54] KJ Martin, 'The Method of Payment in Corporate Acquisitions, Investment Opportunities, and Management Ownership' (1996) 51(4) *Journal of Finance* 1227.

[55] A Cosh, A Hughes, K Lee and A Singh, 'Institutional Investment, Mergers and the Market for Corporate Control' (1989) *International Journal of Industrial Economics* 73; A Cosh, A Hughes, K Lee and A Singh, 'Takeovers, Institutional Investment and the Persistence of Profits' in I Begg and S Henry (eds), *Applied Economics and Public Policy* (Cambridge, Cambridge University Press, 1998); A Cosh and A Hughes, 'Managerial Discretion and Takeover Performance', *ESRC Centre For Business Research, University of Cambridge Working Paper No 216* (2001).

[56] Both surveys evidenced that, although engagement polices are not a key criterion in pension funds' selection of a fund manager, there is growing interest and several funds acknowledged that it is likely to become increasingly important in the future. In this respect, the IMA's survey shows that managers' engagement has increased in the quarter ended 30 June 2004 from the same quarter last year, both in terms of the number of meetings with independent directors to discuss concerns and communications with management over and above routine meetings. Indeed, in the three months to 30 June 2004, managers reported over

It has already been argued, when the pre-emptive and approval rights were examined, that the existence of stricter rules and guidelines in this area can be attributed to a strong influence by professional bodies representing institutional investors.[57] However, when the issue shifts to the takeover decision per se, the role of institutional shareholders in defending shareholders against self-interested or economically bad acquisitions becomes more complex.

Institutional intervention can materialise in two ways: either through exposing the acquirer's management ex post to the discipline of the market, or by actively monitoring and intervening in the takeover decision ex ante. No matter what form the institutional control takes, it is subject to a number of limitations that affect not only its effectiveness, but in certain instances its desirability for the institutional shareholders.

A The Threat of Ex Post Discipline

The value of institutional intervention in takeovers lies not only in the actual monitoring, but also in the threat of the consequences that will follow if management pursues an unwanted acquisition. Institutional shareholders could penalise the bidder by selling their shares, or by accepting a potential offer for the unsuccessful bidder, thus making bidders more susceptible to the price function of capital markets and the market of corporate control.[58]

There are some examples from the UK capital market that support the above disciplinary role of institutional shareholders. One such an example has been the friendly takeover by Easyjet of Go. While the deal was considered as profitable for both companies, disputes over the composition of the board of the combined firm, especially from the side of Easyjet's CEO, threatened the completion of the deal. The deal was eventually completed due to the intervention of the institutional shareholders, who publicly threatened to massively sell their shareholdings in Easyjet and asked the Easyjet's CEO to step down.

Similarly, in the case of the unsuccessful takeover bid by NatWest of Legal and General and the former's successive acquisition by its rival Royal Bank of Scotland ('RBS'), NatWest's institutional shareholders not only opposed their company's bid for Legal and General, arguing that it had overvalued the target and was overpaying, but eventually pressured

1,000 communications with management, nearly two-and-a-half times the level in the same quarter in the previous year. In addition, managers now have an express policy to vote more categories of shares than in 2003. Currently, all 34 managers, with two exceptions, have a policy to vote all their UK shares and the majority vote all or some of their international shares.

[57] See above.

[58] See ch 3 above.

NatWest's board into accepting and recommending RBS's bid. The co-operation of institutional monitoring and the market of corporate control appear to have worked so effectively that they secured for the NatWest's shareholders a 19 per cent premium over NatWest's price before launching its bid for Legal and General, and the control of the combined group.

The effectiveness of the ex post disciplinary role of institutional intervention lies in the assumption that it is economically feasible for an institutional shareholder to exit the bidder. However, there are a number of occasions where this may not be the case. First, institutions may be locked into their shareholdings, or at least cannot sell them without causing an unacceptable adverse movement in the price of the stock they hold.[59] This is more likely in medium sized companies, where institutional shareholdings reach up to 20 per cent of the company's share capital.

Secondly, institutional shareholders may not be able to realistically sell their shares in periods of deep recession.[60] It is not irrelevant that the FSA decided to relax the requirements of equity holdings for insurance companies and pension funds because, otherwise, institutional shareholders would have suffered substantial losses if they were required to sell part of their portfolio to limit their equity exposure.

Finally, there are cases where exit may not be an option, not because of the size of the investment or the market's characteristics, but due to the nature of the institution. There are types of funds, namely indexed or tracker funds, where equity investments are invested in a portfolio of securities that is intended to represent an accurate proxy for the stock market as a whole. Such passive investing seeks not to beat the market, but to duplicate its movements, and, as a result, such investors tend to hold for the long-term. The main benefit of such funds is that they are cheaper than actively-managed funds that try to beat the market and they currently hold a significant percentage of institutional ownership especially in the United States. As a result, the less the institutional shareholders are in the position to sell their shares and thus discipline the bidder, the more they need to monitor the bidder and intervene in the acquisition decision as soon as possible.

B Ex Ante Intervention

The Combined Code requires institutional shareholders to enter into a dialogue with companies based on the mutual understanding of objectives[61] and to make considered use of their votes.[62] Apart from the Code a number

[59] Davies, 'Institutional Investors in the United Kingdom' (n 10 above).
[60] Davies, 'Institutional Investors in the United Kingdom' (n 10 above) 279.
[61] Main Principle E1 of the Combined Code on Corporate Goverance (June 2006).
[62] Main Principle E3 of the Combined Code on Corporate Goverance (June 2006).

of guidelines issued by the relevant professional bodies also portray institutional intervention. However, in them intervention focuses mainly on issues primarily related to directors' remuneration, audits and accounts, dividend payments and in general on issues that are considered as the directors' internal powers.[63] Nevertheless, some guidance is also provided for business decisions, such as takeovers. The Institutional Shareholders' Committee (ISC), in its Statement of Principles on the Responsibilities of Institutional Shareholders and Agents, argues that many issues could give rise to concerns about shareholder value and the company's acquisition and disposal strategy.[64] Compliance with the principles set out in the ISC's Statement of Principles, is also required by the Combined Code.[65] According to the ISC Statement of Principles, institutional shareholders and/or agents should set out the circumstances when they will actively intervene and how they propose to measure the effectiveness of doing so. Intervention should be considered regardless of whether an active or passive investment policy is followed, while being underweight is not, of itself, a reason for not intervening.[66] The statement continues that if boards do not respond constructively when institutional shareholders intervene, then the latter will consider, on a case-by-case basis, whether to escalate their action. In that sense, institutional shareholders could proceed, if they disagree with an acquisition planned by the bidder, in one of the following ways:[67]

— holding additional meetings with management specifically to discuss concerns;
— expressing concern through the company's advisers;
— meeting with the chairman, senior independent director, or with all independent directors;
— intervening jointly with other institutions;
— making a public statement in advance of the EGM in cases where such a meeting is necessary under the Listing Rules, or when authorisation of a new shares issue is needed, or in circumstances where they require the directors to convene one;
— submitting resolutions at shareholders' meetings; and
— finally, voting against the managers' plan to proceed with the specific takeover offer or requisitioning an EGM, possibly to change the board.[68]

[63] See, eg the Institutional Shareholders' Committee, *The Responsibilities of Institutional Shareholders and Agents—Statement of Principles* (2002, Updated June 2007) 1.

[64] *Ibid*, 3.

[65] See Supporting Principle in r E1 of the Combined Code on Corporate Goverance (June 2006).

[66] Institutional Shareholders' Committee, *The Responsibilities of Institutional Shareholders and Agents—Statement of Principles* (2002, Updated June 2007) 3.

[67] *Ibid*, 4.

[68] 'Institutional shareholders and/or agents should vote all shares held directly or on behalf of clients wherever practicable to do so. They will not automatically support the

The above actions fall within three broader categories: first, private communication with the company's management; secondly, public disclosure and dissemination of information to the market and other shareholders relating to the reasons why the company should not proceed with the planned acquisition once an intention to do so is announced; and thirdly, active voting against the proposed acquisition, where applicable.

As it has already been argued, when approval rights were analysed, the commitment of institutions in respect of voting and communication is what, in the end, provides practical substance to the approval requirements of the Listing Rules. Developments at a guidance level encourage institutional shareholders to proceed in that direction.[69] The Combined Code provides that institutional shareholders must make considered use of their votes and that major shareholders should attend AGMs where appropriate and practicable.[70] However, is it necessary for institutional voting in class 1 transactions to be mandatory? Currently, there is no such requirement, although moves by HM Treasury resulting from the Myners Review have been heading in this direction.[71] Til now, however, voting by institutional shareholders remains a subject mainly covered by professional guidelines. For example, the NAPF Corporate Governance Policy provides that informed use of votes is an obligation (although not a legal duty) of owners and an implicit fiduciary duty of trustees and investment managers to whom trustees may delegate this function.[72]

Leaving aside mandatory voting, the real issue is to ensure thoughtful and responsible voting by institutional investors. This requires institutional shareholders to disclose their policies as how they exercise their voting powers in relation to a class 1 transaction. The Combined Code's relevant requirements are limited to provision by institutional investors to their clients of information, on request, on the proportion of resolutions on which votes were cast and non-discretionary proxies lodged.[73] In general, it has been mandatory for pension scheme trustees to disclose in their statement of investment principles their policy on voting rights. Similarly,

board; if they have been unable to reach a satisfactory outcome through active dialogue then they will register an abstention or vote against the resolution. In both instances it is good practice to inform the company in advance of their intention and the reasons why': ISC, *The Responsibilities of Institutional Shareholders and Agents—Statement of Principles* (n 66 above) 4.

[69] Association of Unit Trusts and Investment Funds, *Code of Good Practice; Institutional Investors and Corporate Governance* (2001) 1; ISC, *The Responsibilities of Institutional Shareholders and Agents—Statement of Principles* (n 66 above) 1.

[70] The latter was introduced as a result of the Higgs review to facilitate a more active engagement by institutional shareholders

[71] NAPF, *A Modern Regulatory Framework for Company Law in Europe: A Consultative Document of the High Level Group of Company Law Experts: Response by the National Association of Pension Funds* (2002).

[72] NAPF, *National Association of Pension Funds Corporate Governance Policy* (November 2006).

[73] See Supporting Principles in r E3 of the Combined Code on Corporate Governance (June 2006).

other professional bodies encourage their members to publish their investment and voting policies. However, effective communication requires the dissemination of information specifically related to the transaction in question and not just vague statements of voting policy.

This issue has been subject of a considerable debate, which resulted in the inclusion in the new Companies Act 2006 of section 1277. This section confers a power on the Secretary of State and the Treasury to make regulations requiring certain categories of institutional investor to provide information about the exercise of their voting rights. The power is drawn intentionally widely to enable any mandatory disclosure regime to respond to varied corporate governance arrangements and to capture a range of institutions investing in different markets. The obligation imposed by regulations under this section is enforceable by civil proceedings brought either by the person to whom the information should have been provided or by a regulatory authority specified in the regulations.[74] Information disclosed can cover, under section 1280 the exercise or non-exercise of voting rights, instructions given by the institution and any delegation of a function related to the exercise or non-exercise of voting rights. Currently, there are no relevant rules and disclosure of the exercise of voting rights still remains voluntary.

Similar requirements have been proposed at EU and US level. In its action plan 'Modernising Company Law and Enhancing Corporate Governance in the European Union—A Plan to Move Forward' of 2003, the European Commission proposed a mandatory disclosure of institutional investors' voting behaviour with regard to their portfolio companies, as a medium-term measure. Unfortunately, the Commission's proposal met with strong opposition from commentators when it was presented to the public in 2003. In contrast, in the same year, new Securities and Exchange Commission rules were adopted mandating voting disclosure of investment companies and investment advisers.

Even when shareholders are not awarded any decision rights in relation to a specific acquisition, institutional shareholders could in theory remove the board of directors through an ordinary resolution. In order for institutional shareholders to be able at least to convene the general meeting for that purpose, they should control 10 per cent or more of the acquirer's ordinary shares,[75] and, hence, a coalition between different institutions may be needed. However, if the EGM takes place after the announcement of the offeror's intention to make a bid it is very unlikely that any change in the board or any other opposition to the offer will make the position of the bidder any better. This is because the announcement of an intention to make the offer binds the bidder.[76] In that sense, as already seen, the

[74] Section 1277(4) of the CA 2006.
[75] Section 303 of the CA 2006.
[76] See ch 9 below.

change of control does not instantly permit the bidder to withdraw its offer.

C Limitations and Pre-requisites

Institutional intervention in takeovers may involve substantial costs, such as free ride costs, reputational loss (if the institution supports a takeover that eventually proves to be value reducing), costs associated with the vote casting in the case of class 1 transactions or costs related to the circulation of the institution's views on the takeover.

In addition, if institutional shareholders are to be more active in monitoring takeover activity, such a function must be carried out for the best interests of their beneficiaries. Institutional shareholders' primary duty is to those on whose behalf they invest—for example, the beneficiaries of a pension scheme or the policy-holders in an insurance company—and they must act in their best financial interests. Such a requirement derives from the general principles of trust law and is also repeated in many FSA rules and statements of principles issued by various relevant professional bodies.

A problem arises in cases where information about a potential takeover is disclosed to institutional investors before an official announcement of the bidder's intensions or an actual offer is made. By being involved in pre-announcement discussions about a potential takeover the institutional investor carries the risk of falling within the statutory definition of 'insider',[77] which can hamper its ability to trade in the securities of the bidder.

The Takeover Code also imposes its own restrictions on insider dealing. Rule 4.1 provides that

> no dealings of any kind in securities of the offeree company by any person, not being the offeror, who is privy to confidential price-sensitive information concerning an offer or contemplated offer may take place between the time when there is reason to suppose that an approach or an offer is contemplated and the announcement of the approach or offer or the termination of the discussions.[78]

Nor may such dealings may take place in securities of the offeror.[79] This can result in taking the institution off market in relation both to the bidder's and the target's shares for a long period, until the offer is eventually announced, locking in effect the institution within the bidder.

The public opposition to or support of a bid by an institutional shareholder may also create a number of conflicts of interests. For example, in

[77] As defined in s 118B of the FSMA 2000 and s 57(2) of Part V of the Criminal Justice Act 1993. See also the Code of Market Conduct MAR 1.3.

[78] Rule 4.1(a) of the Takeover Code.

[79] Rule 4.1(c) of the Takeover Code.

the case of a contested bid when the same institution has substantial shareholdings in both bidders, supporting or opposing one bid or another is extremely difficult. In the case of investment funds, an opposition to the bid may conflict with other investment services provided by other divisions of the financial conglomerate, such as underwriting facilities provided to the bidder. Finally, a public announcement that an institutional shareholder will support a specific bid may be considered as an irrevocable undertaking[80] or even as acting in concert[81] with the bidder, especially when the institutional shareholder has also a substantial equity stake in the target. These are situations that an institutional shareholder may not wish to be in.

The above can prove to be substantial disincentives for institutional intervention. But, even if one assumes that institutional shareholders do want to intervene in the course of a takeover decision, it has to be examined to what extent they can effectively do so. Effective intervention at a very early stage of the transaction requires disclosure of important information by the bidder. However, it is questionable whether the bidder can disclose such information to a selective number of institutional shareholders at all. The importance of wide and equal access to information to all shareholders of the same class is emphasised by the Disclosure and Transparency Rules ('DTR') and the Transparency Directive.[82] Moreover, According to the Disclosure and Transparency Rules, selective disclosure to certain third parties is only permitted when accompanied by complete and effective public disclosure of that information via a Regulation Impact Statement ('RIS'),[83] unless there is a reason for disclosure to be delayed. In the latter case, the issuer may selectively disclose that information to persons owing it a duty of confidentiality.[84] The Disclosure and Transparency Rules provide for an exemption in the case of 'major transactions', which includes takeovers. In such cases an issuer needing shareholder support may selectively disclose details of the proposed transaction to major shareholders, as long as the recipients are bound by a duty of confidentiality.[85] Nevertheless it should be noted that this is an exemption which cannot be justified in all cases where selective disclosure is made and public disclosure is delayed. [86] In addition, the wider the group of recipients of inside information is, the greater the likelihood of a leak that will trigger full public disclosure of the information.[87] In addition, the point when disclosure is required is also determined by the Takeover Code.[88]

[80] Rule 2.5, note 3 and r 4.3 of the Takeover Code.
[81] See 'Definitions' in the Takeover Code and r 4.2.
[82] See DTR 6.1.3 and the Transparency Directive, Art 17.1.
[83] DTR 2.5.6 and 2.6.2.
[84] DTR 2.5.7.
[85] *Ibid.*
[86] DTR 2.5.8.
[87] DTR 2.5.9.
[88] See later on in this volume.

Furthermore, any disclosure of this type could contravene General Principle 2 of the Takeover Code as applied before the implementation of the Takeovers Directive, which provided that information should be made available equally to all shareholders, either during the offer or when an offer is in contemplation.[89] The Takeover Panel has in the past forbidden pre-bid discussions with privileged shareholders like institutions on exactly that basis.[90] However, the implementation of the Takeovers Directive resulted in the restatement of all general principles of the Code including General Principle 2. New rule 20.1 now replicates the wording of old General Principle 2 but limits its application only to target shareholders. Nevertheless the rest of rule 20 still imposes restrictions to confidential communication of institutional investors with the bidder. Note 3 on rule 20.1 provides that in any meetings of the offeror that may take place with a small number of institutional shareholders during the offer period, no material new information and no significant new opinions should be disclosed or expressed.[91] Except with the consent of the Panel, an appropriate representative of the financial adviser or corporate broker to the offeror must be present. That representative will be responsible for confirming in writing to the Panel that no material information was forthcoming and no significant new opinions were expressed at the meeting.[92] The above provisions apply to all such meetings held during an offer period, wherever they take place and even if with only one person or firm, unless the meeting takes place by chance.[93] The implication of that rule for the position of the acquirer's institutional shareholders is that, if they want to oppose to an announced takeover offer, they have to do it publicly. However, this reduces the circumstances under which an institutional shareholder will assume the responsibility to publicly oppose a takeover offer.

Another issue that arises is whether the institutional shareholders who intervene act in concert for the purposes of the Code. In this respect, the decisive factor in determining whether shareholders act in concert is whether their action can be characterised as seeking control of the board of the company.[94] In the case where institutional shareholders lobby against a takeover announced by their directors, such determination should be by reference to whether the activist shareholders threaten, either explicitly or implicitly, to make changes to the board of the bidder

[89] Old General Principle 2 of the City Code on Takeovers and Mergers (the Takeover Code).

[90] Stedman, *Takeovers* (n 4 above) 118.

[91] See the Takeover Code, note 3 on r 20.1.

[92] *Ibid*.

[93] *Ibid*.

[94] The Panel on Takeovers and Mergers, PCP 10: *Consultation Paper Issued by the Code Committee of the Panel: Shareholder Activism and Acting in Concert; Revision Proposals Relating to Note 2 on Rule 9.1 of the Takeover Code* (March 2002) 1.2.

if the latter is not disciplined.[95] Even then, the underlying principle of the Code is that the institutional shareholders will be considered to be acting in concert only if they seek on-going control of the bidder, and not if they just intend to pursue a short-term legitimate collective action designed to maximise overall shareholder value.[96]

VI REWARD STRATEGIES, DIRECTORS' REMUNERATION, AND SHARE INCENTIVE SCHEMES

One mechanism that has long been suggested in order to minimise conflicts and align shareholders' and managers' interests is to make managers' compensation sensitive to the firm's performance and share value. This is usually done by structuring part of the directors' remuneration as a share incentive scheme.

The main rationale behind share incentive schemes is that by increasing the share element of the executive's compensation, managerial ownership increases in the firm and, thus, the convergence of interests between managers and shareholders improves. Applying the above hypothesis to the specific case of corporate acquisitions, it is suggested that non-trivial managerial ownership in the bidder decreases the occurrence of value-decreasing takeovers.

Many studies have examined the above hypothesis and report a positive correlation between the acquirer's managerial ownership and the incidence of cash payments in takeovers.[97] However, the correlation between managerial ownership and value-maximising takeovers is more complicated. There are studies which report that firms perform better when managers own a non-trivial fraction of the firm's shares.[98] Nevertheless,

[95] Note 2 on r 9.1 of the Takeover Code.

[96] The Panel believes that the determination of whether a specific collective action will be considered as a board control-seeking proposal is to be carried out by reference to a non-exhaustive list of factors and on a caseby-case basis. See note 2(a) and (b) on r 9.1 See also The Panel on Takeovers and Mergers, RS10: *Shareholder Activism and Acting in Concert. Statement by the Code Committee of the Panel Following the External Consultation Process on PCP 10* (July 2002) 4.3.

[97] M Harris and A Raviv, 'Corporate Control Contests and Capital Structure' (1988) 20 *Journal of Financial Economics* 55; R Stulz, 'Managerial Control of Voting Rights: Financial Policies and the Market for Corporate Control' (1988) 20 *Journal of financial Economics* 25; Martin, 'The Method of Payment in Corporate Acquisitions, Investment Opportunities, and Management Ownership'(n 54 above) 1227; MC Jensen and WH Meckling, 'Theory of the Firm: Managerial Behavior, Agency Costs and Ownership Structure' (1976) 3 *Journal of Financial Economics* 305.

[98] J McConnell and H Servaes, 'Additional Evidence on Equity Ownership and Corporate Value' (1990) 27 *Journal of Financial Economics* 595; BE Hermalin and M Weisbach, 'The Determinants of Board Composition' (1988) 19 *The RAND Journal of Economics* 589; A Agrawal and CR Knoeber, 'Firm Performance and Mechanisms to Control Agency Problems between Managers and Shareholders' (1996) 31(3) *Journal of Financial and Quantitative Analysis* 377.

empirical findings suggest that there is a fine line between convergence of interests and entrenchment. In cases of no or extremely weak managerial ownership, managers tend to overpay,[99] whilst, when managers hold significantly non-trivial fractions of the firm's shares, they tend to engage in non-value-maximising, diversifying acquisitions.[100] Moreover, as seen above, managers with substantial shareholdings in the bidder may have enough voting power to avoid the market of corporate control.[101] In other words, the correlation between managerial ownership and value-maximising takeovers is not monotonic.[102] Morck, Shleifer and Vishny found that as ownership concentration increased from 0 to 5 per cent, performance improved, while performance deteriorated in the ownership range from 5 to 25 per cent.[103] Many other studies of both the US and the UK markets report similar results.[104] Overall, what those studies suggest is that takeovers carried out by managers or directors with either trivial or large stakes in the bidder may manifest managerial self-interests or failure.[105] Accordingly, a successful remuneration strategy should carry a share element big enough to make managers' compensation sensitive to the performance of the acquisition, but not too big to deter managers from pursuing acquisitions in the first place. This leads to the question whether the necessary means are available to the acquirer's shareholders to monitor and structure their directors' remuneration in this way.

Despite the recent implementation of the Companies Act 2006, the statutory regulation of directors' remuneration is mainly confined to dis-

[99] V You, RE Caves, M Smith and J Henry, 'Mergers and Bidders' Wealth: Managerial and Strategic Factors' in LG Thomas (ed), *The Economics of Strategic Planning: Essays in Honor of Joel Dean* (Lexington MA, Lexington Books, 1997); WG Lewellen, C Loderer and A Rosenfield, 'Merger Decisions and Executive Stock Ownership in Acquiring Firms' (1985) 7 *Journal of Accounting and Economics* 209.

[100] DJ Denis, DK Denis and A Sarin, 'Agency Problems, Equity Ownership, and Corporate Diversification' (1997) 52(1) *The Journal of Finance* 135.

[101] E Fama and MC Jensen, 'Separation of Ownership and Control' (1983) 26 *Journal of Law and Economics* 235.

[102] Morck, Shleifer and Vishny, 'Do Managerial Objectives Drive Bad Acquisitions': 31; RG Hubbard and D Palia, 'Benefits of Control, Managerial Ownership, and Stock Returns of Acquiring Firms' (1995) 26(4) *The RAND Journal of Economics* 782; Cosh and Hughes, 'Managerial Discretion and Takeover Performance' (n 55 above).

[103] Morck, Shleifer and Vishny, 'Do Managerial Objectives Drive Bad Acquisitions' 31. After 25 per cent performance improved slowly.

[104] For the US market see Hubbard and Palia, 'Benefits of Control, Managerial Ownership, and Stock Returns of Acquiring Firms': 782; J McConnell and H Servaes, 'Additional Evidence on Equity Ownership and Corporate Value' (1990) 27 *Journal of Financial Economics* 595; Hermalin and Weisbach 'The Determinants of Board Composition' 589. For the UK see Cosh and Hughes, 'Managerial Discretion and Takeover Performance' (n 55 above); H Short and K Keasey, 'Managerial Ownership and the Performance of Firms: Evidence from the Uk' (1999) 5 *Journal of Corporate Finance* 79; M Faccio and M Lasfer, 'Managerial Ownership, Board Structure and Firm Value: The UK Evidence' (1999) *City University Working Papers*.

[105] See for example Cosh and Hughes, 'Managerial Discretion and Takeover Performance' (n 55 above).

closure,[106] audit[107] and approval requirements[108] regarding the details of the remuneration policy, in the same way that the annual accounts are disclosed, audited and approved by the annual general meeting. The new Companies Act provisions are also backed up by the disclosure and approval requirements of the UKLA Listing Rules[109] and chapter B of the Combined Code on Corporate Governance.

According to Main Principle B.1 of the 2006 version of the Combined Code on Corporate Governance, the levels of executive remuneration should be sufficient to attract, retain and motivate directors of the quality required to run the company successfully. In addition a significant proportion of executive directors' remuneration should be structured so as to link rewards to corporate and individual performance.

More detailed rules that govern the structure and the context of reward strategies and try to intervene in the contractual process of the formulation of the reward policy between the company and the managers, are included in the relevant ABI[110] guidelines. The ABI guidelines seek to provide an appropriate framework on remuneration and are currently expressed in a new paper titled 'Executive Remuneration—ABI Guidelines on Policies and Practices'.[111] This means that the implementation of a reward strategy capable of restraining managers from pursuing value-decreasing takeovers relies less on statutory intervention and more on institutional shareholders' pressure.

As described above, a successful remuneration strategy in relation to takeovers must have a convergence effect and should seek to avoid entrenchment. In relation to the convergence effect that a remuneration strategy must have to prevent overpayment, institutional shareholders generally support share incentive schemes that link remuneration to performance and align the interests of participating directors and senior executives with those of shareholders. Moreover, schemes should be designed to encourage share retention, so that directors and other senior executives build up and maintain shareholdings, which are meaningful in the context of their remuneration.[112] Incentive schemes should incorporate the

[106] Sections 420 and 421 of the CA 2006.

[107] Section 422 of the CA 2006.

[108] Sections 439 and 440 of the CA 2006. See also ABI, 2006 *Executive Remuneration—ABI Guidelines on Policies and Practices*.

[109] Para 9.8.6(a). and LR 9.4 of the Listing Rules.

[110] Association of British Insurers.

[111] Although the new text introduced no significant changes and the substance of the Guidelines is largely unchanged, the Guidelines are now in a clearer format with overarching Principles, Main Provisions and more detailed Guidance. The Guidelines incorporate issues dealt with in more detail in *Best Practice on Executive Contracts and Severance—Joint Statement by the Association of British Insurers and the National Association of Pension Funds* (December 2002).

[112] Association of British Insurers, *Executive Remuneration—ABI Guidelines on Policies and Practices* (December 2006) Section III.

requirement to retain a significant portion of shares to which directors become entitled and the targets for shareholding should relate to reward potential.[113] Share awards must also be conditional on satisfaction of certain performance criteria.[114] Performance measures should be fully explained and be clearly linked to the achievement of challenging and stretching financial performance which will lead to enhancement of shareholder value. The vesting of awards with high potential value should be linked to commensurately higher levels of performance. Full vesting should be dependent upon achievement of significantly greater value creation than that applicable to threshold vesting. Sliding scales are a useful way of ensuring that performance conditions are genuinely stretching. Total shareholders' return, relative to a relevant index or peer group, is generally acceptable as a performance criterion.[115] To that effect the definition of Earnings Per Share (EPS) or any other financial measure should fully reflect the performance of the business on a consistent basis in respect of the measurement period. The above criterion could be adequate for providing the right incentives for takeovers, since bad acquisitions are in most circumstances[116] accompanied by negative returns.

In addition, institutional shareholders are not supportive of either transaction bonuses, which reward directors and other executives for effecting transactions regardless of their future financial consequences,[117] or departing directors being rewarded for failure or underperformance.[118] This may further discipline managers by eliminating phenomena, such as the departure of NatWest's CEO with a generous compensation of £3m, after the failure to acquire Legal and General, while NatWest being the target of two hostile bids and having its shares trading at 26 per cent discount of its initial value. Finally, institutional investors insist that options granted under executive (discretionary) schemes should not be granted at a discount to the prevailing mid-market price.[119] This is also required by LR 9.4.4 of the UKLA Listing Rules and the 2006 version of the Combined Code.[120] This further prevents executives from profiting from value-decreasing takeovers when the bidder's share price does not fall beyond the exercise price of the option.

[113] *Ibid.*

[114] ABI, *Executive Remuneration* (n 112 above) Section III.

[115] ABI, *Executive Remuneration* (n 112 above) Section III.

[116] See about the discount hypothesis above under the heading: market of corporate control.

[117] ABI, *Executive Remuneration* (n 112 above).

[118] ABI and NAPF, *Best Practice on Executive Contracts and Severance* (n 111 above) 1.1. The statement continues in 1.2: 'It is unacceptable that failure, which detracts from the value of an enterprise and which can threaten the livelihood of employees, can result in large payments to its departing leaders. Executives, whose remuneration is already at a level which allows for the risk inherent in their role, should show leadership in aligning their financial interests with those of their shareholders'.

[119] ABI, *Executive Remuneration* (n 112 above).

[120] Provision B.1.2 of the Combined Code on Corporate Governance (June 2006).

Apart from the convergence of interests, an effective reward strategy must also account for circumstances of entrenchment. As seen above, large managerial shareholdings may result in undiversified positions that conflict with the interests of other shareholders and are associated with value-decreasing diversifying acquisitions. The ABI guidelines insist that commitments to issue shares under executive (discretionary) schemes should not exceed 5 per cent of the issued ordinary share capital of the company, or 10 per cent when aggregated with awards under all of the company's other schemes.[121]

Finally, any policy against entrenchment at a company level must also take into account any dealings in the bidder's shares by the executive in the aftermarket, which can increase his stake in the company beyond the desired levels. Thus, disclosure rules, included in the Companies Act, the Disclosure and Transparency Rules and especially the Takeover Code, regarding any dealings in the shares of the bidder by its executives help shareholders monitor their managers' stake-building in the bidder and take actions when, under the specific market conditions, it reaches alarming levels.[122]

VII CONCLUSION

This chapter considered the effectiveness of shareholders' voice and reward strategies. The protection afforded to the acquiring shareholders by authorisation rights in cases of share issues has been found to be circumstantial, depending on whether there is adequate authorised capital before the transaction. Pre-emptive rights were also found to protect the acquirer's shareholders from dilution in equity-financed acquisitions, but not in share-for-share exchange offers. Both are useful only when a share issue is necessary in connection to the offer, and provide no protection against debt-financed acquisitions, unless the articles of association provide for the shareholders' approval, in cases where the directors borrow more than the debt limits thereby prescribed.

Approval rights are afforded by the Listing Rules in three cases: substantial acquisitions, related-party transactions and reverse takeovers. Depriving the agent of its decision rights is probably the most direct way to address agency costs and conflicts of interests. However, it is not a panacea. There are costs associated with approval rights in respect of preparing and communicating the information required by the Listing Rules and convening the EGM. Approval rights also demand sophistication and active participation on the part of shareholders. This means that, in the light of the excessive dispersion of UK public ownership and the

121 *Ibid*, 8.

122 According to empirical studies those levels range between as little as 5% to 25%.

documented passivity of private investors, the effectiveness of approval rights lies in the hands of institutional investors.

In addition, the role of institutional shareholders is important in strengthening authorisation and pre-emptive rights of the Companies Act. Claw-backs and limitations to delegation of authorisation power to directors are two areas with considerable influence by institutions. Moreover, and beyond the operation of the class transaction rules, in relation to which institutional activism is essential, recent examples indicate that institutional shareholders can make the acquirer's management more sensitive to the market of corporate control. Furthermore, institutions, by controlling stock lending, can also support the acquirer's market price and protect it from pressures by the operation of risk arbitrageurs. Institutional voting is also an area with considerable developments both in terms of formulating and communicating voting policy and disclosing actual voting. Nevertheless institutional voting or voting disclosure is yet to be implemented at a mandatory level, although, in the latter a first step was taken with regards to section 1277 of the CA 2006.

Finally, share incentives schemes were considered as an alternative way to minimise the conflicts of interests between the acquirer's shareholders and their managers. Empirical findings suggest that there is a positive correlation between managerial ownership and cash payment in takeovers, and a non-monotonic relation between the level of managerial ownership and the emergence of value-decreasing takeovers. This suggests that share incentive schemes may provide the necessary incentives to the bidder's managers to avoid overbidding or value-decreasing diversifying acquisitions. However, there is a fine line between convergence of interests and entrenchment. Accordingly, a share incentive scheme must take both those parameters into consideration. Recent developments at a statutory level, but more importantly institutional intervention in the form of relevant guidelines, create a framework that can contribute to the formulation of an effective reward strategy in takeovers.

6

Auction Risk, Part I: Introduction, Hostile Takeovers and MBOs

I INTRODUCTION

IT HAS BEEN suggested that value-decreasing takeovers for the acquiring shareholders occur, either because of conflicts of interests with their managers, or due to bad business decisions. That being the case, it has been submitted that the main mechanisms to protect the acquiring shareholders are, either to minimise managerial discretion in deciding whether or not to proceed with a takeover, or to align managers' and shareholders' interests.

In this part, the focus shifts from what have been described as internal risks to a set of external risks; in other words, risks that occur irrespective of the existence or not of conflicts of interests and even in cases where the acquisition is sound and potentially value-increasing for the acquiring shareholders. In that respect, three 'external risks' will be identified:

— auction risk, or the risk of losing the target;
— high premium risk; and
— adverse change risk.

All the above risks affect the acquiring shareholders' wealth, either through wealth transfers to the target shareholders or through diminution in the acquirer's share price. They also reflect the fourth explanation for the acquiring shareholders' negative returns provided in the introduction (chapter one), where it was predicted that external sources and especially regulation affect the distribution of gains in takeovers.

II AUCTION COSTS

Once a bidder announces its intention to acquire a target or places its offer, whether the target will accept the offer or not is not its only problem. Another risk that it carries is that its intention to acquire the target discloses information to the market about the value of the transaction, and rivals may enter the contest to acquire the same target. In such a case, an auction situation arises. The City Code on Takeovers and Mergers ('the Takeover Code') does not prohibit auctions and it actually takes for granted that a rival bidder can place a counter offer while the initial offer is still open. Moreover, the Takeover Code includes a number of rules that, directly or indirectly, facilitate auctions. These rules will be further considered below.

A The Costs from Losing the Auction

Auctions are not costless for the initial bidder, who suffers considerable out-of-pocket expenses. A bidder is obliged to invest a considerable amount of money before being able to proceed with the offer. Initially, the acquirer has to invest money in securing the necessary financial resources to be able to implement the offer, as Rule 2.5 of the Takeover Code dictates.[1] Then, the preparation of the necessary takeover documents involves considerable legal and investment banker fees. Finally, engaging in a due diligence process which is necessary to meet the standards of care and skill required, as seen above, demands substantial sums of money. Bidder's costs may also include an investment banker's fee or finder's fee usually paid to a business broker for identifying the target; investment banker's fees for arranging a loan or a securities issue; loan commitment fees or costs involved in the initial steps of public offerings (listing particulars, circulars etc.); underwriting fees and fees to certain outside experts required to value the target. All these costs are borne exclusively by the bidder and most of them need to be covered, even when the bidder loses the auction.

Some of the bidder's costs are also associated with the length of the offer period. Normally, when a competing offer arises, both the initial offeror and the competing bidder are bound by the timetable established by the posting of the competing offer.[2] This means that the announcement of a competing bid usually lengthens the timetable of the initial offer considerably, even over a period of more than 60 days, which is, under the Code, the maximum period that an offer can remain open to acceptances.[3] The

[1] Especially after the amendments performed pursuant to Art 3 of the Takeovers Directive (2004/25/EC), r 2.5 now requires a cash confirmation from a financial adviser or a third party in all cash offers and this applies not only to mandatory bids made pursuant to r 9 of the Code.

[2] Rule 31.6(a)(i) of the Takeover Code, 8th edn (London, Panel on Takeovers and Mergers, May 2006).

[3] According to the Code in the cases of competitive bids, the initial offeror is able to extend its offer for a total period of more than 60 days from the initial posting of the offer documents, with the consent of the panel, which is normally granted under the above circumstances: r 31.6, note 4.

effects of the offer's timetable extension on the bidder's costs are greater when the offer carries a cash alternative.

B The Costs from Winning the Auction

Out-of-pocket expenses are not the only costs carried by the initial unsuccessful bidder. The announcement of an intention to make an offer conveys valuable information to prospective bidders. Subsequent bidders can free ride on the initial bidder's efforts to identify and value the target. In the light of the information that the bidder is required to publish in the context of its offer, rival hostile bidders are likely to find more information about the target in the initial bidder's takeover documents than from any other source. Hence, 'free riding' costs or 'sunk information costs', as they are usually called,[4] arise for the initial bidder.

Auctions can also lead to overbidding. As seen in chapter two, bidders are vulnerable to what is described as 'winner's curse'. That means that, in an auction situation, the bidder is more likely to win when it is willing to pay more than the consensus valuation of the target. But, even if the bidder is disciplined enough not to overvalue the target, still it cannot quantify the risk that its efforts in bidding for the target will be wasted. The bidder has no way of knowing whether its best bid is the highest bid that can be offered by a potential competitive bidder.[5] In other words, the bidder's uncertainty about the offer price concerns not only the value of the subject of the auction, but also the probability and value of rival bids by other potential bidders.[6] Hence, it is very likely that it will try to deter potential competition by raising the bid premium it offers. Empirical studies reveal that an initial aggressive bid is far more effective in deterring competition than a revised offer.[7]

In view of the above, an auction increases the probability of the initial bidder either losing the target and still suffering the initial offer expenses, or overpaying. For the acquiring shareholders this means that they suffer losses, either in the form of a decrease in the acquirer's share price, when the bidder loses, or through wealth transfers to target shareholders, when it wins. Empirical studies submit evidence in support of both these cases:

[4] FH Easterbrook and DR Fischel, 'Symposium: Auctions and Sunk Costs in Tender Offers' (1982) 35 *Stanford Law Review* 1.

[5] WJ Carney, *Mergers and Acquisitions: Cases and Materials*, 1st edn (New York, Foundation Press, 2000) 563.

[6] RL Winkler and DG Brooks, 'Competitive Bidding with Dependent Value Estimates' (1980) 28 *Operations Research* 603.

[7] MJ Fishman, 'A Theory of Preemptive Takeover Bidding' (1988) 19 *Rand Journal of Economics* 88; RM Giammarino and RL Heinkel, 'A Model of Dynamic Takeover Behavior' (1986) 41 (June) *Journal of Finance* 465; IPL P'ng, 'Facilitation of Competing Bids and the Price of a Takeover Target', *Business Economics Working Paper No 87-10* (1987).

first, takeover premia are greater in multiple bids than in one-bidder offers (wealth transfer effect) and secondly, competitive bidders suffer more losses than uncontested acquirers (share price decrease effect).[8]

The existence of the above costs raises two interrelated questions:

1. Would a non-auction rule be more beneficial for the acquiring shareholders? What implications would such a rule have for society, and are these justifiable?

If the answer to that first question is negative, a second question inevitably arises both on a positive and on a normative basis:

2. If a non-auction rule cannot be justified, how can the bidder be protected from a potential rival offer? In normative terms, the same question can be rephrased as: What level of incentives should be provided to the initial bidder? After all, without the first bidder to identify the target there may be no auctions at all.

III PROHIBITING AUCTIONS

A The Debate

The existence of the abovementioned costs inevitably raises the questions of why auctions should be permitted, if they are accompanied by such substantial costs. The most important regulatory implication of a non-auction rule is 'time'. Due to the so-called 'prisoner's dilemma' and the collective action problems associated with a dispersed corporate ownership, target shareholders are not able to act effectively, so as to keep the offer open for a period long enough to induce a prospective buyer to enter

[8] Bradley, Desai and Kim report significant differences in the pattern by which the target's CAR (cumulative average residual) rises in multiple bids as opposed to single bids. In multiple bids the CAR for targets continued to significantly rise over 45% even 80 days after the announcement of the first bid, while in single bids it remained the same with that of the announcement day at 26% on average. The acquirer's abnormal returns appear also more negative in the case of competitive bids. M Bradley, A Desai and EH Kim, 'Synergistic Gains from Corporate Acquisitions and Their Division between the Stockholders of Target and Acquiring Firms' (1988) 21 *Journal of Financial Economics* 3. Weston supports these findings. He reports a 30% increase in the target's returns in single bids and 45% in multiple bids. Also in the former case returns appear to decline after the announcement daywhile in the latter they continue to rise even 40 days after the announcement of the first bid. The acquirer's returns appear positive in single bids and negative in multiple bids. JF Weston, JA Siu and BA Johnson, *Takeovers, Restructuring & Corporate Governance*, 3rd edn (London, Prentice Hall, 2001) 206–7. Varaiya also reports that, on average, the winning bid premium significantly overstates the capital market's estimate of the expected takeover gain. In 67% of the acquisitions in her sample the winning bid premium exceeded the maximum offerable premium conditional on the market's estimate of the expected takeover gain. N Varaiya, 'The "Winner's Curse" Hypothesis and Corporate Takeovers' (1988) 9(3) *Managerial and Decision Economics* 209.

the contest. A rule that facilitates auctions demands that the bidder keep the offer open for a specified period of time, not only in order for the target shareholders to have the time to make an assessed decision, but also because a mandatory delay of the offer period facilitates competing bids. In other words, a non-auction rule does not necessarily need to prohibit auctions directly in cases where an offer is still open. The same result can be indirectly reached by permitting offers to be open for an extremely short period of time. Under both rule variants, the issue is time. In the former case, the initial bidder has the incentive to keep the offer open for as long as possible, while in the latter case it opts for speed.

As has already been argued, auctions are associated with higher takeover premia than one-bidder deals. Bearing this in mind, the importance of the offer timetable in deterring or facilitating auctions is also manifested by the following empirical example.[9] In December 1982, the Stock Exchange Committee ('SEC') in the United States amended rule 14b-8 (passed under the Securities Exchange Act 1934) to require pro rata purchases of shares tendered in a partial offer for the entire period the offer is open, namely, a minimum of 20 days. Previously, only those shares tendered in the first 10 days of a partial offer were required to be taken pro rata. As a result, the period for which a target shareholder could safely wait before tendering his shares was 20 days, as opposed to 10 days before the amendment. This substantially eliminated the benefits of partial offers for the bidder in deterring auctions and inducing shareholders to tender their shares.

In a study by the Office of the Chief Economist on the relative premia of 91 any-or-all offers and partial offers occurring in the 1981–83 period, the above amendments eliminated the differences in premia between the two offer structures. The data suggested that before the SEC amendments, the coercive element of the shorter timetable associated with partial offers had successfully deterred competition, with premia being lower in partial offers (31.3 per cent) than any-or-all offers (63.4 per cent). However, for acquisitions that took place after the SEC amendments such a relationship disappears: 49.4 per cent for partial offers; 49.6% for any-or-all bids.[10]

The Takeover Code regulates both the minimum and the maximum time that an offer can be open. Under rule 31.1 an offer must initially be open for at least 21 days following the date on which the offer document is posted, while under rule 31.6, except with the consent of the Panel, the maximum period that an offer, revised or not, can remain open to acceptances is 60 days.[11]

[9] Data and example provided in RJ Gilson and BS Black, *The Law and Finance of Corporate Acquisitions* 2nd edn (Westbury, NY, The Foundation Press, Inc, 1995) 800.

[10] *Ibid.*

[11] For exemptions see r 31.6(a), cases (i) to (iv) of the Takeover Code.

The desirability or not of a non-auction rule has been the subject of a debate in the early '80s among Professors Easterbrook and Fischel[12] on the one side, who advocated that a non-auction rule maximises investors' wealth overall, and Professors Gilson and Bebchuck[13] on the other, who argued that facilitating competing bids has significant beneficial effects on both target shareholders and social wealth.

The crux of the debate was the relative magnitude of the costs and gains associated with a non-auction rule to the target's shareholders and society, on the one hand, and a rule permitting competing bids on the other. Easterbrook's and Fischel's main argument was that since investors diversify or because it is not pre-determined that a company is always an acquirer or a target, investors may be shareholders, either in a target or in a bidder. As a result, it is only the frequency of takeovers and not the size of the premia that matters. Moreover, raising the price of auctions was argued to reduce the number of acquisitions and thus, the amount of monitoring of the target directors, which eventually reduces the wealth of the target shareholders. The only explicit reference to the acquirer's interests was that a competing bid rule increases the information and searching costs of the initial bidder.

On the contrary, although Gilson and Bebchuck recognised the bidder's costs, they denied their magnitude and importance. They insisted that target shareholders value high premia more than takeover frequency, partly because there is no equal probability that a company may become a bidder or a target. They also submitted the view that a non-auction rule increases the searching costs for the target—divestiture cases—and that competitive bids increase social wealth by reducing value-decreasing takeovers and permitting the movement of assets to the highest value bidders.

In view of the above, when the question shifts to the bidder, both sides seem to agree that auctions impose costs on the initial bidder and that, under a non-auction regime, the initial bidder would be better of. It is the magnitude of those costs and their relative importance as opposed to the target's gains where the two sides seem to disagree.

[12] FH Easterbrook and DR Fischel, 'The Proper Role of a Target's Management in Responding to a Tender Offer' (1981) 94 *Harvard Law Review* 1161; Easterbrook and Fischel, 'Symposium: Auctions and Sunk Costs in Tender Offers' (n 4 above).

[13] L Bebchuck, 'The Case for Facilitating Competing Tender Offers' (1982) 95 *Harvard Law Review* 1028; RJ Gilson, 'A Structural Approach to Corporations: The Case against Defensive Tactics in Tender Offers' (1981) 33 *Stanford Law Review* 819; L Bebchuck, 'The Case for Facilitating Competing Tender Offers: A Reply and Extension' (1982) 35 *Stanford Law Review* 23; RJ Gilson, 'Seeking Competitive Bids Versus Pure Passivity in Tender Offer Defense' (1982) 35 *Stanford Law Review* 51.

B The Costs for the Acquiring Shareholders

The assumption that a non-auction rule can minimise the initial bidder's costs and consequently increase its shareholders' wealth is not unquestioned. What will be argued is that a non-auction rule—either in the form of a prohibition of competitive bidding or through relaxation of the period that an offer must remain open—not only fails to protect effectively the initial bidder from the costs discussed above, but also produces a number of additional costs for the acquiring shareholders and society as a whole.

First of all, a non-auction rule fails to protect the initial bidder from the information costs and free ride costs already mentioned. This is because it is the identification of the target as a corporate opportunity that causes the problem and not the information published, which could have been already publicly available. That, as will be analysed below, is something that the initial bidder cannot avoid even under a non-auction rule. Secondly, a non-auction rule does not necessarily secure the bidder the target shareholders' acceptance of its offer at the end of the day. On the contrary, as will be argued, in a regulatory regime of high takeover frequency generated by a non-auction rule, it is more likely for the target shareholders not to accept the initial offer.

However, the most important complication of a non-auction rule is that it does not necessarily eliminate competition. On the contrary, the view submitted in this book is that a non-auction rule actually increases competition for the initial bidder. First of all, a non-auction rule increases the frequency of takeovers; hence, more potential bidders are around. In addition, competition is fiercer because it is not actual but potential. Under a non-auction rule, auctions may still exist in a more implicit and unregulated form, through announcements by competitive offerors that when the current offer lapses they intend to make a bid for the target. In that way, a non-auction rule does not really minimise the costs of the initial bidder but, actually, those of any competing offeror, in the sense that the latter does not need to devote the resources to make an actual offer; at this point it suffices to make an announcement of its intention to make an offer, and that by itself is enough to deter target shareholders from tendering their shares to the initial bidder.

Even if a potential non-auction rule prohibits such announcements, it is extremely difficult to cover market speculations. Under the current auction rule, whenever a potential bidder has not yet made a formal announcement that it intends to make an offer, and there is considerable speculation in the market that it is about to do so, it may be required by the Panel either to announce its intentions to place an offer[14] or make a

[14] Rule 2.5 of the Takeover Code.

statement that it does not intend to do so.[15] However, under a non-auction rule, the initial bidder would be completely unprotected, because there is no way to clarify such market speculation, since the treatment for the problem—a formal announcement by the potential bidder of its intentions—constitutes the very breach of the rule.

Until now, it has been argued that under a non-auction rule, an initial bidder faces competition from either an identified rival bidder, who announced its intention to make an offer after the initial offer lapses, or an identified rival bidder whose subsequent bid is speculated upon but not confirmed. However, under a non-auction rule, the initial bidder would have to compete even against unidentified potential bidders. This is a direct effect of the increase in the frequency of takeovers. The more likely it is that another offer is 'around the corner', the less likely it is that the target shareholders will accept the first offer. And is there really a more fierce and unfair form of competition than when one does not know the identity of one's competitor?

Overall, the following paradox arises: under a rule that permits auctions, the initial bidder has to compete only against an extremely small number of rival bidders that actually devote the necessary resources and place a rival bid in a short, strictly defined, period of time. Under a non-auction rule, however, though the initial bidder does not have to compete against actual bidders, it faces competition from a larger number of identified bidders (who are going to make an offer but have not yet devoted the necessary resources), or from a number of identified potential bidders (who are speculated to make an offer), or finally, from an even greater number of unidentified potential bidders. In other words, the stricter a non-auction rule is, the more likely it is to increase the potential for different, more implicit, forms of auctions. The above paradox can be schematically presented as shown opposite (figure 3).

As a result, not only does a non-auction rule not protect the initial bidder from the costs discussed above, but it also subjects it to even greater costs. Since auctions are still possible, the initial bidder still suffers the free ride and information costs and it is still subject to the 'winner's curse'. Moreover, because it is subject to greater competition, it still has to pay a considerable premium to persuade the target shareholders to tender their shares. For the same reasons, it is more likely that the initial bidder will make any effort and bear any costs to assure the support of the target's board. In that sense, it is more likely that under a non-auction rule, hostile deals become more difficult to accomplish.

Moreover, the form that auctions take under a non-auction regime further increases transaction costs. Competitive bids are not confined to a specific period of time; rather they spread along a considerable period of

[15] Rule 2.8 of the Takeover Code.

Figure 3: Auction risk under an auction and a non-auction rule:

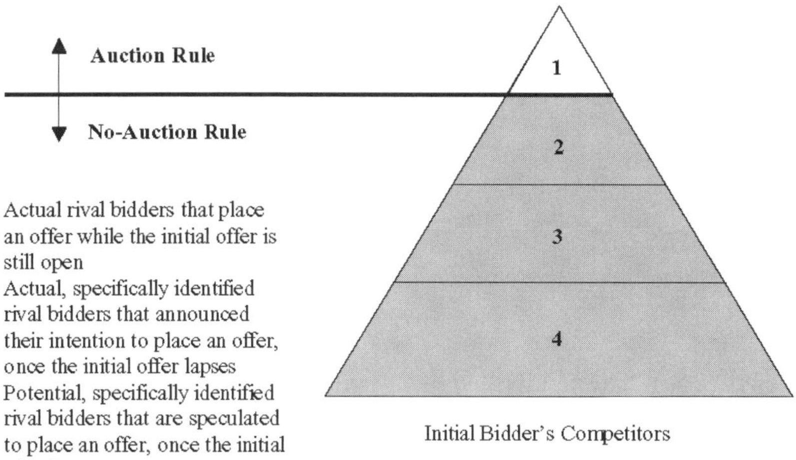

1. Actual rival bidders that place an offer while the initial offer is still open
2. Actual, specifically identified rival bidders that announced their intention to place an offer, once the initial offer lapses
3. Potential, specifically identified rival bidders that are speculated to place an offer, once the initial offer lapses
4. Potential unidentified rival bidders

time in the form of recurring, initial and subsequent or revised bids. Apart from the diseconomies that such a situation creates, to the extent that it elongates the period during which the target is under siege, it also increases some of the bidder's costs, such as underwriting fees, since such facilities must either remain open for a long and uncertain period of time, or be re-arranged every time a revised bid is attempted. The same applies to other types of fees as well.

IV BIDDER'S PROTECTIVE MECHANISMS

The above analysis revealed that both the acquiring shareholders and society benefit from a rule that permits competitive bidding more than from a rule that prohibits auctions. However, this does not eliminate the acquirer's costs described in the first part of this chapter. As a result, the main question remains unanswered: What level of protection does or should the acquirer enjoy in the event of an auction?

Protecting the initial bidder in an auction situation does not result only in gains for the acquiring shareholders. There are also strong arguments that the right level of protection of the initial bidder promotes allocative efficiency and increases the overall social wealth. There is a significant concern about the ability of regulation to provide the necessary incentives to the initial bidder. In the absence of the first bidder to identify a specific opportunity and initiate the auction, no competitive bidding will occur and the assets in question will not be transferred to the highest-value use.

The means of protecting the acquirer in an auction are not universal, but depend on the specificities of the different situations that arise. Three cases can be identified:

— friendly takeovers;
— hostile takeovers; and
— auctions, where the competitive bidder is either a 'white knight' or a management buy-out ('MBO').

V HOSTILE TAKEOVERS

By contrast with friendly takeovers, in hostile bids the acquirer cannot count on the support of the target's board. Accordingly, it is deprived of the contractual protection available in friendly deals and has to rely primarily on its own resources and efforts. Despite the fact that there are various ways in which a bidder can increase the desirability of its offer, this chapter is not concerned with the various techniques that make a specific bid more desirable to a specific set of target shareholders. Rather, the focus of this part is to identify the acquirer's interests in the case of competitive bids and examine whether they are considered at a regulatory level or not.

According to the Takeover Code, a competitive situation will normally arise following a public announcement of the existence of a new offeror or a potential offeror, whether named or not.[16] This is in accordance with the definition of 'offer period', which states that an offer period will commence on the announcement of a 'proposed or possible bid'. Other circumstances may also constitute a competitive situation.[17] In its Statement on the Irish Distillers Group Plc offer of 17 November 1988, the Panel ruled that an approach by Pernod Ricard to Irish Distillers shareholders, seeking irrevocable commitments in respect of over 50 per cent of the target's shares, as a prelude to an offer in itself, amounted to a competitive offer.[18] Similarly, a competitive situation may arise pursuant to a strategic review announcement made by the target where specific reference is made to an offer (or a merger or a search for an alternative buyer) as an option to be considered as a part of the strategic review. The same will apply pursuant to an announcement made upon the Executive's request in cases where an offer will be actively considered (as opposed to being imminent), or where

[16] There is no broad definition of the term 'competitive situation' in the Takeover Code. However in two instances in the Code the public announcement of an imminent named or unnamed bidder, does provide the starting point for a 'competitive situation': see r 32.2 and r 31.5.

[17] Rule 32.2, note 2 of the Takeover Code.

[18] Irish Distillers Group plc, Panel Statement 1988/26 of 17 November 1988.

there is a rumour or speculation about a possible offer, or an untoward movement in the target's share price. It is obvious that such strategic review announcements when an offer has already been made may coincide with the target directors' duties (a) to comment on the offer[19] and (b) not to implement any frustrating action without the consent of their shareholders.[20] However, strategic review announcements will not normally be considered frustrating actions according to the meaning of the Takeovers Directive, since Article 9 explicitly excludes solicitation of rival bidders as a defensive action requiring shareholders' approval.[21] Although this exception is not explicitly mirrored in new rule 21 of the Takeover Code, previous practice and the narrower concept of frustrating action provided by the regime previous to the implementation of the Directive[22] serve to corroborate the argument that a strategic review announcement by the target's board that identifies the opportunity or the intention for soliciting an offer by an identified or unidentified bidder does not constitute a frustrating action requiring the approval of the target shareholders.

For the purposes of the present analysis, it will be assumed that all bids in an auction are hostile. In the next part of this chapter, special consideration will be given, though, to auctions where one of the competing bidders is a 'white knight' or an MBO. The view submitted in this paper is that in auctions where all the competing bids are hostile the acquiring shareholders and the initial bidder have four main concerns:

1. The existence of an orderly framework for auctions permits the initial bidder to respond to competitive offers.
2. An orderly framework should also protect the initial bidder from speculative offers that may reduce the likelihood of success of its bid.
3. The timetable for the auction is also important: achieving finality through the imposition of a strict timetable that explicitly deals with circumstances where an auction may chronically escalate throughout a considerable amount of time minimises the bidder's transaction costs and uncertainty.
4. The final concern evolves around toeholds or, in other words, the ability of the bidder to increase its stake in the target before or after the announcement of the offer. Extra-offer purchases of shares in the target are valuable to the initial bidder for two reasons: first, they may provide the initial bidder with a way to deter potential rival bidders; and secondly, and more importantly, they allow the initial bidder to recoup the information costs associated with the identification of the target. The latter is achieved when the initial bidder, after having lost the auction,

[19] Rule 25.1 of the Takeover Code.
[20] Rule 21.1 of the Takeover Code.
[21] Art 9.2 of the Takeovers Directive (2004/25/EC).
[22] See The Takeover Panel, Statement 2005/10, 21.

tenders its shares to the competing bidder at a premium over the purchase price.

A The Bidder's Right to Revise its Offer

The initial bidder is the first to go public with its intention to acquire the target. Consequently, one of its concerns during the period that its offer is open is to be able to respond to a counter-offer by increasing its initial bid. Such a rule increases the incentives of the initial bidder by providing it with more security. In the same way, it takes the acquiring shareholders' interests into consideration. Under a no-revision rule, the initial bidder would have to make a pre-emptive bid by offering in advance a greater premium to deter potential bidders. However, this would have detrimental effects to the bidder's shareholders, because it would be more likely for the bidder to overpay.

Overall, the Takeover Code recognises two types of offer revisions: first a revision of an offer before day 46 from the announcement of the last competitive bid, and secondly, a revision of an offer after day 46. The latter type of revision will be considered in the next part of this chapter, because it is closely related to the notion of finality, as will be further explained there. As far as the 'early revision' is concerned, the restrictions imposed by the Takeover Code in rules 32.1 and 32.2[23] are as follows:

Rule 32.1 provides that an offeror can revise its offer, provided that a non-increase statement was not made and no revised offer may be posted in the 14-day period ending on the last day of the offer becoming unconditional as to acceptances. This is, for competing situations, the 60th day of the last competing offer, since, under rule 31.6(a)(i) the initial bidder is bound by the competing bid's timetable. This practically means that the bidder will not normally be able to revise its offer after day 46 from the announcement of the competing offer.[24] When the bidder offers equity or convertible securities, the rule applies also to announcements which may increase the value of the offer, such as trading results, profit or dividend forecasts, asset valuations, merger benefit statements or proposals for dividend payments.[25]

In cases where the bidder made a non-increase statement, rule 32.2 provides that the bidder is normally prohibited from increasing its offer, unless the right to do so has been specifically reserved at the time of the

[23] Both rr 32.1 and 32.2 of the Takeover Code remained unchanged in the 'post-Directive' regime, apart from the inclusion of a requirement to post a revised offer document, see below.

[24] However, see below under case 3.

[25] Rule 32.1, note 1 of the Takeover Code. See also Siebe Gorman's offer for Tecalemit, Panel Statement 1983/11 of 5 December 1983.

non-increase announcement.[26] Putting this into perspective in competitive situations, the bidder can choose to disregard the previous non-increase statement and revise its offer, provided that it reserved the right to set aside its statement in circumstances where a counter-bid is made.[27] The specific circumstances under which the non-increase statement can be set aside must be clearly stated in the first document sent to the target shareholders[28] and will be strictly interpreted by the Panel.

In an appeal by Miller against the Executive's ruling in Miller 1999 plc and Dotterel Ltd's bids for Cala plc, the Panel refused to permit Miller to increase its bid if Dotterel were to announce an increased offer at a price equal to, but not higher than, Miller's offer, on the grounds that Miller had made a non-increase statement reserving the right to increase its offer only in the event that another offeror made an offer higher than Miller's. The rationale behind the Panel's decision was that Miller was not permitted to set aside its non-increase statement in circumstances where it had not specifically reserved the right to do so.[29] If the bidder is not bound by a non-increase statement, it is also under the deadline to give notice of its intention within four business days after the day of the firm announcement of the competing offer.[30]

In cases where an opt-out provision in a non-increase statement was not reserved by the bidder, the Panel would allow an offer to be revised in 'wholly exceptional circumstances'.[31] According to the Panel, 'wholly exceptional circumstances' is not a term of art.[32] The term cannot be confined to a limited number of specific factual situations. Rather, whether such circumstances exist is a consideration that should be based on the facts of each particular case. An example of wholly exceptional circumstances occurred in an appeal in relation to the offer by Service Corporation International plc for Great Southern Group plc.[33] In that case, the Panel was satisfied that the failure of the offeror to expressly reserve its right to revise its offer in the event of a competitive situation was attributable to a proven administrative mistake on the part of the offeror's advisers.[34] However, the Panel's ruling in Miller's appeal considered above was different. Despite the proven novelty of the situation, the Panel ruled that, in that specific case, no wholly exceptional circumstances arose from the fact that the counter-bidder made an equal offer and the initial

[26] Rule 32.2 of the Takeover Code.
[27] Rule 32.2, note 4 of the Takeover Code.
[28] Rule 32.2, note 4 of the Takeover Code.
[29] Cala plc, Dotterel Ltd, and Miller 1999 plc, Panel Statement 1999/08.
[30] Rule 32.2, note 2(a) of the Takeover Code.
[31] Rule 32.2, note 4 of the Takeover Code.
[32] Panel Statement 1999/08 (n 29 above).
[33] Service Corporation International plc, Great Southern Group plc, the Loewen Group Inc, Panel Statement 1994/08.
[34] Panel Statement 1994/08 (n 33 above).

offeror had reserved the right to revise its offer only if a higher offer was made.[35] In addition, the recommendation by the board of the offeree company is not enough to permit the bidder to revise its offer.[36]

Finally, it should be noted that when the bidder is not allowed to increase its offer it is also prohibited from placing itself in a situation where it has to revise its offer.[37] The latter will be normally required in circumstances where the offeror, or any person acting in concert with it, purchases shares in the target at above the offer price, or it becomes obliged to make a cash offer under rules 11 and 9 of the Takeover Code.[38]

Subject to the prior consent of the Panel, and only to the extent necessary to implement an increased or improved offer, the offeror may introduce new conditions (eg, obtaining shareholders' approval or the admission to listing, or admission to trading, of new securities).[39]

Prior to the amendments to the Code to implement the Takeovers Directive, when an offer was revised, although there were no specific requirements in the Code, the bidder would usually send the target shareholders a revised offer document and the target company's board would usually send them a circular commenting on the revised offer. Pursuant to the implementation of the Takeovers Directive, rule 32.1 has been amended[40] and rule 32.6[41] has been added to the Takeover Code to formalise the requirements for a revised offer document and target board's circular to target shareholders.

B Speculative Offers: 'The Put Up or Shut Up' Approach

The initial bidder may find itself in a situation where there is speculation in the market that a competing offeror is about to make a bid for the target. This, as seen above, can substantially decrease the probability that its offer will be accepted by the target shareholders, at least until such rumours are clarified. Such rumours, if not addressed at a point way

[35] Panel Statement 1999/08 (n 29 above).

[36] Rule 32.2, note 4 of the Takeover Code.

[37] Rule 32.1, note 3 of the Takeover Code.

[38] Rule 32.1, note 2 of the Takeover Code.

[39] Rule 32.4 of the Takeover Code.

[40] According to r 32.1, if an offer is revised, a revised offer document, drawn up in accordance with rr 24 and 27, must be posted to shareholders of the offeree company. On the day of posting the offeror must put the revised offer document on display in accordance with r 26 and announce in accordance with r 2.9 that the document has been posted and where the document can be inspected.

[41] According to r 32.6, the board of the offeree company must post to the company's shareholders a circular containing its opinion on the revised offer under r 25.1(a), drawn up in accordance with rr 25 and 27. On the day of posting, the offeree company must put the circular on display in accordance with r 26 and announce in accordance with r 2.9 that the document has been posted and where the document can be inspected.

earlier than the last day that the offer can remain open as to acceptances, may even effectively frustrate the offer.

Rule 2.2 of the Code requires an announcement to be made as a result of rumours and speculation that a potential offeror is contemplating making an offer for the target company, but is not yet in a position to commit itself to make a firm offer. Under such circumstances, the potential offeror is usually permitted by the Panel, under rule 2.4 of the Code, to announce merely that it is considering making an offer for the target.[42] Following such an announcement, there is no fixed deadline in the Code by which the potential bidder must clarify its intentions. In non-competitive situations, the timing of any subsequent announcement will depend on the readiness of the prospective bidder and the reaction of the offeree's board.[43] If the offeree's board requests so,[44] that being the case when the potential offeror is unwelcome, the Executive of the Panel may intervene by requiring the potential bidder to either make a firm announcement of its intention to bid under rule 2.5 or disclose its intention not to place an offer.[45]

However, the above approach cannot work in competitive situations, since it is imperative for the initial bidder that such speculation be resolved at a certain point during its offer timetable. The Code partly deals with this issue in rule 19.3, where it is emphasised that

> [p]arties to an offer or potential offer and their advisers must take care not to issue statements which, while not factually inaccurate, may mislead shareholders and the market or may create uncertainty'.

Under note 1 on Rule 19.3, a competing offeror's statement that is considering making an offer is treated as a holding statement, and it is stipulated that in the later stages of the offer period, 'it is not acceptable for such statements to remain unclarified for more than a limited period of time'. Before any statements of this kind are made, the Panel must be consulted as to the period allowable for clarification.

The Rule was further clarified by the Panel in the case of the Bank of Scotland's and Royal Bank of Scotland's bids for NatWest.[46] After the announcement of the Bank of Scotland ('BOS') bid for NatWest there was considerable speculation in the market about various competing offerors, including the Royal Bank of Scotland ('RBS'). As a response to excessive

[42] The Takeover Panel's Annual Report 2002. See also The Panel on Takeovers and Mergers, PCP 2004/2 *Consultation Paper: Possible Offer Announcements. Revision Proposals Relating to Rule 2.4 of the Takeover Code*, for a number of changes proposed, not affecting though the rule in principle.

[43] The Takeover Panel's Annual Report 2002.

[44] See r 2.4(b) of the Takeover Code. The Panel on Takeovers and Mergers, PCP 2004/1 *Consultation Paper: 'Put up or Shut up' and No Intention to Bid Statements. Revision Proposals Relating to Rules 2.4, 2.8 and 35.1 of the Takeover Code.*

[45] *Ibid*; see also the Takeover Panel's Annual Report 2002.

[46] National Westminster Bank plc, Bank of Scotland, The Royal Bank of Scotland Group, Panel Statement 1999/19.

press speculation, RBS made an announcement that was considering placing an offer for NatWest. Four days after the posting of the offer document by BOS, and while in the meantime references in the press to RBS as a potential competing offeror increased, BOS requested the Executive to rule that pursuant to rule 19.3, RBS should be required to clarify its position.

The Executive ruled that it would not set a firm deadline for RBS to make such an announcement but would, depending on the circumstances, require clarification no later than 10 days prior to the end of the 60-day offer timetable, in order for the target shareholders to make acceptance decisions in the light of knowledge of all parties' intentions. BOS appealed against the Executive's ruling, but the Panel affirmed the Executive's view. The Panel held the view that the objective of the rule in determining 'limited time' is achieved by providing sufficient time for the target shareholders to reach a decision on whether or not to accept an offer,[47] while any uncertainty, in the mean time, was similar to that which necessarily persists during the currency of a hostile bid. As a general rule, the Panel considered day 50 as the latest appropriate day for clarification. Nonetheless, according to the Panel, circumstances may arise which would point to an earlier or later date as being more appropriate, and this is upon the Executive to decide in the first instance, in the light of the circumstances prevailing at the time.[48]

A similar frustrating effect may arise in cases of comments predicting a possible improvement of an already-posted competitive offer. Rule 19.3 of the Code therefore prohibits an offeror from making a statement to the effect that it may improve its offer without committing itself to doing so and specifying the improvement. The Code also requires that information about companies involved in an offer must be made equally available to all shareholders as nearly as possible at the same time and in the same manner.[49] Hence, the Code imposes a duty on all parties involved in takeovers and their advisers to take the utmost care in any discussions, whether formal or informal, with shareholders and others (such as journalists or investment analysts) not to release any material new information or significant new opinions relating to the offer.[50]

C Transaction Costs: Achieving Finality of a Competitive Situation

As has already been identified, a means of protecting the acquiring shareholders from excess deterrent overbidding in competitive situations is to

[47] The Royal Bank of Scotland Group, Panel Statement 1999/19 (n 46 above) 3.
[48] Panel Statement 1999/19 (n 46 above) 4.
[49] See General Principle 1 of the Takeover Code.
[50] See, eg Offer by Silvestor UK Properties Ltd for Canary Wharf Group Plc, Panel Statement 2004/07.

allow the bidder to revise its offer once a competitive offer arises. At the same time, though, keeping an auction open for an indefinite amount of time increases transaction costs and exposes the acquiring shareholders to lengthier market-price pressures. As a result, there must be a trade-off between an unrestricted right to revise an offer and an indefinite auction timetable. This trade-off is achieved with the notion of finality.

According to the Panel, finality means ensuring that both offerors in a competitive situation make bids which are final, in the sense that they are not capable of further revision even with the consent of the offeree board.[51]

Following the announcement by an offeror of a firm intention to make an offer under rule 2.5, the Code provides a standard timetable comprising up to 28 days in which to post the formal offer document to the offeree company's shareholders[52] (rule 30.1); a further 60 days within which the offer must become or be declared unconditional as to acceptances (rule 31.6); and a further 21 days within which all other conditions to the offer must be either satisfied or waived (rule 31.7). In addition, after an offer has become or is declared unconditional as to acceptances, the offer must remain open for acceptance for not less than 14 days after the date on which it would otherwise have expired.[53] Assuming that the closing date will generally be day 60, the offer cannot close before day 74 if it has become unconditional as to acceptances on day 60. The Takeovers Directive provides that the time allowed for acceptance of an offer is between 14 and 70 days from the posting of the offer document. The offer period may be extended, however, beyond 70 days provided the bidder gives at least 14 days' notice of its intention to close the bid. To that effect, rule 31.2 has been amended so as to provide that if an offer remains open for acceptance beyond day 70, at least 14 days' notice in writing is given to those shareholders who have not accepted before the offer is closed.

Once the 60-day period has started, the bidder can revise its offer subject to the qualifications described already, provided it does so before day 46. The Code does not explicitly require, though, the posting of the revised offer on day 46 at the latest. This can be deduced from rule 32.1, which states that the offer must be kept open for at least 14 days following the date on which the revised offer document is posted. Therefore, no revised offer document may be posted in the 14 days ending on the last day when the offer can become unconditional as to acceptances. In that context, a question arises in relation to the revision of the offer after day 46. This is where finality becomes relevant as a policy concern. Finality should not be

[51] The Panel on Takeovers and Mergers, PCP7: *Consultation Paper Issued by the Code Committee of the Panel: Resolution of Competitive Situations. Revision Proposals Relating to Rules 31.6, 32 and 35 of the Takeover Code* (October 2001).

[52] See r 32.1(b) of the Takeover Code.

[53] Rule 31.4 of the Takeover Code.

interpreted as a static 'final day rule'. According to the Code, offer revisions are permitted after day 46 but within an extremely strict and short timetable.[54]

According to the Panel, the rationale behind finality is that the target shareholders should not be exposed to an excessive period of siege.[55] Shareholders should be given a period of certainty within which to make the investment decision, which the competing offers present them with. Certainty requires that both offers are final. Finality, however, is equally important to the acquiring shareholders for a number of reasons.

First, by the time that day 46 of the competitive offer lapses, it could be that the initial bidder has kept its offer open for up to four months, assuming that another bidder has emerged, to whose timetable the initial bidder is bound as well. As seen above, during that period, the acquirer's shares are subject to market pressures and volatility. The existence of competing offerors further enhances the uncertainty over the outcome of the bid and thus, drives the acquirer's share price further down. Achieving finality does not completely eliminate the above risks but, at least, prevents auctions from escalating to an indefinite amount of time. Finality also minimises transaction costs, because the bidder can more or less identify in advance the maximum period that its offer could remain open and arrange its underwriting or financing facilities accordingly.

The Panel in recent years had to consider, on a number of occasions, how to provide such a framework. In order to resolve the competitive situation in an orderly fashion, the Panel has employed sealed bids procedures governing the making of increased offers on day 46. However, before its recent amendments, the Takeover Code included no specific provisions of the procedure that should be followed in the case of late auctions.

A new rule has been added on late competitive situations. Rule 32.5 requires revised offers to be published in accordance with an auction procedure, the terms of which will be determined by the Panel. This procedure will normally require final revisions to competing offers to be announced by day 46 following the posting of the competing offer document, but will enable an offeror to revise its offer within a set period, in response to any revision announced by a competing offeror on or after day 46. The procedure will not normally require any revised offer to be posted before the expiry of a set period after the last revision of either offer is announced. However, the Panel will consider applying any alternative procedure which is agreed between competing offerors and the board of the offeree company. The Panel also reserves the right to impose a final time limit to revisions of competing offers, taking into account represen-

[54] See r 32.5 of the Takeover Code.

[55] The Panel on Takeovers and Mergers, PCP7 (n 51 above) para 4.3.

tations by the board of the offeree company, the revisions previously announced and the duration of the procedure.[56]

The procedure that the Panel has followed is what the Code Committee described in its consultation document as an 'open auction'.[57] An 'open auction' procedure denotes a set of rules that permit the normal competitive bid process which runs up to day 46 to continue after day 46, but on an accelerated and controlled basis. The main principle of such a procedure is that, once a revised offer is made on day 46, each offeror has one day to respond to any revised offer announced by its competitor. This process continues until one or the other offeror fails to announce a revised offer within the time specified,[58] or up to a date that the Panel explicitly specified as the last date for the posting of any revised offers.[59] There is no requirement that the increase of the offer price should be material.[60] However, the Panel has the right either to specify a minimum increase in the consideration offered by that bidder, but not necessarily greater that the competitive bidder's offer[61] or the right to 'guillotine' the procedure, if it believes that the process is unduly prolonged.[62]

A typical example of an open auction procedure is the procedure followed to resolve the competitive bids of Tata Steel UK Limited and CSN Acquisitions Limited for Corus Group plc.[63] The auction procedure consists of a maximum of nine rounds, comprising up to eight rounds in which each offeror is able to lodge a fixed-price bid in cash followed by—if the auction procedure has not by then concluded—a final round. In the final round each offeror is able to lodge either a fixed-price bid in cash, or a cash bid, calculated by reference to a formula, pursuant to which an offeror can lodge a bid at a specified amount in cash more than the other offeror subject to a specified maximum cash amount.

In respect of the first eight rounds of the auction procedure, a subsequent round only takes place if the offeror that has the lower cash bid as at the beginning of that round (or, if at that time the highest cash bids of both offerors are the same, either offeror) lodges an increased cash bid in that round. Such a cash bid must be not less than 5p higher than the higher cash bid as at the beginning of that round (or, if at that time the highest cash bids of both offerors are the same, not less than 5p above the price of those bids). The auction procedure may complete in circumstances where

[56] Rule 32.5, note 2 of the Takeover Code.

[57] The Panel on Takeovers and Mergers, PCP7 (n 51 above) para 8.4.1.

[58] The Panel on Takeovers and Mergers, PCP7 (n 51 above) para 8.4.1.

[59] See above.

[60] The Panel on Takeovers and Mergers, PCP7 (n 51 above) 8.4.3.

[61] See, eg Tiger Acquisition Corporation Plc ('Tiger') and Beleggingsmaatschappij Florissant NV ('Florissant') v Qxl Ricardo plc ('Qxl'), Panel Statement 2005/16.

[62] Rule 32.5, note 2 of the Takeover Code.

[63] Tata Steel UK Limited and CSN Acquisitions Limited v Corus Group plc, Panel Statement 2007/03.

the revised cash offers, which the offerors are required to announce under rule 2.5 of the Takeover Code, are the same. In addition none of the offerors, nor any person acting in concert with it, may deal in relevant securities of the target or take any steps to procure, amend or renew any irrevocable commitment or letter of intent in relation to its or the other offeror's offer. Following the conclusion of the auction procedure, neither offeror is permitted to revise the price of its offer or to introduce any new alternative offer (unless, under the normal provisions of the Code, a third party announces a firm intention to make an offer for the target).

Another alternative procedure that actually has been implemented by the Panel in two cases[64] is that of sealed formula price bids. Formula price bids are bids, which are expressed as a formula by reference to the competitor's bid. The principal attraction of a sealed bid procedure allowing formula price bids is that it operates very much like an open auction. As in an open auction, the winner is the bidder prepared to offer the highest price, but it is not compelled to pay its maximum price, only a price that exceeds the next highest offer by a specified amount. Thus, formula offers can be expected to produce the same outcome as an open auction but without any extension of the bid timetable.[65] From the perspective of the acquiring shareholders, the main objections to sealed formula offers are that, first, too much importance is placed on the premium offered and second, they fail to take into account other qualitative characteristics that may differentiate each offer, making more likely for the acquirer to overpay.

Achieving finality in a late auction may also involve avoiding tactical opportunities by competitive bidders with the purpose of defeating the procedural rule of late auctions. For example, a bidder may not revise its existing offer on day 46, but then allow that offer to lapse on a closing date prior to day 60, with the intention of buying offeree shares in the market at above the competing offeror's offer price and thereby frustrating that offer. A new rule 35.4 addresses the issue by prohibiting any competing bidder whose offer has lapsed from acquiring shares in the offeree company on better terms than those made available under its lapsed offer, until each of the competing offers has either been declared unconditional in all respects or has itself lapsed.[66] Similarly, in the case of the offers by Tiger Acquisition Corporation Plc ('Tiger') and Beleggingsmaatschappij Florissant NV ('Florissant') for Qxl Ricardo Plc ('Qxl'), the Panel Executive ruled that neither bidder, nor any person acting in concert with it, could deal in any of the target's relevant securities (as defined in note 2 on rule

[64] Texas Utilities Company, Pacificorp v the Energy Group Plc, Panel Statement 1998/08; St David Capital Plc and WPD Limited v Hyder Plc, Panel Statement 2000/13.

[65] The Panel on Takeovers and Mergers, PCP7 (n 51 above) para 8.3.4.

[66] Other rules, like 31.6 and 35.1 of the Takeover Code were amended to address other tactical opportunities that might arise. For further details see the Panel on Takeovers and Mergers, PCP7 (n 52 above).

8) during the 'late auction period', other than with the consent of the Panel. However, there was no restriction on either bidder obtaining irrevocable commitments or letters of intent during this period.

D Free Ride Costs: Toeholds and Extra-offer Dealings

(i) *The Strategy of Stake-building*

The previous section of this chapter discussed finality as a policy of minimising transaction costs for the bidder. However, the initial bidder is still exposed to free ride or information costs. These are costs associated with the identification of the target and the information that the offer conveys to potential bidders as to the existence of a corporate opportunity. In that way, the competitive bidder can free ride on the efforts of the initial bidder, offering a higher premium without incurring the search and identification costs from which the initial bidder suffers.[67] One way for the initial bidder to protect itself is by building a stake in the target.

Stake-building is the accumulation by an acquirer of a portion of shares in the target other than through the offer, usually before an actual offer is announced. Stake-building is valuable to the initial bidder and its shareholders for three main reasons: first, it deters competition, because the larger the portion of the target shares the initial bidder has in its possession, the fewer shares need to be tendered for its offer to become wholly unconditional. Secondly, there is a coercive element in any offer when the bidder carries a large block of target shares, since a potential hostile bidder is unlikely to place a bid if it feels that its counter-bidder is already in an advantageous position. Alternatively, stake-building may permit the initial bidder to recoup its cost of identifying the target by tendering its shares to the competing bidder at a premium, in case it loses the auction.

In strategy terms, there are considerable differences between acquiring shares to deter competition and purchasing shares to recoup the offer costs. In the first case, the bidder has to acquire a considerable stake in the target and it is not usually concerned for the price it pays for these shares. In the second case, the bidder usually has to acquire only a small stake in the target, which preferably remains below a disclosure threshold—usually called a toehold. Also, the price at which it acquires the target shares is extremely important. In order for a recouping strategy to work, the bidder has to acquire the shares at a price lower than the winning offer price. The lower the price at which it buys, the smaller the toehold it has to hold in the target. Inevitably, this means that the initial bidder is extremely interested in trying to establish such a toehold as soon as possible, and before any trading activity in the target increases due to its offer

[67] See above about auction costs.

announcement. Secrecy is also important, because a disclosure at a very early moment may alert the target to the potential bid and provide it with the opportunity to take effective pre-bid defensive action.

For society, pre-emptive stake-building may produce a number of diseconomies. First, there is a coercive element in substantial stake-building, in the sense that the more the stake of the bidder increases in the target the bigger the target shareholders' 'prisoner's dilemma' is. Secondly, substantial stake-building deters competition and thus, may deprive target shareholders of a higher premium, therefore preventing the target's assets from being moved to their highest value. Such diseconomies are not associated with toeholds, namely, accumulations of limited amounts of shares in the target. Toeholds are expected to increase the incentives of the initial bidder and minimise its costs. They also seem to carry an element of fairness, since they are an effective way of getting the initial bidder compensated for identifying the target.

In view of the above, it is logically expected that substantial stake-building which may deter competition faces more regulatory restrictions than purchasing a small toehold. In other words, heavier restrictions are expected as the bidder's stake builds up. In the United Kingdom, stake-building has been, 'til recently, regulated, as far as automatic disclosure is concerned, by Part VI of the Companies Act 1985 ('CA 1985'). However, the automatic disclosure requirements of Part VI of CA 1985 have been abolished by the Companies Act 2006 and replaced by new provisions inserted in the Financial Services and Markets Act 2000, implementing the Transparency Directive in the United Kingdom.[68] The City Code on Takeovers and Mergers ('the Takeover Code') and the provisions on market abuse[69] and insider dealing[70] are also relevant. Stake-building in the recent past was also substantially regulated by the Rules on Substantial Acquisitions of Shares ('SARs'), which have been abolished from 20 May 2006. The application of SARs excluded the application of the Takeover Code and vice versa,[71] and had the practical effect of slowing down the speed at which the bidder was able to raise its stake between 15 and 30 per cent minus one share.

The above sets of rules, although they form an extremely detailed and complicated framework, have two things in common. First, they all provide, in short, the same types of restrictions on the initial bidder, namely

[68] Section 1266 of CA 2006 inserts seven new sections into Part 6 of the FSMA 2000: ss 89A, 89B, 89C, 89D, 89E, 89F and 89G. Part 6 of the FSMA deals with certain aspects of the regulation of securities that are traded on regulated markets in the UK. These new sections make provision about rules that may be made by the 'competent authority' (which is the Financial Services Authority ('the Authority')) for the purposes of the Transparency Directive (2004/109/EC)—'transparency rules'.

[69] Section 118 of the FSMA 2000.

[70] See the Criminal Justice Act 1993.

[71] See below.

prohibition of dealings and mandatory disclosure. Secondly, they all deal with possible evasions of the disclosure and prohibition of dealings requirements, by demanding, for the purposes of the relevant thresholds, the aggregation of any shareholdings of all parties that—in each specific situation and under the specific rules applied—are deemed or considered to 'act in concert'.[72]

Next, an attempt will be made to identify the key elements of both the previous and present legal and regulatory frameworks and assess the ability of the initial bidder to implement such stake-building strategies. In terms of regulatory interest, a stake-building strategy can take the form of extra-offer dealings either before or after an announcement is required.

(ii) *The Legal and Regulatory Treatment of Extra-offer Dealings*

(a) Undetected purchases—the previous regime

Under the regime in place prior to the Companies Act 2006 and the implementation of the Transparency Directive (TD),[73] before a formal announcement of an offer, UK law permitted undetected purchases of up to three per cent of the target's share capital. Once reaching the threshold of three per cent, the specific purchaser was obliged under section 198 of CA 1985 to notify the company about its interest in its shares, and to do so every time such a percentage increased or decreased by one per cent.[74] The provisions related only to shares carrying votes and the three per cent threshold related to the nominal value of the shares bought. Accordingly, a purchaser breached that threshold if the nominal value of the shares bought exceeded the three per cent of the total voting share capital, irrespective of the actual percentage of the votes that those shares carried.[75]

Section 206 of the CA 1985 required that the notification was to be made within two days of the purchaser knowing that it had breached the three

[72] For the differences in the definition of concert parties between the Companies Act and the Takeover Code, see Davies, *Gower's Principles of Modern Company Law*, 6th edn (London, Sweet & Maxwell, 1997) 488–92. For the differences in definition of concert parties between the Takeover Code and the Rules Governing substantial Acquisitions of Shares ('SARs') (persons acting by agreement or understanding) see G Stedman, *Takeovers* (London, Longman, 1993) 142. What suffices to be said here is that for the purposes of this section, whenever the terms purchaser, acquirer or potential acquirer are used in respect of one's shareholdings it is implied that those shareholdings are the aggregated shareholdings of all its concert parties, such as for example its investment bankers or financial advisers.

[73] Directive 2004/109/EC of the European Parliament and of the Council of 15 December 2004 on the harmonisation of transparency requirements in relation to information about issuers whose securities are admitted to trading on a regulated market, and amending Directive 2001/34/EC.

[74] Sections 198–200 of the Companies Act 1985.

[75] Section 198(2)(a). This is usually the case when a company has more than a class of voting shares that each carry one vote but their nominal value is different. See Davies, *Gower's Principles of Modern Company Law* (n 72 above) 486.

per cent threshold.[76] This provided the initial bidder with the following tactical opportunity: once it breached the three per cent threshold, and during the two subsequent days, it could acquire as many shares of the target as possible so as to disclose at the end of the two days the aggregate of its dealings.[77] The above strategy permits the bidder to enjoy the full benefits of undetected stake-building, since, once a notification is made, this conveys to the market the signal that a takeover offer may be imminent. As a result the target share's price increases. In that sense, the above type of stake-building is the only way for the bidder to acquire shares in the target without paying the premium that the speculation of its offer adds to the target shares.

As part of the Companies Act reform and the United Kingdom's implementation of the Transparency Directive (TD), the Companies Act 2006 repealed the major shareholding disclosure provisions of the CA 1985 and responsibility for the major shareholding notification regime passed from the DTI to the FSA. To that effect, section 1266 of the Companies Act 2006 inserts five new sections into Part 6 of the FSMA 2000: sections 89A, 89B, 89C, 89D and 89E. Part 6 of the FSMA 2000 deals with the regulation of securities that are traded on markets in the United Kingdom. These new sections enable the FSA to make transparency rules. To this extent the FSA published the Disclosure and Transparency Rules as part of the UKLA Rules. These require, amongst other things, vote-holders to notify issuers of shares and others, of the number of votes attached to shares of such issuers controlled by people who hold a specified proportion of those votes and set out—as sections 198–206 of the CA 1985 did—the circumstances under which, and the method through which and time within, vote-holders must notify a change in the proportion of voting rights.

The TD minimum requirements in relation to each of these elements can be compared to those of the CA 1985, which sets out the United Kingdom's former major shareholder disclosure regime. However, the CA 1985 requirements are constructed differently, with notification requirements triggered by reference to 'interests in shares' rather than control over the exercise of voting rights. Although occupying some common ground with the TD, the former CA 1985 provisions are in some respects more extensive and stringent than the minimum TD requirements. For example, with regard to notification thresholds, under the TD, shareholders must notify the issuers when the proportion of voting rights held reaches, exceeds or falls below the thresholds of five per cent, 10 per cent, 15 per cent, 20 per

[76] This was not always easy to determine. There also special provisions for persons acting in concert as to under what circumstances are deemed to acquired such knowledge. See, eg s 207 of the CA 2006.

[77] Under the previous regime, the amount of shares that the purchaser could acquire within those two days was subject to the restrictions imposed by the SAR. See below.

cent, 25 per cent, 30 per cent, 50 per cent and 75 per cent.[78] In comparison, under the CA 1985, shareholders must make a notification when an acquisition or disposal of an interest in a public company's shares takes that interest over or below the threshold of three per cent and then every one per cent thereafter. The CA 1985 qualifies this disclosure requirement in the sense that only 'material interests' have to be notified from three per cent to 10 per cent. In addition, with regard to notification deadlines, under the TD, a shareholder must notify an issuer as soon as possible—but not later than four trading days—after any notification threshold has been reached, exceeded or fallen below.[79] The issuer must then make the information public no later than three trading days after receiving the notification.[80] In contrast, under the CA 1985, a shareholder must notify the company within two days following the day on which the obligation to notify arose. Under the previous version of the Listing Rules, the listed company had then to notify a Regulation Impact Statement as soon as possible and not later than the end of the business day following receipt of the information.

As the TD is a minimum harmonisation Directive, the FSA could either choose to implement the Directive's minimum thresholds or, alternatively, retain the existing, more stringent, thresholds. In any case, this implementation could have been a suitable opportunity to consider the desirability of retaining what would become super-equivalent requirements relative to the minimum TD requirements and whether the United Kingdom's current regime produces more useful information or just additional costs. For the acquirer an important issue arises in the context of such a debate: What threshold permits the initial bidder to fully recoup the costs of identifying the target?

In the United States, the relevant threshold is five per cent, after which the purchaser is required to file a notification to the Securities and Exchange Commission, the appropriate stock exchange and the target company, explaining what happens and what can be expected.[81] The previous EC Directive[82] from which the UK requirements emerged also provided for a higher threshold of 10 per cent, with fewer exceptions though.[83] The TD imposes an initial notification requirement when five per cent is reached.[84] Nevertheless, the FSA decided to retain the CA 1985 three per cent threshold for UK issuers.[85]

[78] See Art 9 of the Directive.

[79] Article 12.2 of the Directive.

[80] Article 12.6 of the Directive.

[81] Schedule 13D of the Securities Exchange Act 1934 ('the Williams Act').

[82] Directive 88/627/EC.

[83] For an analytical account see Davies, *Gower's Principles of Modern Company Law* (n 72 above) 485.

[84] See above.

[85] DTR 5.1.2, which, however, sets the minimum notification threshold for non-UK issuers at 5% instead of 3% for UK issuers.

Overall, since undetected purchases of a small stake in the target (as opposed to larger scale stake-building that is usually accompanied by the diseconomies discussed above) provide incentives to the initial bidder, and protect its shareholders from the identification costs in case of auctions, it seems that the regulatory treatment of those toeholds should be more relaxed. Whether the three per cent threshold is enough to permit the bidder to recoup its costs or to what extent it should be increased are matters which require further empirical research. Nevertheless, regulation should address the issue in principle.

As far as the notification deadlines are concerned, it should be noted that the same result as increasing the notification threshold for the acquirer can be achieved by allowing for a longer notification deadline, during which the acquirer can increase its shareholdings as described above under the CA 1985 regime. However, the wording used in the Directive seems to suggest that, even if the rules transposing the Directive allow for a longer notification period, it will be very difficult for a 'delayed notification' strategy to be allowed, since despite the four days that the Directive provides as a the deadline for notification, it requires notification as soon as possible. The Disclosure and Transparency Rules retained the super-equivalent two-day period for UK issuers, while providing for a four-day period in the case of non-UK issuers.[86] Nevertheless, in transposing the TD, it seems that a strategy of acquiring additional shares by knowingly delaying the notification until the two-day deadline does not seem to be in line with the TD's duty to notify 'as soon as possible', despite the fact that the notifying period is shorter under the Disclosure and Transparency Rules.

The TD does not affect Companies Act rules giving a listed company powers to make enquiry of those it believes to have an interest in its shares using notice served by the target company. These investigation provisions are repealed and restated, with no significant amendments, by the Companies Act 2006. Under section 793 of the Companies Act 2006 a public company is allowed to issue a notice requiring a person who it knows, or has reasonable cause to believe, has an interest in its shares (or to have had an interest in the previous three years) to confirm or deny the fact, and, if the former, to disclose certain information about the interest, including information about any other person with an interest in the shares. To that effect undetected stake-building may be hampered.

(b) Purchases after notification of the acquirer's interest in the target shares

Once notification is made, the interests of the initial bidder or its strategy shifts from cautiousness and undetected purchases to swift and decisive

[86] DTR 5.8.3.

stake-building. And it is not just the information that the above dealings convey to the market and the increase in the target's share price that demands speed. It is true that once disclosure is made a race begins. The sooner the bidder increases its stake the less it pays, since the target's price gradually increases to reflect the market's appreciation of the probable value of a potential offer.

At this point, and apart from any disclosure requirements imposed by the Disclosure and Transparency Rules or the Companies Act, the potential offeror is not entirely free to acquire as many shares as it wants. Before the Takeover Code reform on May 2006, the speed at which a potential offeror could build up a stake in the target was regulated mainly by the SARs.[87] The SARs did not apply to purchases by an offeror who had already announced its intention to make an offer, the posting of which was not subject to any pre-conditions being fulfilled. Such purchases under the above circumstances were considered as dealings during the offer and were, and still are, subject to the Takeover Code's relevant provisions.

Rule 1 of the SARs stipulated that a person, or any concert party,[88] could not, in any period of seven days, acquire voting shares or rights over such shares, representing 10 per cent or more of the voting rights of the target, if such acquisitions when added to any shares already held by the potential offeror would result in carrying 15 per cent or more, but less than 30 per cent[89] of the voting shares of the target. The SARs did not impose absolute prohibitions on the acquisitions of shares, but they had the effect of slowing down the acquisitions of shares by the bidder to effectively prevent 'dawn raids'.[90]

Rule 2 of SARs provided exemptions from the above prohibition in circumstances where the acquisition was by a single shareholder, if it was the only acquisition within any period of seven days.[91] The purchases were also accepted, provided that they were made pursuant to a tender offer in accordance with rule 4. The latter, though, was very unlikely, to the extent that a potential bidder would not prefer to make an offer for less than 30 per cent of the target's shares as part of a takeover strategy because of the delay and costs involved. Finally, purchases were also exempted, provided that they were made immediately before the person announcing a firm intention to make an offer, the offer would be publicly recommended by the target's board, and the acquisition was conditional upon the announcement of the offer.[92] Again, this provided little help to a hostile bidder.

[87] See the Rules Governing Substantial Acquisitions of Shares (SARs).
[88] Not the actual term used, see the SARs, r 4.
[89] At that point the Takeover Code applies.
[90] Stedman, *Takeovers* (n 72 above) 142 and the SARs r 2.
[91] The SARs, r 2(a).
[92] The SARs, r 2(c).

The SARs applied to purchases that added to the shares the potential offeror already held, increasing its aggregate to more than 15 per cent but less than 30 per cent. If the aggregate exceeded the 30 per cent threshold, it was rules 5 and 9 of the Takeover Code that applied and still apply.[93] As already mentioned, the SARs have been abolished, permitting thus a potential bidder to reach the 30 per cent minus one vote threshold with no delays, provided that there is sufficient market for the acquisition of such a stake.

The main policy argument in favour of the SARs' application was to prevent 'dawn raids', which could deter competition in takeovers. This was because substantial shareholdings could deter competition, while, by delaying a potential bidder in building a stake in the target, time was given to rival bidders to enter the contest. In other words, the SARs facilitated auctions. However this argument is not incontestable. As described already, regulation must provide greater focus and facilitate auctions where both bidders commit the required resources and express a real commitment to acquiring the target. In this way market is not distorted and target shareholders are not deprived of value-maximising offers.

The Takeover Code includes provisions (including provisions related to the offer timetable), which, as discussed already, facilitate auctions. At the same time, the benefits of formalising such auctions within the offer timetable have been already analysed in detail above. Furthermore, markets do respond to dawn raids, since a swift acquisition program of a substantial stake in the target will lead to upward market movements in the target's shares. According to the Takeover Code, such abnormal market movements may impose a duty on the potential offeror to consult the Panel[94] and the Panel may request the potential bidder to clarify its position.[95] In addition, as will be analysed in detail in chapter eight, any dealings made as part of a stake-building strategy are well reflected in the type of consideration and the price of the offer. Hence, equality is achieved between the target shareholders that tender their shares pursuant to the offer and those who sold their shares before the posting of the offer. Finally, the SARs provided for a distinction between friendly and hostile takeovers and sales of blocks of shares by a single shareholder and stake-building through the market.[96] In that way a potential friendly offeror was in a more favourable position than a hostile potential offeror, in building

[93] The SARs also cease to apply once the bidder announces its intention to make an offer or is required to do so by the Takeover Code (see r 2.2 of the Code).

[94] See rr 2.2 and 2.3 of the Takeover Code. Whether or not a movement in the share price of a potential target is untoward for these purposes is a matter for the Panel to determine. The Panel will consider all relevant facts (eg general market and sector price movements and publicly available information relating to the target) and not simply the absolute percentage movement in the share price.

[95] See r 2.2 of the Takeover Code.

[96] See above, the SARs, r 2.

a stake in the target. To that effect the abolition of the SARs has led to the equal treatment of all potential offerors.

The abolition of the SARs leaves only the Takeover Code to regulate pre-offer dealings. It should be noted that this is done only exceptionally in a restrictive approach. In contrast, the approach used by the Code is, with the exception of rule 5, permissible. However, the conduct of the offeror during the pre-offer stage affects its offer in a number of ways.

Rule 5 applies irrespective of whether the potential bidder made an announcement of its intention to make an offer or not. According to rule 5, a person that holds shares that carry less than 30 per cent of the voting rights of a company may not acquire any shares carrying voting rights in that company or any rights over such shares which, when aggregated with the shares that it holds, would carry 30 per cent or more of the voting rights.

Rule 5.2 provides exceptions to the restrictions imposed by rule 5.1, which are similar to the exceptions provided by the SARs, rule 2.[97] However, it also states that, in relation to a hostile bidder, the restrictions imposed by rule 5.1 cease to apply in two occasions: first, after the closing date of that offer or after any competing offer has passed—this is day 21—provided that the proposed takeover is cleared by any anti-trust implications[98]; and secondly, immediately after a competing offeror has announced an offer that has been publicly recommended by the target's board.[99] However, an acquisition permitted by rule 5.2 may result in an obligation to make a mandatory offer under rule 9, in which case an immediate announcement of such an offer must be made.[100]

Conclusively, with the abolition of the SARs, pre-offer dealings are substantially regulated through disclosure requirements, rather than in a restrictive way.

(c) Dealings after the offer is announced

A toehold strategy may continue after an offer is announced, albeit less effectively, since the market has been already informed about the terms of the offer. The Takeover Code does not prohibit extra-offer dealings. Restrictions, however, may arise. Under rule 6.2 of the Code, the offeror is obliged to make an increased offer if it buys, during the offer period, any shares of the target at a higher price than the offer price. This effectively means that the offeror is not permitted to make any further purchases over

97 Rule 5.2, especially cases (a) and (b). The main difference is that once the bidder makes an acquisition from a single shareholder it is not permitted to make any further acquisitions except in the circumstances set out in r 5.2(b),(c),(d) and (e):r 5.3 of the Code.

98 Rule 5.2(c)(iii)(1) and (2) of the Takeover Code.

99 Rule 5.2(c)(ii) of the Takeover Code.

100 Rule 5.2, note 2 of the Takeover Code.

the offer price in circumstances where it is not allowed to increase its offer, namely, as seen above, after day 46 and in cases where it made a no-increase statement. In addition, during an offer period, the offeror and persons acting in concert with it must not acquire an interest in any securities in the offeree company through any anonymous order book system, or through any other means, unless, in either case, it can be established that the seller, or other party to the transaction in question, is not an exempt principal trader connected with the offeror.[101]

In addition, after the announcement of an offer, disclosure rules become more stringent. Once a firm intention to make an offer has been announced, the requirements of the Takeover Code about disclosure of dealings also kick in alongside the general disclosure requirements as described above. While rule 8 of the Code is quite complicated, its practical effect is that the bidder is obliged to disclose any dealings in the target's shares irrespective of any thresholds reached.[102] The rule also catches various deviation tactics that may be used by the bidder, since all dealings made by associates of the bidder must also be notified[103] as well as any irrevocable undertakings received by target shareholders.[104] The advantage that the announcement of the offer confers on the bidder is that the Code increases the frequency at which potential competitive bidders need to disclose their dealings in the target's shares. According to rule 8.3, if,

> [d]uring an offer period . . . a person, whether or not an associate, is interested (directly or indirectly) in 1% or more of any class of relevant securities of an offeror or of the offeree company or as a result of any transaction will be interested in 1% or more, dealings in any relevant securities of that company by such person (or any other person through whom the interest is derived) must be publicly disclosed in accordance with Notes 3, 4 and 5.

(d) Other considerations

In addition to the aforementioned requirements, a bidder must also take into account a number of other issues when devising and implementing its stake-building strategy. This is because the Code includes a number of additional requirements that are triggered by extra-offer dealings in the target shares, before or after the offer is posted. The detailed rules will be considered in chapter eight. However, it suffices to be said here that such requirements include the requirement to offer the highest price paid for shares bought outside the offer[105] or to make a cash offer.[106]

[101] Rule 4.2(b) of the Takeover Code.
[102] Rule 8.1 of the Takeover Code.
[103] *Ibid*.
[104] See r 8.4 of the Takeover Code.
[105] Rule 6.1 of the Takeover Code, see ch 8 below.
[106] If the 10% threshold is reached: r 11. See ch 8 below.

Moreover, since the Code prohibits special deals that are not extended to all shareholders,[107] the bidder in building its stake must ensure that it does not enter into any special arrangements with any of the selling shareholders that are not extended to all shareholders. In particular, a purchase cannot be made on terms that the bidder will make up the difference to the selling shareholder in the event that an offer is subsequently announced at a price greater than that received by the selling shareholder.[108] One of the exceptions provided by rule 16 is where the shareholder who is the subject of the special deal may properly be considered to be a joint offeror in the offer for the target company.[109]

In addition, any purchases made prior to the commencement of the offer period will be added to the bidder's holdings and, accordingly, will be excluded from the total of the 90 per cent acceptances that the bidder has to receive in order to be able to squeeze out any minority interest remaining in the target, under sections 428–430 of the Companies Act 1985.[110] A similar approach is taken by the Companies Act 2006,[111] despite the fact that a dual test has been implemented. This makes the threshold harder for the bidder to reach, because it reduces the pool from which the acceptances can be received.[112] In contrast, irrevocable undertakings received by the potential bidder will normally count towards reaching the 90 per cent threshold.[113] Finally, shares purchased by the bidder after the time of the offer may be counted towards reaching the 90 per cent threshold.

The insider dealing provisions of the Criminal Justice Act 1993 are also relevant, since any stake-building strategy involves purchases of securities on a regulated market, unless such securities are purchased from a target shareholder off the market and without the assistance of a financial intermediary.[114] However, this is more likely to be the case in connection to a friendly takeover (irrevocable undertakings) and will be further considered below.

Under normal circumstances, pre-offer stake-building will fall under the market information defence of the Act. Under Schedule 1 of the Criminal Justice Act 1993, where a person's only inside information is 'market information', no offence will be committed if he deals, or encourages another to deal, in connection with and to facilitate a particular transaction—in this case the takeover bid. 'Market information' for these purposes is, broadly, information about the acquisition and disposal of

[107] See r 16 of the Takeover Code.
[108] See note 1 on r 16 of the Takeover Code.
[109] See Indigo Capital LLC and Regus Plc, Panel Statement 2003/05.
[110] Section 430E(1) of the CA 1985.
[111] Section 974(2) of the CA 2006.
[112] See Stedman, *Takeovers* (n 73 above) 148 and MA Weinberg and MV Blank, *Takeovers and Mergers*, 2nd edn (London, Sweet & Maxwell, 1989) 3365.
[113] See s 975(2) of the CA 2006.
[114] Sections 52(3) and 59 of the Criminal Justice Act 1993.

securities. Accordingly, stake-building will not constitute an offence, provided that the only price-sensitive information on the basis of which trading is taking place is that the bidder is considering or will make a bid.

In contrast, this is not the case if the bidder possesses any additional price-sensitive information. One such case is when the takeover bid is subject to merger control and informal clearance has been secured from the relevant regulator. In such a situation, the bidder may have to refrain from any extra-offer dealings until the particular piece of information is made public.

In addition to the statutory provisions on insider dealing, the Takeover Code also contains restrictions on dealings in shares of the target. The Code does not prevent pre-offer dealings by the offeror itself on grounds of price-sensitive information. However, as expected, it prevents anyone who has confidential price-sensitive information about the offer or contemplated offer, other than the offeror, from acquiring shares in the target at any time during the period when there is reason to suppose an offer is contemplated prior to the offer being announced. In addition, no person who is privy to such information may make a recommendation to any other person as to dealing in the relevant securities.

Rule 4.1 does not catch behaviour that is not already prohibited by the Insider Dealing and Market Abuse regime. However, the practical advantage of the rule is that even when behaviour that is contrary to the rule succeeds in escaping the application of the insider dealing provisions of the Criminal Justice Act 1993 (due to the erroneous standards of proof required or the application of the market abuse provisions of the FSMA 2000), and no matter whether such behaviour is characterised as insider dealing or market abuse, the Panel has—especially pursuant to its enhanced new statutory status resulting from the transposition of the Takeover Directive—the power to impose sanctions including financial penalties. It should be noted, however, that such power cannot extend to a power to order compensation for a breach of rule 4 of the Takeover Code, since the circumstances in which the Panel is able to require the payment of compensation have already been set out in section 10(c) of the Introduction to the Code that was introduced in the new edition of the Code and are restricted to a breach of any of rules 6, 9, 11, 14, 15, 16 or 35.3.

Contrary to the main rule 4, note 3 on rule 4 provides for an important yet controversial exception with regards to a practice called 'warehousing', which permits parties acting in concert with the offeror or potential offeror to deal in interests in the target's securities as long as the dealing is on a no-profit or no-loss basis, that is that the bidder itself takes the risk of fluctuations in share values. In addition, persons acting in concert may be compensated for normal expenses or carrying costs but arrangements which contain a benefit or potential benefit to the person acting in concert (beyond normal expenses and carrying costs) are normally prohibited. In cases of doubt, the Panel must be consulted.

Similarly the Code includes a provision for consortium offers. According to note 2 on rules 4.1 and 4.2, it will not normally be acceptable for members of a consortium to acquire interests in offeree company securities unless there are appropriate arrangements to ensure that such acquisitions are made proportionate to members' interests in the consortium company or under arrangements which give no profit to the party making the acquisition.

These rules, however, should not be regarded as exceptions from the provisions on market abuse of the FSMA 2000[115] or the Code of Market Conduct (MAR 1), which is published by the FSA, on the basis of the authority conferred on it by section 119. To that effect and notwithstanding the provisions of rule 4 of the Takeover Code, a person may be precluded from dealing or procuring others to deal by virtue of restrictions contained in the FSMA 2000 regarding market abuse.

Although the implementation of the Market Abuse Directive ('MAD')[116] resulted in the restriction of statutory safe-harbours from the Market Abuse regime only in relation to price-stabilising and share buybacks, wording has been changed and the Takeover Code compliance exemption of the pre-MAD regime was retained. This states that compliance with the Code provisions is not likely to give rise to behaviour that would amount to market abuse. More precisely, the Code retains the previous wording that behaviour conforming with certain rules of the Takeover Code[117] relating to announcements, disclosures and other communications and releases of information, the timing, dissemination or availability and contents thereof, and the standards of care that need to have been met in relation to these matters,[118] or relating to restrictions on dealings by the offeror,[119] did not amount, in general, to market abuse. However, this exception would not apply if the behaviour was in breach of any General Principle of the Takeover Code.[120] To that effect, stake-building and warehousing was enjoying a safe-harbour status, provided that it was done in accordance with the Code and that the rest of the requirements of the Code regarding persons acting in concert and the disclosure of dealings in the shares of the target were met.

In addition under the previous regime, the Code of Market Conduct explicitly provided a blanket statement that a person should not be prevented by the market abuse regime from acquiring shares in a potential target in order to pursue a takeover bid, or from engaging in other forms of market operations, simply because he knew that he would be making a

[115] Section 118 of the FSMA 2000.
[116] Directive 2003/6/EC.
[117] And the SARs under the previous regime.
[118] See the Code of Market Conduct, MAR 1.10.5.C and MAR 1.10.4.C.
[119] Rule 4.2 of the Takeover Code. See the Code of Market Conduct, MAR 1.10.6.C.
[120] MAR 1.10.4 and MAR 1.10.4 of the Code of Market Conduct.

bid.[121] The new Code still provides that behaviour based on inside information relating to another company in the context of a public takeover bid or merger for the purposes of gaining control of that company or proposing a merger with that company does not of itself amount to market abuse (including seeking irrevocable undertakings from shareholders, making arrangements for the underwriting or placing of securities that are to be offered as consideration, and making arrangements for a cash alternative).[122] For these purposes, inside information is considered as information that a bidder or potential offeror is going to make, or is considering making, an offer for the target; or information that a bidder or potential bidder may obtain through due diligence.[123] The Code of Market Conduct continues that the following factors are to be taken into account in determining whether or not a person's behaviour is for the purpose of him gaining control of the target, namely, whether the transactions concerned are in the target company's shares; or whether the transactions concerned are for the sole purpose of gaining that control or effecting that merger.[124]

To that effect, stake-building will not normally be caught, according to the FSA, by the market abuse provisions, since it normally amounts to trading activity of a bidder who trades on the target shares on the basis of information that it is going to make an offer to acquire control of the target, and the transactions performed are for the sole purpose of effecting the acquisition of control in the target. Similarly, the wording is wide enough to cover (although not explicitly) the practice of warehousing, which as a practice could be caught by the market abuse regime either as dealing on inside information or as improper disclosure as well. As far as the former is concerned, warehousing is not likely to be caught by MAR 1.3 since it meets the criteria imposed by the rule:

1. The bidder procures the party in the warehousing agreement and the other party deals on the basis of inside information relating to *another* company in the context of a public takeover bid for the purposes of gaining control of that company.
2. Inside information is considered as information that a potential offeror is going to make, or is considering making, an offer for the target.
3. The transactions concerned are in the target company's shares.
4. The transactions concerned are for the sole purpose of gaining that control or effecting that merger.
5. No own benefit is conferred to the concert party.

In contrast, according to the Code of Market Conduct, examples of market abuse consist of cases where, in the context of a takeover, an offeror or

[121] The Code of Market Conduct, MAR 1.4.30E.
[122] MAR 1.3.17C of the Code of Market Conduct.
[123] MAR 1.3.18G of the Code of Market Conduct.
[124] MAR 1.3.19E of the Code of Market Conduct.

potential offeror enters into a transaction in a qualifying investment on the basis of inside information concerning the proposed bid, that provides merely an economic exposure to movements in the price of the target company's shares (for example, a spread bet on the target company's share price); or where a person who acts for the offeror or potential offeror deals for his own benefit in a qualifying investment or related investments on the basis of information concerning the proposed bid which is inside information.[125]

As far as improper disclosure is concerned, it can be directly derived from section 118(3) of the FSMA 2000 that a disclosure of inside information made in the proper course of the exercise of one's employment, profession or duties cannot be regarded as improper. MAR 1.4.5E further clarifies that in the opinion of the FSA, the following factors are to be taken into account in determining whether or not the disclosure was made by a person in the proper course of the exercise of his employment, profession or duties, and are indications that it was:

(1) whether the disclosure is permitted by the rules of a prescribed market, of the FSA or the Takeover Code; or
(2) whether the disclosure is accompanied by the imposition of confidentiality requirements upon the person to whom the disclosure is made and is:
    (a) reasonable and is to enable a person to perform the proper functions of his employment, profession or duties; or
    (b) reasonable and is (for example, disclosure to a professional adviser) for the purposes of facilitating or seeking or giving advice about a transaction or takeover bid; or
    (c) reasonable and is for the purpose of facilitating any commercial, financial or investment transaction (including prospective underwriters or placees of securities); or
    (d) reasonable and is for the purpose of obtaining a commitment or expression of support in relation to an offer which is subject to the Takeover Code.

It should be noted, however, that the Code of Market Conduct is not exhaustive in its descriptions of behaviour which may or may not amount to market abuse and has only evidential effect to the extent that the Code contains descriptions of behaviour which, in the FSA's opinion, does not amount to market abuse. That means that, at least in theory, market abuse could occur even if the above factors were fulfilled, and equally absence of the factors does not necessarily mean that market abuse has occurred.

The UKLA Transparency and Disclosure Rules ('the DTR') that implemented the disclosure requirements of the MAD also impose duties for the

[125] MAR 1.3.2E of the Code of Market Conduct.

bidder additional to the Takeover Code. Although the announcement of a firm intention is regulated by the Panel and the Takeover Code, the DTR may also be relevant in the case of a listed bidder. Delaying the announcement of the decision to acquire the target would require the bidder to control and monitor the selective disclosure of such inside information. The requirements imposed as to the control of the inside information are broader than the requirements imposed by the Takeover Code as to pre-bid secrecy and announcements, and to that effect, one could argue that in practice it is unlikely that a bidder will fail to satisfy the standard of care required by DTR if it satisfies the requirements of the Takeover Code. However, one noticable addition is the requirement for the bidder to maintain insider lists, namely to draw up, and promptly update, lists of persons working for it with access to inside information relating directly or indirectly to the company, whether on a regular or occasional basis.[126] The lists must be kept for at least five years and be available to the FSA on request.[127] The obligation also extends to persons acting on the company's behalf. To that extent a listed bidder must ensure that their advisers or other non-listed concert parties agree to compile and maintain a list for at least five years, and take any other necessary measure to ensure compliance of the bidder with the relevant requirements of the Disclosure and Transparency Rules.

(e) Shaping the acquirer's stake-building strategy

Under the previous regime, the initial bidder could implement the following strategy when building a stake in the target:

- Buy an undetected three per cent of the target shares.
- Buy as many shares up to 14.99 per cent as possible, during the two-day period within which it is required to notify the potential target. After that the market is expected to push up the target's share price.
- Once reaching the 15 per cent threshold, the SARs apply. This means that, provided that the potential bidder already holds 14.99 per cent of the target's voting rights, it can buy up to 10 per cent more of the voting rights of the target company seven days after the first disclosure of its interests, or make an excepted purchase by a single shareholder.
- Assuming that it has increased its shareholdings to 24.99 per cent, the potential bidder has to wait for another seven days before making any subsequent acquisitions. However, this time, it can only purchase five per cent of the target's voting rights because of the restrictions imposed by rule 5.1 of the Takeover Code, unless it acquires shares from a single shareholder or receives the recommendation of the target board. In the

[126] DTR 2.8.1.
[127] DTR 2.8.5 and DTR 2.8.2.

latter cases, it may be obliged, though, to make a mandatory offer under rule 9 of the Takeover Code.

— If at any point the initial bidder makes an announcement that intends to make an offer or is required to do so by the Takeover Code, the SARs cease to apply. This means that from that point the bidder is free to make any acquisitions of the target shares up to 29.99 per cent without the interval time delays imposed by the SARs. 21 days after the commencement of the offer or after a competing bid receives a public recommendation by the target board, the bidder can exceed the 30 per cent threshold. However, by that time, the target's share price has already risen to reflect the takeover premium offered. In that sense, the bidder must have in mind that when purchasing shares in the target over the market price, it will be required to revise its offer to accommodate the highest price paid. Moreover, the bidder is prohibited from making purchases over the offer price in circumstances where it is restricted from revising its offer. In addition, exceeding the 30 per cent threshold triggers the application of rule 9, which means that the bidder will be required to make a mandatory offer.

— Finally, the bidder should refrain from making any purchases in the market if it is in possession of any price-sensitive non-public information, to avoid any implications in relation to the insider dealing and market abuse offences.

Under the new regime the position of the initial bidder is substantially simplified because of the abolition of the SARs.

— Buy an undetected three per cent or five per cent of the target shares (depending on the approach that the FSA will follow in transposing the Transparency Directive).

— Buy as many shares as possible (up to 30 per cent minus one vote), during the period within which it is required to notify the potential target. After that the market is expected to push up the target's share price. (However, see concerns above about the wording used in the Directive)

— Continue to buy, making the necessary disclosures pursuant to the Disclosure and Transparency Rules, until it reaches the 30 per cent minus one vote threshold because of the restrictions imposed by rule 5.1 of the Takeover Code, unless it acquires shares from a single shareholder or receives the recommendation of the target's board. In the latter cases, it may be obliged, though, to make a mandatory offer under rule 9 of the Code.

— Rule 5.1 still applies even if the bidder announces its firm intention to make an offer. However, 21 days after the commencement of the offer or after a competing bid receives a public recommendation by the target's board, the bidder can exceed the 30 per cent threshold. However, by that time, the target's share price has already risen to reflect the takeover premium offered. In that sense, the bidder must have in mind that when purchasing shares in the target over the market price, it will be required to revise its offer to accommodate the highest price paid. Moreover, the bidder is prohibited from making purchases over the offer price, in circumstances where it is restricted from revising its offer. In addition, exceeding the 30 per cent threshold triggers the application of rule 9, which means that the bidder will be required to make a mandatory offer.

— Finally, the bidder or any concert parties should refrain from making any purchases in the market, if it is in possession of any price-sensitive non public information, to avoid any implications in relation to the insider dealing and market abuse regimes.

VI 'WHITE KNIGHTS' AND MBOS

A 'White Knights' and Equality of Information

In the previous section of this part, the analysis focused on cases of competing bids where all the offerors were treated as hostile by the target's board. If this is not the case, then the initial bidder or any other hostile bidder faces the threat that a competitor may have access to better information about the target. Hostile bidders are vulnerable to two types of offerors: first, 'white knights' and secondly, management buy-outs (MBOs). A 'white knight' is a friendly acquirer who is supported by the target's board and seeks to acquire the target as a response to a hostile takeover. In an MBO, the existing target's management offers to purchase the target shares at a premium and take the company private.

Both these types of offerors have an information advantage over a hostile offeror that permits them to make more accurate valuations of the target, and thus offer a higher premium. From the hostile bidder's perspective, this means that in order to be able to win the auction it needs to have access to the same amount and quality of information as the friendly acquirer, so as to be able to determine the price that it can offer on an equal basis.

Equality of information among competing offerors is a concern of the Takeover Code as well. The rationale behind the Panel's approach is that the provision of inside information to competing, but less welcomed, offerors facilitates auctions and increases the probability of the target shareholders receiving a better offer for their shares.[128] Nonetheless, the very same approach serves the interests of the hostile bidder and its share-

[128] The Panel on Takeovers and Mergers, PCP3 *Consultation Paper Issued by the Code Committee of the Panel: Equality of Information to Competing Offerors. Revision Proposals Relating to Rule 20.2 of the Takeover Code* (September 2001) 2.1.1.

holders. Rule 20.2 stipulates that any information, including particulars of shareholders, given to one offeror or potential offeror must, on request, be given equally and promptly to another offeror or bona fide potential offeror, even if that other offeror is less welcome. Such requirement does not necessarily arise only when there has been a public announcement of the existence of the offeror or potential offeror to whom the information has been given, as older versions of the Code gave the impression because of their wording. Recent amendments to rule 20.2 clarified the issue by emphasising that there is no need for the bidder to be named and there is no need for a public announcement, as long as the offeror or bona fide potential offeror requesting information under this rule has been informed authoritatively of the existence of another potential offeror.[129]

The Panel does not provide an explicit interpretation of the term *'authoritatively informed'*, so as not to restrict the flexibility of the Executive in applying rule 20.2.[130] However, this is usually the case when an offeror or a potential offeror seeking to invoke rule 20.2, has been informed by a person who has actual knowledge of the existence of another potential offeror, or who is connected with the offeree company or such other potential offeror and could, therefore, be said to be an authoritative source of information. Such a person would include advisers to, or employees of, either the offeree company or such potential offeror.[131]

The initial bidder, who has already received information from the offeree company, is entitled to invoke rule 20.2 and request additional information, provided that it is not bound by an agreement with the target to the contrary. According to the Panel, the Executive does not intervene where conditions as to the provision of information by the target board are imposed on a first offeror, because rule 20.2 does not apply at that stage since no information has been provided to another bidder.[132] This means that if the offeror enters, at that stage, into an agreement with the target not to seek additional information and does not explicitly reserve the right to set aside such an agreement, and the target subsequently furnishes additional information to another more welcomed bidder, it will not be possible to invoke rule 20.2.

In policy terms, it is beyond any doubt that the target's board should be able to seek to protect its company, when it furnishes valuable information

[129] See r 20.2 of the Takeover Code as amended after the implementation of the changes discussed in PCP3 (n 129 above). See The Panel on takeovers and Mergers, RS3 *Equality of Information to Competing Offerors: Statement by the Panel Following the External Consultation Process on PCP3* (December 2001). Prior to the Code amendments the Panel had expressed the same view in its 2000 Annual Report.

[130] *Ibid*, para 4.8.

[131] *Ibid*, para 4.8.

[132] The Panel on Takeovers and Mergers, PCP3 (n 129 above) 2.1.2. See also The Panel on Takeovers and Mergers, *Practice Statement No 3: Rule 20.2—Controlled Auctions* (February 2004).

to a potential offeror by binding the latter to commit to its offer and not seek to impose any conditions requesting the provision of additional information before proceeding with the bid. However, such agreements, although undoubtedly understandable in cases that only one offeror exists, seem less acceptable when a subsequent bidder appears. Under the above Panel's interpretation of rule 20.2, while the target will be required to disclose, upon request of the subsequent bidder, all information that had furnished to the initial bidder, any undertakings by the target, if present, not to provide such information to subsequent bidders may not be binding.[133] It should be noted though, that in extreme cases, the provision of more favourable information to a subsequent bidder, in circumstances where the initial bidder is not eligible to request such information, may constitute, in theory, a prohibited frustrating action under rule 21.1, or a breach of the target directors' duties to their shareholders, since it deprives shareholders from a subsequent more favourable offer.[134]

In the light of the above interpretation of rule 20.2, it is important to an initial bidder who enters into a binding agreement with the target not to subsequently seek additional information, to explicitly include an opt-out clause covering cases where the target provides additional information to a subsequent competing bidder.

However, even when the initial bidder is not subject to such contractual restrictions, it can be practically difficult to ask for any information subsequently given to a more welcomed bidder. Rule 20.2 provides that a competing offeror should specify the question to which it requires answers. Thus it is not entitled, by asking general terms, to receive all the information supplied to its competitors.[135] A less welcomed bidder may be in a position, where not only does it not know the context of information provided to a friendly bidder, but also it has no way to know that such disclosure was made at the very first place. Thus, rule 20.2 imposes on the less welcomed bidder the task to speculate the existence, the context and the timing of such disclosures, by submitting analytical and detailed questionnaires in the hope to catch all pertinent information, and by renewing such requests many times during the offer.[136]

At the same time, a competitive bidder can make its offer subject to the condition that it receives, should this prove satisfactory, any information provided to the existing bidder as long as it is specifically requested. This was the case with the competing bids of Lloyds and HSBC Holding plc for Midland Bank plc. As soon as the Lloyds made their bid announcement subject to the above condition, its financial advisers requested specific information from Midland in accordance with rule 20.2. Both the

133 See ch 7 below about friendly takeovers.
134 See ch 7 below about no-shop agreements.
135 Rule 20.2, note 1 of the Takeover Code.
136 See also Stedman, *Takeovers* (n 73 above) 277.

Executive and the Panel in Midland's appeal ruled that Midland must comply with rule 20.2.[137]

Some comfort can be provided by the fact that, according to the Panel, it would not be acceptable for an offeree to provide information covered by rule 20.2 to an existing or potential offeror, when it might be unable to provide this information to another existing or potential offeror on an equal basis. For example, if an offeree wishes to release information to an offeror or potential offeror that is subject to a confidentiality agreement with a third party, the offeree must ensure that it has authority to pass that information to the other competing bidders.[138]

Finally, while it has been suggested that, under normal circumstances, the target board is free to impose any conditions it desires when furnishing information to a bidder, this is not the case, when an auction situation arises. Until recently, offerors seeking information under rule 20.2 frequently agreed to the imposition of conditions, even though they were not obliged to do so. Such conditions included, most notably, standstill or no hostile bid arrangements (whereby the recipient of the information was restricted from acquiring shares in the offeree company or from making a hostile offer for it).[139] Now, note 2 on rule 20.2 has clarified the issue and allows three types of conditions: confidentiality agreements, reasonable restrictions forbidding the use of the information passed to solicit customers or employees,[140] and 'hold harmless agreements' whereby the offeror agrees that it cannot hold the firm of accountants, or other third party, who produced the information, liable for any loss arising from their relying on such information.[141] According to the Code, any such conditions imposed should be no more onerous than those imposed on any other offeror or potential offeror.[142]

B Management Buy-outs and Less Welcomed Bidders

MBOs also impose considerable problems on less welcomed bidders. In cases of MBOs, the main concern of a less welcomed bidder is not what information is disclosed to a competing bidder, but the fact that MBOs have unlimited access to inside information, because it is the target's managers, the same persons who run the company, that seek to acquire it. This, inevitably, has a number of implications.

[137] HSBC Holding plc and Lloyds Bank plc offers for Midland Bank plc, Panel Statement 1992/15.

[138] Panel's Annual Report 1999.

[139] The Panel on Takeovers and Mergers, PCP 3 (n 129 above) para 2.1.3.

[140] The Panel on Takeovers and Mergers, RS3 (n 130 above) para 4.1.

[141] It is another issue whether such a clause is reasonable under s 2(2) of the Unfair Contract Terms Act 1977.

[142] Rule 20.2, note 2(1) of the Takeover Code.

First, due to the target management's involvement, MBOs constitute a bigger threat to a less welcomed bidder. Secondly, because of the managers' unsurpassed knowledge of the target's affairs and their substantial involvement in an MBO, the amount of information that needs to be passed to another competing bidder in order to achieve equality of information is greater. Finally, rule 20.2, in the form described above, is not effective in protecting the initial bidder, because no information is actually disclosed during the negotiation of a competing offer. In contrast, information is passed by the target's management to the external financiers of the MBO.

As a result, the Code stipulates that the information, which rule 20.2 requires to be given to competing offerors, is information generated by the offeree company, which is passed to external providers or potential providers of finance to the MBO.[143] Information generated by the target company also includes information generated by the management of the offeree company, acting in their capacity as such for the purposes of the transaction.[144] A business model, for instance, will normally include the management team's opinions, estimates and projections based on the team's knowledge of the offeree company, its business and the markets in which it operates and accordingly it will be disclosable in its entirety. Due diligence reports prepared by professional advisers (accountants, lawyers, property consultants) are likely to be disclosable, since they will derive from information supplied by the offeree company, reviewed by the management for accuracy and shown to the financiers.[145]

VII CONCLUSION

In this chapter, it has been suggested that an auction increases the probability that the initial bidder will, either lose the target and still suffer the initial offer expenses, or overpay. For the acquiring shareholders, that means that they suffer losses, either in the form of a decrease in the acquirer's share price, when the bidder loses, or through wealth transfers to target shareholders, when it wins. Empirical studies submit evidence on both cases: first, takeover premia are greater in multiple bids than in one-bidder offers, and secondly, competitive bidders suffer more losses than uncontested acquirers. It has also been suggested that a rule that prohibits auctions generates more costs for the initial bidder and its shareholders, since it increases implicit competition. At the same time, it has been submitted that it is important to provide the initial bidder with adequate

[143] Rule 20.2, note 3 of the Takeover Code.

[144] *Ibid*. See also r 20.3 of the Takeover Code.

[145] See r 20.3 of the Takeover Code. There is no apparent reason why the same interpretation cannot apply in r 20.2. In any case the Executive should be consulted in cases of doubt.

incentives to initiate the auction. Otherwise, no competitive bidding will occur and the assets in question will not be transferred to the highest possible value use. Accordingly, the initial bidder's protection in a takeover auction is not an issue of importance only to the acquiring shareholders but to society as a whole.

The initial bidder's main concerns in auctions can be addressed at a regulatory level, through permitting the initial bidder to revise its offer, or by providing restrictions to speculative offers, or by achieving finality in takeover contests. In this way overpayment concerns are addressed and the bidder is protected against losing the target from speculative offers. In addition, by permitting undetected stake-building, regulation can allow the initial bidder to recoup some of its identification costs, if it eventually loses the auction. Proper incentives are thus provided to initial bidder, whose efforts initiate the operation of the market of corporate control.

Contrary to auctions where all offers are hostile, in the case of auctions that involve a 'white knight' or an MBO, the hostile bidder's main concern is that the former have better access to inside information. The Code provides for equality of information among actual and potential competing bidders, with the main intention to secure that the target shareholders are not deprived of an opportunity for a higher offer. However, the same rule, leaving aside some practical difficulties that have been discussed above, protects, at least in principle, less welcomed hostile bidders as well. It also provides the initial bidder with considerable incentives, apart from the case that the latter finds itself in a binding agreement not to seek additional information. The Code also addresses the case of management buyouts and expands the amount and type of information that needs to be passed to competing bidders.

Overall, in the United Kingdom, regulatory intervention at this level appears to be just a positive externality of regulatory concerns, either for the welfare of target shareholders or for the creation of an 'orderly framework for competitive situations'. In addition, whether the current permitted level of undetected toeholds allows the bidder to recoup its costs, demands additional fieldwork. The recent public discussion however pursuant to the implementation of the Transparency Directive requirements did not involve this concern. However, due to the importance of providing the necessary incentives to the initial bidder, the interests of bidder's shareholders in auctions should be recognised explicitly and directly at a regulatory level and be addressed as a policy concern. However, at the same time, the fact that regulatory choices designed to protect the interests of target shareholders also protect the acquiring shareholders' interests, only serves to corroborate with the fact that the interests of those two parties in a takeover transaction do not necessarily and always collide. This makes any trade-offs that regulation has to make, if it has to consider the interests of the bidder's shareholders, easier and less severe.

7

Auction Risk, Part II: Friendly Takeovers

I INTRODUCTION

IN A FRIENDLY takeover, the initial bidder is able to protect itself against the emergence of a rival bidder, as well as to recoup some of the 'sunk' or transaction costs associated with the takeover, in a way that is not available in hostile bids. Such protection derives from securing the target board's support. In friendly takeovers, the bidder usually insists on a number of 'exclusivity' undertakings or covenants, usually, but not necessarily, expressed in the form of a formal merger agreement. There are two main types of such deal-protective measures: exclusivity non-financial undertakings and break fees.[1] The first category includes undertakings made by the target's board that it will take a specific action or refrain from taking such an action, with the main purpose of securing the consummation of the deal. In contrast, break fees provide that the target will confer a benefit to the bidder in case the deal fails.

In addition, the bidder can also secure the support of major shareholders in the bidder. This is usually achieved by seeking irrevocable undertakings from the target's shareholders that they are going to tender their shares when the offer is announced. Next, an attempt will be made to examine those deal protective measures and their practical, regulatory and legal limitations.

II SECURING THE SUPPORT OF THE TARGET'S BOARD

A Exclusivity Provisions—Non-financial Undertakings

(i) *Introduction, Types, and Functions.*

Non-financial undertakings can either be positive—for example, the target's directors undertake to negotiate for a specific period of time with the

[1] JF Sneirson 'Merger Agreements, Termination Fees, and the Contract-Corporate Tension' (2002) *Columbia Business Law Review* 573; SM Bainbridge, 'Exclusive Merger Agreements and Lock-Ups in Negotiated Corporate Acquisitions' (1990) 75 *Minnesota Law Review* 239.

bidder, or to recommend the offer (lock-in agreements)—or negative—for example, not to solicit any other bids for a specific period of time (lock-out agreements). In practice, non-financial undertakings take the form of best effort clauses, no-shop covenants, and no-negotiation or no-talk covenants.[2]

Best effort clauses require both parties to use their best efforts to consummate the deal. This usually means that the target's board makes the undertaking that it will recommend the offer to the target's shareholders. Best effort clauses are usually, but not always, accompanied by explicit let-outs in circumstances where the target's board may be in breach of its fiduciary duties to its shareholders or in breach of the requirements of the City Code on Takeovers and Mergers ('the Takeover Code'). These fiduciary or code outs may either state that nothing contained in the agreement shall relieve the target's board of its fiduciary duties or its duties under the Takeover Code, or they relieve the target's board of its obligation to recommend the bid, if a better offer emerges.

No-shop covenants have a more negative form and prohibit the target's board from actively soliciting bids by other prospective offerors. However, they usually permit the target's board to consider and negotiate unsolicited takeover offers. A typical no-shop clause provides that

> [t]he company and its subsidiaries will not directly or indirectly . . . solicit, initiate or encourage submission of proposals or offers from any person relating to any acquisition or purchase of all or . . . a portion of the assets of, or any equity interest in the Company.[3]

Under no-talk or no-encouragement provisions, the target's board assumes the responsibility to refrain from any kind of negotiation with a prospective bidder, either up until a specific point of the takeover timetable, or until the first offer lapses. A typical no-talk covenant could have the following wording:

> the target company shall not participate in any negotiations regarding, or furnish to any other person any information with respect to, or otherwise cooperate in any way with, or assist or . . . participate in, facilitate or encourage, any effort or attempt . . . to do or seek to acquire a substantial part of the assets or equity of the company.[4]

Such a clause is usually accompanied by the explicit let-out that the target's board must comply with the requirement of the Takeover Code that an offeree company provide all offerors with the same information.[5]

[2] The latter are a more strict form of no-shop covenants.

[3] See Bainbridge, 'Exclusive Merger Agreements and Lock-Ups in Negotiated Corporate Acquisitions' (n 1 above)note 13.

[4] See Bainbridge, 'Exclusive Merger Agreements and Lock-Ups in Negotiated Corporate Acquisitions' (n 1 above) note 15.

[5] See the Dawson International and Coats Paton merger agreement, in *Dawson International plc v Coats Paton plc*, 1993 SLT 80 (OH).

(ii) *Regulatory Issues*

The Takeover Code affects the interpretation of such clauses in a number of ways. Under rule 3.1, the board of the offeree company must obtain competent independent advice on any offer and the substance of such advice must be made known to its shareholders. The implications of this rule are obvious. First, the Code affects the level of care required by the target's board when binding itself in such agreements. Secondly, even if the target's directors find themselves bound by such agreements they still have to consider any future hostile offers, get independent advice and disclose such advice to the target's shareholders. Also, although they are not required by the Code to respond to any attempt by a potential bidder for a friendly takeover, in the end, they have to comment on any formal offer made by any bidder irrespective of how welcomed it is.[6] In addition, as seen above, the target's directors are required by the Code to provide, upon request, to a subsequent less welcomed bidder any information given to the initial bidder.[7] Accordingly, any exclusivity clauses must be accompanied by specific let-outs in circumstances where they could potentially lead to a breach of the Code.

A number of cases and academics identify a separate duty of the target's directors to their shareholders, when they are required to advise them under the Takeover Code about the merits of a specific offer.[8] In addition, any exclusivity undertakings that are in breach of the Code could potentially be struck out by the courts on the basis of public policy concerns, as expressed by the Court of Appeal in *Fulham Football Club v Cabra Estates plc.*[9] Although in that specific case public policy concerns were not enough to justify the illegality of the agreements in question, this might be possible if the bidder were to ask for judicial intervention to enforce a no-talk clause that did not provide a let-out for the application of rule 20.2.[10] The same would apply with regard to an absolute undertaking to recommend an offer, in breach of the Takeover Code duty of the target's directors. Whether such breaches of the Code are enough to set aside an agreement on public policy grounds has yet to be examined by the courts. However,

[6] Rule 25.1(a) of the Takeover Code. See also the wording in note 3 on r 3.1.

[7] Rule 20.2 of the Takeover Code; see ch 6 above.

[8] *Gething and Others v Kilner and Others* [1972] 1 All ER 1166 (ChD); *Heron International Ltd v Lord Grade, Associated Communications Group plc* [1983] BCLC 244 (CA); see, eg PL Davies, *Gower's Principles of Modern Company Law*, 6th edn (London, Sweet & Maxwell, 1997). Not all cases support this view, though they reach similar conclusions in different ways. Eg, in *John Crowther Group v Carpets International* [1990] BCLC 460 (HC) the court rejected the idea of a secondary duty to the shareholders. However, it interpreted the interests of the company as the interests of its shareholders.

[9] *Fulham Football Club v Cabra Estates plc* [1994] 1 BCLC 363, [1992] BCC 863 (CA).

[10] The public policy argument has been supported in the relevant literature with reference though to *Dawson International* case (n 5 above). See Davies, *Gower's Principles of Modern Company Law* (n 8 above).

in the past, the Panel rejected the argument that the Code absolutely prohibited a target's directors from fettering their discretion to recommend a subsequent higher offer.[11] The ruling of the Panel, though, should be read in the light of the fact that under Irish law, which was applicable in the specific case, such fettering was legal.

Furthermore, the Takeover Code requirements are also important when it comes to the examination of the existence or not of a contractual relationship between the bidder and the target's board. It has been held that announcements made by the target's board in relation to the recommendation of a specific offer result from the obligations of the target's board under the Code and under normal city practice, and not necessarily from a particular contractual requirement, upon which the bidder relies.[12] Accordingly, in cases where the target's board recommends the offer to its shareholders after negotiations with a potential bidder, such statement and any undertakings assumed in relation to implementing the offer—even in joint announcements—should not be considered as obligatory and contractual in nature, unless explicit wording used suggests so. On the contrary, such announcements derive from the Takeover Code's obligations imposed on the target's directors, and any subsequent undertakings may be considered, in view of normal city practice,[13] as statements of common intention, which can 'be relied upon as a matter of honesty and trust, and not as a matter of obligation and law'.[14]

The question that arises is how the new statutory status of the Panel could potentially change this approach in the light of the fact that now such announcements are obligatory, especially when considering that the announcement of the target board's views, including expressing or not its support for the bid, is a requirement deriving from European Community Law as well. However, nothing in the law or the Takeovers Directive could be interpreted to support the view that the target board's duty to publish its views on the offer could give rise to the conclusion of a contract with the bidder, or the provision of an irrevocable undertaking, unless expressly given as such.

The above means that the bidder must either insist on a pre-announcement written agreement between the two parties, or insist on explicit terms in any announcement required by the Takeover Code, that any undertakings assumed by the target's board for the consummation of the offer are obligatory and result from a contractual agreement reached by the two parties. In view of the above, it is clear that the Takeover Code plays an important role, in terms of the interpretation of exclusivity

[11] See Irish Distillers Group plc, Panel Statement 1988/25 (November 1988).

[12] *Dawson International plc v Coats Paton plc*, 1993 SLT 80 (OH) 93. See also rr 1(a), 2.2 and 2.5 of the Takeover Code.

[13] *Dawson International* (n 12 above) 98.

[14] *Dawson International* (n 12 above) 97.

promises, by both affecting the level of care required by the target's board in assuming such obligations, on the one hand, and on the other hand, by affecting the determination of the existence of a contract, if any, with the bidder.

(iii) *The Legal Treatment of Exclusivity Provisions*

The present analysis assumes that the directors in the target do not put themselves in a conflict of interest situation. A conflict arises where the bidder offers side-payments or payments for a loss of office or any other type of inducement to the target's directors, in order to achieve their recommendation. In those cases, a completely different set of issues arises that goes beyond the scope of the present analysis. What suffices to be said is that in circumstances where a conflict of interest arises, exclusivity clauses become more problematic. For the scope of the present analysis, though, it is assumed that the directors, in exercising their power to enter in such an agreement, do so without putting themselves in a conflict of interest situation.

On that basis, two main concerns arise in terms of the legal treatment of exclusivity clauses:

1. The enforceability of exclusivity agreements under contract law.
2. The law of fiduciary duties and the possibility that exclusivity clauses may constitute a breach of the fiduciary duties of the target's directors.

In other words, the legality of exclusivity provisions can be described, as has been stated in the US case law,[15] as 'a delicate interplay of principles of both contract and corporate law, neither wholly controlling the outcome'. Overall, it should be noted at the outset that, as far as contractual law is concerned, the case law seems to differentiate between positive and negative undertakings, while as far as the law of fiduciary duties is concerned, a distinction seems to arise between undertakings that relate to decisions that are to be made by the target's shareholders, for which the target's directors need to provide advice, and decisions that rest with the board of the target.

Finally, it should be noted that such undertakings do not cause any of the financial assistance concerns discussed below under break fee agreements, because no financial assistance is given, and any liability that arises from breach of such clauses cannot constitute financial assistance, since it is not usually anticipated at the time of giving the covenants that there will be any liability thereunder.[16]

[15] See *ConAgra Inc v Cargill Inc*, 222 Neb 136 at 153, 382 NW2d 576 at 586. See also Bainbridge, 'Exclusive Merger Agreements and Lock-Ups in Negotiated Corporate Acquisitions' (n 1 above) 250.

[16] See *Barclays Bank plc v British & Commonwealth Holdings plc* [1996] 1 All ER 381 (CA) and *Chaston v SWP Group plc* [2002] EWCA Civ 1999, [2003] 1 BCLC 675. See below.

(a) Contract law concerns (positive v negative undertakings)

It is well established in the case law that an agreement that obliges the seller to negotiate with the purchaser—even if such negotiations are confined to a specific period of time, and a consideration is provided in return—cannot be enforced.[17]

In contrast, negative undertakings (or lock-out agreements) can be enforced, provided that are made for a reasonable fixed period[18] and are accompanied by a consideration. The buyers' promise to proceed with the purchase within a specified period of time has been considered by the courts as a sufficient supporting consideration for the lock-out agreement, because he limits his discretion to exchange contacts within a specified period.[19] Alternatively, execution of the lock-out agreement under seal releases the purchaser from the need to support the negative undertaking with a consideration[20] and avoids the potential problems associated with the judicial interpretation of what is a sufficient consideration.

Accordingly, positive undertakings that the target directors will continue negotiations with the bidder, even though they are confined to a short period of time, are most likely to be unenforceable under English law. However, the bidder can easily circumvent the problem of exclusive negotiations by structuring the undertaking in a negative way, for example in the form of a no-shop agreement. Similarly, the bidder can make its offer conditional upon the fulfilment of such undertakings, since the prohibition on enforceability of positive undertakings does not cover conditions in contracts.[21] The legal and regulatory issues associated with such conditions will be further considered in chapter nine.

(b) Fiduciary duties implications (shareholders' decisions v board powers)

Even if an exclusivity agreement is cleared at a contract law level, it can potentially be problematic for the bidder if the application of the target's directors' fiduciary duties can provide a let-out from the agreement. Even if there is no doubt that the target's directors act in good faith for the best interests of their company at the time they give the exclusivity undertakings, the issue that arises is whether such undertakings will be enforceable after the situation changes, namely when a second bidder actually emerges.

[17] This was the unanimous opinion of the House of Lords in the *Walford v Miles* [1992] 2 AC 128; see also *Radiant Shipping Co Ltd v Sea Containers Ltd* [1995] CLC 976.

[18] *Walford v Miles* (n 17 above). See however *Global Container Lines Ltd v State Black Sea Shipping Co* [1999] 1 Lloyd's Rep 127 (CA), where the judge dealt with the issue of certainty in cases where the clause does not provide for a fixed period of termination.

[19] *Pitt v PHH Asset Management Limited* [1993] 4 All ER 961 (CA).

[20] *Walford v Miles* (n 17 above).

[21] See *Global Container Lines Ltd v State Black Sea Shipping Co* [1999] 1 Lloyd's Rep 127 (CA).

Two questions arise: first, are target's directors obliged to respect the undertakings given, even if they feel that by doing so they no longer act in the best interests of their shareholders? Secondly, do the target directors fetter their future discretion at all when entering in such agreements, or do they just lawfully exercise their present discretion to bind the company? The case law seems to answer both questions similarly, by making a distinction between decisions that fall into the scope of the boards' powers and decisions that rest with the shareholders to take.

In *John Crowther Group v Carpets International*[22] and in *Rackham v Peek Foods Ltd*[23] it was held that any agreement between the acquirer and the target's board, according to which the latter has to recommend a specific offer to its shareholders, must be read subject to the fiduciary duty of the target's directors to act in the interests of the company and to make a full and honest disclosure to the shareholders. Vinelott J's judgment is quite emphatic of the let-out role of fiduciary duties:

> The terms of the agreement (to recommend the offer) must clearly be read in the light of the fact known to all parties that directors owe a fiduciary duty to act in the interests of their company and to make full and honest disclosure to shareholders before they vote on such a resolution. It seems to me that it must have been understood by all that, if the undertaking was to use reasonable endeavours to procure the passing of the resolution, it was necessarily subject to anything which the directors had to do in pursuance of that fiduciary duty.[24]

Even more straightforward is the wording in *Rackhman v Peek Foods Ltd* case:

> Of course, directors normally recommend a conditional agreement because otherwise they would never have allowed the company to enter into the agreement itself. But, if, after the date of the conditional agreement, the directors consider that the bargain has become unacceptable from the point of view of the shareholders, it is the duty of the directors so to advise the shareholders and that advice by the directors does not constitute a breach of the 'best endeavours' covenant by the company.[25]

In addition, in the Scottish case of *Dawson International v Coats Paton*, the court held that even without recourse to the specialities of fiduciary duty, under a broader principle of general law, clauses to recommend an offer would not be enforceable in cases of 'bona fide change of mind'.[26] The Scottish Court of Session took the view that the target's directors owed a negative duty to their shareholders not to give misleading advice.[27]

[22] *John Crowther Group v Carpets International* [1990] BCLC 460 (HC).

[23] *Rackham v Peek Foods Ltd* [1990] BCLC 895 (HC).

[24] *John Crowther Group v Carpets International* [1990] BCLC 460 at 464–5 (HC).

[25] *Rackham v Peek Foods Ltd* [1990] BCLC 895 at 898 (HC).

[26] *Dawson International plc v Coats Paton plc,* 1993 SLT 80 (OH) 96 (Lord Prosser). The issue was also partly covered by early judgments on the case: see 1988 SLT 854 and 1989 SLT 655.

[27] *Ibid* (Lord Cullen).

However, the court continued that under the same general law principles, the obligant could not be free to take steps to change the underlying circumstances, so as to be able to drop out of its obligations, accepting thus the enforceability of no-shop and no-talk clauses.

The potential width of the above cases has been subsequently confined by the Court of Appeal in *Fulham Football Club Ltd v Cabra Estates plc*.[28] The main legal issue was whether at the point that the directors of a company entered into a binding agreement with a third party, they fettered their future discretion or they rather just exercised their present discretion. The former is not allowed.[29] However, once the latter is held, then it is for the court to examine whether the directors in doing so acted in good faith and fulfilled the level of care required by them.

Fulham is based on different facts than the previous cases, which directly referred to exclusivity agreements in the context of a takeover offer. The court heavily relied upon a previous Australian authority, *Thorby v Goldberg*,[30] which was cited neither in *Crowther* nor in *Rackham*. Accordingly, the Court of Appeal confined these decisions to their particular facts, and expressed the view that they should not be read as laying down a general proposition that directors can never bind themselves as to the future exercise of their fiduciary powers. In the wording of the court 'if they could be so read then they would be wrong'.[31]

In *Fulham*, the court was primarily concerned with directors' powers to bind the company to an agreement with a third party for an action taken by the company as represented by them towards another third party. Accordingly, the decision in question fell into the scope of directors' external powers.[32] The board can exercise such powers in its discretion, provided that, in doing so, it believes it is in the best interests of its company and meets the requirements of the duty of care. Hence, undertakings not to put the target into the market by not soliciting other bidders, or undertakings not to assist any bidders more than is required for the purposes of compliance with the Takeover Code, do not constitute an unlawful fettering of the target directors' future discretion and any subsequent changes cannot render them void.

Of course, at the time that the target directors provide such covenants, they must meet the standards of care required, and honestly believe that by doing so they act for the best interests of their company. In identifying what is in the best interests of the target company in a takeover situation, it has been held that, where it is clear that a company is to be taken over

[28] *Fulham Football Club Ltd v Cabra Estates plc* [1994] 1 BCLC 363 (CA).

[29] *Boulting v ACTT* [1963] 2 QB 606.

[30] *Thorby v Goldberg* (1964) 112 CLR 597 (High Ct Aust).

[31] *Fulham Football Club Ltd v Cabra Estates plc* [1994] 1 BCLC 363, last paragraph.

[32] For the distinction between external and internal powers, see Nolan, 'The Proper Purpose Doctrine and Company Directors' in BA Rider (ed), *The Realm of Company Law* (London, Kluwer Law International).

and the only question is which of the competing offers should be recommended, the interests of the company are to be judged by reference to the interests of the current shareholders, and that the duty of the directors is to obtain the best price.[33]

In *Heron International Ltd v Lord Grade,* Lawton LJ formulated the following test: when deciding whether to commit the company to a particular bidder, the directors should ask themselves whether there was a reasonable possibility of obtaining a higher bid from a third party, or whether it was vitally necessary, in the interests of the company and of the existing shareholders, that the present offer should be immediately accepted.[34] The fact that the financial state or the state of the management of the target company prevent the target's directors from waiting for a higher bid, or the fact that the offer in question would have lapsed if it had not been accepted, are not sufficient by themselves to justify the directors' actions.[35] However, the court accepted that in the specific case, the directors had not behaved unreasonably in securing the first bid, as it was clear to them that there were reasons why the second bid could never have succeeded.[36]

The codification of director's fiduciary duties in the Companies Act 2006 supports the approach of *Fulham* and *Heron*. Section 173 of the CA 2006 codifies the current principle of law under which directors must exercise their powers independently, without subordinating their powers to the will of others, whether by delegation or otherwise (unless authorised by or under the constitution to do so). The section also provides that directors must not fetter the future exercise of their discretion unless they are acting: (a) 'in accordance with an agreement' which has been 'duly entered into by the company'; or (b) 'in a way authorised by the company's constitution'.

While in the case of negative undertakings, such as no-shop or no-talk covenants, the target's directors seem to exercise their present discretion, this is not the case with absolute undertakings to recommend a specific offer. The directors do not have the discretion to inform or provide impartial and accurate advice to their shareholders, but rather the duty to do so.[37]

[33] *Heron International Ltd v Lord Grade, Associated Communications Group plc* [1983] BCLC 244 (CA); *Morgan Crucible Co Plc v Hill Samuel Bank & Co Ltd* [1990] 3 All ER 330 (Hoffman J), decision reversed by *Morgan Crucible Co Plc v Hill Samuel Bank Ltd* [1991] 2 WLR 655 (CA). However, in *Dawson International plc v Coats Patons plc* [1991] BCC 276 it was stressed by the lower court that the interests of the current shareholders may conflict with the interests of the company.

[34] See *Heron International* (n 33 above).

[35] See *Heron International* (n 33 above).

[36] See *Heron International* (n 33 above).

[37] See r 25.1 of the Takeover Code and the wording of the cases: *Gething and Others v Kilner and Others* [1972] 1 All ER 1166 (ChD); *Heron International Ltd v Lord Grade, Associated Communications Group plc* [1983] BCLC 244 (CA); *Morgan Crucible Co plc v Hill Samuel Bank Ltd* [1991] Ch 295, [1991] BCLC 178 (CA).

Accordingly, the target's directors cannot exercise their discretion according to the meaning of *Thorby* and *Fulham* simply because they do not have such discretion. In this case, their discretion is limited to identifying what offer they consider, in their personal opinion, as the best for their shareholders. It is the target's shareholders who have the discretion to accept or reject an offer. Hence, once a better deal arises in the directors' view, they have the duty not to lie to their shareholders and honestly to advise them on both deals. If, in doing so, they have to change their recommendation or refrain from making such a recommendation, despite a contractual agreement to the contrary, it is the principles established in *Crowther* and *Rackham* that apply.

One way for the bidder to circumvent this problem is to make its offer conditional on the actual recommendation of its offer by the target's directors instead of relying on the undertaking itself. The legal and regulatory issues associated with such conditions will be further considered in chapter nine. Finally, subject to the limitations that will be analysed in the next part of this chapter, the bidder could include the non-recommendation of its offer by the target's directors as one of the events that could trigger the payment of a predetermined termination fee.

(iv) *Practical Considerations*

Leaving aside any legal issues discussed above, the exclusivity undertakings with no financial element do not really provide substantial protection to the contractual bidder. First, the above exclusivity provisions do not prevent any rival bidders from bypassing the target's board and making an offer directly to the target's shareholders at a higher price. This puts substantial pressure on the target's directors for having just recommended a lower price offer. Moreover, the Takeover Code's provision about equality of information among more and less welcomed bidders[38] further decreases the need for the target board's support. In that sense, exclusivity clauses do little to deter competition.

Neither are they effective in recouping the bidder's costs. First of all, the initial bidder can potentially retrieve any costs only in cases of a breach of contract by the target's board. However, this may be extremely difficult to be established, considering the many explicit and implicit let-outs that usually accompany that kind of clause. Then, it has to pursue any such claims judicially. But, even in circumstances that it can establish such a breach of contract in a courtroom, it has also to establish a measure of damages. The pursuer's claims would probably be for any underwriting costs or other transaction-associated costs and fees, such as tax liability for having to sell any shares that the bidder bought in the market as part of its takeover strat-

[38] See ch 6 above.

egy. In that sense, the bidder's claims would be for abortive or wasted expenditure. In such cases of breach of contract, the basic rule is that the pursuer be put where it would have been, had the contract been performed.[39] For that purpose, it would be necessary to show not merely that the expense had been incurred, but that it would have been recovered if the breach of contract had not occurred. Accordingly, it was held in *Dawson International plc v Coats Paton plc*[40] that the bidder's costs would have been irrevocable even if the actions relied upon as constituting breach of contract had never been taken. The probabilities were, as the court's reasoning continued, that the counter-bidder would have made a higher hostile bid without the defender's recommendation.[41] Even if the initial bidder had made a new higher offer, the cost of underwriting for the initial offer would have been wasted and not recovered.[42] This means that for the initial bidder to claim any damages it has to either prove that the rival bidder would not have proceeded with a hostile bid without the recommendation of the target's board, or establish its claims on a different basis, for example misrepresentation on behalf of the target's board about material facts such as the existence of a rival bidder at the point that the agreement was reached.[43]

B Inducement, Termination or Break Fees

(i) *Definition and Functions*

Given the relative weakness of exclusivity provisions as a cost-hedging and bidding deterrent mechanism, transaction planners came up with a different device, often described as a break, termination or inducement fee.[44] Such agreements have been extremely common in the United States[45] and are becoming increasingly popular in the United Kingdom as well, partly because of pressure by US bidders.[46]

[39] *Dawson International plc v Coats Paton plc*, 1993 SLT 80 (Ct Sess); *Houldsworth v Brand's Trustees* (1877) 4 R 369 (HL)).

[40] *Dawson International* (n 39 above).

[41] *Dawson International* (n 39 above) 100.

[42] *Dawson International* (n 39 above). The analysis of Lord Prosser primarily involved underwriting costs. A similar approach was followed in relation to other expenditure by way of fees, although it has been accepted that in theory they may include elements, which might have made them recoverable.

[43] *Dawson International* (n 39 above) 101.

[44] As described by r 21.1 of the Takeover Code.

[45] In 1998, lock-up agreements appeared in 80% of the friendly merger deals over $50m compared to 40% ten years ago. For further information see JC Coates and G Subramanian, 'A Buy-Side Model of M&a Lockups: Theory and Evidence' (2000) 53 (November) *Stanford Law Review* 307. In the UK almost all recent big takeovers were accompanied by a form of inducement fee agreement. For a list see M Wippell and G Knighton, 'Inducement Fees: A Us Import Takes Root' (2004) 15(3) *PLC* 31.

[46] W Charnley and B Breslin, 'Break Fees: Financial Assistance and Directors' Duties' (2000) *Company Lawyer*.

A break fee agreement is an arrangement between an offeror or a potential offeror and the offeree company pursuant to which the target's management promises to confer a benefit on the offeror if certain specified events occur, such as the offeror ultimately losing the bidding contest, or events that have the effect of preventing the offer from proceeding or causing it to fail (eg the recommendation by the offeree company's board of a higher competing offer). Before examining the legal and regulatory treatment of such fees, it is essential to understand their function through a simple example:

Bidder B examines the possibility of entering into a friendly acquisition agreement with target T, which is valued at £80m. A rival bidder, R, enters the contest valuing the target at £83m. In the absence of any break fee agreement, R is more likely to free ride on bidder B and acquire the target. If a break fee of £2m is signed between B and T, R is not able to offer £83m, since it will be obliged to pay the break fee in case it acquires the target. Accordingly, its offer price needs to be reduced to £81m to account for the fact that the break fee must be paid.[47] Yet, it still acquires the target. However, if the break fee is £4m, the rival bidder cannot offer more than £79m. Consequently, either the second bidder does not make an attempt to make an offer or, if it has already expressed an interest in the target, it loses the contest.

In view of the above, the initial bidder benefits from an inducement fee agreement in a number of ways. First, it recoups the costs of identifying the target and placing an offer. Secondly, it minimises its financial risk associated with the offer, thus enabling the bidder to make the offer in the first place or to bid even more aggressively. For example, if the initial bidder expects to gain £20m if it acquires the target, and lose £2m if it fails, then, assuming a probability of 50 per cent for each outcome, the value of the project for the bidder is £20m – £2m ÷ 2 = £9m. In contrast, in the event of a fee of £2m, the same project is valued by the bidder at £20m – £0m ÷ 2 = £10m. Finally, a break fee may also deter potential competition. The latter effect mainly depends on the size of the inducement fee.

Target shareholders may be deprived of the possibility of receiving a higher offer where the costs imposed by the inducement fee on the rival bidder defeat its higher valuation of the target. However, at the same time, the break fee agreement may give the opportunity to the initial bidder to offer a higher price, which could not have been offered without the break fee. In addition, had the target been identified by the initial bidder the rival hostile offer may have never occurred.

Finally, the second bidder, although it loses when the costs of the inducement fee out-perform its higher valuation of the target, may still win the contest if the difference in its reservation price is higher than the

[47] £81m + 2m = £83m. Assuming the rival bidder does not want to exceed its target's estimation of £83m.

inducement fee. This means that, in cases where the inducement fee represents just the initial information sunk costs of the first bidder, the second bidder wins only if its higher valuation does not represent only an exploitation of, or a free ride on the first bidder's efforts. In that sense, hedging inducement fees do not deprive target shareholders of offers by higher-value bidders, but only of offers by bidders who free ride on the identification costs incurred by the initial bidder. In contrast, deterring break fees may prevent higher-value bidders from making an offer and represent a potential loss for target shareholders.

(ii) *The Typology of Inducement or Break Fees*

(a) Types of inducement fees

Break fees can be distinguished according to the function they serve, the time at which they occur in relation to the posting of the offer and the type of the benefit promised.

Break fee agreements may have three purposes: first, the bidder seeks to retrieve the costs of the offer in cases where its offer eventually lapses (hedging fees)[48]; secondly, break fees may make the target too expensive for a potential rival bidder and thus they may deter potential competition (deterring break fees)[49]; and finally, target firms may also grant such agreements to 'white knight' bidders in response to hostile takeovers (second bidder break fees). A second bidder break fee may produce some additional legal and, especially, regulatory concerns,[50] mainly when the target has already entered into an inducement fee agreement with the initial bidder (multiple break fee situation).

In certain circumstances, the bidder may also be required to provide break fees to the target. Such fees, though unusual, may serve to cover the costs of the target's professional advice in respect of the proposed offer and may be triggered in cases where the bidder fails to announce an offer. This may also be the case when the acquisition falls within the definition of a class 1 transaction and the bidder's directors assume the responsibility to recommend the offer to their shareholders for approval, or when the acquisition has to be cleared by regulatory approval for antitrust purposes. Both requirements may constitute conditions that can trigger the

[48] Such lock-ups serve as a hedging mechanism against the acquisition costs and accordingly are quantitatively confined to reflect those costs. They are also called non-anticipatory by part of the literature. See eg M Kahan and M Klausner, 'Lockups and the Market of Corporate Control' (1996) 48 (July) *Stanford Law Review* 1539.

[49] These are lock-ups that can prevent a higher-valuing party from acquiring a target company. Also called anticipatory or foreclosing lock-ups (I Ayres, 'Analysing Stock Lock-Ups: Do Target Treasury Sales Foreclose or Facilitate Takeover Auctions?' (1990) 90 *Columbia Law Review* 682 at 704.

[50] Especially in relation to the aggregated size of the inducement fees. See below about the Takeover Code's treatment of multiple lock-ups.

payment of the break fee to the target. In all these cases, it is likely that both target and bidder will enter into a mutual break fee agreement. Mutual break fees may also accompany friendly takeovers that are announced to consummate merger agreements.[51]

Inducement fee agreements can be entered into either when the bid is announced (post-announcement inducement fees) or at a much earlier stage, during the pre-bid due diligence process that the bidder undertakes (pre-announcement inducement fees).[52] The conditions under which pre-announcement inducement fees are triggered mainly seek to protect the due diligence costs from the risk that the transaction will fail before the offer is actually announced. Pre-announcement inducement fees usually accompany non-financial undertakings, described above.

(b) Trigger mechanisms

Among the events that can trigger the payment of an inducement fee and are usually included in lock-up agreements are:[53]

1. Any person not connected to the bidder announces its intention to make an offer, which has not been withdrawn prior to the lapse or withdrawal of the offer of the bidder that is the party to the lock-up agreement, and at any time thereafter such competing offer is declared unconditional as to acceptances.
2. The target's directors (independent or executive) withdraw or adversely modify their recommendation of the offer.
3. The target's directors recommend a competing offer.
4. Prior to the announcement of the offer by the potential bidder, or while the offer is still open to acceptances, the target's directors or advisers solicit or encourage or enter into discussions with another potential bidder or purchaser of a substantial business or asset of the company.
5. Prior to the announcement of the offer by the potential bidder, or while the offer is still open to acceptances, the target's directors or advisers provide information to a potential competitive offeror (except to the extent required by rule 20.2 of the Takeover Code).
6. Prior to the announcement of the offer and while the bidder's advisers confirm the willingness of the bidder to make an offer at a pre-negotiated price, the target's directors (independent or not) refuse to recommend the offer.

[51] See, eg the P&O Princess and Carnival Corporation merger agreement. Merger announcement dated 8 January 2003. See also and Wippell and Knighton, 'Inducement Fees: A US Import Takes Root' (n 45 above) 33.

[52] The latter are becoming more and more popular in the UK market: Wippell and Knighton, 'Inducement Fees: A US Import Takes Root' (n 45 above).

[53] Some of the examples taken from Wippell and Knighton, 'Inducement Fees: A US Import Takes Root' (n 45 above) 39.

7. Any disposal of target's assets of a predetermined value without the consent of the bidder. This was the case in Morrison Supermarkets' bid for Safeway. The lock-up agreement provided for Safeway to pay Morrison a fee if it agreed to dispose, without the consent of Morrison, of assets of an aggregate value of £30m before the termination of the lock-up agreement, or £300m if the disposal was agreed at any time within 12 months of the date of the inducement fee agreement.[54]
8. For any other reason for which the proposed bid is unsuccessful. This was a condition to an inducement fee agreement of £7.8m (0.5 per cent of the bid value) between MSREF and Canary Wharf, that formed a part of Silvestor UK Properties' recent bid for Canary Wharf.[55]

Inducement fee agreements can extend over the period for which the bid has to remain open and after it lapses (see, for example, the Morrison and Safeway agreement). Pre-announcement inducement fees may not even require the announcement by the bidder of its intention to make an offer as a triggering condition. According to such an agreement, the target has to pay the fee, provided that the bidder and its advisers assure every week that they commit themselves to make an offer.[56] No announcement of a firm intention to make an offer is necessary for the condition to be satisfied and the fee is just payable upon the completion of the due diligence process. What such an agreement results in, in practice, is the target bearing the cost of the due diligence process up to a predetermined and calculated amount. This was the case in Baroness Retail's bid for Debenhams, in which, under the inducement fee agreement, Debenhams assumed the responsibility to pay a £6m fee, provided that Baroness reaffirmed each week its strong commitment to proceed with the offer and notified Debenhams before the end of September 2003 if it no longer wished to proceed with the offer.[57] Under such arrangements, payments of fees up to a predetermined value may accrue week by week.[58]

In view of the above wide typology of inducement fees, the question that arises next is what is the regulatory and legal treatment of inducement fees in the United Kingdom.

(iii) *The Position of the Takeover Code*

A fundamental objective of the Takeover Code has been to prevent the target's board from taking any actions which would frustrate an offer against the wishes of their shareholders. The above objective is encapsulated in General Principle 3 of the Code and rule 21. General Principle 3,

[54] Wippell and Knighton, 'Inducement Fees: A US Import Takes Root' (n 45 above) 39.
[55] Wippell and Knighton, 'Inducement Fees: A US Import Takes Root' (n 45 above) 39.
[56] Wippell and Knighton, 'Inducement Fees: A US Import Takes Root' (n 45 above) 39.
[57] Wippell and Knighton, 'Inducement Fees: A US Import Takes Root' (n 45 above) 39.
[58] Wippell and Knighton, 'Inducement Fees: A US Import Takes Root' (n 45 above) 38.

introduced as part of the amendments to the Code made pursuant to the introduction of the Takeovers Directive and in order to mirror the principle stated therein, supports rule 21.1 by providing that the target's board must not deny the holders of securities the opportunity to decide on the merits of the bid. Prior to the amendments to the Code that have been made to implement the Takeovers Directive, old General Principle 7 also embodied this principle of no frustrating action.

In addition to General Principle 3 the main prohibition of frustrating actions lies in rule 21.1. Pursuant to the amendments resulting from the implementation of the Takeovers Directive, rule 21.1 states:

> During the course of an offer, or even before the date of the offer if the board of the offeree company has reason to believe that a bona fide offer might be imminent, the board must not without the approval of the shareholders in general meeting take any action which may result in any offer or bona fide possible offer being frustrated or in shareholders being denied the opportunity to decide on its merits.

Furthermore, it provides, by way of example, a list of specific actions that are deemed to constitute frustrating actions and which cannot be entered into by the target's board without obtaining the explicit consent of the target's shareholders.[59]

The amendments performed in rule 21.1 had the effect of widening the obligation on the board of the target to seek shareholders' approval, since the old rule 21.1 referred to a list of particular actions that were regarded as being frustrating actions while the new version of the rule includes reference to such particular actions but only by way of examples.

The prohibition of frustrating actions applies—as was the case under the regime in place prior to the implementation of the Takeovers Directive—during the period of the offer or even before, as long as the board of the offeree company has reasons to believe that a bona fide offer might be imminent.[60] Accordingly, as has been identified by the Code Committee, where a target is in discussions with a potential offeror, it can, in theory, enter into a contractual agreement with that potential offeror, which might have the effect of frustrating an offer by another, yet unidentified, potential bidder.[61] This is where the issue of inducement fees kicks in. Before the implementation of the Takeovers Directive, the Panel had indicated that it does not consider prima facie inducement fees as frustrating actions, provided that they meet certain requirements.[62] The same

[59] Rule 21.1 of the Takeover Code.

[60] Rule 21.1 of the Takeover Code.

[61] See The Panel on Takeovers and Mergers, PCP 11: *Consultation Paper Issued by the Code Committee of the Panel: Dual Listed Company Transactions and Frustrating Action. Revision Proposals Relating to the Definition of an Offer and Rule 21.2 of the Takeover Code* (April 2002) para 9.4.

[62] *Ibid*. See also r 21.2 of the Takeover Code.

approach is retained after the implementation of the Directive, since the Takeover Code's approach on break fees remained unchanged

The main requirement imposed by rule 21.2 is that the value of the inducement fee cannot exceed one per cent of the offer value.[63] According to note 1 on rule 21.2, the above de minimis rule will apply to any other favourable arrangements that have similar or comparable financial or economic effects, even if such arrangements do not actually involve any cash payments.[64] Moreover, the note continues that

> such arrangements will include for example, break fees, penalties, put or call options or other provisions having similar effects, regardless of whether such arrangements are considered to be in the ordinary course of business. In cases of doubt the Panel should be consulted.[65]

In view of the above, rule 21.2 also catches payments made pursuant to exclusivity agreements. Payments for any breach of such agreements that have the effect of preventing the offer from proceeding or causing it to fail (because, for example, the offeree board successfully solicits a higher bid) are regarded as falling within rule 21.2. Therefore, the maximum total payments to the offeror for such breaches (including any inducement fee) should be one per cent of the value of the offeree company, as set out in the rule. In contrast the Executive of the Panel recognises that payments by the offeree company for breaches that have not prevented the offer from succeeding or caused it to fail will fall outside rule 21.2.[66] The Executive will also normally require that all relevant agreements include a clause as follows:

> Nothing in this agreement shall oblige [the offeree company] to pay any amount which the Panel determines would not be permitted by Rule 21.2 of the Takeover Code.[67]

The one per cent limit can be calculated on the basis of the fully diluted equity share capital of the offeree company.[68] On a securities exchange offer, the value of the offeree company for these purposes will be fixed by reference to the value of the offer at the time of the announcement of the

[63] Rule 21.2 of the Takeover Code.

[64] Note 1, second paragraph on r 21.2 of the Takeover Code.

[65] Note 1, third paragraph on r 21.2 as added by the Code Committee in RS11. The Panel on Takeovers and Mergers, RS 11: *Dual Listed Company Transactions and Frustrating Action. Statement by the Code Committee of the Panel Following the External Consultation Process on PCP 11* (August 2002).

[66] The Panel on Takeovers and Mergers, *Practice Statement No 15: Inducement Fees—Agreements between the Offeror and the Offeree Company etc* (November 2005).

[67] *Ibid.*

[68] Only options and warrants which are 'in the money' may be included in the calculation. When determining the value of the fully diluted share capital, the value to be attributed to such warrants and options is their 'see-through' value, taking into account the offer price for the relevant shares and any exercise price. The value attributable to convertible securities is the offer price multiplied by the conversion ratio; *Practice Statement No 15* (n 66 above).

transaction, and will not fluctuate as a result of subsequent movements in the price of the consideration securities.[69] In addition, where the inducement fee is agreed prior to a firm announcement of an offer, the value of the offeree company will be determined by reference to the expected value of the offer at the time the fee is agreed.[70] It should be noted that, since an inducement fee exceeding the one per cent limit will be regarded by the Panel as a frustrating action for a competing offeror, the one per cent limit can be exceeded with the agreement of the target's shareholders, as is the case with the validation of other frustrating actions.[71]

The bidder should also receive an undertaking that the target board will take any necessary steps to ensure compliance with the Takeover Code's requirements in rule 21.2, amongst other things, to obtain a confirmation by the target's financial advisers that the inducement fee is in the best interests of the target's shareholders. Written confirmations must also be provided to the Panel. Apart from the directors' and the target advisers' opinions on the fairness of the arrangement, such confirmations must confirm (amongst other things) that the inducement fee resulted from normal commercial negotiations, explain the trigger conditions of the payment of the fee, and provide all relevant information concerning any other undertakings in connection to the fee or any other possible competing offers—including, for example, the status of discussions of the timing of the offer.[72] Finally, any inducement fee should be fully disclosed in the announcement made pursuant to rule 2.5 of the Code and in the offer document.[73]

More specific issues arise in relation to multiple break fees. As discussed above, there are cases where the target may enter into lock-up agreements with more than one bidder, either during or before the announcement of an offer. In such cases, the issue that arises is whether the aggregate value of those lock-ups may exceed the one per cent limit. In a recent practice statement, the Executive interpreted rule 21.2 as permitting an offeree company to agree multiple inducement fees, each up to the relevant one per cent limit, regardless of the fact that, in certain circumstances, the aggregate amount payable by the offeree company might exceed the one per cent limit.[74]

[69] The Panel on Takeovers and Mergers, *Practice Statement No 4: Rule 21.2—Inducement Fees* (February 2004).

[70] *Ibid.*

[71] See r 21.1 of the Takeover Code.

[72] The Panel on Takeovers and Mergers, *Practice Statement No 4* (n 69 above).

[73] Rule 21.2 of the Takeover Code.

[74] See The Panel on Takeovers and Mergers, *Practice Statement No 4* (n 69 above). Prior to that clarification, practitioners used to structure inducement fees given to a second bidder in a way that at no time the target should pay a fee exceeding the 1% limit. See for example the CVC's bid for Debenhams and Gondola Express's bid for Pizza Express. See Wippell and Knighton, 'Inducement Fees: A US Import Takes Root (n 45 above) 38.

In the previous version of the UKLA Listing Rules there were no specific rules in the class tests regarding inducement fees. Despite the fact that an inducement fee agreement, although restricted to a fee of one per cent of the value of the bid, could still exceed the 25 per cent threshold imposed by the Listing Rules, requiring thus the approval of the target's shareholders. According to the old LR 10.2.4, 'any agreement or arrangement with a party', not being a member of the listed company's group,

> under which a listed company agrees to discharge any liabilities for costs, expenses, commissions or losses incurred by or on behalf of that party, whether or not on a contingent basis [and]
>
> 'under which the maximum liability is equal to or exceeds an amount equal to 25% of the average of the company's profits[75] for the last three financial years,
>
> is to be treated as class 1 transaction.

This meant for inducement fees that when the target had a high market value (and accordingly, the size of the fee would be higher) but was hampered by low or negative profitability during the last three years, it was likely for the inducement fee to fall into the definition of a class 1 transaction.

The new version of the UKLA Listing Rules follows the approach of the Takeover Code and defines a break fee as

> a fee payable by a listed company if certain specified events occur which have the effect of materially impeding a transaction or causing the transaction to fail.

Rule 10.2.7R of the Listing Rules provides that a break fee payable in respect of a transaction is to be treated as a class 1 transaction 'if the total value of the fee or the fees in aggregate exceeds':

— In the case of acquisition of a listed company, '1% of the value of the listed company calculated by reference to the offer price' on the basis of the fully diluted equity share capital of the listed company.[76]

— 'In any other case, 1% of the market capitalisation of the listed company'.

While the approach of the Listing Rules resembles that of the Takeover Code in respect of the one per cent threshold in case of takeovers, the Listing Rules depart from the Takeover Code approach in case of multiple break fees. According to the Listing Rules, where a company enters into more than one break fee arrangement, the break fees are to be aggregated for the purposes of the one per cent threshold, whereas under the

[75] See LR 10.13 of the Listing Rules.

[76] Except to the extent that it is recoverable, VAT payable is to be taken into account in determining whether the 1% limit would be exceeded. For a securities exchange offer, the value of the listed company is fixed by reference to the value of the offer at the time the transaction is announced.

Takeover Code, multiple break fees are not aggregated. In that respect, there may be cases where break fees which do not exceed the one per cent threshold imposed by the Code may still require the target's shareholders' approval if the target has already provided similar termination fees in other transactions and deals entered by the Panel, either other takeover offers or not. This approach imposes additional due diligence burdens on the bidder, despite the fact that failure to receive approval does not render the break fee void or unenforceable. Furthermore, this approach provides a substantial benefit to the first bidder who received a break fee, since a break fee given to a second bidder is very likely to require shareholders' approval under the Listing Rules. This clearly affects equality between competitive bidders and is not in line with the approach adopted by the Takeover Code as analysed in chapter six, resulting in an unsatisfactory regulatory conflict between the FSA and the Takeover Panel manifested more clearly in this area.

In addition the approach of the Listing Rules differs from that of the Takeover Code in being broader than the one adopted by the Takeover Panel, seeking also to regulate break or termination fees in other transactions as well. To that extent, fees payable by the bidder on a mutual basis to give effect to a merger agreement or simply in order to assure the exclusive support of the target's board are not restricted by the one per cent limit of the Takeover Code. In contrast, they still fall into the definition of the Listing Rules and thus can be considered as class 1 transactions should they exceed the calculations provided by the Listing Rules. In such cases the approval of the offering company's shareholders would be required.

(iv) *The Legal Implications of Break Fee Agreements*

The courts have yet to examine the validity of break fee agreements in the United Kingdom, although transactions and practices with similarities, such as poison pills[77] and undertakings by the target to pay professional fees associated with the offer (for example accountants' fees)[78] have been the subject of judicial review. In contrast, in the United States, break fee agreements have long been in the centre of high-profile legal battles.[79] Although break fees are not invalid per se, they have been the subject of close scrutiny by the US courts, and in many circumstances they have been enjoined.[80] The question of how break fee agreements are to be treated by

[77] See, eg *Criterion Properties Plc v Stratford UK Properties LLC* [2002] EWCA Civ 1883, [2003] 1 WLR 2108, [2003] 2 BCLC 129 (CA).

[78] *Chaston v SWP Group plc* [2002] EWCA Civ 1999, [2003] 1 BCLC 675.

[79] See, eg the Revlon and Paramount Communication cases: *Revlon, Inc v Mac Andrews & Forbes Holdings, Inc* 506 A2d 173 (Del 1986); *Paramount Communications, Inc v QVC Networks, Inc*, 637 A 2d 34 (Del 1993).

[80] In contrast, US commentators have taken a less strict view toward lock-ups. For an analytical account of US literature and the views of various commentators, see Kahan and Klausner, 'Lockups and the Market of Corporate Control' (n 48 above).

English courts can be split into three sub-questions, one related to contract law concerns and the other two related to company law concerns:

- — Do any restrictions arise from the law of liquidated damages and penalties?
- — Does a break up fee agreement constitute a 'financial assistance' prohibited by section 678(1) of the Companies Act 2006?
- — Could break up fee agreements constitute a breach of directors' fiduciary duties?

(v) *The Law of Liquidated Damages and Penalties*

Under a break fee agreement, bidder and target agree beforehand what shall be payable by way of damages if the target breaches one of its promises made under the agreement, for example, if the target's board fails to recommend the offer to its shareholders, or it recommends a rival bid.

The question whether a break fee, under those circumstances, is actually a liquidated damage or a penalty is a legal one with considerable practical implications. In general, if the inducement fee is a genuine pre-estimate of the loss that will be caused to the bidder, if the contract is broken—for example when the target directors recommend a rival offer to their shareholders contrary to an opposite agreement with the bidder—then the inducement fee is a liquidated damage. However, if the inducement fee is held over the target's board 'in terrorem', as a security to the bidder that the deal will be consummated, it is a penalty. There is an element of oppression in every penalty.[81]

The issue becomes even more important, once considering that an inducement fee always needs to have a predetermined value. This is not only because of the one per cent limit imposed by the Takeover Code, but also because, as it will be argued below, an unlimited agreement to cover the due diligence costs of the bidder will easily fall within the definition of indemnity and thus, will constitute a prohibited financial assistance without any consideration to the materiality of the agreement.[82]

The main difference between the fee being characterised as a liquidated damage and as a penalty is that, in the former case, the fee is enforceable irrespective of the actual loss suffered,[83] while in the latter case, the bidder will only be entitled to a sum equal to its actual loss[84] and the agreement

[81] For a general analysis see HG Beale (ed), *Chitty on Contracts* vol 1, 28th edn (London, Sweet & Maxwell, 1999); also M Furmston, *Law of Contract*, 14th edn (London, Butterworths, 2001).

[82] See below, next part.

[83] *Wallis v Smith* (1882) 21 Ch D 243 at 267.

[84] Beale (ed), *Chitty on Contracts* (n 81 above) para 27-103; Furmston, *Law of Contract* (n 81 above) 689.

will be unenforceable as to the excess.[85] In addition, penalties have for long been under the scrutiny of equity jurisdiction and have in most cases been considered as irrecoverable.[86] It should also be noted that the law of penalties applies not only to break fees where the payment is a sum of money, but also to break fee agreements where the promise is an option or an asset. This is because the law of penalties also applies to a clause, which, upon breach, obliges the party that breaches the contract to transfer some form of property to the innocent party.[87]

The law of penalties does not apply to events that do not constitute breaches by one of the parties. This means that when the inducement fee is triggered by the occurrence of other events, such as a rival bid being eventually accepted by the target shareholders, then the law of penalties and liquidated damages does not apply and the fee is enforceable irrespective of its value relative to the bidder's actual loss, since it is considered a contractual duty.[88] However, if the fee is extravagant, it may be considered as a 'disguised penalty clause' by the court.[89]

Conclusively, inducement fees may be subject to the law of penalties and liquidated damages, mainly when they are used as enforcement of non-financial undertakings, as discussed above (for example not to solicit another bid). In such cases, the value of the inducement fee must be a genuine estimate of the actual loss that the bidder will incur if the deal is not consummated. If the size of the inducement fee is excessive, then the court may enforce it only up to the sum that represents the actual loss. However, if the inducement fee depends on events that are beyond the control of the target's board, no such restrictions apply, as long as the fee is not so extravagant that it could conceal a disguised penalty clause. This means that the bidder is better off, when the break fee agreement provides for a payment in cases where the offer lapses or when a rival bidder acquires the target, than when it attempts to enforce exclusivity provisions, such as no-shop or no-talk covenants or undertakings by the target's board to recommend the offer to the target shareholders.[90]

[85] *Dunlop Pneumatic Tyre Co Ltd v New Garage and Motor Co Ltd* [1915] AC 79 (HL).

[86] See Beale (ed), *Chitty on Contracts* (n 81 above) para 27-102. The onus of showing that the specified sum is a penalty lies upon the party who is sued for its recovery: *Robophone Facilities Ltd v Blank* [1966] 1 WLR 1428. The term used by the parties is not restrictive for the court: *Dunlop Pneumatic Tyre Co v New Garage and Motor Co* [1915] AC 79. See also Furmston, *Law of Contract* (n 81 above) 688–93.

[87] *Jobson v Jobson* [1989] 1 WLR 1026 (CA).

[88] The leading case is *Export Credits Guarantee Department v Universal Oil Products Co* [1983] 1 WLR 399 (HC). See also *Jervis v Harris* [1996] Ch 195. However, see also *Campbell Discount Co Ltd v Bridge* [1961] 1 QB 445. For further discussion on the issue refer to Beale (ed), *Chitty on Contracts* (n 81 above) para 27-111.

[89] *Interfoto Picture Library Ltd v Stiletto Visual Programmes Ltd* [1988] 1 All ER 348 (CA) 358 (Bingham LJ).

[90] Commentators find the common law position in relation to penalties unsatisfactory. See, eg Beale (ed), *Chitty on Contracts* (n 81 above).

(vi) *Financial Assistance*

Another area of concern in relation to the legality of break fee agreements derives from sections 677–683 of the Companies Act 2006, which replace sections 151–154 of the Companies Act 1985. These sections prohibit the provision of financial assistance from a company for the acquisition of its own shares. The key change is that the prohibition on private companies providing financial assistance for a purchase of own shares is not carried forward. The general prohibition on the giving of financial assistance by a public company is required by the Second Company Law Directive,[91] and this prohibition is retained in sub-section (1) of section 678 of the CA 2006. As under the previous regime, the prohibition extends to post-acquisition assistance.[92]

Answering the question of whether an inducement fee falls into the scope of the prohibition in sections 677–683 CA 2006 requires the examination of the following three sub-questions:

1. Does an agreement to pay inducement fees constitute 'financial assistance'?
2. If so, is it one of the forms of 'financial assistance' caught by section 677 of the Companies Act 2006?
3. And, finally, is the financial assistance given for the purpose of the acquisition, or for the purpose of reducing or discharging a liability that has been incurred for the purpose of the acquisition?[93]

(a) Does an agreement to pay inducement fees constitute 'financial assistance'?

As was the case with the Companies Act 1985, the new Act does not provide any definitions of the term 'financial assistance'. Even section 677, which is entitled 'meaning of financial assistance' repeats the supposedly defined term 'financial assistance' as part of the definition. The courts have traditionally considered that what constitutes a financial assistance should be an issue of commercial judgement.[94] Some cases seem to suggest that agreements that only provide encouragement, inducements or

[91] Second Company Law Directive 77/91/EEC.

[92] See s 678(3) of the CA 2006.

[93] See s 678(1) and (3) of the CA 2006.

[94] See *Chaston v SWP Group plc* [2002] EWCA Civ 1999, [2003] 1 BCLC 675; *Charterhouse Investment Trust Ltd v Tempest Diesels Ltd* [1986] BCLC 1; *Barclays Bank plc v British & Commonwealth Holdings plc* [1996] 1 All ER 381. See also *MacNiven (HM Inspector of Taxes) v Westmoreland Investments Ltd* [2001] UKHL 6, [2003] 1 AC 311. Also, E Ferran, 'Corporate Transactions and Financial Assistance: Shifting Policy Perceptions but Static Law' (2004) 63 *Cambridge Law Journal* 225.

incentives[95] or, in general, reassurance[96] to the bidder should not be regarded as financial assistance. This corrective approach lies in the assumption that the financial assistance must have a direct or indirect effect on the price of the acquisition, thus conferring on the purchaser the benefit of making the acquisition partly with the company's money.[97]

Putting this argument into the perspective of inducement fees, it could be argued that if the transaction goes through no payment will be triggered and the bidder will acquire the target's shares by relying fully on its own resources. Thus, the argument continues, inducement fees do not financially assist the bidder to acquire the target's shares by diminishing the price it has to pay. Rather, they only provide it with certain reassurance that the target company is committed to effectuate the deal. The fact that the fee will help the bidder to meet some of its costs if the deal does not take place can only be seen as an additional incentive or a concurrent benefit.

However, such a strict interpretation of the term financial assistance was not accepted by the Court of Appeal in the case of *Chaston v SWP Group plc*.[98] Although the Court in *Chaston* did not directly deal with inducement fees,[99] the case carried considerable similarities, especially with pre-announcement inducement fees. The court held the view that the payments of the accountant's fees in question were to facilitate the progress of the negotiations and to enable the bidder to conclude its due diligence exercise, and, having done so, then to make up its mind whether or not to acquire the shares in the target.[100]

On that basis, the court held it unnecessary for a 'financial assistance' to have an impact on the acquisition price, and effectively suggested that it is sufficient for any inducements or additional benefits to minimise transaction costs for the purchaser, in order to constitute financial assistance, since 'as a matter of commercial reality, they smooth the path to the acquisition of shares'.[101] Hence, *Chaston* leaves little room for arguing that

[95] *MT Realisations Ltd (in liquidation) v Digital Equipment Co Ltd* [2002] EWHC 1628 (Ch), affirmed [2003] EWCA Civ 494.

[96] In *Barclays Bank plc v British & Commonwealth Holdings plc* [1996] 1 All ER 381, [1996] 1 BCLC 1 (CA) 40.

[97] See Ferran, 'Corporate Transactions and Financial Assistance: Shifting Policy Perceptions but Static Law' (n 94 above) 225 Charnley and Breslin, 'Break Fees: Financial Assistance and Directors' Duties' (n 46 above).

[98] *Chaston v SWP Group plc* [2002] EWCA Civ 1999, [2003] 1 BCLC 675.

[99] The case was about the assumption of responsibility by a subsidiary of the target to pay the accountant's fees for the short and long form reports in respect of the transaction.

[100] *Chaston v SWP Group plc* (n 98 above) para 38.

[101] The argument that the prohibition of financial assistance is a penal section and accordingly the definitions of financial assistance in s 152 (now 677 of CA 2006) should not be strained to cover transactions, which are not fairly within them does not help since, according to *Chaston*, the question is whether, from a commercial point of view, the transaction impugned amounts to financial assistance. If the company's participation in the transaction meets that test, no straining of the statutory language occurs. See *Chaston v SWP Group plc*

inducement fees or termination fees do not constitute financial assistance for the purposes of section 151 of the Companies Act 1985 (now section 678 of the Companies Act 2006).[102] This is especially the case with all break fees that seek to anticipate the occurrence of certain events that eventually trigger the payment.

However, what if the break up fee is just a liquidated damage for a breach of covenant given by the target directors? In *Barclays Bank plc v British & Commonwealth Holdings plc* the court accepted that the covenants given by the target company as to the future conduct of its business could not 'financially assist' anyone to buy shares.[103] Although the court in *Chaston* refused to interpret that ruling as a submission that an assistance which merely acted as an inducement to a transaction could never be financial assistance, it seems to have accepted 'en passant' that, when it is not anticipated at the time of giving the covenants that there will be any liability thereunder, any liability that arises from the breach of such covenants cannot constitute financial assistance.[104]

The above case has many similarities to break fee agreements, where the trigger mechanism is a breach of a negative undertaking given by the target's directors, the only difference being that in the latter case an attempt is made to calculate in advance the loss of the bidder and effectively to limit the exposure of the target, in order to ensure compliance with rule 21.2 of the Takeover Code.[105] As a result there may be a case, even after *Chaston*, that such break fees may not constitute financial assistance.

(b) Inducement fees and the types of financial assistance caught by section 152

The second question that arises is whether inducement fees fall within one of the types of financial assistance caught by section 677 of the Companies Act 2006. This is extremely important, since, as was the case under the Companies Act 1985, only those forms of financial assistance are prohibited. Section 677 repeats the types of financial assistance recognised by section 152 of the Companies Act 1985. Two of the types caught by section 677 are relevant in the case of inducement fees: guaranties, securities and

(n 98 above) para 39 of the Court of Appeal decision. See also *Charterhouse Investment Trust Ltd v Tempest Diesels Ltd* [1985] 1 BCLC 10; *Barclays Bank plc v British & Commonwealth Holdings plc* [1995] BCC 1059, [1996] 1 BCLC 1.

[102] The same argument is reached by a number of commentators as well. See Ferran, 'Corporate Transactions and Financial Assistance: Shifting Policy Perceptions but Static Law' (n 94 above) 225; Wippell and Knighton, 'Inducement Fees: A Us Import Takes Root' (n 45 above) 31; C Pearson 'Practice Note: Break Fees' (2004) *www.practicallaw.com/a29103*.

[103] *Barclays Bank plc v British & Commonwealth Holdings plc* [1996] 1 All ER 381, [1996] 1 BCLC 1 (CA) 40.

[104] *Chaston v SWP Group plc* (n 98 above) para 44 (Arden LJ).

[105] However, see about the problems that may arise with such clauses in respect of the law of penalties and liquidated damages.

indemnities under section 677(1)(b)(i) and any other method that results in a material reduction in the net assets of the company that provides the financial assistance (section 677(1)(d)).

By contrast with the term financial assistance, the term indemnity is a legal concept and has a specific technical meaning. An indemnity is a contract by one party to keep the other safe against a loss.[106] An inducement fee can constitute an indemnity if it is structured in a way that seeks to cover all the related costs of the bidder (for example a pre-announcement agreement that the target will cover all the due diligence costs of the bidder). Theoretically, there maybe a case that despite the one per cent cap on inducement fees imposed by the Takeover Code, an agreement may still constitute an indemnity if it seeks to cover all the bidder's costs, and the anticipated costs are not expected to exceed in value the one per cent of the value of the transaction. However, in practice, it is highly unlikely that the Panel will be satisfied with the target assuming an unlimited liability in respect of the acquisition costs.

This leaves section 677(1)(d) as the most relevant type of financial assistance in the case of inducement fees. The difference between case (d) and all other types identified in section 677(1) is that a materiality test is required for the financial assistance to be prohibited. Accordingly, in order for an inducement fee to be considered a prohibited financial assistance, it must result in a material reduction in the net assets of the target.[107]

But what is an acceptable size of an inducement fee? In the United Kingdom, the courts have not yet got the chance to deal with this issue. In the United States the Delaware courts have approved termination fees of up to five per cent of the value of the acquisition, but they have found a termination fee of six or seven per cent unreasonable.[108] The Takeover Code, as seen above, provides that for the purposes of the Code, an inducement fee is acceptable if it does not exceed one per cent of the value of the offer. However, at the same time, the Code stipulates in note 2 on rule 21.2 that the

> view expressed by the Panel in relation to such fees or arrangements can only relate to the Code and must not be taken to extend to any requirements of the Companies Act or any other relevant law.

Similarly, the Listing Rules provide, as seen above, that break fees that exceed one per cent of the value of the company based on the value of the

[106] See E Ferran, *Company Law and Corporate Finance* (New York, Oxford University Press, 1999) 388. See also *Yeoman Credit Ltd v Latter* [1961] 1 WLR 828 (CA) 830; *Barclays Bank plc v British & Commonwealth Holdings plc* [1995] BCC 1059 (CA).

[107] Or where the company has no net assets: s 677(1)(d)(ii).

[108] See *Paramount Communications, Inc v QVC Networks, Inc*, 637 A 2d 34 (Del 1993); *Phelps Dodge Corp v Cyprus Amax Minerals Co* 1999 WL 1054255 [Del Ch Sept 27 1999]. For various example of US inducement fees see Wippell and Knighton, 'Inducement Fees: A US Import Takes Root' (n 45 above) 31.

offer are to be considered as class 1 transactions, which means that they are considered material enough to require shareholders' approval. Nevertheless, this does not predetermine that the same materiality threshold will apply in the case of financial assistance. This is because the purpose of the class 1 rule is to shift decision-making from the board to shareholders, whereas the financial assistance rule provides an absolute prohibition on deviations from the share capital requirements. The Court of Appeal has also stated that there is no specific rule and the question must be answered on the facts of each particular case.[109]

(c) Inducement fees and the purpose of financial assistance

The final question that needs to be answered is whether the break fee is financial assistance actually given for the purpose of the acquisition,[110] or for the purpose of reducing or discharging a liability that has been incurred for the purpose of the acquisition.[111] As Ferran argues,

> interpreting the purpose requirements in s. 151 (now s. 678) is perhaps the trickiest aspect of the law on financial assistance,

and the court in *Chaston* provided little guidance on its interpretation.[112] A full analysis goes beyond the scope of the present work and it suffices to present only certain conclusions that are relevant to inducement fee agreements. First, a transaction could be regarded as a breach of section 678 of the CA 2006 even if a bidder is only proposing an acquisition.[113] This means that the actual occurrence of the acquisition is not an essential element of the offence and thus, a fee paid—even if the transaction fails—can be regarded as given for the purpose of the acquisition.

In addition, it is the time that the break fee agreement is entered into that matters (at which point the potential bidder would be proposing to acquire shares in the target). This is the time when the possible financial assistance is given,[114] and at that time it is likely that there is financial assistance 'for the purposes of the acquisition', since, without the break fee agreement in place, the bidder would not continue with its offer. Since a proposed acquisition suffices for the purposes of section 678 of the CA 2006 (as the case was with section 151 of the Companies Act 1985), there seems to be no difference if an offer is actually posted or announced or even if the break fee agreement is entered before the announcement of the offer and the bidder is still examining whether to announce its firm

[109] *Parlett v Guppys (Bridport) Ltd (No 1)* [1996] 2 BCLC 34, [1996] BCC 299 (CA).
[110] Section 678 (1) of the CA 2006.
[111] Section 678(3) of the CA 2006 (post-acquisition financial assistance)
[112] Ferran, 'Corporate Transactions and Financial Assistance: Shifting Policy Perceptions but Static Law' (n 94 above) 232.
[113] *Chaston v SWP Group plc* (n 98 above) para 42 (Arden LJ).
[114] *Parlett v Guppys (Bridport) Ltd (No 1)* (n 109 above).

intention to make an offer or walk away. Even in the latter case, the purpose of the agreement is to facilitate the bidder to conclude its due diligence process and make up its mind whether to acquire the target on not. The same facts were enough for the court in *Chaston* to consider that the financial assistance was given for the purpose of the acquisition.[115]

However, what if the inducement fee is not given, or at least not given solely, with the purpose of conferring a financial benefit on the bidder, but seeks to ensure a higher price for the target shareholders? Similarly, what if both bidder and target provide similar break fees as part of a merger agreement, they are relatively equal in terms of bargaining power, and the break fee has as its purpose to facilitate the merger (mutual fees)? In both cases the purpose, or at least one of the purposes, of the inducement fees could be argued to be the negotiation of a higher offer price or the consummation of a merger of equals that has been initiated and planned by both parties.

One issue that arises, in respect of the first situation, is whether the prohibition of section 678 extends to financial assistance given to vendors.[116] A break fee that is given to increase the price of the offer eventually benefits the target's shareholders. Since the payment of the fee is also triggered only if the deal does not materialise—for examplem, the offer is rejected by the target shareholders—the target does not contribute financially to the increased premium that is to be paid. Thus, by assuming the liability to pay a break fee to the bidder, the target company indirectly assists its shareholders, who can dispose of their shares at a higher price. Whether they are going to accept or not the offer is a matter that rests within their complete discretion. And, if the fee seeks to distort or interfere with the exercise of such discretion, it is a matter of the law of fiduciary duties or the Takeover Code, and not the law of financial assistance to intervene.

Arden LJ saw no mandate for reading into the financial assistance provisions that the prohibition applies only to financial assistance given to the purchaser.[117] However, the issue in question was whether the fact that the direct recipient of the financial assistance was someone other than the purchaser of the shares precluded or not the situation from falling within the ban on financial assistance, if the purchaser indirectly benefited as well. In our situation, the issue is exactly the opposite, namely that, although the party to the inducement fee is the bidder, it is the target shareholders who indirectly benefit from the fee by receiving a higher premium.

This is an area where the principal or larger corporate purpose exemptions of section 678 (2) and (4) (restating section 153 of the Companies Act

[115] See *Chaston v SWP Group plc* (n 98 above) para 56 (Ward LJ).

[116] For an analysis of the policy concerns associated with the financial assistance to vendors see Ferran, 'Corporate Transactions and Financial Assistance: Shifting Policy Perceptions but Static Law' (n 94 above) 225.

[117] *Chaston v SWP Group plc* (n 98 above) para 40.

1985 as interpreted by the House of Lords in *Brady v Brady*[118]) could be relevant. In the case of inducement fees, this could mean that the principal purpose is to increase the offer price; and in the case of mutual fees the larger corporate purpose required by section 153 (now 678(2) and (4)) could be the consummation of the merger agreement between the two companies.

Overall, such an interpretation does not sit well with the court's views in *Chaston*, where it held that section 153 (now 678(2) and (4)) made it clear that a transaction could fall within section 151 (now 678(1) and (3)) even if only one of the purposes for which it was carried out was to assist the acquisition of shares.[119] However, in *Brady v Brady*, Lord Oliver, giving the definition of the principal purpose, stated that

> the inquiry (in the principal purpose exemption) is whether the assistance given was principally in order to relieve the purchaser of shares in the company of his indebtedness resulting from the acquisition or whether it was principally for some other purpose—for instance, the acquisition from the purchaser of some asset which the company requires for its business.[120]

Nevertheless, discharging the directors' fiduciary duties to their company, which in the case of takeovers is translated as seeking the highest price for their shareholders, cannot constitute by itself a purpose and, even less, a principal purpose within the meaning of the prohibition in the Act.[121] Similarly, the narrow interpretation of the larger corporate purpose test, on whose meaning little guidance has been given by the courts,[122] provides no clear-cut assurance that a merger of equals could be the larger purpose required by section 678.

Overall, it could be argued that, although there seems to be some room (even after *Chaston*) for interpretations that can navigate inducement fees, under specific circumstances, out of the minefield of the financial assistance provisions, any protection can only be circumstantial and thus, of little practical use. The Companies Act 2006 also has not changed this position since any changes introduced were primarily related to the abolition of the prohibition for private companies. In addition, in practice, any such inquiry is less necessary, since most of the inducement fees are more likely to be exempted on the basis of the materiality test of section 677(1)(d), partly because of the Takeover Code one per cent limit in that respect.

[118] *Brady v Brady* [1989] AC 755 (HL).

[119] *Chaston v SWP Group plc* (n 98 above) para 50.

[120] *Brady v Brady* [1989] AC 755 (HL) 779 (Lord Oliver). In addition, the court must be satisfied that the company's directors gave the assistance in good faith for the bests interests of the company after having also considered that the assistance does not jeopardise the company's ability to pay its debts to its creditors: *ibid*, 777.

[121] See *Chaston v SWP Group plc* (n 98 above) para 46.

[122] *Chaston v SWP Group plc* (n 98 above) para 46. See also Ferran, *Company Law and Corporate Finance* (n 106 above) 393.

Finally, it should also be noted that reverse inducement fees, namely fees payable by the bidder in return for exclusivity by the target, do not fall under the scope of the prohibition of section 678, since they are not given for the purpose of an acquisition but to facilitate a disposal of shares. The exception is share-for-share exchange offers, where the same problem arises for the acquirer's side, since such a reverse break fee may be considered as indirect financial assistance given to target shareholders for acquiring shares in the bidder in exchange for their target shares.

(vii) *Fiduciary Duties*

As with exclusivity undertakings, break fees may raise problems from the perspective of target directors' fiduciary duties. Generally, the same test established in *Heron* and subsequently in *Fulham* applies. This means for the case of break fees the following.

When deciding whether to enter a break fee agreement with a particular bidder, the target's directors should act in the best interests of their company, and with due care. As seen above, in the case of takeovers, the best interests of the company have been judged to reflect the interests of the current shareholders, and the target directors were found to discharge their duty by seeking to obtain the best price.[123] Accordingly, the target's directors discharge their duties if, at the time they enter the break fee agreement, they honestly believe that the bidder, first, is seriously contemplating making an offer and has secured the necessary funds, and secondly, would not offer the same price or would not make an offer without the break fee clause. In addition, the target directors should not be aware or reasonably expect that the fee will prevent them from negotiating with a rival bidder who is offering a higher price, or prevent such a rival bidder from making a higher offer, unless they have reasons to believe that it will not be successful (for example, the second bidder has difficulties in securing the necessary funds). Finally, as established in the *Criterion Properties* case,[124] the target directors should exercise their discretion to provide an inducement fee for proper purposes, and not with the purpose to entrench their position against a less welcomed rival bidder.

But even in cases where it could be found that a break fee was given for an improper purpose, the position of the case law was, until recently, that such a break fee was not automatically unenforceable unless the bidder knew enough about the motivations of the target's board.[125] In deciding

[123] See the analysis of fiduciary duties for exclusivity undertakings.

[124] *Criterion Properties Plc v Stratford UK Properties LLC* (n 77 above). Although the court was concerned with a poison pill agreement, there is no reason for a different treatment of a break fee agreement, if under the specific circumstances it entrenches the position of the target management. However, see the more general analysis on the multipurpose test in ch 4 above.

[125] *Bank of Credit and Commerce International (Overseas) Ltd v Akindele* [2001] Ch 437; [2000] 3 WLR 1423 (CA); *Criterion Properties Plc v Stratford UK Properties LLC* (n 77 above); See also

whether to set aside the agreement it did not suffice that the bidder had knowledge of the relevant facts. In contrast, it was necessary to consider the actions and knowledge of the parties in the context of their commercial relationship as a whole.[126] However, the House of Lords has recently rejected this approach and held that it suffices to examine whether the parties had the authority to enter into the specific agreement, making the issue of the conscionability or unconscionability of the bidder's behaviour in seeking to hold the target to the break fee agreement completely irrelevant.[127] The House of Lords' decision does not entirely clarify whether an agreement—for example, a break fee agreement—that under the specific circumstances constitutes a breach of the target directors' duties to their company, can nonetheless be found to be one which the target directors had ostensible authority to enter into, or whether any breach of duty on behalf of the board would mean that it lacks ostensible authority and so cannot bind the company, no matter how much in good faith the other contracting party is.[128]

If the former is correct, then the question of the other contracting party's knowledge is important. In this case the bidder can enforce the break fee agreement, relying on the target board's ostensible authority, provided it does not know the board does not have actual authority to enter into the contract.[129] If the latter is correct, then the bidder needs to establish that there is no breach of duty on the part of the board when putting forward the agreement.

The statutory codification of Director's duties is not likely to affect the aforementioned analysis on the implications of fiduciary duties law on break fees. Nevertheless, an implication may arise out of the wording of section 172 of the Companies Act 2006. The statutory duty of section 172 codifies the current law and enshrines in statute what is commonly referred to as the principle of 'enlightened shareholder value'. The duty requires a director to act in the way he or she considers, in good faith, would be most likely to promote the success of the company for the benefit of its members as a whole and, in doing so, and have regard to the factors non-exhaustively listed in the section. The question that arises is to what extent it is permissible under section 172 for the target board to provide a break fee when it knows that the bidder, for example, is expected to

Manchester Trust v Furness [1895] 2 QB 539 (CA); *Eagle Trust plc v SBC Securities* [1993] 1 WLR 484 (ChD) 497; *Re Montagu's Settlement Trusts, Re, Duke of Manchester v national Westminster Bank Ltd* [1987] Ch 264 (Ch); *Belmont Finance Corp v Williams Furniture Ltd (No 2)* [1980] 1 All ER 393(CA).

126 *Criterion Properties Plc v Stratford UK Properties LLC* (n 77 above) para 40 (Carnwath LJ). It should be noted though that the case was a summary judgment and the issue was whether the action will go on trial. The court considered the enforceability of a poison pill agreement.

127 *Criterion Properties Plc v Stratford UK Properties LLC* [2004] UKHL 28, [2004] 1 WLR 1846.

128 *Ibid*, see the analysis in paras 28–9 (Lord Scott). See also above in ch 4 for a more thorough discussion on the House of Lords decision.

129 *Criterion Properties Plc v Stratford UK Properties LLC* (n 127 above) para 31.

absorb or even dissolve, or asset-strip the company. How does such a break fee promote the 'success of the company'? A strict approach would suggest the exact opposite. The success of the company is not synonymous with the shareholders receiving the highest price for their investment, especially under the principle of the 'enlightened shareholder value', where, for example, the interests of the employees must be considered as well. The same applies of course in the case where the target's board decides whether or not to recommend the bid and provide its support for the offer, but providing a break fee further increases its commitment and support for the bid, and amplifies its responsibility. It remains to be seen how this new wording is going to be interpreted by the courts, and it is worth exploring in the form of empirical studies how this new approach affects the target board's attitude in committing to offers made and providing break fees.

In most cases, fiduciary complications are, in practice, minimised by the size limit imposed by the Takeover Code on break fees and the class 1 requirement for shareholders' approval that is specific to break fees. However, a specific concern arises in cases where payment of a break fee is triggered if the target directors decide either not to recommend the offer or recommend an offer made by a rival bidder. Are such break fees enforceable, in the light of the fact that the target's directors, as analysed above, cannot fetter the exercise of their duty to provide honest and accurate advice to their shareholders about the proposed offers?[130]

The answer partly lies in the law of liquidated damages and penalties examined above. If the fee is given as a liquidated damage or penalty for the breach of the undertaking to recommend the offer to the target shareholders, then it is more likely that it will not be enforceable.[131] This is because the courts are more likely to subordinate the break fee to the standard of review of the primary agreement whose breach triggers the fee.[132]

However, the bidder can bypass this problem by structuring the fee as a contractual duty that is triggered by the occurrence of the event that the (independent) directors in the target do not recommend the offer or recommend another offer, or even that the offer fails or a competing offer is successful. In such cases, the break fee has no impact on the actual exercise of the directors' duty to advise the target's shareholders. If, subsequently, the target directors feel that the situation has changed so as not to be able to recommend the offer, they are free to do so. Accordingly, the standard of review established in the *Crowther* and *Rackham* cases is not relevant. However, if the size of the fee is such that, under the specific circumstances, it prevents the target's directors from changing their views and

[130] See the *John Crowther Group v Carpets International* and *Rackham v Peek Foods Ltd* cases (nn 8 and 23 above).

[131] See above about penalties.

[132] See above about penalties.

recommending another offer, then it is most likely that they have in the first place breached their fiduciary duties or their duty of care, at the time that they entered the break fee agreement.

The same applies to break fees payable in cases where the target's shareholders decline an offer. If such agreements prevent the target's shareholders from freely exercising their power to elect not to accept the offer, then it is most likely that the fee will be found to have been given for an improper purpose in the very first place.

III SECURING THE SUPPORT OF MAJOR SHAREHOLDERS

A Irrevocable undertakings

An irrevocable commitment consists of an undertaking to accept the offer and not to exercise any right to withdraw such acceptance, usually accompanied by the qualification that the commitment will not have any effect if the bidder fails to receive the required amount of tenders to declare its bid unconditional as to acceptances.[133]

From the above description it follows that irrevocable undertakings do not allow the initial bidder to recoup some of its identification costs, as toeholds do.[134] This is because the bidder actually does not acquire any shares which it can subsequently tender at a premium to another bidder. However, irrevocable undertakings do help to deter competition and increase the probability of an offer being accepted. There are a number of advantages and disadvantages associated with using irrevocable undertakings in the course of a takeover offer and prior to it.

Irrevocable undertakings did not immediately give rise to a disclosure of a concert party agreement under section 204 of the Companies Act 1985, since such a disclosure was only triggered on the first acquisition of the shares pursuant to the agreement.[135] That meant that they did not count for breaching the threshold of three per cent. Rather, their disclosure was deferred until the actual announcement of the bidder's intention to make an offer.[136]

However, the automatic disclosure obligations contained in sections 198 to 211 of Part 6 of the 1985 Act were repealed and replaced by regulations under the authority given to the FSA by new section 89A of the Financial Services and Markets Act 2000 (as inserted by section 1266 of the Companies Act 2006), in implementation of the Transparency Directive. In

[133] For a further analysis of the context of irrevocable undertakings see G Stedman, *Takeovers* (London, Longman, 1993) 186.

[134] See ch 6 above.

[135] See s 204(2)(b) of the CA 1985.

[136] See r 2.5(b)(iii)(c) of the Takeover Code.

the regulations, a different concept of 'interest in voting rights' is adopted in order to implement the Transparency Directive. This basic notification requirement in relation to changes in voting rights is extended to entitlements to acquire, dispose of, or exercise voting rights in certain situations. The situations include those: where an agreement is concluded between two or more parties, which obliges the holders of voting rights to adopt a lasting common policy towards the management of the issuer and vote their rights in concert; or where a person or entity may exercise voting rights at its discretion, in the absence of specific instructions from shareholders by way of a proxy.

Transparency Directive-based notification requirements are also extended to include arrangements that result in an entitlement to acquire, on such party's own initiative alone, under a formal agreement, shares already issued to which voting rights are attached.[137] To that extent, normal irrevocable undertakings still will not constitute a notifiable arrangement under the new rules, since they will normally be conditional on the outcome of the offer or the emergence of a new bidder. However, there may be circumstances where the wording of such undertakings gives rise to a notification requirement. This is when for example:

- undertakings are given pursuant to an option agreement entered into between the potential bidder and the target shareholder; or
- voting rights attached to the shares subject to the irrevocable commitment are transferred for the interim period to the bidder; or
- the bidder can exercise such voting rights as a proxy without instructions by the target shareholder; or
- the takeover is effected through a scheme of arrangement and the irrevocable undertakings have the form of an undertaking to vote in favour of proposed scheme.

On top of the above circumstances, the question that arises is whether irrevocable commitments, followed by an undertaking to vote in favour of the offer in any resolution that the target may have to pass in the context of the offer, would be considered as notifiable entitlements over voting rights or not. The answer to the question lies in identifying whether the purpose for the voting is the 'adoption of a lasting common policy towards the management of the company'. For example, could voting against a possible proposal by the target's board to implement defensive measures be considered as part of a lasting common policy towards the management of the company, to the extent that it facilitates the takeover offer? A strict interpretation of the Directive could suggest so, since it is clear that the intention of the Transparency Directive is to impose ongoing obligations on shareholders in respect of acquisitions and disposals of both

[137] Article 10 of the Transparency Directive. See also the table in r 5.2.1 of the Disclosure and Transparency Rules Instrument 2006.

shares and voting rights.[138] In other words, there is an element in such irrevocable undertakings that kicks in before the actual completion of the offer and regulates the voting in the target with the purpose of facilitating the change of control in the company.

However, this approach is not in line either with the treatment of irrevocable commitments under the Takeover Code or the meaning that the Panel attributes to shareholders' actions that are considered as board-control seeking. One could argue, though, that the Disclosure and Transparency Rules and the Code are two different sets of rules with different mandates and rationales. The Disclosure and Transparency Rules seek to promptly alert the market about major shares and voting rights movements, while the relevant Takeover Code rules seek to identify circumstances where joint behaviour amounts to acquisition of control for the purposes of the Code or affects the terms on which such acquisition of control will be made.

The Panel's position with regard to shareholders' voting is that an expression of support for one side or the other (and hence a commitment to vote in any way in favour of the offer),[139] including the granting of a proxy, would not of itself result in the shareholders approached being deemed to be acting in concert with that side. There may, however, be other factors evidencing this.[140]

In addition, the Code's definition of interests in shares is drafted in a way that excludes irrevocable undertakings except in the case where a person is restricted by the Code from exceeding the 30 per cent threshold (rule 5). This means that although irrevocable undertakings are considered by rule 5 as restricted transactions in circumstances where, once aggregated with the bidder's shareholdings, the latter pass the 30 per cent threshold, rule 9 is not triggered by irrevocable undertakings.[141] Accordingly, it is possible for a bidder, when it is allowed by rule 5, to pass the 30 per cent threshold by virtue of irrevocable commitments, without having to make a mandatory offer.[142]

While before the announcement of the offer, the treatment of irrevocable undertakings as to whether they constitute notifiable events depends on their structure and terms of the agreement, as described above—with the general rule being that under normal circumstances no notice will be

[138] CESR's Final Technical Advice on Possible Implementing Measures of the Transparency Directive (June 2005) 29.

[139] The wording in brackets was added by the author.

[140] See The Panel on Takeovers and Mergers, PCP 10 *Consultation Paper Issued by the Code Committee of the Panel: Shareholder Activism and Acting in Concert; Revision Proposals Relating to Note 2 on Rule 9.1 of the Takeover Code* (March 2002) para 2.5 and below.

[141] See the definitions section of the Takeover Rules: a person is defined as 'having an interest in securities' if— '(5) in the case of Rule 5 only, he has received an irrevocable commitment in respect of them'. See also, regarding the pre-Takeovers Directive regime, Stedman, *Takeovers* (n 133 above) 190.

[142] See r 5.2 in conjunction with r 9 of the Takeover Code.

triggered when normal undertakings are received—during the offer, the position of the bidder with regard to irrevocable undertakings or letters of intent received must be publicly disclosed and updated any time changes occur, in accordance with rule 8.4 of the Code. A disclosure of the procuring of an irrevocable commitment or a letter of intent must provide full details of the nature of the commitment or letter including:

— the number of relevant securities of each class to which the irrevocable commitment or letter of intent relates;
— the identity of the person from whom the irrevocable commitment or letter of intent has been procured;
— in respect of an irrevocable commitment, the circumstances (if any) in which it will cease to be binding; and
— in the case of an irrevocable commitment or a letter of intent procured prior to the announcement of a firm intention to make an offer under rule 2.5, the value (and any other material terms) of the possible offer in respect of which the commitment or letter has been procured.

The effectiveness of irrevocable undertakings is also hampered by a number of regulatory restrictions and practical limitations. First, seeking irrevocable commitments before an actual announcement of the offer is not easy in the light of the Panel's scrutiny about secrecy before the announcement of offers.[143] In addition, once an announcement has been made, the bidder who wishes to contact a small number of private individuals or small corporate shareholders with a view to seeking an irrevocable commitment to accept or refrain from accepting an offer, must consult the Panel in advance.[144] The Panel will wish to be satisfied that the proposed arrangements will provide adequate information as to the nature of the commitment sought, and a realistic opportunity to consider whether or not that commitment should be given and to obtain independent advice, if required.[145] In addition, such arrangements should not contain any special inducements beyond those extended under the offer to the other shareholders of the same class.[146] Rule 16 provides that

> [e]xcept with the consent of the Panel, an offeror or persons acting in concert with it may not make any arrangements with shareholders and may not deal or enter into arrangements to deal in shares of the offeree company, or enter into arrangements which involve acceptance of an offer, either during an offer or when one is reasonably in contemplation, if there are favourable conditions attached which are not being extended to all shareholders.

[143] Rule 2.1 of the Takeover Code.
[144] Rule 4.3 of the Takeover Code.
[145] Note on r 4.3 of the Takeover Code. The Panel must also be consulted before a telephone campaign is conducted with a view of gathering irrevocable commitments in connection with an offer. See r 19.5 note 3.
[146] See r 16 of the Code and General Principle 1.

An irrevocable commitment to accept an offer, combined with an option to put the shares should the offer fail, will also be regarded as such an arrangement.[147]

Irrevocable undertakings could also give rise to concerns about acting in concert for the bidder. The Takeover Code's definition of acting in concert primarily provides (at note 9) that

> a person will not normally be treated as acting in concert with an offeror or an offeree company by reason only of giving an irrevocable commitment. However, the Panel will consider the position of such a person in relation to the offeror or the offeree company (as the case may be) in order to determine whether he is acting in concert if either:
>
> (a) the terms of the irrevocable commitment give the offeror or the offeree company (as the case may be) either the right (whether conditional or absolute) to exercise or direct the exercise of the voting rights attaching to the shares or general control of them; or
> (b) the person acquires an interest in more shares.
>
> The Panel should be consulted before the acquisition of any interest in shares in such circumstances.

Although gathering irrevocable undertakings is usually made off the market, there may be circumstances, especially before the bidder is going public, where such dealings may fall within the scope of the insider dealing provisions of the Criminal Justice Act 1993. This may be the case when such dealings involve a 'professional intermediary', such as the bidder's financial adviser.[148] However, two statutory defences may be available: first, that there is no expectation of any profit attributable to the inside information (because the information will be reflected in the offer price),[149] or secondly, that the offer would have proceeded anyway, at the same price, in the absence of the inside information.[150] This is because, neither the offeror buys shares in the target nor does the target shareholder, who gives the undertaking, sell his shares at the time when the undertaking is given. The actual transfer of shares takes place after the offer is announced, on the terms of the announced offer, which are available to all target shareholders, and only if the offer is accepted by the target shareholders. Finally, in relation to market abuse, irrevocable undertakings raise similar concerns to any other form of stake-building.[151]

Irrevocable undertakings are also accompanied by other practical limitations. First of all, seeking irrevocable undertakings may constitute an investment advertisement—now 'financial promotion' under section 21 of

[147] Rule 16, note 1 of the Takeover Code.
[148] Sections 52(3) and 59 of the Criminal Justice Act 1993.
[149] See s 53(1)(a) of the Criminal Justice Act 1993.
[150] See s 53(1)(c) of the Criminal Justice Act 1993.
[151] See ch 6 above.

the FSMA 2000. In addition, institutional shareholders rarely wish to give irrevocable undertakings, since they want to have as many choices open as possible, and if they do so, they will probably insist on a qualification that the commitment can be withdrawn if subsequently a higher bid is made. Ruling out institutional shareholders, the main target group left in seeking irrevocable commitments is any block-holders in the target. This is the main reason why seeking irrevocable undertakings is a technique that has more mileage going for it in relation to friendly, rather than hostile takeovers.

B Financial Undertakings by Major Shareholders: The Case of Shareholders' Break Fees

(i) *Typology*

There may be cases where it makes commercial sense for the bidder to require from major shareholders in the target a more substantial form of commitment to its offer than a (semi-hard) irrevocable undertaking. Shareholders' break fees can take various forms similar to the ones described above in respect of break fees assumed by the target's directors.

Normally, under such an agreement, the target's shareholder assumes the obligation to pay a fee to the bidder in cases where the former decides not to accept the bidder's offer, or when a competitive bid at a higher value (of a certain percentage of the first offer) is accepted. Break fee agreements may also be given by the offeror rather than by the target's shareholders. The bidder may have to enter into such an arrangement with major shareholders in return for a period of exclusivity over a competitive bidder.

A notable example, in the UK practice, of a break fee given by target shareholders was the break fee agreement that accompanied Gannett's offer for Newsquest in 1999: Gannett (the bid vehicle) entered an agreement with KKR and Cinven (venture capitalists), both major shareholders in Newsquest, under which KKR and Cinven would, if a competing offer was made and they did not accept the Gannett offer, pay Gannett a fee on a very complicated basis. Depending on the disposal price per share, in its most extreme form, the break fee amounted to almost 10 per cent of the value of Gannett's offer for each of Newsquest's shares.[152] This was possible because break fees given by target shareholders are not subject to the

[152] If the disposal price per share was more than 400p, but less than 495p, KKR and Cinven should pay an amount per share equal to 22.6 % of the excess over 400p; if the disposal price per share was 495p or more but less than 600p, an amount per share of 21.5p was payable, plus an amount equal to 20.4% of the excess over 495p; if the disposal price per share was 600p or more, an amount per share of 42.9p was payable. See Pearson, 'Practice Note: Break Fees' (n 102 above).

one per cent cap of the Takeover Code.[153] For that, shareholders' financial undertakings not only serve as a hedging mechanism for recouping the costs occurred during the due diligence process, but also they represent a more effective deterring mechanism than normal break fees, which are subject to the size limitations of the Takeover Code. However, material break fees may be subject to other provisions of the Code.[154]

(ii) *Legal and Regulatory Concerns*

Break fees given by major shareholders do not constitute financial assistance by definition and are unlikely to cause any problems with fiduciary duties, unless the shareholder promising the fee has an involvement in the management of the target and is found to be a shadow director. However a number of regulatory issues arise.

During the offer period, an agreement conferring a substantial break fee may (apart from raising a requirement of disclosure as an irrevocable undertaking under note 14 on rule 8.4 of the Code) also, subject to its specificities, constitute a dealing in shares that is discloseable under rule 8, and under the Disclosure and Transparency Rules.[155] Before the abolition of SARs, a disclosure could be required under rule 3 of the SARs in cases where the agreement was entered before the commencement of the offer period, depending on the value of the break fee, the size of the shareholdings that it referred to, and the size of the bidder's stake in the target.[156]

In addition, a break fee agreement is likely to fall within the definition of an indemnity arrangement, or an agreement which may be an inducement to deal or refrain from dealing, according to note 6 on rule 8 of the Takeover Code. In such cases, not only will any person who is party to such an agreement with the bidder be considered, for the purposes of the Code, as an associate of the offeror, but it is very likely to mean that such a person is acting in concert with the offeror. In such a case, rules 4, 5, 6, 9 and 11 of the Code will apply.[157]

Although the analysis of these rules is deferred for the next chapter, it suffices to say that their application affects the speed at which the bidder can build a stake in the target (rule 5), or even the ability of the bidder or its concert parties to acquire additional rights (rule 4), the price at which the bidder will have to make the offer (rule 6) and the consideration offered (rule 11). The bidder may also be required to make a mandatory offer, according to the requirements of rule 9. Since the parties to such a

[153] See above for normal break fees.
[154] See below.
[155] See above.
[156] See r 3 of the SARs. However, see above the discussion about transparency rules, that equally applies to break fees received by major shareholders as well.
[157] Rules 7 and 24 of the Takeover Code will also apply.

break fee agreement will be deemed to act in concert, the shareholdings to which the break fee refers will be added to the bidder's stake in the target for the purposes of rule 9.

Finally, in the case of break fees payable by the bidder to selected major shareholders, such arrangements may constitute a breach of General Principle 1 and fall under the prohibition of special deals with favourable conditions in rule 16 of the Takeover Code, and the bidder may be required to extend the terms of the arrangement to all shareholders. According to note 1 on rule 16,

> an arrangement to deal with favourable conditions attached includes any arrangement where there is a promise to make good to a vendor of shares any difference between the sale price and the price of any subsequent successful offer. An irrevocable commitment to accept an offer combined with an option to put the shares should the offer fail will also be regarded as such an arrangement [namely, one conferring a private benefit to certain shareholders].

In addition,

> arrangements which contain a benefit or potential benefit to the person acting in concert (beyond normal expenses and carrying costs) are . . . normally prohibited'.[158]

Rule 16 also covers cases where the inducement fee has as a purpose the remuneration of a shareholder in an offeree company for the part that he has played in promoting the offer. However, the Panel will normally consent to such remuneration, provided that the shareholding is not substantial and it can be demonstrated that a person who had performed the same services, but had not at the same time been a shareholder, would have been entitled to receive no less remuneration.[159]

Finally, there may be cases where the inducement fee payable to the target's shareholder consists of the purchase of an unwanted company asset of the target or the offeror by the target's shareholder on favourable terms, or the retaining of a management interest of the shareholder in the target. In such cases, the arrangement is not practically capable of being extended to all shareholders.[160] The Panel is likely to consent to such arrangements provided that the arrangements are subject to a publicly discloseable independent valuation of their fairness and reasonableness and the transaction is approved by the remaining acquiring or target's shareholders, depending on which entity the benefit is accruing from.[161]

[158] Note 1 on r 16 of the Takeover Code.
[159] See note 3 on r 16 of the Takeover Code.
[160] See note 2 on r 16 of the Takeover Code.
[161] See notes 2 and 4 of r 16 of the Takeover Code. In cases of a retaining of a managerial interest, shareholders' approval is only required if the shareholder in question and the bidder hold more than 5% of the target's shares. See note 4 of r 16 of the Code.

IV CONCLUSION

This chapter builds on the analysis of the previous chapter and addresses auction risks in friendly takeovers. In a friendly takeover, the bidder's protection is contractual in nature. An exclusivity agreement with the target's board can include either non-financial undertakings, such as no-shop, no-talk or recommendation covenants by the target's board, or financial undertakings in the form of inducement or termination fees. Non-financial undertakings were found to be less effective both for legal and practical reasons. Positive undertakings to negotiate and undertakings by the target's directors to recommend the offer to their shareholders were found to be unenforceable, while no-talk covenants must include a let-out that permits the target to comply with the Takeover Code requirements on the provision of equal information to all competitive bidders. In contrast, termination fees can protect the initial bidder by permitting it to recoup some of its due diligence and transaction costs.

Law and regulation, though, prevent the initial bidder from effectively eliminating competition, by limiting the size of the inducement fee. The Takeover Code permits inducement fees provided that they do not exceed one per cent of the value of the bid, although higher inducement fees can be agreed with the approval of the target shareholders. Changes in the Listing Rules, however, make the size of the break fee dependent on the aggregate value of all similar termination fees given by the target on other occasions. Financial assistance provisions, under which inducement fees are initially caught, also provide for a materiality exemption. However, the size permitted by the Code, although indicative, does not necessarily bind courts in determining the permissive level of inducement fees under the financial assistance provisions. Moreover, the approval by the target's shareholders of a larger inducement fee is not enough to set aside the application of the financial assistance prohibition. Finally, the wording used in section 172 of the Companies Act 2006 regarding the directors' duty to promote 'the success of the company' raises questions on how the section is going to be interpreted by the courts in cases of inducement fees and exclusivity undertakings. In this respect, it is worth exploring in the form of empirical studies how this new approach affects the target board's attitude in committing to offers made and providing break fees.

Limiting the size of inducement fees to reflect a genuine attempt of the bidder to retrieve its actual loss, in cases where it loses the target, achieves an efficient trade-off between the interests of the parties involved, since it protects the bidder's shareholders from the costs of making an unsuccessful bid, and does not deprive the target's shareholders of a genuinely higher-value offer. However, further research is required to determine whether the current level of permitted break fees provides an adequate protection to the initial bidder.

In addition, although it could be more appropriate for the break fee agreements to be entirely excluded from the statutory financial assistance prohibition (since they represent a negotiated arrangement that benefits not only the bidder but also the target shareholders through an increase in the offer price), unfortunately no steps were taken in the statutory review of the prohibition through the Companies Act 2006, to alter the previous regime apart from excluding altogether private companies from the financial assistance regime. Such an approach could allow the Panel to raise the current level of permitted break fees. At the same time, any abuse of the target directors' power to enter into break fee agreements with the purpose of interfering with their shareholders' decision, can be effectively addressed by the Takeover Code's prohibition of defensive actions without the consent of the target shareholders and the general law of fiduciary duties. In contrast, the revisions performed in the Listing Rules—ie the aggregation requirement—effectively resulted in limiting the circumstances where no shareholders' approval is required for the conclusion of a break fee agreement and, hence, limiting in practice the one per cent threshold.

Finally, the bidder can seek the support of major shareholders in the target, who can provide either semi-hard irrevocable undertakings that they are going to accept the offer, or termination fees similar in structure to those provided by the target's board. Such fees may not carry the financial assistance and fiduciary duties complications, but they may affect the position of the bidder, since such shareholders could be considered for the purposes of the Takeover Code as persons acting in concert. This may affect the price and consideration that the bidder has to offer, or even expose the offeror to the requirement to make a mandatory offer.

8

Regulatory Risk: Equality Rules and Transaction Costs

I INTRODUCTION

IN THE FIRST part of this paper, where internal risks have been considered, it has been argued that wealth transfers from the acquiring to the target shareholders may be associated with conflicts of interests between the acquiring shareholders and their managers—such as empire building and hubris—or with overpayment. Similarly, in the two previous chapters, it has been suggested that the existence of a rival bidder, actual or potential, may give rise to an increase in the takeover premium offered to the target's shareholders, as a result of either an actual auction or a deterring bid by the initial bidder. It has also been emphasised that any rule that increases the period for which an offer must remain open increases auction likelihood and, accordingly, takeover premia.[1] However, as will be analysed in this chapter, there is a more direct relation between regulation and high takeover premia.

An important aspect of many takeover regulatory regimes is a concern for horizontal equity.[2] Many rules seek to protect the target's minority shareholders and ensure that they will be fairly treated by receiving the opportunity to tender their shares on equal terms. Such rules usually demand an equal treatment of all shareholders of the same class, both in respect of the price and the type of the consideration offered. The level of horizontal equity desired varies among jurisdictions, from 'highest price' and mandatory cash offer rules[3] to just pro rata acceptance of shares in over-subscribed offers.[4] In other cases, such considerations may simply be limited to fairness concerns without any direct reference to equal treatment.[5] Some rules may

[1] See also Romano 'A Guide to Takeovers' in KJ Hopt and E Wymeersch (eds), *European Takeovers: Law and Practice* (London, Butterworths, 1992).

[2] *Ibid*.

[3] The City Code on Takeovers and Mergers and the EU Directive on Takeover Bids (Directive 2004/25/EC at OJ L142/12 2004).

[4] See s 14(d)(6) of the Securities Exchange Act 1934 ('the Williams Act') (US).

[5] Some of the US State anti-takeover laws.

also prohibit the acquirer from engaging in any coercive actions, such as two-tier or partial bids.[6]

The inclusion of such provisions in a takeover regulation lies in three assumptions. First, the company law rules protecting minority interests within the company or a group of companies may not be adequate in protecting the target's shareholders—who are not given the opportunity to tender their shares—against a new transferee or acquirer of control.[7] This is a strong position of the new Takeovers Directive, which does not allow the Member States to use the existing statutory protection for minority shareholders in a company as an excuse for not providing for a mandatory offer rule.[8]

Secondly, not all shareholders have the same access to the market. On that basis, non-controlling shareholders should be treated equally with majority owners, corporate shareholders and institutional investors. At a market level, this enhances market confidence and encourages minority investment.[9]

Thirdly, target shareholders should be entitled to make an undistorted choice. This derives from the fact that, in the context of a takeover, the whole weight of deciding the outcome of an offer lies in the hands of the target's shareholders. In that sense, and taking into account the collective action problems that they face, the bidder may engage in a number of coercive actions that can pressurise the target's shareholders into accepting an offer that is not in their best interests. The main efficiency concern is that such coercive actions may defeat or jeopardise the operation of the market of corporate control, on which so much importance is bestowed by commentators and regulators alike.[10]

Horizontal equity is a cornerstone principle of takeover regulation and this is an additional reason that makes it imperative to assess the effects of such a policy on the other half of a takeover transaction, namely the acquirer and its shareholders.

[6] The City Code on Takeovers and Mergers and many US State anti-takeover laws.

[7] See,eg the French example of the development of a minority exit mechanism in relation to transfers of control prior to a mechanism for accumulation of control. PL Davies, 'The Notion of Equality in European Takeovers' in J Payne (ed), *Takeovers in English and German Law* (Oxford, Hart Publishing, 2002).

[8] According to the new EU Directive on Takeover Bids, Justification on Amendment 21, Art 6(3)(e): 'The offeror should always be required to acquire 100% of the securities. He must therefore accept any offer to sell securities at the bid price during the validity of his takeover bid. The purpose of takeover law is among other things to protect minority shareholders. Restrictions involving specific shares in a company cannot be the purpose of safeguarding minority shareholders under takeover law'. Report on the proposal for a European Parliament and Council Directive on Takeover Bids. (COM(2002) 534–C5-0481/2002–2000/0240(COD)).

[9] Davies, 'The Notion of Equality in European Takeovers' (n 7 above).

[10] For a further analysis of the rationales behind equality rules see Davies, 'The Notion of Equality in European Takeovers' (n 7 above).

II THE TAKEOVER CODE'S EQUAL TREATMENT RULES

The City Code on Takeovers and Mergers ('the Takeover Code') includes a substantial number of equality provisions. These equality rules not only refer to the actual offer itself, but also seek to cover any tactical opportunities that the offeror may devise through extra-offer dealings to defeat the terms of the offer. It should be noted from the outset that the position of the Takeover Code has not been changed since the implementation of the Takeovers Directive, since the Code already has a more detailed and developed set of horizontal equality rules. Four principal requirements can be identified.

First, all target shareholders must have an equal opportunity to tender their shares, irrespective of the class that their shares belong to. This is manifested by General Principle 1 of the Takeover Code and rule 14, which require that when a company has more than one class of equity shares a comparable offer must be made for each class. In addition, according to rule 36, partial offers are not permitted, unless with the consent of the Panel, which is expected to be granted only in exceptional circumstances—normally in cases of offers that could not result in the offeror holding shares carrying 30 per cent or more of the voting rights of the target company.[11] In contrast, consent will not normally be granted for partial offers that could result in the offeror holding shares carrying 30 per cent or more but less than 100 per cent of the target's voting shares, when the offeror or any person acting in concert have acquired, selectively or in significant numbers, shares in the offeree company during the 12 months preceding the application for the Panel's consent.[12]

Secondly, all target shareholders of the same class must receive the same price not only for shares tendered within the terms of the offer but also for share purchases during the offer period or share purchases for a certain period preceding the offer. Rule 6 stipulates that the level of consideration offered to the target's shareholders must equal the highest price paid for target's shares of the same class in the three months preceding the offer, while rule 16 also prohibits any special deals with favourable conditions which are not being extended to all shareholders. Rule 6 also catches derivate, or call and put option deals, and special rules exist as to the determination of the call option, put option or derivative value so as to determine the offer price[13].

Thirdly, in most cases, target shareholders must receive the same type of consideration. Under rule 11, if the offeror or its concert parties pur-

[11] *The Takeover Code*, 8th edn (London, Panel on Takeovers and Mergers, May 2006), r 36.1. See, however, below about GPG's partial offer for De Vere Group.

[12] Rule 36.2 of the Takeover Code.

[13] Note 4 on r 6, points (b) to (e) of the Takeover Code.

chase for cash any shares during the offer period, or shares of the target carrying 10 per cent or more of the voting rights within 12 months prior to the offer, then the offeror is obliged to make a cash offer or provide a cash alternative at not less than the highest price offered for those shares. The Panel has the discretion to require cash to be made available even when the 10 per cent threshold is not met where, according to the Panel, there are circumstances which render such a course necessary in order to give effect to General Principle 1.[14] This could be the case, for example, in related-party transactions, where the vendors of the shares are the directors of one of the companies involved or closely associated with those companies.[15]

In addition, rule 11.2 provides for a share alternative where purchases have been made of any class of the offeree company's shares carrying 10 per cent or more of the voting rights, by an offeror in exchange for securities in the three-month period prior to the commencement of, and during, the offer period. However, this does not override the overlapping cash offer requirement imposed by rule 11.1, unless the vendor is required to hold the securities received either until the offer has lapsed or the offer consideration has been posted to the accepting shareholders.[16] This means that if the bidder acquired shares in the target in exchange for its securities in the three-month period preceding the commencement of the offer, it may be required to offer both a cash alternative on the basis of the value of the offered securities when the purchase took place, and a share alternative on the basis of the number of the offered securities.[17]

Finally, the fourth principal requirement of the Takeover Code deprives the bidder of its discretion to post an offer or not when its shareholdings in the target reach a certain threshold. Rule 9 demands that the bidder, when the 30 per cent threshold is reached, makes a cash offer or provides some short of cash alternative, even though it might not initially have wished to place an offer for the rest of the shares. Furthermore, once Rule

[14] Rule 11.1 of the Takeover Code.

[15] Note 4 on r 11.1 of the Takeover Code.

[16] Rule 11.2 and note 5 on r 11.1. The Panel did not feel it necessary to mirror the provisions of r 11.1(a) as regards the timing of the purchases made. As a result, only purchases made during the three months prior to the offer may count for the 10% threshold that has to be reached in order for a share's offer to be required. There are two main reasons behind this thinking. First, because cash is frequently regarded as a more attractive consideration than securities, the Panel has, in most cases where the relevant purchases have preceded the offer by a significant period, felt that the offeror's obligations would be satisfied by the provision of cash. Secondly, the possible volatility of the offeror's share price can give rise to further inequalities in the treatment of target shareholders, if securities are the only form of consideration available. Accordingly, where the relevant purchases have taken place some time before the offer, the Panel has tended to regard cash as the more equitable form of consideration. See The Panel on Takeovers and Mergers, PCP 6. *Consultation Paper Issued by the Code Committee of the Panel: Purchases by the Offeror of Shares in the Offeree in Exchange for Securities. Revision Proposals Relating to Rule 11 of the Takeover Code* (October 2001).

[17] See rr 11.1 and 11.2 of the Takeover Code.

9 is triggered, the bidder is not allowed to attach any conditions to the offer, not even to set the level of acceptances higher than 51 per cent.[18] Rule 9.7 also imposes a number of additional restrictions in terms of how the bidder can exercise its rights in the target prior to making an offer.

Overall, it could be argued that the greater the stake the bidder builds in the target, the greater the Code's concerns about the equal treatment of target shareholders and the stricter the rules become. The Code's requirements for acquisitions of shares before and during the offer period can be classified according to the threshold reached as follows:

Table 5: Share purchases before and during the offer period

		Share purchases before the offer period		
Shares acquired by the bidder	*Highest price requirement*	*Determination of the consideration offered*	*Mandatory offer Requirement*	*Additional requirements*
< 10%	Highest price during 3 months prior to the offer	No requirement to make a cash or a share offer. However, if the value of the securities offered falls on the first business day after the offer is announced the Panel should be consulted.[19]	Not applicable	If the vendors of the shares are the directors of one of the companies involved or closely associated with those companies, the Panel has the discretion to require cash or other securities to be made available.[20]
10% to < 30%	Highest price during 12 months prior to the offer for cash offers and / or highest number of shares offered for purchases in exchange for shares during 3 months prior to the offer	Need to make a cash offer or offer some sort of cash alternative and / or a share offer.	Not applicable	

[18] Rule 9.3(a) of the Takeover Code.
[19] Note 3 on r 6 of the Takeover Code.
[20] Note 4 on rule 11.1 and note 2 on rule 11.2 of the Takeover Code.

Table 5: *cont.*

		Share purchases before the offer period		
Shares acquired by the bidder	*Highest price requirement*	*Determination of the consideration offered*	*Mandatory offer Requirement*	*Additional requirements*
= or > 30%	As above.	As above. However, the cash offer or the cash alternative must remain open for at least 14 days after the date on which it would otherwise have expired.[21]	Required. The offer should only be conditional upon the offeror receiving acceptances of 50% of the target's shares. The bidder cannot set a higher level of acceptances as a condition or include any other type of conditions.[22]	Except with the consent of the Panel, no nominee of an offeror or persons acting in concert with it may be appointed to the board of the offeree company, nor may an offeror or persons acting in concert with it exercise the votes attached to any shares held in the offeree company, until the offer document is posted.[23]
		Share purchases during the offer period		
< 10%	— The bidder is under an obligation to increase its offer, if it acquires shares in the target company during the offer period and pays or agrees to pay a higher price than that offered in the takeover. — If the offeror acquires any shares in the target during the offer period, it is required, according to rule 11.1(b), to change its offer to cash for that specific class of shares or offer a form of cash alternative at not less than the highest price paid during the offer period. The above applies unless the bidder acquires shares in exchange for securities, which the vendor of the offeree company shares is required to hold, either until the offer has lapsed or the offer consideration has been posted to the accepting shareholders.			
= or > 10%	— Purchases made in exchange for securities during the offer period may also trigger the obligation for the bidder to make a share offer, if the aggregate percentage of those purchases and purchases made within a period of three months prior to the offer reaches 10%.[24]			

[21] Rule 9.5. See also r 31.4 of the Takeover Code.

[22] Rule 9.3 of the Takeover Code. See, however, note 3 on r 9.3, which provides for a number cases that dispensation may be granted.

[23] Rule 9.7 of the Takeover Code.

[24] See also above.

Equality extends not only before and during the offer period but even afterwards. Even after the closure of a successful offer rule 35.3 prohibits, for a period of six months, the offeror or his concert parties from acquiring shares in the target on better terms than the terms included in the offer.[25] Special deals with favourable conditions attached may also not be entered into during that six-month period.[26] In addition, once the level of acceptances of the offer reaches the 90 per cent threshold, the remaining minority shareholders are given the opportunity to sell their shares on no less favourable terms, subject to a number of requirements imposed by section 983 of the Companies Act 2006, which amended section 430A of the Companies Act 1985 pursuant to the implementation of the Takeovers Directive.[27]

Finally, equality also extends to management-related deals. This is one major change that came with the implementation of the Takeovers Directive. While General Principle 1 required *similar* treatment for all shareholders of the same class the Takeovers Directive's relevant principle imposes an *equivalent* treatment requirement. Note 4 on rule 16 has therefore been amended to reflect this principle. The Panel will now always require shareholder approval for any such special arrangements with management and not just where the offeror and management of the offeree together hold more than five per cent of the equity share capital of the offeree, as was the case prior to the implementation of the Directive. Similarly, an independent adviser to the offeror must state publicly that, in its opinion, any other forms of ongoing incentive offered to members of management of the offeree company to ensure their continued involvement in the management of the business after completion of the transaction are fair and reasonable. Such incentives might be enhanced contractual terms, share option grants from the offeror or a position on the board of the offeror.

Overall, breaches of the above rules may have severe financial consequences for the bidder. In Guinness plc's offer for Distillers Company plc,[28] the Takeover Panel ruled that it had jurisdiction to make a compensatory money order, even after the completion of the takeover in question, and accordingly, ordered Guinness to pay compensation of £85m to the former shareholders of Distillers for breach of rule 11 of the Code.

In addition, under the statutory powers that the Panel obtained pursuant to the implementation of the Takeovers Directive and as set out in section 11 of the Introduction to the Takeover Code, the Panel may impose sanctions on a person who has acted in breach of rules made by the Panel or who has failed to comply with a direction given by the Panel.

25 Unless the Panel gives its consent.

26 Rule 35.3 of the Takeover Code.

27 See below.

28 Guinness plc v The Distillers Company plc, Panel Statement 1989/13 of 14 July 1989.

Furthermore, the Panel has the power to apply to the court for enforcement where there is a reasonable likelihood that a person will contravene, or where there has already been contravention of, a Code rule-based requirement.[29] However as noted earlier in chapter four, contravention of a rule-based requirement will not give rise to any right of action for a breach of statutory duty and nor will any such contravention make any transaction void or unenforceable or otherwise affect its validity or the validity of anything relating to it.[30] It would seem that the main purpose of such provisions is to avoid, where possible, tactical litigation on bids.

III SHOULD REGULATION PROMOTE EQUALITY IN THE CONTEXT OF A TAKEOVER?—THE ACQUIRER'S PERSPECTIVE

A Introduction

The effects of equal treatment rules—and especially those rules that require the participation of the target's minority in sales or accumulations of control, such as mandatory bids or the prohibition of partial offers—have long been the subject of a considerable debate. This part seeks to approach the above debate from the acquirer's perspective and examine the efficiency and distribution effects of equality rules for the bidder and its shareholders.

On the one hand, there are obvious costs for the acquiring shareholders generated by the application of such rules. Equality rules increase takeover premia. Hence, it is argued that regulation produces the transfer of wealth from the acquiring to target shareholders (distributory effect).[31]

[29] Section 955 of the Companies Act 2006.

[30] Section 956 of the Companies Act 2006.

[31] A number of empirical studies in the United States associate regulation with negative returns for acquirers. Many of those studies measure the impact of major regulatory events, like the implementation of the Williams Act (see n 4 above) and many anti-takeover State laws, on the abnormal returns of acquirers with active acquisition programs at the point that such regulatory amendments occurred. Unfortunately no similar studies exist assessing the impact of the implementation of the Takeover Code and any subsequent significant amendments to bidders' returns in the United Kingdom. R Smiley, 'The Effect of the Williams Amendment and Other Factors on Transaction Costs in Tender Offers' (1975) 3 *Industrial Organization Review* 138, finds that the Williams Amendment increased the abnormal returns to target firms by 13%. G Jarrell and M Bradley, 'The Economic Effects of Federal and State Regulations of Cash Tender Offers.' (1980) 23 *Journal of Law and Economics* 371, report similar results. The average abnormal returns for targets increased from 22% before the implementation of the Williams Act to 40% for targets regulated by the Williams Act. At the same time bidders' average returns declined from 9% to 6%. Similar evidence is provided by P Asquith, R Bruner and D Mullins, 'The Gains to Bidding Firms from Merger' (1983) 11 *Journal of Financial Economics* 121: average abnormal returns for acquirers declined from 4.4% to 1.7%. K Schipper and R Thompson, 'The Impact of Merger-Related Regulations on the Shareholders of Acquiring Firms.' (1983) 21 *Journal of Accounting Research* 184, also report –1.3% returns for acquirers during the 15 months when four regulatory amendments took place, including the Williams Act Amendment and Extension. A number of other studies also

In addition, higher costs may chill otherwise profitable deals. Equality rules cause disincentives to both the bidder and the target's block-shareholders, affecting the free transfer of control and thus, the operation of the market of corporate control (efficiency effect).[32]

In contrast, other commentators argue that the chilling effect of equality rules is not obvious, either analytically[33] or in theory,[34] or that equality rules provide other efficiency gains.[35] From the acquirer's perspective, as will be analysed below, the absence of equality rules could lead to an exploitation of the *bidder's minority* by the majority shareholders; the majority owner in the bidder could 'snatch' any potential profits generated by the synergies expected, by selling its shareholdings after the deal has been consummated. Looking into the above debate from the perspective of the acquirer, it is logical to expect that the second issue, which relates to the distribution of the acquisition profits, is more likely to emerge in acquirers with concentrated shareholdings. In contrast, such benefits are less evident in acquirers with dispersed ownership.

show a decline from positive abnormal returns for acquirers in the 1960s to roughly zero returns in the 1970s. The decline in acquirers' returns coincided with the introduction of the Williams Act provisions in the late '60s. M Bradley, A Desai and EH Kim, 'Synergistic Gains from Corporate Acquisitions and Their Division between the Stockholders of Target and Acquiring Firms' (1988) 21 *Journal of Financial Economics* 3, reported a decline from 4.1% to 1.3%, G Jarrell, J Brickley and J Netter, 'The Market for Corporate Control: The Empirical Evidence since 1980' (1988) 2 *Economic Perspectives* 49, noted a decline from 4.4% to 1.2%, while C Loderer and KJ Martin, 'Corporate Acquisitions by Listed Firms: The Experience of a Comprehensive Sample' (1990) (Winter) *Financial Management* 17, noted a decline from 1.7% to 0.6%. Although the Williams Act does not include profound equality rules like mandatory bids, the regulatory rules passed under it do include provisions related to the period that an offer must remain open (rule 14d-10) and pro rata participation of all shareholders who tendered, once an offer becomes unconditional as to acceptances (s 14(d)(6) of the Act), prohibitions of share purchases outside the offer (rule 10b-13) etc. Such rules are also found to have an impact on the acquirer's ability to implement coercive actions. See also the previous chapter about the impact of the period for which the offer is required to remain open.

[32] See FH Easterbrook and DR Fischel, *The Economic Structure of Corporate Law*, 4th edn (Cambridge, MA, Harvard University Press, 1998). Davies also provides an analysis of the concerns over the disincentives created by equality rules: Davies, 'The Notion of Equality in European Takeovers' (n 7 above).

[33] See J Hackl and R Testani, 'Note, Second Generation State Takeover Statutes and Shareholder Wealth: An Empirical Study' (1988) 97 *Yale Law Journal* 1193; J Karpoff and P Malatesta, 'The Wealth Effects of Second Generation Takeover Legislation' (1989) 25 *Journal of Financial Economics* 291; L Schumann, 'State Regulation of Takeovers and Shareholder Wealth: The Case of New York's 1985 Takeover Statutes' (1988) 19 *Rand Journal of Economics* 557; R Romano, 'The Political Economy of Takeover Statutes' (1987) 73 *Virginia Law Review* 111. All studies appear to indicate that fair price rules included in various anti-takeover statutes do not have negative share price effects. See also Romano, 'A Guide to Takeovers' (n 1 above).

[34] Romano, 'A Guide to Takeovers' (n 1 above); M Bagnoli and B Lipman, 'Successful Takeovers without Exclusion' (1988) 1 *Review of Financial Studies* 89.

[35] JC Coffee, 'Regulating the Market for Corporate Control: A Critical Assessment of the Tender Offer's Role in Corporate Governance', (1984) 84 *Columbia Law Review* 1145.

B Facilitating Transfers of Control v Encouraging Minority Investment (The Case of Acquirers with Concentrated Shareholdings)

The issue of equal distribution of acquisition profits, identified above, raises the question whether the acquiring shareholders prefer a rule that increases the probability of acquisition of control but results in unequal distribution, to a rule that ensures equal sharing but decreases the number of control transactions. From the perspective of the target's shareholders, the implementation of equality rules assumes that the latter prefer equality to the increased likelihood of a takeover. However, this perception has been questioned by some commentators, who, assuming that for each company there is an equal probability of being a bidder or a target, come to the conclusion that shareholders prefer a policy that facilitates transfers of control to one of equal treatment.[36]

Equality rules can have chilling effects on transfers of control, creating disincentives for bidders. It is also true that in the presence of equality rules the bidder is required to pay a control premium to non-controlling shareholders as well.[37] This not only increases the acquisition costs, but also produces disincentives to majority owners in the target, who may wish to receive more for their controlling shares than the price paid to non-controlling shareholders. Offering the same price to all shareholders may mean for majority owners that they are deprived of a control-premium and thus, they may be more reluctant to accept an offer.[38] In addition, equality rules make it extremely difficult for block-shareholders to be compensated for any private benefits of control that they may enjoy.[39]

On the other hand, equality rules may have certain benefits for the acquirer's shareholders. First of all, as seen above, every company has roughly equal probabilities of being the acquirer or the target at one time or another. Even if this is not the case, equality rules ensure that all shareholders in the bidder will equally share the benefits of the acquisition. In the absence of such rules, a majority owner in the bidder could sell control in the acquirer after the acquisition is consummated, receiving a premium that reflects the synergies gained by the acquisition and the control over the target as well. Under such a situation, minority shareholders in the acquirer would have been left in a similar position to minority shareholders in the target. At the same time, the new majority owner in the acquirer would have acquired control over both the acquirer and the target, being in a position to exploit the minority shareholders in both companies.

It is not necessary that the actual transaction takes place for the acquirer's shareholders to be affected. The risk of unequal distribution is

36 See, eg Easterbrook and Fischel, *The Economic Structure of Corporate Law* (n 32 above).
37 See below.
38 Davies, 'The Notion of Equality in European Takeovers' (n 7 above).
39 Davies, 'The Notion of Equality in European Takeovers' (n 7 above) 27.

enough to discount the market value of their investment in the acquirer. The market assesses the probability of unequal distribution of the gains of the acquisition and, accordingly, it discounts the market price of the acquirer's shares which are not part of a controlling block.

As a result, in cases of concentrated ownership, equality rules ensure equal distribution and contribute to the regulatory goal of free and equal marketability of all shares of the same class, thus increasing confidence in the market. This puts the issue of equality regulation into a different perspective: the benefits of equality rules are not confined to protecting the minority interests in the target; they also protect the minority interests in the acquiring company and have a market confidence function from which all investors benefit.

However, as already identified, equality rules are not without costs for the acquirer's shareholders, and the purpose of the above analysis is not to undermine this fact, especially in the case of acquirers with dispersed shareholdings, where the minority's protection from an exploitation by the majority ceases to be a policy concern.

C Maximising the Number of Bids and The Acquirer's Costs (The Case of Acquirers with Dispersed Shareholdings)

A number of commentators argue that, although the aim of equality rules is to ensure that the premium of control is not paid only to one or more of the target's shareholders but is equally shared among all the target shareholders, it is possible that the same rules increase the cost of acquiring control in the target, and thus discourage a number of otherwise profitable and efficient transactions.[40]

The prohibition of partial offers and the mandatory offer rule mean that the bidder has to bid for the whole share capital of the target, even though it needs a lesser percentage to secure control in the target. This not only increases acquisition costs, but also creates disincentives from the perspective of potential acquirers, who would otherwise have purchased or accumulated only a controlling block in the target. Mandatory bids and cash offer requirements impose additional costs on the bidder, when under different circumstances it would have been free to make a share offer. Cash offers are usually associated with high debt-servicing costs or

[40] See C Bradley 'Corporate Control: Markets and Rules' (1990) 53 *Modern Law Review* 170 at 193; Romano, 'A Guide to Takeovers' (n 1 above); PL Davies and KJ Hopt, 'Control Transactions' in R Kraakman, PL Davies, H Hansmann, G Hertig, KJ Hopt, H Kanda and EB Rock (eds), *The Anatomy of Corporate Law: A Comparative and Functional Approach* (Oxford, Oxford University Press, 2004); Deakin and Slinger, 'Hostile Takeovers, Corporate Law and the Theory of the Firm' in S Deakin and A Hughes (eds), *Enterprise and Community: New Directions in Corporate Governance* (Oxford, Blackwell Publishers); Easterbrook and Fischel, *The Economic Structure of Corporate Law* (n 32 above).

underwriting fees. Moreover, as already analysed, requirements for a minimum time period that the offer must remain open create the opportunity for rival bidders to emerge, and thus increase acquisition costs and the likelihood of deterring overbidding.[41] Finally, the restriction of the acquirer's ability to utilise coercive strategies to induce target shareholders to tender their shares makes the latter more reluctant to accept an offer, unless it is accompanied by a huge premium over the market price.

Consequently, it is a logical deduction that equality rules minimise the number of potential bids. From the perspective of society, it is clear that, as Davies points out, there seems to be no public policy in favour of simply maximising the number of bids. Especially,

> offers motivated by the prospect of maximising the private benefits of control (a particular risk with partial bids) or implemented by techniques which pressurise target shareholders into accepting an offer may not be driven by either of the justifications of the market for corporate control,

namely, disciplining incumbent managers and shifting resources to higher values.[42]

A number of commentators have also pointed out that high premia may just discourage business combinations that would have failed anyway.[43] After all, as Coffee argues, the more a bidder is willing to invest in its own judgement, the greater the confidence that society can also place in it.[44] The high occurrence of takeovers may also lead to excess deterrence for target company managers,[45] who demand in turn a higher compensation for the risk of losing their job. High deterrence may also shift managerial behaviour towards higher risk preference. Managers may engage in a number of defensive activities to secure their jobs, such as high leverage or defensive acquisitions. Since any acquirer can be at any time a potential target, such behaviour affects the acquirer's shareholders as well.[46]

From a policy perspective, a two-fold conclusion can be derived. First, maximising the number of bids cannot constitute a public policy by itself, so as to be able to justify a departure from equality rules. Secondly, there is no doubt that equality rules increase the risk that bidders may overpay. Such overpayment needs to be addressed on a case-by-case basis.

[41] See the previous chapter.

[42] Davies, 'The Notion of Equality in European Takeovers' (n 7 above) 26.

[43] Romano, 'A Guide to Takeovers' (n 1 above); Coffee, 'Regulating the Market for Corporate Control: A Critical Assessment of the Tender Offer's Role in Corporate Governance' (n 35 above).

[44] Coffee, 'Regulating the Market for Corporate Control: A Critical Assessment of the Tender Offer's Role in Corporate Governance' (n 35 above).

[45] Coffee, 'Regulating the Market for Corporate Control: A Critical Assessment of the Tender Offer's Role in Corporate Governance' (n 35 above).

[46] See ch 2 above.

IV SHOULD REGULATION DEVIATE FROM EQUALITY GOAL IN SPECIFIED CASES?—ADDRESSING THE CONCERNS OF THE BIDDER AND ITS SHAREHOLDERS

A Introduction

As seen above, accepting equality rules as a policy choice is one thing and raising concerns over the effects of specific rules within the boundaries of the above policy is a different issue. In certain cases, some rules cannot be justified and exceptions should be provided, namely when they merely result in wealth transfers from the acquirer's to the target's shareholders, or in cases where other regulatory policies should prevail. This is because, on the one hand, wealth distribution cannot be the purpose of regulatory intervention, and on the other hand, regulation should respond to circumstances where one party is expected systematically to lose. Accordingly, the question that arises is whether there are circumstances where the Takeover Code's rules, as described above, should be, could be, or are actually relaxed to reflect concerns about the acquirer's shareholders.

Three types of concerns are identified. First, rules that promote equality among target shareholders produce externalities in the form of costs and disincentives that could affect the bidders and their shareholders.[47] Secondly, the application of the mandatory rule can produce problems of choice distortion for the acquirer's shareholders, when they are given the right to approve the acquisition. Finally, as analysed above, there is no justification for pressurising target shareholders as a public policy to increase takeover occurrence. However, a level of coercion may be necessary to enhance the bidder's ability to acquire 100 per cent of the target's shares, in circumstances where it is imperative to do so, in order for the acquisition synergies to materialise, and in order to discourage adverse incentives of the target's shareholders that may cause a value-adding offer to fail.

B Mitigating the Externalities of Target Shareholders' Equality

As described above, there are in general three types of equality rules: rules that regulate the price offered to target shareholders ('highest price' rule in the Takeover Code); rules that regulate the medium of payment offered (cash or share offer requirements); and rules that require the participation of all shareholders in a takeover offer or an acquisition or transfer of control (mandatory offer rule and prohibition of partial offers). Each of these

[47] See above.

rules seeks to protect the target's shareholders, but produces externalities for the acquirer and its shareholders. Such externalities are or can be addressed by relaxing the relevant rules.

(i) *Dispensation from the 'Highest Price' Rule*

The highest price rule exposes the bidder to price changes during the period between the time when pre-acquisition dealings in the target's shares take place and the announcement of the formal offer. The bidder fully bears the volatility risk of the target's shares three months before the offer commences in the case of voluntary offers, or 12 months before if it acquires a stake of 10 per cent or more in the target,[48] or buys shares from the target's directors or other persons connected to the company,[49] or from any other person during the offer period.[50]

The above, unqualified form of highest price rule originating in the United Kingdom and the Takeover Code is no longer just a UK phenomenon. It has also been adopted in Germany as the basis of calculation of the offer price for voluntary and mandatory offers[51] and is also repeated in the European Takeovers Directive.[52] The German Takeover Act does make a reference to an 'average weighed stock market price test' as the basis for the calculation of the offer's price. However, this is only in circumstances where no target shares are acquired by the acquirer prior to the commencement of the offer and during the period in question.[53]

Some jurisdictions during the pre-Takeovers Directive regime allowed for some automatic protection against such fluctuations in the target's market price. The Italian law, for example, required that the offer price be the arithmetical mean of the highest price paid by the offeror in the 12-month period prior to the offer and the average market price over that period.[54] Swiss law also required that the offer price only be 75 per cent of the highest price paid by the bidder over a 12-month period prior to the

[48] Rule 11.1(a) of the Takeover Code.

[49] Note 4 on r 11.1 of the Takeover Code.

[50] Rule 11.1(b) of the Takeover Code.

[51] At least with regards to the regime prior to the implementation of the Takeovers Directive. See the Act on the Acquisition of Securities and Takeovers (Wertpapiererwerbs- und Übernahmegesetz, or WpÜG), which entered into force on 1 January 2002.

[52] Directive 2004/25/EC, Art 5(4), first sub-paragraph.

[53] At least under the regime prior to the Takeovers Directive. See s 31(I) of the WpÜG (n 51 above).

[54] Legislative Decree 58 of 24 February 1998, Art 106(2). See also Davies and Hopt, 'Control Transactions' (n 40 above). The same rational is carried forward even after the implementation of the Takeovers Directive. New par 106(2) reads as follows: *For each class of shares referred to in paragraph 1, the offer shall be made within thirty days at a price no lower than the arithmetic mean of the weighted average market price in the last twelve months and the highest price agreed in the same period by the offeror for the purchase of shares of the same class; if no purchases have been made, the offer shall be made at the weighted average market price in the last twelve months or the shorter period for which market prices are available.* Nevertheless, this approach seems unlike to be in line with the Takeover Directive for the reasons explained below.

offer, and no less than the market price of the target, when the offer is made.[55] Similarly, Austrian law permitted an offer to be made on the basis of the average price paid for target shares within a period of six months prior to the offer, as long as it was not lower than 85 per cent of the highest price paid within the 12 months preceding the offer.[56] The Takeover Directive does not affect the power of the Member States to address market fluctuations in calculating the mandatory bid price when market price is taken into account. Nevertheless this price may not be lower than the highest price paid by the bidder in that period. According to Art 5 par 4 of the Takeover Directive 4:

> The highest price paid for the same securities by the offeror, or by persons acting in concert with him/her, over a period, to be determined by Member States, of not less than six months and not more than 12 before the bid referred to in paragraph 1 shall be regarded as the equitable price.

To that effect market fluctuations that can affect the average market price of the target shares within the aforementioned period can only be taken into account, provided that Member States wish so, only when they affect the mandatory bid upwards rather than downwards.

The Takeover Code does not go that far, but still provides for a dispensation of the highest price rule subject to the approval of the Panel and only in exceptional circumstances. The Code includes a number of factors that the Panel might take into account when considering the application of any adjusted terms in relation to the price of the offer. In relation to voluntary offers, the Code includes the following factors:[57]

(a) whether the relevant acquisition was made on terms then prevailing in the market;
(b) changes in the market price of the shares since the relevant acquisition;
(c) the size and the timing of the relevant acquisition;
(d) the attitude of the offeree board;
(e) whether interests in shares have been acquired at high prices from directors or other persons closely connected with the offeror or the offeree company; and
(f) whether a competing offer has been announced for the offeree company.

Similar factors need to be considered by the Panel in relation to voluntary offers where a cash offer is required, or in relation to mandatory offers, except for market fluctuations.[58] Bearing in mind the fact that the period for which the highest price rule applies in these cases is 12 months,

[55] Art 32, para 4 of the Federal Act on Stock Exchanges and Securities Trading (Switzerland).
[56] Section 26, para 1 of the Takeover Act, Federal Law Gazette (1998) I 127, 14 August 1998 (Austria).
[57] Note 1 on r 6.1 of the Takeover Code.
[58] Note on r 11.3 of the Takeover Code, for voluntary offers where a cash offer is required, and note 3 on r 9.5, for mandatory bids.

as opposed to three months for voluntary offers, market fluctuations are not included as factors to be considered, exactly when they are more likely to occur and the bidder is more exposed to them.

Of course, the factors recited in the Takeover Code are not exhaustive. However, such an omission may indicate a policy choice for a stricter application of the highest price rule in the case of mandatory bids. The Panel has not yet exercised its discretion in permitting an offer to be made on adjusted terms strictly on grounds of market fluctuations, but according to the Panel's approach in similar situations—for example in relation to market changes that permit the offeror not to proceed with the offer[59]—it is more likely that in order for the market fluctuations to justify dispensation from the highest price rule, they should be completely unforeseeable, material and of an exceptional nature.

Alternatively, a de minimis exception may also be accepted under exceptional circumstances, provided that the target's board agrees on the adjusted price. The Panel Executive in the Knightswood (Property & Investments) Co Limited (KPI) offer for PCT Group plc (PCT)[60] ruled that the highest price rule in relation to rule 9 was satisfied by a price that was not the highest price paid but the price at or below which the greater majority of shares has been purchased.[61] In reaching its decision, the Executive disregarded a higher price paid for shares representing 0.01 per cent of the target's share capital, on de minimis grounds.

Similarly, shares offered by the market and purchased at the market price, but later sold, and thus not counting for the acceptance condition to be met, are also likely to be disregarded. In the same offer of Knightswood for PCT, 200,000 shares (2.26 per cent of the share capital) were bought at a price (163p) that was higher than the offer price, and later sold at 155p. That purchase was at market price, there were no other buyers around and the shares were offered by the market. The Executive decided that in the light of the above circumstances the above purchase price should be ignored.[62] However, it should be noted that in both the above cases, the target's board agreed on the lower price, and the fairness of the price at which the offer was made was confirmed by the target's financial advisers.[63]

59 See below under adverse change risk.

60 Knightswood (Property & Investments) Co Ltd offer for PCT Group plc, Panel Statement 1996/16 of 24 September 1996.

61 *Ibid*, 2.

62 Panel Statement 1996/16 (n 60 above).

63 'Four independent Directors of PCT together with PCT's Rule 3 advisers have confirmed that they are satisfied that a price of 130p per share is adequate to discharge the obligations under Rule 9' (Panel Statement 1996/16 (n 60 above) 2.

(ii) *Qualifications of the Medium of Payment Requirement*

As described above, the Takeover Code includes quite an elaborate and complicated set of requirements in respect of the type of consideration that the bidder has to offer. What is quite unique to the Takeover Code is that the bidder may be required, depending on the circumstances, to make either a cash or a share offer or even both of them, while under different regulatory regimes equal treatment is usually satisfied with only a requirement to make a cash offer. Those dual requirements, although designed to serve the equal treatment of the target's shareholders,[64] produce a number of concerns for the bidder. On the one hand, mandatory cash offers impose additional costs on the bidder in circumstances where it could otherwise make a share offer, since cash offers are usually associated with high servicing and underwriting costs. On the other hand, mandatory share offers may produce disincentives to both the acquiring and target majority shareholders.[65]

Overall, the 'medium of payment' related requirements of the Takeover Code may cause the bidder three types of concerns:

- First, in the case of targets with dispersed shareholdings, the cash offer requirement may diminish the bidder's benefit from building a toehold before the actual offer. Toeholds increase the initial bidder's incentives to identify a target and prepare itself to engage in a potential auction.
- Secondly, in the case of targets with concentrated shareholdings, the share offer requirement impairs the desirability of friendly deals for both bidder and target block-holders,[66] without any substantial benefit being conferred to minority shareholders, who could have been equally satisfied with a cash offer.
- Thirdly, as identified above, there may be circumstances where the bidder will be obliged to make both a cash and a share offer at the same time, but on a different valuation basis. In such cases, the issue that arises is how such requirements can be accommodated in a single offer. This is more a practical than a policy concern.

(a) Cash offer requirement and toehold strategies

A logical argument against any attempt to identify concerns that equal treatment rules cause to the offeror is that it is the bidder who puts itself in the position to be required to make a cash or mandatory offer. In that

[64] And especially institutional shareholders. See the reasoning behind the amendments in The Panel on Takeovers and Mergers, PCP 6. *Consultation Paper Issued by the Code Committee of the Panel: Purchases by the Offeror of Shares in the Offeree in Exchange for Securities. Revision Proposals Relating to Rule 11 of the Takeover Code* (October 2001) para 2.1.6.

[65] See below.

[66] See below under (b).

sense, the best way for the bidder to protect itself is to refrain from such market behaviour.

The latter seems quite reasonable in relation to market purchases during the offer period. The bidder should be expected to have confidence in its offer. While under different regulatory regimes, such as the Williams Act,[67] the bidder is not permitted to make any purchases while its tender offer is still open, the Takeover Code offers the bidder the flexibility to make such purchases, as long as the offer terms are changed to reflect any higher price paid for shares acquired outside its offer.

However, pre-offer purchases are more likely to be part of a toehold strategy. Cash offer requirements associated with pre-offer market purchases may provide disincentives to the initial bidder to build a small stake in the target in order to protect itself from losing the target in a potential auction. As already identified in chapter six, toeholds play an important role in providing the necessary incentives to the initial bidder to make an offer, and thus identify the target and signal to the market an opportunity for an auction to start.

The Takeover Code tries to mitigate the effects of rule 11.1 on toeholds, by allowing the bidder to acquire less than 10 per cent of the target's shares prior to the offer, as long as such shares are not acquired from the target's directors or persons connected to them.[68] In the words of the Panel,

> in the context of purchases of offeree shares for cash prior to an offer it has long been recognised that there is an apparent inconsistency between General Principle 1 and Rule 11.1(a) in that up to 10% of the voting rights of any class of the offeree can be purchased for cash prior to an offer before a full cash offer is required to be available. It is, however, generally accepted that an offeror should be permitted limited buying freedom prior to an offer and the concept that aggregate purchases for cash below 10% do not lead to a requirement for a full cash offer has not, in practice, given rise to General Principle 1 concerns.[69]

It should also be noted that purchases made earlier than 12 months prior to the offer do not count for the purposes of rule 11.1.

In addition, the Code recognises the increased costs that a cash requirement may impose on a bidder who intended to structure its takeover as a share-for-share exchange offer. In such cases, compliance with rule 11.1 would require that at least a cash alternative be offered to the target's shareholders. Cash alternative fees are calculated not only on the basis of the amount of cash that is made available, but also on the basis of the period of time for which the cash alternative must remain open. The offeror's problem lies in the fact that it does not know ex ante how many of the target's shareholders will elect to receive cash, and it does not know

[67] Rule 10b-13 of the regulatory rules passed under the Securities Exchange Act 1934 ('the Williams Act').

[68] Note 4 on r 11.1 of the Takeover Code.

[69] The Panel on Takeovers and Mergers, PCP 6. (n 64 above) para 2.1.4.

how long it will take to complete the offer, especially if a second bidder emerges.[70] While the former is a risk that the bidder bears as a logical result of the target's shareholders' equal treatment, the latter is addressed by rule 33.2. This provides that, in cases where the value of a cash underwritten alternative provided by third parties is at the time of the announcement more than half the maximum value of the offer, the bidder is not obliged to keep the alternative open after the offer is declared unconditional as to acceptances, provided that it gave notice to shareholders in writing that intends not to do so.[71] The ability of the bidder to shut out a cash alternative also imposes an acceptable level of coercion that might induce irresolute shareholders to tender their shares.

(b) Securities offer requirement and transfers of control

Share offer requirements may decrease the bidder's opportunities for acquiring control in companies where shareholdings are concentrated, since in such cases, it is more likely for a friendly deal than a hostile one to succeed. A block-holder may be willing to sell his shareholdings provided that it participates in the distribution of the future benefits incurred by the acquisition. While an institutional shareholder will probably be satisfied with a healthy profit through realising its investment, in companies with family ties it is very likely that majority owners will be more interested in a more long-term investment. Accordingly, share exchange deals may be more valuable to them. However, at the same time, such deals may become undesirable for the bidder and its shareholders, if they have to be extended to all target shareholders, because of the diluting effect that share exchange offers carry. Furthermore, the desirability of a pre-offer private sale of shares in exchange for securities in the acquirer may diminish for the majority owner, if all shareholders are entitled to receive the acquirer's securities on the same terms.

Prior to the Code's amendments, the equality requirement was satisfied by requiring the bidder to make a cash offer at the highest price that the securities offered to the majority owner had reached, when the exchange took place. In that way, while the equal treatment requirement was satisfied in price terms, there was a level of play that satisfied a majority owner's need to receive some sort of an added benefit for sealing a friendly deal. That approach was based mainly on the assumption that cash is a more attractive consideration than securities, and constituted an effective trade-off between two rather conflicting policies, a policy that promotes minority investment and a policy that facilitates transfers of control.[72]

[70] See chs 5 and 6 above.

[71] Rule 33.2 of the Takeover Code. It should be noted that the rule will not apply to a cash alternative provided to satisfy the requirements of r 9. Note 2 on r 33.2.

[72] On the interaction of equality treatment and those two policies, see Davies, 'The Notion of Equality in European Takeovers' (n 7 above).

The Panel, though, felt that there are circumstances where a cash offer is not enough to satisfy the requirements of General Principle 1 where there have been purchases for securities. According to the Panel, there may be cases where securities of the acquiring company are issued at a level which is, or appears to be, advantageous to the vendor of the target shares. In addition, offeree shareholders accepting cash are not always able to purchase securities in the offeror on the same terms as those received by a vendor. In addition, the market in the offeror securities may be illiquid and, in any event, the market impact of significant buy-orders is likely to cause an increase in the price of the bidder's shares.[73]

However, the above may not be of much importance to minority shareholders. First, if the level at which the acquirer's shares are issued is advantageous, then this will be reflected, due to the highest price rule, on the price that the offer should be made at, irrespective of the medium of payment offered. Secondly, if the market in the offeror securities is illiquid, this is a very important reason for the target's shareholders to want to be paid in cash. Finally, a consistent result of many empirical studies is that the acquirer's share-price is more likely to decline than to increase, prior to and during a takeover. In that sense, from the perspective of the target's shareholders, it is better for the offer to be made on the basis of maintaining the value rather than the number of the securities offered. As the regulatory requirements of the Takeover Code stand now, the former is achieved through a cash offer requirement, while the number of the securities offered forms the basis of the mandatory share offer requirement of the Code.[74] Accordingly, it is dubious whether the benefits of a share offer requirement exceed the costs that it produces, both in terms of incentive diminution and dilution.

The Takeover Code provides some opportunities to circumvent the simultaneous application of rules 11.1 and 11.2, which may give rise to the unfortunate situation for the bidder, where, under the Code, it might have to make both a cash and a share offer. The fact that only purchases made within three months prior to the offer count towards the 10 per cent threshold to be reached—in contrast to the 12-month period that applies in respect of purchases for cash or purchases that are deemed to be made for cash—seems initially to allow the bidder to circumvent the application of rule 11.2 if it delays the offer announcement for at least three months after a substantial purchase of shares in exchange for securities is made. In addition, the application of rule 11.1 is circumvented and no cash offer is required, even though the 10 per cent threshold is reached, when the securities offered carry selling restrictions.

However, this is not entirely the case. This is because the Panel may require securities to be offered on the same basis to all other holders of

[73] The Panel on Takeovers and Mergers, PCP 6 (n 64 above) para 2.1.6.

[74] See above under II.

shares of that class, even though the amount purchased is less than 10 per cent or the purchase took place more than three months prior to the commencement of the offer period.[75] This discretion will normally be exercised when the vendors of the relevant shares are directors of, or other persons closely connected with, the offeror or the offeree company.[76] Hence, where the bidder acquires a toehold in exchange for securities from a block-holder that has some form of involvement in the management of the target—which is the norm in companies with concentrated shareholdings—the bidder will be required, in most circumstances, to extend the offer of the same securities to all the target's shareholders. Finally, even if the Panel does not exercise its discretion, it may still require the bidder, due to the nature and the size of the purchases in question, to go forward and make a statement as to whether or not it wishes to proceed with the offer. This effectively means that the bidder may not have the choice to wait for three months before proceeding with its offer.

While purchases in exchange for securities are not an issue either in companies with dispersed shareholdings, or in companies with concentrated shareholdings as long as minority shareholders receive the same price in cash, it may be an issue of importance where shareholdings are divided among different institutional shareholders who have substantial, but yet non-controlling, shareholdings in the same firm.

In this case and when the market suffers from illiquidity, it is important to institutional shareholders, in a very competitive environment, to be able to participate equally in vendor placings or other share issues with terms more favourable than the market provides. In that sense, it could be argued that the share offer requirement is a regulatory response to a new form of company structure, where dispersed shareholdings are replaced by concentrated, but not controlling, institutional ownership, and proclaims the institutional heritage of the Takeover Code.

(c) Accommodating a dual requirement to offer both cash and shares in a single offer

One of the potential problems that the simultaneous application of rules 11.1 and 11.2 can lead to is that the offeror may need to make both a cash and a share offer in order to satisfy the Takeover Code's requirements. Share offers issued directly to target shareholders do not carry any preemption rights for the acquirer's shareholders, and underwriting costs or debt-servicing costs related to cash offers are quite substantial, especially when they are associated with long commitment periods. What is even more important for the bidder, though, is the uncertainty involved in a dual offer.

[75] Note 2 on r 11.2 of the Takeover Code.
[76] *Ibid.*

Dual offer requirements create the following problem for the offeror, namely how many shares it should issue and how much cash it will need to raise. There is a considerable number of potential combinations of percentages of cash and shares that the target's shareholders may elect. This means that, in circumstances where the bidder is obliged to make both a cash and a share offer, it needs to have double the resources available that it would otherwise need to have.

One way to mitigate this problem is by combining the two offers in one. Usually, this can be achieved through a cash underwritten alternative arrangement. A cash underwritten alternative is an arrangement under which the bidder offers its own shares to the target's shareholders and then arranges for an underwriter—usually a merchant bank—to offer to buy all or a proportion of these shares from accepting shareholders who wish to receive cash instead.[77] In that way, the bidder offers its shares directly to target shareholders to satisfy the share offer requirement and arranges for the underwriter to buy them at the highest price paid to satisfy the cash offer requirement.

The dynamics of a cash underwritten alternative, other than combining the two offers in one, stem also from two other major sources. First, shares are issued directly to the target's shareholders, and thus merger relief and merger accounting may also be available; and secondly, the Takeover Code treats a cash alternative more favourably than a cash offer, in terms of the period for which the underwriting commitment has to be kept open.[78]

On the side of the drawbacks, one could identify the fact that the acquirer's shareholders do not have any pre-emption rights. This is because the consideration shares are issued for shares in the target company (thus for a non-cash consideration), and section 89 of the Companies Act 1985 only applies to new issues for cash.[79] The deficit in the acquiring shareholders' protection can be mitigated through an 'open offer' or 'clawback'.[80] However, it should be noted that such a practice leaves underwriters facing two risks: first, whether the target's shareholders will elect to retain the consideration shares or they will wish to receive cash; and secondly, whether the acquirer's shareholders will elect to take advantage of the open offer and as a result affect the underwriting fees.[81]

In addition, following the implementation of the Takeovers Directive's requirement for cash confirmation even in voluntary offers, where the financing of an offer in whole or in part is by the issue of securities, the

[77] G Stedman, *Takeovers* (London, Longman, 1993) 4.

[78] Rule 33.2 of the Takeover code. See also above.

[79] Stedman, *Takeovers* (n 77 above) 98; E Ferran, *Company Law and Corporate Finance* (New York, Oxford University Press, 1999) 347.

[80] See above ch 5.

[81] Stedman, *Takeovers* (n 77 above) 99.

option of conditional confirmation has been abolished, leaving full responsibility on the bidder and its financial adviser to take all reasonable steps before the offer announcement to satisfy themselves that the securities issue will be successful. To that effect, if there are conditions attaching to cash raising though a share issue, the bidder can be considered as having ensured the availability of the cash only if fulfilment of these conditions is within the bidder's control. Consequently, it obvious that any condition that is not within the bidder's control will need to be included as a condition of the offer, as otherwise the bidder will not have ensured that it has the cash to fund the offer.[82] This leads to the issue of what can be a permissible condition attached to an offer, but this will be further explored in the next chapter.

(iii) *Mandatory Offers, Partial Offers and Transfers of Control*

Mandatory offers raise a number of concerns for the bidder. Of course, there are a number of dispensations of the mandatory offer rule on grounds of practical considerations. For example, the Panel may not require a mandatory offer if a person incurs such an obligation due to an inadvertent mistake.[83] Dispensations from the requirement to make a mandatory offer are also provided to allow for certain types of market and business practices to operate, such as shares underwriting,[84] enforcement of security for a loan,[85] or rescue operations.[86] However, the important question is whether dispensations should be available on grounds of policy choices.

There is little to be argued in favour of the bidder on grounds of facilitating a toehold strategy, since the mandatory rule applies once the 30 per cent threshold is reached, which by any means is quite high to prevent the bidder from building a pre-offer stake in the target. After all, it is the bidder who puts itself in a position to have to make a mandatory offer. Also, as has already been argued earlier in this chapter, the fact that the bidder may wish to acquire majority control in the target without having to extend the offer to all the target's shareholders is not by itself a justification for granting a dispensation from the mandatory offer rule. It has also been shown that the mandatory offer rule provides benefits to the acquirer's shareholders as well and any decrease in the occurrence of takeovers resulting from its application does not impair the operation of the market of corporate control.[87]

[82] The Panel on Takeovers and Mergers, *Practice Statement No 10: Cash Offers Financed by the Issue of Offeror Securities* (April 2005).

[83] Note 4 on dispensations from r 9 of the Takeover Code; see also Hillsdown Holdings/S&W Beresford, Panel Statement 1986/21 (May 1986).

[84] Note 1 on dispensations from r 9 of the Takeover Code.

[85] Note 2 on dispensations from r 9 of the Takeover Code.

[86] Note 3 on dispensations from r 9 of the Takeover Code.

[87] See above under III.

However, although a dispensation from the mandatory offer rule, as a policy choice, cannot be justified in general terms, there may be cases where a dispensation can be granted. Three cases are identified:

- First, when the justification behind protecting minority interests is missing. This could be the case, for example, when such dispensation from the mandatory offer rule is included in the articles of association of the target, or when the remaining shareholders give their consent to disapply the mandatory offer rule, or when there is a number of quality controls in respect of partial offers.
- Secondly, in order to address the disincentives that the mandatory offer rule produces from the perspective of potential sellers of majority blocks.
- Finally, when the bidder acquires de jure control through a single transfer of such control by a majority owner.

(a) Minority approval, quality controls and partial offers

Many regulatory regimes permit some sort of relaxation of a mandatory offer rule, in the form of partial offers, or even a complete dispensation of the mandatory offer rule, when the remaining target's shareholders value the change of control. For example, Swiss regulation permits the target's shareholders to change, by provision in the articles of association, the threshold of the mandatory bid requirement from one-third to 49 per cent or even completely disapply the requirement.[88] Similarly, Italian law permits partial offers subject to the approval of the majority of the remaining target shareholders.[89] However, the partial offer must be for at least 60 per cent of the target's shares and the offeror must not have acquired any shares in the target during 12 months prior to the partial offer.[90]

In the United Kingdom, partial offers are subject to the approval of the Panel, which is given in exceptional circumstances. Recently, the Panel cleared a hostile partial offer for De Vere Group by Guinness Peat Group ('GPG'), which sought to add 25 per cent more to its 10 per cent stake with the purpose of appointing two directors to the De Vere board.[91] This represents the first partial offer for a number of years. Consent will not be normally granted for partial offers that could result in the offeror holding shares carrying 30 per cent or more but less than 100 per cent of the target's voting shares, when the offeror or any person acting in concert has acquired, selectively or in significant numbers, shares in the offeree

[88] Federal Law on Stock Markets and Securities Dealing (Loi federale sur les bourses et le commerce des valeurs mobiliers, LBVM), Arts 32(1) and 22(2) (Switzerland).

[89] Legislative Decree 58 of 24 February 1998, Consolidated Law on Financial Intermediation, Art 107.

[90] *Ibid*. See Davies, 'The Notion of Equality in European Takeovers' (n 7 above) 27.

[91] R Martin, 'Guinness Peat Group Partial Offer. Breaking the Mould' (2004) 15(4) *PLC* 10.

company during the 12 months preceding the application for the Panel's consent.[92] Even in the cases where the Panel's consent is obtained, the Code provides a number of additional safeguards for the target's shareholders.

First, an offer for 30 per cent or more of the target's shares requires approval by 50 per cent of the target's shareholders, normally signified by means of a separate box on the form of acceptance.[93] However, such a requirement may be waived, if over 50 per cent of the voting rights of the offeree company are held by one shareholder.[94] Special warning should also be given about the offeror holding shares carrying over 49 per cent of the target's voting rights,[95] while any shares tendered should be accepted on a pro rata basis.[96]

There are many reasons why a partial offer could make more business sense than a full offer for both the bidder and the target. In friendly takeovers, a bidder may be presented as a strategic business partner, and in hostile bids as a forerunner or an advocate of a change in the target's management or business.[97] In addition, there may be situations where the bidder may wish to retain a separate listing of the target. Since LR 3.21 of the Listing Rules requires that a minimum of 25 per cent of shares be in public hands, such a condition will remain satisfied after a partial offer, while making a full offer means that the bidder carries the risk that its shareholdings will rise to more than 75 per cent. At the same time, retaining a separate listing means that the remaining target shareholders enjoy the protection of the market and the Listing Rules.

(b) Disincentives from the perspective of the vendors of controlling blocks

It has already been emphasised that equality rules may produce disincentives to majority owners to sell their controlling blocks, since it is very likely that they will expect to receive an additional premium as compensation for losses of private benefits they enjoy.[98] One way to mitigate this problem is to permit such shareholders to receive some sort of additional premium. This is achieved by many jurisdictions, such as Austrian and Swiss laws, by a relaxation of the equal treatment requirement: Austrian law permits controlling holders in the target to receive an additional premium of 15 per cent, and Swiss law, a premium of 25 per cent.[99] The

[92] Rule 36.2 of the Takeover Code.
[93] Rule 36.5 of the Takeover Code.
[94] Rule 36.5 of the Takeover Code.
[95] Rule 36.6 of the Takeover Code.
[96] Rule 36.7 of the Takeover Code.
[97] See above about the GPG offer for De Vere Group. Martin, 'Guinness Peat Group Partial Offer. Breaking the Mould' (n 91 above).
[98] See above.
[99] See above under B(i) 'Dispensation from the "Highest Price" rRule'.

Takeover Code does not provide for such allowances, mainly because, as Davies argues, concentrated shareholdings are not a common phenomenon in the United Kingdom.[100]

(c) Transfers of de jure control

Regulation treats transfers and accumulations of control in the same way. The bidder is obliged to make a mandatory offer, irrespective of whether it accumulates control through many open market purchases or through one private transaction. However, there is a notable difference: in the absence of any regulatory intervention, an investor in a company with dispersed shareholdings buys shares on the basis of the rational expectation that the shares he buys can be combined with others to affect control in the target. Hence, such shares carry a control premium. This makes the company more susceptible to the operation of the market of corporate control and that is reflected on the value of the shares.

In contrast, in a company with concentrated shareholdings, where control rests in the hands of a majority owner, an investor knows in advance that the shares he acquires cannot affect control in the target. Accordingly, minority shares are not expected to carry a control premium, since the market discounts them to reflect precisely the fact that they cannot change control in the target. In addition, due to the existence of a majority block in the company, hostile takeovers are effectively prevented, and thus the investor can only rely on the company law minority protection to avoid majority oppression or self-dealing.

As a result, when a bidder acquires control in a target with previously dispersed shareholdings, the minority shareholder suffers a loss in his investment. Such a loss equals the loss of the control premium expectation plus the increase in the investment's vulnerability to managerial conflicts of interests, since the company is now less susceptible to the operation of the market of corporate control. Assuming that capital markets are efficient, such an increase in agency risk is also expected to be reflected in the market price of the remaining publicly-traded shares.

In contrast, when majority control just shifts from one owner to another, the position of the minority shareholder does not structurally change. Thus, the minority shareholder suffers no loss at least from structural changes, other than when the target becomes a member in a group when it used to be an independent company. However, even in such cases, an investor that buys shares in a company where control lies in the hands of a majority owner accepts the risk that he is vulnerable to changes in control, and such a risk is also reflected in the market price of the shares he buys.

[100] Davies, 'The Notion of Equality in European Takeovers' (n 7 above).

Hence, there is a qualitative difference between accumulations of control and transfers of existing control blocks. Taking also into account the costs that a mandatory bid rule produces for the bidder and the disincentives it causes to majority owners, there are fewer persuasive arguments in favour of mandatory offers in the case of transfers of existing control than in the case of accumulations of control. This means that there is room for relaxing the mandatory offer rule to address the bidder's interests and facilitate transfers of control and majority investment, without irredeemably affecting minority interests.

The Takeover Code does not recognise such form of dispensation from the mandatory bid rule, probably because, as noted elsewhere, transfers of de jure control blocks are not the norm in the UK capital markets. Nevertheless, from the wording of rule 9.1(b) it can be derived that any person who, together with persons acting in concert with him, holds more than 50 per cent of the voting rights, is not required to make a mandatory bid if he acquires additional shares which increase his percentage of the voting rights in the target.

Although that rule is far from disapplying the mandatory bid requirement for transfers of de jure control, it still makes a notable and similar distinction to that in the above analysis, between acquisitions once de facto control (more than 30 per cent) is obtained, and acquisitions once de jure control (more than 50 per cent) is achieved. In the former case such acquisitions fall within the application of rule 9, mainly to avoid so-called creeping takeovers, where the bidder can, over a long period of time, obtain de jure control in the target. However, when the bidder does enjoy de jure control additional acquisitions are exempted from the application of rule 9 of the Code.

(iv) *The Acquiring Shareholders' Undistorted Choice*

One of the main rationales behind equality regulation is to ensure that the bidder will not be able to force the target's shareholders to accept the offer. However, undistorted choice is not only a concern for target shareholders. As regulation puts the whole weight of decision-making on the target's shareholders, in respect of accepting an offer or not, there are some cases—especially in transactions that fall within the description of class 1 transactions of the Listing Rules—where the acquirer's offer is subject to the approval of its shareholders as well. In such circumstances, it is imperative that a requirement to make a mandatory offer does not affect the acquiring shareholders' decision-making. If the bidder's management is able to circumvent their shareholders' right to approve the transaction, by just acquiring shares in the market and putting the bidder under an obligation to make a mandatory offer, then the very purpose of the shareholder's approval rule is defeated.

The Takeover Code addresses this problem. Rule 9.3(b) explicitly prohibits any acquisitions of shares which would give rise to a requirement for an offer under rule 9 to be made, if the making or implementation of such offer would or might be dependent on the passing of a resolution at any meeting of shareholders of the offeror. This means that when the transaction is classified as a class 1 transaction, the bidder's management cannot put the bidder in a situation where it is obliged to make a mandatory bid.

C Qualifying the Prohibition of Coercive Actions: The Acquirer's Need to Freeze Out the Remaining Target Shareholders

It has already been emphasised that one of the main rationales behind equality rules is to prevent the bidder from implementing any coercive actions that could distort the target's shareholders' decision and force them to accept an offer which they do not find satisfying. Despite the costs that such a policy imposes on the bidder, there seem to be no persuasive arguments that permitting such coercive tactics could lead to efficiency gains. However, there may be cases where an acceptable level of coerciveness is necessary in terms of both the bidder and society. Such circumstances may arise when the bidder needs first to acquire 100 per cent of the target and secondly, to discourage the free riding of target shareholders.

(i) *Why Acquiring 100 Per cent of the Target May Be Important*

As will be analysed below, there are a number of reasons why the bidder may wish to acquire 100 per cent of the target's share capital. If a small group of shareholders does not tender its shares, then the outcome of a deal accepted by the majority of the target's shareholders is jeopardised. The bidder can of course protect itself from getting into a situation of acquiring control in a company, where the existence of minority interests affects the business benefits from the acquisition, by simply not relaxing its acceptance condition.[101] However, this may lead to many otherwise profitable acquisitions failing, although they are accepted by the majority of the target's shareholders. Such a situation raises efficiency concerns, because a small minority may effectively decide the outcome of a deal that has been widely accepted by the majority in the target.

The acquirer may wish to obtain 100 per cent of the target for four reasons: first, to be able to freely conduct the target's business within a group without the participation costs of a minority; secondly, to be able to have access to the assets of the target; thirdly, to be able to eliminate the costs of

[101] See above.

public ownership; and finally, because 100 per cent ownership provides additional accounting and tax benefits.

When a bidder acquires control of a target a group situation arises. Control of the target's assets lies in the hands of a central management, which inevitably has to take decisions of allocating opportunities within the group, in order for the acquisition synergies to materialise. Such a strategy of unequal distribution of synergies within members of a group may be important to the bidder to effectively generate the synergies expected from the acquisition. However, it may be difficult to implement such a strategy, in cases where a minority interest remains in the target that may oppose the transfer of the target's business to another member of the group, or oppose any other unequal division of the costs and the benefits of the synergies generated from the acquisition. Litigations and judicial actions sought by minority shareholders impose substantial costs and may be extremely time consuming. Therefore, it may be in the interest of the bidder to eliminate in advance the risk of legal actions.

The problem is even more acute when the bidder wants to have access to the target's assets or eradicate the costs of public ownership. The existence of a minority in the target may prevent it from doing so, which may by itself prevent the bidder from acquiring the target in the first place, if it intends to finance the acquisition by using part of the target's assets. Of course, the elimination of minority interest is not by itself enough to prevent the application of financial assistance provisions,[102] since they also serve to protect the interests of the target's creditors, but it eradicates this problem by permitting the bidder to re-register the company as a private company to which the financial assistance prohibition does not apply.[103]

When a hostile bidder wants to finance the acquisition with the target's assets to pay for a leveraged bid, it may be instructed by its financiers to eradicate the minority, despite the fact that re-registration as a private company requires the bidder to have control of at least 75 per cent of the target (in order to be able to pass a special resolution to that effect).[104] This is because section 98 of the Companies Act 2006 permits a minority of five per cent or 50 shareholders to apply to the court for cancellation of the resolution. Accordingly, only by acquiring over 95 per cent of the target, or by reducing the minority to fewer than 50 shareholders, is it possible for the bidder to be sure that it can convert the company to a private one.

Under the Companies Act 1985 the bidder could also face opposition, even after having succeeded in re-registering the target as a private company. A minority of 10 per cent could apply under section 157(2) of the

[102] See under ch 7 above.

[103] Section 678 of the Companies Act 2006 replaces s 151(1) and (2) of the 1985 Act and restates s 153(1) and (2) of that Act. The key change is that the prohibition on private companies providing financial assistance for a purchase of own shares is not carried forward.

[104] Section 97 of the Companies Act 2006.

Companies Act 1985 for cancellation of the special resolution authorising the financial assistance. However, in the Companies Act 2006 the prohibition of financial assistance for private companies is not carried forward. Nevertheless, dissentient shareholders in the target may still be able to apply for a petition on the grounds of unfair prejudice under section 994 of the Companies Act 2006. For such a petition, minority shareholders do not need to hold any specific percentage. Irrespective of whether such a petition will succeed or not, it may still delay the bidder and may prevent it from meeting deadlines agreed with its financiers. Moreover, even the probability of such petition succeeding is enough for the financier to make finance available, but subject to the bidder acquiring the 100 per cent of the target or in practice at least 90 per cent for reasons discussed below.

Other than financing a leveraged bid or just eliminating the costs of public ownership, there may be also additional accounting and tax benefits from acquiring 100 per cent of the target. Although the analysis of such benefits goes beyond the scope of the present work, it suffices to be said that when the bidder fully owns the target, it can benefit from merger relief or merger accounting or a number of tax reliefs, such as the dispensation of a requirement to pay a stamp duty.[105]

(ii) *The Bidder's Free Riding Problem*

It has been argued[106] that another critical concern for the bidder is that the target's shareholders may free ride on its efforts. It has already been analysed that potential bidders may free ride on the initial bidder's announcement to acquire the target. In the case of minority shareholders' free riding, the bidder faces the same externalities as any shareholder that devotes resources to improve management. Small shareholders have neither the resources nor the incentives to devote resources to ensuring better management. Accordingly, such shareholders free ride on the efforts of larger shareholders. If target shareholders expect that the profits from the change of the management in the target will exceed the price offered, even though the latter equals the highest price paid by the bidder, they are more likely not to tender their shares and remain in the target.

Grossman and Hart[107] argue that the above free rider problem has efficiency implications. Takeovers are used as a disciplinary mechanism for managers who do not act in the best interests of their shareholders. Proper management of a company is a public good to all shareholders. Accordingly, if one shareholder devotes resources to ensure proper man-

[105] In general, see MA Weinberg and MV Blank, *Takeovers and Mergers*, 2nd edn (London, Sweet & Maxwell, 1989) and Stedman, *Takeovers* (n 77 above).

[106] SJ Grossman and OD Hart, 'Takeover Bids, the Free-Rider Problem, and the Theory of the Corporation' (1980) 11(1) *The Bell Journal of Economics* 42.

[107] *Ibid*.

agement, all shareholders benefit. Because of the costs associated with hostile bids, the only way to create proper incentives for the production of this public good, namely the disciplinary effect of hostile takeovers, is to exclude non-payers from enjoying the benefits of the public good.[108]

In addition, in the absence of any coerciveness, target shareholders may wish not to tender their shares and to remain in the target under the new management, because they just infer that when a takeover offer is made, the acquirer must believe that the target is worth more than the price offered or else it would not have made the offer. If this is the case, as Gilson and Black argue,

> target shareholders may respond strategically by not tendering, instead free-riding on the acquirer's discovery of the target's real value.[109]

The argument continues that, because of the collective action problem, if every target shareholder believes that his decision not to tender does not affect the chances of the offer succeeding, then it becomes more likely that the bidder will fail to acquire control.[110] Hence, a level of coerciveness is necessary to eliminate free riding and the adverse selection problem that it produces.

(iii) *Allowing a Level of Coerciveness to Permit the Bidder to Acquire 100 Per cent of the Target*

As described above, equal opportunity means that all target shareholders are given the chance to decide whether they want to tender their shares on equal terms or not. One way for the bidder to ensure that all shareholders tender their shares is to be able to deprive the minority shareholders of the opportunity not to tender, in other words, by squeezing out the remaining minority shareholders. This can be achieved mainly in two ways.

Sections 974 to 991 of the Companies Act 2006 set out the compulsory acquisition procedure that will apply (in place of the procedure set out in sections 428–430F of the Companies Act 1985) to all takeover offers within the scope of the Takeovers Directive. In contrast to section 429 of the Companies Act 1985, section 979 of the Companies Act 2006 permits the bidder to compulsorily acquire the minority shares, as long as a dual test is satisfied. A bidder needs to have acquired or unconditionally contracted to acquire both 90 per cent of the shares to which the offer relates and 90 per cent of the voting rights in the company to which the offer relates. In practice, however, this new dual test should not make a real difference

[108] Grossman and Hart, 'Takeover Bids, the Free-Rider Problem, and the Theory of the Corporation' (n 106 above) 59.

[109] RJ Gilson and BS Black, *The Law and Finance of Corporate Acquisitions*, 2nd edn (Westbury, NY, The Foundation Press, Inc, 1995) 1238.

[110] See *ibid*; and Grossman and Hart, 'Takeover Bids, the Free-Rider Problem, and the Theory of the Corporation' (n 106 above) 42.

since the percentage of total capital-carrying voting rights in a company and the percentage of voting rights will normally be the same.

Under the Companies Act 1985 regime, the 90 per cent threshold must have been reached within four months from the date of the original offer[111] and the bidder must had exercised its right within two months after it reached the 90 per cent threshold.[112] Under the new provisions the bidder can activate the compulsory acquisition procedure, provided that it does so before the expiry of three months from the last day on which the offer can be accepted.[113] Consequently, in contrast to the posting of the offer as the starting point under the previous regime, the deadline for service of the notice is now three months after the last day on which the offer can be accepted. This means that the longer a bidder leaves the offer open for acceptances, within the timeframe allowed by the Takeover Code, the longer the squeeze-out procedure is available to a bidder. However, in practice, a bidder will if possible issue a squeeze-out notice before it is obliged to issue a notice to shareholders informing them of their right to require to be bought out.[114] It should be noted that, in calculating whether the 90 per cent threshold is reached, shares held by the bidder prior to the offer do not count.[115]

In terms of the consideration offered, if the offer provided the target shareholders with the choice to elect between alternative forms of consideration (cash or shares), the bidder would have to offer a similar choice. This applies irrespective of whether according to the Takeover Code the bidder is able to close a cash alternative earlier, or the underwriter who supplied the cash alternative is no longer able or bound to provide it. This practically means that, in the case of cash alternatives, the offeror must arrange in advance how it will be able to provide cash to the remaining 10 per cent of the target's shareholders. Finally, section 978 of the Companies Act 2006 provides a procedure for the acquisition of untraceable shareholders, since a problem may arise in respect of the acquisition of the shares of such shareholders, especially when the bidder needs to acquire 100 per cent of the shares.[116]

Alternatively, the bidder can use the court scheme procedure.[117] In that case, it needs to receive the approval of 75 per cent of the target's share-

[111] See s 429 of the Companies Act 1985 and *Musson v Howard Glasgow Associated Ltd* [1960] SC 371.

[112] Section 429 of the Companies Act 1985.

[113] Section 980 of theCompanies Act 2006.

[114] According to s 984(3) of the Companies Act 2006, such an obligation arises one month after the thresholds of 90% of all target shares and 90% of the voting rights have been achieved.

[115] Since they were not acquired 'by virtue of acceptance of the offer': see PL Davies, *Gower's Principles of Modern Company Law*, 6th edn (London, Sweet & Maxwell, 1997) 808. See also s 974(2) of the Companies Act 2006.

[116] See also s 430(5)–(8) of the Companies Act 1985.

[117] Section 895 of the Companies Act 2006.

holders in order for the scheme to be approved. In that way, it can squeeze out 25 per cent of minority shareholders since, once the scheme has been approved by the target shareholders and the court, it is binding on all shareholders. This can be an advantage, particularly when the bidder already holds a significant number of shares.

A court scheme procedure may be implemented even when the bidder triggers the obligation to make a mandatory bid. Once the bidder acquires 30 per cent of the target's shares in the market and triggers the requirement to make a mandatory offer under rule 9 of the Takeover Code, the Panel may allow it to discharge this requirement through a court scheme. The Panel is more likely to accept a court scheme subject to the acquirer assuming the responsibility of making a mandatory cash offer if the scheme fails, and the offeror's financial adviser confirming that the bidder has the resources to make the cash offer.[118] However, it should be noted that any stake built by the bidder does not count for the purposes of the 75 per cent threshold. This is because the scheme must be approved by the remaining shareholders, who usually form, for that purpose, a separate class of members.[119] Hence, any market purchases by the bidder may make it more difficult to receive the approval of 75 per cent of the remaining shareholders.

Although a court scheme is a lengthy procedure, compared to a normal takeover offer (it might take up to 10 weeks),[120] the court scheme can be quicker than relying on the compulsory acquisition provisions of section 979 of the Companies Act 2006 since the latter may take up to six months.[121] Nevertheless, the fact that a court scheme takes longer than a conventional offer to complete means that the bidder remains exposed to rival offers for a longer period of time.

A court scheme demands the cooperation of the target, since it is an arrangement between the company and its shareholders. The bidder will normally appear by counsel at the court hearing to give its undertakings to comply with its obligations under the scheme.[122] On the side of the benefits, though, when the bidder wishes to obtain authorised financial assistance by the target, it may find court schemes more effective and quick, since it may be possible for financial assistance to be proposed and be provided as part of the court scheme.[123] However, the benefits of such

[118] See Weinberg and Blank, *Takeovers and Mergers* (n 105 above) 3411; Stedman, *Takeovers* (n 77 above) 199.

[119] Section 899 of the Companies Act 2006 and *Re Hellenic & General Trust Ltd* [1975] 3 All ER 382, [1976] 1 WLR 123 (ChD)(Templeman J).

[120] Stedman, *Takeovers* (n 77 above) 38.

[121] Stedman, *Takeovers* (n 77 above) 36.

[122] Theoretically, the bidder may be able to apply to the court under s 902 of the Companies Act 2006, if it is a shareholder in the target. Stedman, *Takeovers* (n 77 above).

[123] According to s 900 of the Companies Act 2006 the court has extensive powers to make such ancillary orders as necessary to secure that the reconstruction or amalgamation is fully

procedure are minimised with the enactment of the Companies Act 2006, since the abolition of the financial assistance prohibition for private companies means that there is no need to wait for the private company exemption procedure to be followed. To that effect, the bidder will wish to obtain authorised financial assistance in the context of the court scheme, only when he cannot wait for the target to re-register as a private company.

Apart from the compulsory sale and court scheme procedures, it is debatable whether deviations from the right of any shareholder to retain or dispose its shares can be achieved, when the bidder obtains constitutional majority, by changing the articles of association. More precisely, the bidder, at least in theory, could potentially compel a sale of the minority's shares, or impose a selective reduction of capital by altering the articles of association. Both these procedures are very likely to be fiercely opposed by the minority, who will seek to take judicial action on grounds of oppression of the minority or unfair prejudice. There is no UK judicial precedent of such cases in respect of public companies. However in a relevant Australian case,[124] the High Court held that before the majority could proceed with an expropriation of the minority's shares by way of an alteration of the company's constitution, they had to satisfy two requirements: first, the majority had to prove that the alteration of the articles of association was fair, and secondly, that it was for proper purpose.

(iv) *Allowing a Level of Coerciveness to Discourage Free Riding*

Grossman and Hart,[125] who first identified the free riding problem for the bidder, as analysed above, argue that in order to discourage free riding it is important that the bidder be able to squeeze out non-tendering shareholders. However, this is only one method for discouraging free riding.[126] Although a squeeze out rule can be supported in cases where the bidder wishes to acquire 100 per cent of the target, there are other ways by which the right incentives can be created for the target shareholders to tender their shares.

First, company law rules on minority treatment heavily rely on the notion of fairness rather than equality. A fair treatment does not necessarily preclude that the majority owner, in this case the bidder, will enjoy additional benefits from the acquisition. This means that there is room for differential treatment of minority interests, as long as such treatment is fair.

and effectively carried out. See also the court scheme exemption in relation to financial assistance of s 681(1) and (2) of the Companies Act 2006.

[124] *Gambotto v WCP* (1995) 182 CLR 432 (H Ct Aust).

[125] Grossman and Hart, 'Takeover Bids, the Free-Rider Problem, and the Theory of the Corporation'(n 106 above).

[126] See also Gilson and Black, *The Law and Finance of Corporate Acquisitions* (n 109 above) 1238.

In addition, empirical studies suggest that the benefits produced from the acquisition of the target are not accessible to minority shareholders that do not tender their shares and instead remain in the target, because the acquiring companies do not necessarily profit from an increase in the value of the target's market price—which could be shared with the target shareholders—but through an increase in the acquirer's stock price, as a result of the ability to control the target's resources.[127] The above indicate that equality in the context of takeover regulation does not continue as an underlying principle, once the bid is consummated and a group situation emerges. This, as well as realities and practical difficulties, make it a less attractive investment for minority shareholders to remain in the target and not to tender their shares.

Still, one could argue that minority shareholders may be satisfied with just a fair treatment, as long as they still have the ability to realise their investment in an open market, and they enjoy the added protection of the Listing Rules. According to LR 5.2.2 of the Listing Rules, if the bidder acquires over 75 per cent of a class of the target's shares, the percentage of shares of this specific class in the hands of the public falls below 25 per cent and this may result in a cancellation of listing pursuant to the FSA's request. In addition, under previous versions of the Listing Rules, the de-listing decision lay in the hands of the company's directors. For example, after the acquisition of Tempus by WPP, the bidder's directors, who also had majority of the target, delisted the target to pressurise minority shareholders into selling out. The current version of the Listing Rules provide that in order for an issuer to request the cancellation by the FSA of the listing of its shares it needs to obtain, at a general meeting, the prior approval of a resolution for the cancellation, from a majority of not less than 75 per cent of the holders of the listed securities.[128] However, this will not substantially ameliorate the position of minority shareholders, as long as the bidder has already in its hands more than 75 per cent of the target's shares pursuant to the takeover offer.

Through de-listing, the bidder can effectively reduce the marketability of the shares in the target. While this might not be a problem for the bidder, it is more likely to impose substantial costs on minority shareholders. This is because not only the risk of their investment increases—as they do

[127] M Bradley, 'Interfirm Tender Offers and the Market for Corporate Control' (1980) 35 *Journal of Business* 345. Bradley examined the post takeover performance of target companies' stock following successful partial tender offers in the US. While it is logical for free riding to be profitable since the stock performance of the targets should increase, he actually found out that it fell on average by 13%. He attributed that on the fact that the acquiring firms benefit not from increases in the target's market price but from increases in their own stock price; see also Jarrell and Bradley 'The Economic Effects of Federal and State Regulations of Cash Tender Offers.' (n 31 above) and Gilson and Black, *The Law and Finance of Corporate Acquisitions* (n 109 above) 1239.

[128] See LR 5.2.5 of the Listing Rules.

not have a viable exit option—but also they cannot benefit anymore from any increases in the target's market price resulting from the bidder's management of the target. In addition, the withdrawal of the listing also means that minority shareholders are deprived of the protection of the Listing Rules, especially in respect of pre-emption rights[129] and the free-transferability of shares.

V CONCLUSION

This chapter examines the assumption that wealth transfers from the acquiring to target shareholders may be attributed to the horizontal equity rules of takeover regulation. Although these costs are evident by increases in the target's premia, in acquiring firms with concentrated shareholdings, equality rules ensure equal distribution of the acquisition profits between majority and minority, by preventing the former from selling control just after the acquisition is consummated and 'making a grab' at the full benefits of the combined control. In that way, the benefits of equality rules are not confined to protecting the minority interests in the target, but can also protect the acquiring shareholders and have a market confidence function from which all investors benefit.

However, the costs that equality rules impose on bidders should not be underestimated, especially in the case of bidders with dispersed shareholdings, where no minority concerns exist. Overall, three types of costs concerns have been identified. First, rules that promote equality among target shareholders produce externalities, in the form of costs and disincentives that affect the bidder and its shareholders. Secondly, the application of the mandatory offer rule can produce problems of choice distortion for the acquirer's shareholders, when they are bestowed with the right to approve the acquisition. Finally, while there is no justification for pressurising target shareholders or in increasing takeover occurrence as a public policy, a level of coercion may be necessary for two reasons. First, the bidder should be able to acquire 100 per cent of the target's shares, in circumstances where it is imperative to do so, in order for the acquisition synergies to materialise. Secondly, the bidder should be able to discourage target shareholders from free riding on its efforts, which can cause a value-adding offer to fail.

[129] See above ch 3.

9

Adverse Change Risk—Withdrawing an Offer

I INTRODUCTION

DURING THE PERIOD that the offer remains open, it is not only the intervention of a rival bidder or the operation of risk arbitrageurs that may cause problems to the initial offeror. A number of events may occur that go beyond the control of the bidder, and that may alter the profitability of the offer to the extent that it is no longer desirable to acquire the target. The issue is further amplified by the fact that a takeover offer, as has been already argued, is a time-consuming mechanism. The Takeover Code requires the offer to remain open for a specific period of time and even to be extended under certain circumstances.[1] Moreover, the emergence of a counter-bidder further extends the offer timetable. The above expose the bidder to market or other target-specific risks for a substantial window of time. Adverse changes during the offer period could include market price declines in the acquirer's or target's value that make the deal economically unfavourable, or deteriorations of the assets, business, financial or trading position, profits or prospects of the target.

There are three points during or before the commencement of the offer timetable when the offeror may find itself in a position where it wants to withdraw its offer: first, after a potential bidder makes an announcement that it is considering making an offer, (possible offer announcement) either because it is required to do so under rules 2.2 and 2.9, or wishes to make such an announcement; secondly, after the bidder has announced its firm intention to place an offer and during the 28-day period within which it needs to post the offer document; and thirdly, after the bidder has posted the offer document but in any case before day 21, which is the first closing date of the announced offer.[2]

[1] See ch 6, above.

[2] Provided that the bidder did not announced its intention to extend its offer.

II WITHDRAWAL AFTER A POSSIBLE OFFER ANNOUNCEMENT

Rule 2.4(a) provides that where an announcement is made as a result of an obligation arising under rule 2.2, a brief statement confirming that talks are taking place or that the offeror is considering making an offer, is all that is required by the Takeover Code. Otherwise, the Code does not make express provision as to what information can be included in an announcement relating to a possible offer, except that note 1 on rule 2.4 requires prior consultation with the Panel if a person intends to refer to any pre-condition to the making of an offer in a possible offer announcement. However,

> [a]ny such pre-conditional possible offer announcement must:
>
> (a) clearly state whether or not the pre-conditions must be satisfied before an offer can be made or whether they are waivable; and
>
> (b) include a prominent warning to the effect that the announcement does not amount to a firm intention to make an offer and that, accordingly, there can be no certainty that any offer will be made even if the pre-conditions are satisfied or waived.[3]

The Code also does not impose any obligation on a potential offeror making a possible offer announcement to proceed with an offer. Until a firm intention to make an offer is notified, a potential offeror may withdraw its interest in proceeding with the offer at any time. Hence, the purpose of a possible offer announcement is only to inform shareholders and the market of the possibility that an offer might be made for the offeree company. It provides no certainty as to whether, or when, such an offer will in fact take place, or on what terms.[4] However two exceptions apply to the above general rule:

First, if any a statement in relation to the terms on which an offer might be made is included in an announcement by a potential offeror, the potential offeror will be bound by the statement if an offer for the offeree company is subsequently made, unless it reserved the right not to be so bound at the time the statement was made. In any case the Panel must be consulted. Where the statement concerned relates to the price of a possible offer, except with the consent of the Panel, the potential offeror will not be allowed subsequently to make an offer at a lower value, unless there has occurred an event which the potential offeror specified in the statement as an event which would enable it to be set aside.[5]

[3] Note 1 on r 2.4 of the Takeover Code.

[4] The Panel on Takeovers and Mergers, PCP 2004/4: *Consultation Paper Issued by the Code Committee of the Panel: Conditions and Pre-conditions. Revision Proposals Relating to Rules 2.4, 2.5, 2.7, 9.3, 13, 23, 24.6, 34, 35.1 and 38.3 of the Takeover Code and the SARs* (August 2004).

[5] Rule 2.4(c) of the Takeover Code.

Secondly, at any time following the announcement of a possible offer (provided the potential offeror has been publicly named), the offeree company may request that the Panel impose a time limit for the potential offeror to clarify its intentions with regard to the offeree company. If a time limit for clarification is imposed by the Panel, the potential offeror must, before the expiry of the time limit, announce either a firm intention to make an offer for the offeree company in accordance with rule 2.5 or that it does not intend to make an offer for the offeree company, in which case the announcement will be treated as a statement to which rule 2.8 applies.[6]

III WITHDRAWAL AFTER THE FIRM ANNOUNCEMENT AND PRIOR TO THE POSTING OF THE OFFER

A Rule 2.7 and Subsequent Developments

The position of the Panel on the ability of the bidder to disengage from an announcement to proceed with an offer is encapsulated in rule 2.7 of the Takeover Code and for long has been based on Panel Statements 1974/02 and 1974/07. This position was further interpreted by the Panel's adjudication in the appeal by WPP against the Executive's ruling in WPP's offer for Tempus plc,[7] and has undergone an extensive review by the Code Committee,[8] which resulted in the wording of rule 2.7 being changed

According to the rule's previous wording when there had been an announcement of a firm intention to make an offer, the offeror was obliged, except with the consent of the Panel, to proceed with the offer, unless the posting of the offer was subject to the prior fulfilment of a specific condition and that condition had not been met. Furthermore, note 1 on rule 2.7 continued that a change in general 'economic, industrial or political circumstances' would not justify failure to proceed with an announced offer. To justify a decision not to proceed, circumstances of an exceptional and specific nature were required. Similarly, in a statement issued at a time of major market decline in 1974, the Panel emphasised that general market risks or changes in legislative policy, which might suggest that a proposed acquisition would not be as advantageous for the offeror company as it had been hoped, when the intention to offer was first announced, were to be borne by the offeror. In order

> to justify a unilateral withdrawal, the Panel would normally require some circumstance of an entirely exceptional nature and amounting to something of the kind that could frustrate a legal contract.[9]

[6] Rule 2.4(b) of the Takeover Code.
[7] See n 10 below.
[8] The Panel on Takeovers and Mergers, PCP 2004/4 (n 4 above).
[9] Changes in circumstances, Panel Statement 1974/02 (January 1974).

It has been a firm view of the Panel that a lower test would permit the bidder to defeat the purpose of rule 2.7 and Panel Statement 1974/02.[10] According to the latter,

> the terms and timing of an announcement of intention to offer and of the posting of offer documents are, subject to the Code, entirely in the hands of the offeror. It is therefore right, that an offeror should accept the risk of a change of circumstances in the intervening period. Once an offer is announced, the market in the shares of the offeree company is likely to be, at least to some extent, supported by the price at which the offer has been fixed. It follows that withdrawal would contribute to the market having been a false one.

Similarly, under General Principle 6 of the Code, it is the duty of the bidder, along with the other parties to the offer, to prevent the creation of a false market in the securities of the target and itself.

The above position of the Panel dates back from a period when normally no conditions were attached to the announcement or the posting of an offer. However, since it has been in recent years a standard practice for a number of conditions and pre-conditions to accompany an announcement of a firm intention to place an offer, the wording of rule 2.7 has changed to reflect such practice.[11]

Under the present wording, two categories of circumstances are recognised under which the bidder may not post the announced offer. In the first case the bidder may not post the offer by seeking recourse to the conditions or pre-conditions attached to the announcement of the offer, while in the second case the bidder may not post its offer upon the occurrence of certain events for which no reference is required in the conditions attached to the announcement. More specifically, rule 2.7 provides that, in cases where there has been an announcement of a firm intention to make an offer, the offeror must normally proceed with the offer unless:

— the offeror is permitted to invoke a pre-condition to the posting of the offer; or
— would be permitted to invoke a condition to the offer if the offer were made.

Under what circumstances the bidder will be able to invoke such conditions is to be determined by rule 13.[12] In the absence of specific conditions, and on the basis of the above analysis and the history of the rule, it could be argued that the bidder might be able to walk away with the consent of the Panel under the same circumstances that a legal contract could be frustrated. To that effect according to note 1 on rule 2.7 an offeror need not proceed with posting its offer if, in the mean time, a competitor has already

[10] Offer by WPP Group Plc for Tempus Group Plc, Panel Statement 2001/15 (6 November 2001) para 16.
[11] The Panel on Takeovers and Mergers 2004, PCP 2004/4 (n 4 above).
[12] See below.

posted a higher offer.[13] The effect of a higher competitive offer announcement is automatic and there is no need for the Panel's consent to be sought. The Takeover Code also includes as a quasi presumption of such a significant event the announcement or the approval by the target's shareholders of any frustrating action, meaning that, once the target shareholders approve a frustrating action, such an approval qualifies as a significant event that permits the bidder to withdraw its offer with the prior approval of the Panel.[14]

B Pre-conditions

Pre-conditions are conditions attached to an announcement of a firm intention to proceed with an offer, whose satisfaction or waiver is necessary for the offer to be posted. In that sense, they differ from any other offer conditions that permit the bidder to withdraw its offer once posted and, according to rule 2.5(b)(iv), they also need to be included in the announcement of the bidder's firm intention to proceed with the offer. The difference is that, while the latter must be satisfied or waived within 21 days after the offer is declared unconditional as to acceptances,[15] the satisfaction or waiver of pre-conditions is required for the standard Takeover Code offer timetable to commence.[16]

Initially, the Panel in its 1998–99 Annual Report seemed to suggest that pre-conditions could, under certain circumstances, be subjective. However, the Panel's decision in WPP's offer for Tempus[17] seemed to suggest that the same principles which underlie note 2 on rule 13 also apply in the case of pre-conditions. This means that the bidder will be allowed to rely on such conditions, provided that they meet the objectivity and materiality requirements imposed by the Takeover Code and the Panel.[18] This approach has been upheld by the Code Committee. To that effect, rule 13 has been revised so as to explicitly cover pre-conditions as well, and it is considered that the guidance contained in the above Annual Report has no continuing application.[19] The main rationale behind the Code revisions

[13] Note 1 on r 2.7 of the Takeover Code.

[14] Rule 2.7 and note 5 on r 21.1 stipulate that the Panel may allow an offeror not to proceed with its offer if, at any time during the offer period prior to the posting of the offer document either the offeree company passes a resolution in general meeting as envisaged by r 21.1, or the Panel has given consent for the offeree company to proceed with an action or transaction to which r 21.1 applies without a shareholders' meeting.

[15] Rule 31.7 of the Takeover Code.

[16] This is because no posting of the offer document will follow unless all pre-conditions are met. See rr 30.1 and 31.7 of the Takeover Code.

[17] Panel Statement 2001/15 (n 10 above).

[18] See below.

[19] The Panel on Takeovers and Mergers 2004, PCP 2004/4 (n 4 above) 36. See also below about r 13.

was that a firm announcement under rule 2.5 is a step forward from a possible announcement under rule 2.2 or 2.9. The bidder can always structure its announcement as a possible announcement, attaching any conditions it may find necessary. In addition, permitting more subjective or wider pre-conditions to be included in a firm announcement could defeat the offer timetable and put the target under siege for a longer period of time than permitted.[20]

According to new rule 13.3,

> the Panel must be consulted in advance if a person proposes to include in an announcement any pre-condition to which the posting of the offer will be subject.[21]

This seems to bring the application of the materiality test of rule 13.4, in the case of pre-conditions, forward in time: the bidder is not merely prevented from invoking a pre-condition which was included in the announcement of its firm intention and does not meet the materiality requirements of the Panel—it is actually not allowed to make the posting of its offer subject to such a pre-condition in the first place. At least, this approach provides more certainty to the bidder, who can choose in advance whether to proceed or not with the announcement without the pre-condition.

However, there may be circumstances where a pre-conditional offer structure is more preferable than a conventional offer structure. Unfortunately, the circumstances identified by the Takeover Code have nothing to do with the bidder's protection, but provide more certainty to the target shareholders. These are cases where a competition clearance or other regulatory clearances cannot be obtained within the normal offer timetable. In such cases, under the previous regime, the offeror would normally be allowed to rely on posting a new offer pursuant to the exceptions provided by rule 35.1. To that effect, and in the absence of any relevant pre-conditions for the posting of the offer, once the offeror's initial offer has lapsed, the offeror can only make a further offer with the recommendation of the offeree company's board once the clearance is subsequently received.[22] The Panel may also grant its consent in circumstances where

> it is likely to prove, or has proved, impossible to obtain material official authorisations or regulatory clearances relating to the offer within the Code timetable.[23]

On the same basis, the Code permits only pre-conditions that relate to clearance from competition authorities, or involve another material official authorisation or regulatory clearance relating to the offer, provided

[20] The Panel on Takeovers and Mergers 2004, PCP 2004/4 (n 4 above) 20.
[21] Rule 13.3 of the Takeover Code.
[22] Note (a)(i) on r 35.1 of the Takeover Code.
[23] Note (b) on r 35.1 of the Takeover Code.

also that either the offer is recommended by the board of the offeree company or the Panel is satisfied that it is likely to prove impossible to obtain the clearance within the usual Takeover Code timetable.[24] This is to ensure that the offeror will definitely proceed with its offer if the authorisation is given, since under the previous regime there was no certainty that the second offer would be made, or that the offeror would be bound by its original offer price when making the second offer.[25]

According to new rule 13, financing pre-conditions may also be permitted, but only in exceptional circumstances: in cases, for example, where a regulatory clearance is necessary and where the regulatory timetable is likely to be unusually lengthy.[26] However, the Code Committee does not consider that the timetable for obtaining any necessary OFT/Competition Commission and/or European Commission clearances would typically satisfy this requirement.[27] In addition, it should be noted that pursuant to the implementation of the Takeovers Directive, in all cases where there is a cash element to an offer the firm offer announcement has to

> include confirmation by the financial adviser or another appropriate person that resources are available to the offeror sufficient to satisfy full acceptance of the offer.[28]

This rule is backed up by a new General Principle 5, which provides that

> an offeror must announce a bid only after ensuring that he/she can fulfil in full any cash consideration, if such is offered, and after taking all reasonable measures to secure the implementation of any other type of consideration.

Similarly, under rule 13.4(b),

> following the announcement of a firm intention to make an offer, an offeror should use all reasonable efforts to ensure the satisfaction of any conditions or pre-conditions to which the offer is subject.

To that effect:

(a) any pre-condition on financing 'must be satisfied (or waived), or the offer must be withdrawn, within 21 days after the satisfaction (or waiver) of any other pre-condition or pre-conditions permitted by [rule 13]'; and
(b) 'the offeror and its financial adviser must confirm in writing to the Panel before announcement of the offer that they are not aware of any reason why the offeror would be unable to satisfy the financing pre-condition within that 21 day period'.[29]

24 Rule 13.3. See also The Panel on Takeovers and Mergers, PCP 2004/4 (n 4 above) 22.
25 The Panel on Takeovers and Mergers, PCP 2004/4 (n 4 above) 22.
26 The Panel on Takeovers and Mergers, PCP 2004/4 (n 4 above) 26.
27 The Panel on Takeovers and Mergers, PCP 2004/4 (n 4 above) 26.
28 Rule 2.5(c) of the Takeover Code.
29 Note on rrule 13.1 and 13.3 of the Takeover Code.

The Code Committee[30] considered the circumstances in which the Panel might exercise the discretion given to it by rule 13.3 and concluded that

> the circumstances in which the Panel should be prepared to consider exercising its discretion to allow pre-conditions outside the permitted categories are likely to be very limited.

According to the Code Committee's statement,

> such circumstances might arise, exceptionally, when the requested pre-condition:
>
> — relates to a matter concerning the offeree company that is likely to be incapable of resolution within the normal offer timetable (so that a condition would not be appropriate); and
> — crucially, is a matter without which it would be unreasonable to expect the offeror to make the offer at all (and it would not, in the circumstances, be in the interests of offeree company shareholders to make the offeror wait to bid).

However, according to the Code Committee, the granting of allowance to pre-conditions is an area in which the Panel should act with circumspection and be aware of the risk of undermining the certainty provided by General Principle 3. To that end, the consent of the offeree's board to a proposed pre-condition is not a factor that should determine the granting of such allowance by the Panel. Similarly, a pre-condition related to the offer receiving the recommendation of the board will not be acceptable either.[31] Similarly, pre-conditions relating to matters such as the completion of a transaction by the target or the resolution of litigation in which either the bidder or the target is involved will either be considered by the Panel as a matter that should be a condition to be dealt with in the normal Code timetable, or the bidder should make a possible offer announcement instead.[32]

Conclusively, the current position of the Code on pre-conditions is as follows:

— The announcement of any pre-conditions to which the posting of the offer is subject requires the Panel's previous consent.
— Allowed pre-conditions will normally relate to regulatory clearances.
— Financing pre-conditions may also be permitted, but only in exceptional circumstances.
— The consent of the offeree's board to a proposed pre-condition is not a factor that should determine the granting of a relevant consent by the Panel.

[30] The Panel on Takeovers and Mergers, RS2004/4 *Conditions and pre-conditions—Statement by the Code Committee of the Panel following the external consultation process on PCP 2004/4* (April 2004) para 4.5.9.

[31] *Ibid*, 10.

[32] The Panel on Takeovers and Mergers, RS2004/4 (n 30 above).

— A pre-condition related to the offer receiving the recommendation of the board is not acceptable.
— The Panel's consent will not be granted in cases where the bidder could either make a possible offer announcement or where the issue can be resolved within the offer timetable by posting the offer under a condition similar to the requested pre-condition.

C Other Offer Conditions

While the above approach in respect of pre-conditions seems very strict, some comfort can be given to the bidder, in that it may be permitted not to proceed with posting of the offer, not by relying on a pre-condition but by invoking one of the other offer conditions that normally can be relied upon after the offer is posted. Such conditions, as seen above, are required to be disclosed at the time of the announcement of the firm intention.[33] In such circumstances, where it becomes clear after the announcement of a firm offer, but before posting the offer document, that one or more offer conditions (as distinct from pre-conditions) are breached (and not capable of remedy) or otherwise incapable of satisfaction in accordance with the usual materiality standards applicable under rule 13,[34] it has been the Panel's practice to grant a dispensation from the otherwise pointless obligation under rules 2.7 and 30.1 to post the offer document.[35] New rule 2.7 reflects this practice by permitting the bidder not to post its offer if it would be permitted to invoke a condition to the offer if the offer were made.

IV WITHDRAWALS AFTER THE POSTING OF THE OFFER

The confinement of rule 2.7 to the period between the announcement of the bidder's firm intention to make an offer and the posting of the offer documents leaves little room for a posted offer to be withdrawn, in cases where the bidder cannot rely on a condition that it has included in the offer. Nevertheless, since it is now standard practice for bidders to include a number of conditions in their offer, a key part of the regulatory treatment of offer withdrawals is rule 13.4(a) of the Takeover Code, which provides that the circumstances that give rise to the right to invoke a condition must be 'of material significance to the offeror in the context of the offer'. The only conditions to which the rule does not apply are the acceptance and

[33] Rule 2.5(b)(vi) of the Takeover Code. See above.
[34] See below.
[35] The Panel on Takeovers and Mergers, PCP 2004/4 (n 4 above) 23.

EC/UK antitrust conditions.[36] Similarly, rule 13.4 does not apply, in practice, to other conditions required to give effect to some overriding statutory or regulatory requirement necessary to implement the offer or to issue any consideration securities under the terms of the offer (such as a listing condition or a class 1 shareholder approval condition).[37]

Accordingly, the answer to the question of whether the bidder is able to withdraw its offer after it is posted depends first on examining what conditions the bidder is permitted to include in its offer, and secondly, on determining what constitutes a 'material significance to the offeror in the context of the offer'.

A Conditions Attached to the Offer

The typology of the conditions that a bidder can attach to its offer depends on the type of the offer and varies between mandatory and voluntary, hostile and friendly offers.

Under rule 9.3, mandatory offers

> must be conditional only upon the offeror having received acceptances in respect of shares which, together with shares acquired before or during the offer, will result in the offeror and any party acting in concert with it, holding shares carrying more than 50% of the voting rights.

Moreover,

> no acquisition of any interest in shares which would give rise to a requirement for a mandatory offer under [rule 9] may be made if the making and the implementation of such offer [is subject to] the passing of a resolution at any meeting of shareholders of the offeror or upon any other conditions, consents or arrangements.[38]

This effectively means that if the offeror finds itself in a position to make a mandatory offer, it must bear entirely the risk of any adverse changes or events during the period that a mandatory offer must remain open, since it cannot attach any kind of conditions to the offer other than the acceptance condition. It does not even have a viable exit from its offer by manipulating the level of acceptances it wishes to receive, since the Code sets the level of acceptances at 50 per cent and not the 90 per cent that acquirers usually set.

Things are different in relation to voluntary offers, but again there is a number of restrictions and qualifications in relation to the nature of the conditions that can be attached. First, the bidder cannot include conditions

[36] See rr 13.4 and 12.1(c) of the Takeover Code. See also proposed r 13.2. The Panel on Takeovers and Mergers 2004 PCP 2004/4 (n 4 above).

[37] The Panel on Takeovers and Mergers, PCP 2004/4 (n 4 above) 27.

[38] See r 9.3(a) and (b) of the Takeover Code. The only exception is conditions related to clearance from the Competition Commission and the European Commission: r 9.4.

that can be triggered by the subjective judgement of the offeror's directors or the fulfilment of which is in their hands.[39] However, the Takeover Code provides that

> the Panel may be prepared to accept an element of subjectivity in certain circumstances where it is not practicable to specify all the factors on which satisfaction of a particular condition or pre-condition may depend, especially in cases involving official authorisations, the granting of which may be subject to additional material obligations for the offeror or the offeree company (as the case may be)..[40]

Conditions must be objective and refer to events and changes that go beyond the control of the offeror before and during the offer period. Such conditions may relate to securing all the necessary regulatory consents and authorities or the absence of any actions taken by any competent regulatory authority, usually in relation to competition and antitrust policies.[41] In the latter case, the offeror is required according to rule 12.1, to include such a condition in its offer.

The bidder is also not able to rely on conditions where their breach is caused by its failure to show the necessary standard of care in the preparation of the offer.[42] Under rule 2.5(a) of the Takeover Code,[43] offers should be announced, only 'after the most careful and responsible consideration[44].'

In other words, events that could have been avoided if the offeror had showed the required standard of skill and care cannot be used as conditions whose breach may permit the bidder to withdraw its offer. Even if the latter succeeds in withdrawing its offer, it is very likely that it will face disciplinary proceedings.[45]

The bidder is also not permitted to make an offer conditional upon financing becoming available.[46] This is further emphasised by rule 2.5(c)

[39] Rule 13.1 of the Takeover Code.

[40] *Ibid.*

[41] See r 12.1 of the Takeover Code.

[42] This issue has already been addressed in ch 4 above.

[43] Previously General Principle 3 of the Takeover Code. Pursuant to the implementation of the Takeovers Directive, General Principle 3 was deleted as a principle and its wording was incorporated in r2.5.

[44] See also the wording in r 13.4(b) of the Takeover Code.

[45] See Proposed Offer by Wm Low and Co plc for Budgens plc, Panel Statement 1989/14 (August 1989). Although Low's board made the offer conditional on its estimates being appropriately verified, the Panel emphasised that it is not enough for the bidder to discharge its duty of care by just including conditions in the offer, and held that relying on a computer model for the target's projections was not enough to discharge the offeror's and its advisers' duty of care under General Principle 3, especially in a friendly takeover. However, the Panel, upon agreement by the target's board, decided to permit the bidder not to proceed with its offer. At the same time, though, it considered disciplinary proceedings for breach of General Principle 3. See also ch 4 above.

[46] See note on rr 31.1 and 13.3 of the Takeover Code.

which, pursuant to the implementation of the Takeovers Directive, requires that a cash confirmation[47] is required to be included in the rule 2.5 announcement for all cash offers and not just in the case of a mandatory offer. In addition the Takeover Code stipulates that a bidder should only announce an offer when it has every reason to believe that it can and will continue to be able to implement the offer.[48]

An issue arises in circumstances where the bidder wishes to finance its offer with a share issue. In such cases the Takeover Code introduces an exemption from the general rule that no financing conditions are permitted, since it provides that in such cases the offer must be made subject to any condition required, as a matter of law or regulatory requirement, in order validly to issue such securities or to have them listed or admitted to trading. Conditions which will normally be considered necessary for such purposes include:

(i) the passing of any resolution necessary to create or allot the new securities and / or to allot the new securities on a non-pre-emptive basis (if relevant); and
(ii) where the new securities are to be admitted to listing or to trading on any investment exchange or market, any necessary listing or admission to trading condition.[49]

Such conditions, however, must not be waivable and the Panel must be consulted in advance.[50]To that effect, it will not be appropriate for the offer to be conditional upon any placing, underwriting or underpinning agreement in relation to the issue of the new securities becoming unconditional and / or not being terminated. A condition of this nature is not necessary as a matter of law or regulatory requirement in order to issue the new securities or, therefore, to implement the offer.[51] Similarly, the implementation of the Takeovers Directive resulted in the abolition of the Panel's discretion to allow conditional cash confirmation.[52]

A discussion arose with regard to the acceptability of financing conditions relating not to the offer itself but to the working capital requirements of the enlarged offeror group after the completion of the offer.[53] 'Working capital' in this context means any third party debt of the enlarged offeror group that is required for reasons other than satisfying the cash consider-

[47] Pursuant to r 24.7 of the Takeover Code.

[48] Rule 2.5(a). This is also deduced by r 1(c) and r 24.7. See also G Stedman, *Takeovers* (London, Longman, 1993) 218. However, see above about the cases where the bidder will be allowed to include a financing pre-condition above.

[49] See also r 24.9 of the Takeover Code.

[50] See note on rr 31.1 and 13.3 of the Takeover Code.

[51] The Panel on Takeovers and Mergers, *Practice Statement No 10: Cash Offers Financed by the Issue of Offeror Securities* (April 2005).

[52] Paragraph 2 of old r 24.7 of the Takeover Code.

[53] The Panel on Takeovers and Mergers, *Practice Statement No 11: Working Capital Requirements in Cash and Securities Exchange Offers* (April 2005).

ation due under the offer. In line with the above analysis, the Executive held the view that no such financing conditions are acceptable unless they are of an exceptional nature such as those described in the note on rule 13.3 on the acceptability of financing pre-conditions.[54] In addition if working capital concerns arise after the announcement of the offer, the offeror will be able to allow its offer to lapse only if it is material enough to be able to invoke one of the conditions to the offer in accordance with the usual application of rule 13.4(a).[55]

The bidder will also seek to secure that no material adverse changes will take place that may affect the value of the target. Such material adverse change clauses ('MAC clauses') can either refer to a specific event or be more general in their wording. Examples of specific clauses are: that the target shall not declare any unexpected and substantial dividends; that no material litigations will emerge; that the target will not engage in any material contracts or sales of its assets beyond the ordinary course of business; that no loss of any material contract or loan or asset as a result of the change of control will take place, etc. All such clauses must satisfy the materiality test required by the Takeover Code.[56]

Specific clauses can also be drawn without any reference to materiality ('bespoke clauses'). In those cases, the bidder specifically determines the exact circumstances that may give rise to a right to withdraw its offer. Such bespoke conditions may, for example, stipulate that the 'net debt' of the offeree company shall not exceed a particular amount; or if the offeree company is a property investment company, that no event occurs (such as an act of terrorism) as a result of which a particular percentage of the portfolio is rendered unoccupiable for a particular period of time.[57]

A standard general clause may provide that

> no material adverse change or deterioration shall occur in the business, assets, financial or trading position or profits or prospects of the target or its group.

While specific clauses may provide more certainty as to what constitutes a material change for the bidder, they carry the risk that certain events may have not been anticipated. This is why a general MAC clause is normally present in most offers, irrespective of the existence of other more bespoke clauses.

In friendly takeovers, the MAC clause may not appear as a condition to the bidder's obligation to close the offer but as a recurrent representation or warranty by the target's board, repeated during the period of the offer, stating that no material adverse change has occurred in the target's

[54] *Ibid*. See also above in relation to pre-conditions.

[55] See below.

[56] See r 13.4(a) of the Takeover Code.

[57] Sample clauses taken from The Panel on Takeovers and Mergers, PCP 2004/4 (n 4 above) 7.

financial position since the relevant accounting date.[58] In any case, conditions attached to friendly takeover offers, especially specific ones that do not just represent standard practice, are more likely to be heavily negotiated and included in the offer with the consent of the target.

B The Materiality of the Adverse Change

The Panel was provided with the opportunity to interpret the 'material significance requirement' of rule 13.4(a)[59] in respect of MAC clauses in its decision on WPP Plc's offer for Tempus Plc. WPP sought to invoke the general MAC condition included in its offer for Tempus, believing that the terrorist attacks on 11 September 2001 had had a material adverse impact on the prospects of Tempus. However, the Panel refused to allow WPP to invoke its MAC clause.[60]

There are four key elements in the Panel's decision.

First, the materiality test applied by the Panel does not relate only to the interpretation of a material adverse change as anticipated by a general MAC clause. It is wider and refers to the 'material significance' required by rule 13.4, which is required every time the bidder wants to invoke any condition attached to its offer. Hence, the materiality interpretation introduced by the Panel is not confined to the case of general MAC clauses, but applies to any condition that the bidder seeks to invoke,[61] irrespective of how specifically and objectively it may be drafted.[62]

Secondly, while the wording of r 13.4(a), which, as already argued, is the key test applied when the bidder wishes to withdraw its offer, seems to suggest that the test is subjective–'the condition must be of material significance *to the offeror* in the context of the offer' (emphasis added)—the Panel has chosen an objective test and reserved itself the right to determine whether the test is met. More precisely, the Panel considers that the issue of material significance to the offeror in the context of an offer is to be determined objectively. This does not prevent the Panel from being

[58] K Birkett, 'Untying the Knot: Material adverse change clauses' (2002) XIII (March) *PLC* 17.

[59] Then note 2 on rule 13.

[60] Panel Statement 2001/15 (n 10 above). The case referred to a cash offer made by WPP Plc for the whole of the shares in Tempus Plc not already owned by WPP. After the 11 September attacks and the announcement of Tempus interim reports for the six months following the terrorist attacks, and although WPP's offer became unconditional as to acceptances, WPP announced that it was to seek a ruling from the Panel Executive that it was entitled under the Code to invoke its material adverse change condition. The Panel Executive ruled that WPP should not be permitted to invoke the material adverse change condition.

[61] Except for the acceptance and antitrust regulation provisions.

[62] See The Panel on Takeovers and Mergers, *Practice Statement No 5: Note 2 on Rule 13—Invocation of Conditions* (April 2004). See, however, below about negotiated or bespoke conditions.

heedful of the view of the offeror's board on that question, and any other informed views such as those of the offeree, but giving those views such weight as seems appropriate in the light of all the evidence.[63] However, at the same time, the burden of proof is on the bidder to prove that a material adverse change affecting the target has occurred and that this is of material significance to the offeror in the context of its offer.[64] What also makes the bidder's task even more difficult is the fact that, as practitioners argue, the WPP/Tempus case shows that the Panel will be very reluctant to require an offeree company to disclose information that could be helpful to the bidder in that respect.[65]

Thirdly, the confinement of r 2.7 to pre-posting situations, as seen above, means that a change in general economic circumstances may legitimately be relied upon when seeking to invoke the relevant condition, but only to the extent that by doing so the materiality and objectivity requirements of the Panel are met.[66] This means that general or sectoral economic declines that were known to the bidder or could have been foreseen at the time the offer was announced cannot be legitimately relied upon.[67] Since the Panel's adjudication on the Offer by WPP Group Plc for Tempus Group Plc, rule 2.7 has changed to the extent that reference to general economic terms was deleted even for pre-posting situations.

Fourthly, the Panel in considering the materiality test of rule 13.4, reached the opinion that meeting this test requires a circumstance of an entirely exceptional nature[68] and an adverse change of very considerable significance, striking at the heart of the purpose of the transaction in question, analogous to something that would justify frustration of a legal contract.[69]

In that context, the Panel refused to accept that it is enough for the offeror to show that there has been

> a change which undermines, from the offeror's perspective, the rationale for having made the offer at the price and on the terms specified.[70]

Similarly, the Panel made clear that a temporary effect on profitability was not, under the specific circumstances, of itself sufficient for the bidder to invoke a withdraw condition. The adverse change has to be long lasting, since a purchaser of 100 per cent of a company for strategic reasons is clearly investing for the long term and, therefore, something of material

[63] See Panel Statement 2001/15 (n 10 above) para 20.
[64] Panel Statement 2001/15 (n 10 above) para 21.
[65] Birkett, 'Untying the Knot: Material adverse change clauses' (n 58 above).
[66] Panel Statement 2001/15 (n 10 above) para 17.
[67] See above about the types of conditions that are allowed to be included in an offer.
[68] See Panel Statement 1974/02 (n 9 above).
[69] See Panel Statement 1974/02 (n 9 above) and Panel Statement 2001/15 (n 10 above) para 16.
[70] Panel Statement 2001/15 (n 10 above) para 16.

significance to such an offeror in the context of the offer has to be long term.[71]

It should be noted that, after the Panel's decision in WPP's offer for Tempus, the Executive retreated from the frustration analogy, insisting, though, on the other qualitative elements of the Panel's analysis of the materiality test of rule 13.4.[72] Similarly, the Code Committee upheld the Executive's interpretation.[73] However, in the case of the offer of Kellen Acquisitions Limited for East Surrey Holdings Plc the Executive ruled that it was not permitting a bidder to invoke a condition even though there had been developments since the bid was announced which had not been anticipated by either party. This was because the developments were found to be 'not of sufficient substance' to permit invoking a condition.[74]

Conclusively, the bidder is able to withdraw an offer by benefiting from the satisfaction or waiver of a condition attached to its offer, as long as the circumstance that the condition seeks to cover satisfies the following conditions:

— It is not a consequence of the bidder's failure to show the necessary standard of care required by the Takeover Code in the preparation of the offer.
— It is of an entirely exceptional nature, meaning that it could not have reasonably been foreseen at the time of the announcement of the offer.
— It is of a very considerable significance, striking at the heart of the purpose of the transaction in question. This means that it usually should have a material long-term effect on the offeror that substantially alters the continuing strategic benefits of proceeding with the bid. Short-term effects are not usually enough to justify withdrawal.
— The materiality of the effect that the event has on the bidder must be able to be determined objectively. A material change which undermines only from the offeror's perspective the reasons for having made the offer at the price and on the terms specified is not enough to invoke a withdraw condition. The term 'reason' should not be confused with the term 'purpose'. The bidder may have many reasons for selecting a specific price and including specific terms in the offer, but those reasons are not the same as the purpose of initiating the transaction in the first place.

[71] Panel Statement 2001/15 (n 10 above).

[72] The Panel on Takeovers and Mergers, *Practice Statement No.5* (n 62 above).

[73] The Panel on Takeovers and Mergers, PCP 2004/4 (n 4 above).

[74] Kellen Acquisitions Ltd and East Surrey Holdings Plc, Panel Statement 2005/40 (October 2005).

C The Doctrine of Frustration

The frustration analogy of the Panel's materiality test requires a brief examination of the doctrine. A contract is said to be frustrated when a supervening event occurs which so fundamentally affects the performance of the contract that, in the eyes of the law, the contract comes to an end and both parties are discharged from any future duty to perform. The contractual obligation becomes incapable of being performed when the circumstances in which performance is called for would 'render it a thing radically different from that which was undertaken by the contract'.[75] Supervening impossibility of performance is the most obvious ground of frustration, such as destruction of the subject matter of the contract,[76] subsequent legal changes,[77] or supervening illegality.[78] Financial loss in performing the contract, or hardship or inconvenience would not justify frustration of a legal contract.[79] The test of frustration is an objective test,[80] and a party cannot rely on self-induced frustration[81] or, prima facie, on foreseen and foreseeable events.[82]

If a contract is frustrated it automatically comes to an end. If not, the parties must perform, however burdensome the contract may have become, and no matter how much the circumstances may have changed. There is no duty for the parties to renegotiate the contract terms, nor does the court have power to modify the contract on the grounds of hardship.[83]

A clause in a contract that is intended to deal with the event which has occurred will normally preclude the application of the doctrine of frustration.[84] This means that the parties are free to allocate the risk of an adverse change in any way they want, by including relevant conditions in their contract. Such conditions exclude the strict test of frustration and it is the intentions of the parties and the proper construction of the contract that determine whether circumstances have occurred that could permit the contract to be terminated without performance.

When the offeror places an offer a contractual relationship arises between the offeror and the accepting shareholders, the determination of which is a matter of law. Under general law, conditions attached to the

[75] *Davis Contactors Ltd v Fareham UDC* [1956] AC 696(HL) 729.
[76] *Taylor v Caldwell* (1863) 3 B & S 826 (QB).
[77] *Baily v De Crespigny* (1869) LR 4 QB 180.
[78] *Metropolitan Water Board v Dick, Kerr & Co Ltd* [1918] AC 119.
[79] *Davis Contactors Ltd v Fareham UDC* (n 75 above).
[80] *Davis Contactors Ltd v Fareham UDC* (n 75 above).
[81] Ie, a frustration due to one's own conduct: *Bank Line Ltd v Arthur Capel & Co* [1919] AC 675 (HL) 700.
[82] *Davis Contactors Ltd v Fareham UDC* (n 75 above). However, it is also a matter of construction of the contract: see *Chandler Bros Ltd v Boswell* [1936] 3 All ER 179 (CA).
[83] R Goode, *Commercial Law*, 2nd edn (London, Penguin Books, 1995) 140.
[84] *Joseph Constantine SS Line Ltd v Imperial Smelting Corp Ltd* [1942] AC 154 (HL) 163.

offer the waiver or fulfilment of which permit the bidder to withdraw its offer exclude the strict frustration test. However, the Panel's initial approach departs from general law by requiring that such conditions can only be legitimately invoked when requirements analogous to the frustration test are met. From a strict legal perspective, this renders the inclusion of conditions completely useless, since any contract can be frustrated without the need to rely on specific conditions. As mentioned above, the Panel subsequently retreated from its frustration analogy,[85] without, though, altering the qualitative characteristics of its materiality test that gave rise to such an analogy in the first place.

Accordingly, despite its subsequent retreat from the frustration analogy, whilst, under general law, the parties are free to determine the severity of the events that can frustrate their contract, the Panel takes it upon itself to determine whether the frustrating event stipulated by the parties is material and objective enough to justify unilateral withdrawal. Hence, the Panel makes mandatory an objectivity and materiality rule, which under the law of frustration is only a default rule.

This stricter approach of the Panel raises the issue of whether the bidder could seek, in a courtroom, termination of its contract with the accepting target shareholders on the basis of the conditions attached to its offer and irrespective of the Panel's decision. However, this might be difficult in that the courts will more likely take the view that the parties to the offer have contracted under a regulatory regime which specifies that the Code and the Panel dictate what is allowed and what is not, as far as withdrawal is concerned, and this regime will be seen as replacing the general law.

D Negotiated or Bespoke Conditions

As seen above, the Panel's overriding materiality requirements apply even in cases of negotiated conditions or bespoke conditions—where the bidder explicitly describes the circumstances that may give rise to the right to invoke them—without any reference to materiality determination.[86] Such a strict approach gives rise to a number of concerns that have also been identified by the Code Committee of the Panel.[87] First, the bidder should be able to rely on conditions whose significance is specifically identified in advance. The same applies to conditions that the bidder heavily negotiated with the target and which, hence, reflect the views of both parties on materiality and fairness. Secondly, such conditions may be accompanied by a higher price offered, as a result of the reduction in the bidder's interim risk. Thirdly, the market is, in advance, fully aware of the specific circum-

[85] See above.
[86] For examples see above.
[87] The Panel on Takeovers and Mergers, PCP 2004/4 (note 4 above) 8–9.

stances when the offer may be withdrawn; hence, there is no risk that a false market may arise.[88] Finally, excessive restrictions on the ability of the bidder to determine the conditions which its offer is subject to may prevent otherwise profitable deals from taking place.

Despite the above concerns, the Code Committee expressed the view that rule 13.4 and the overriding materiality requirements imposed by the Panel should equally apply in the case of negotiated and bespoke conditions, and that the bidder should not be able to contract out of the application of the relevant rules.[89] However, it proposed that in applying the overriding materiality test, the Panel should also consider among others the following factors:

— whether the condition in question was negotiated with the target's board;
— whether the condition was expressly drawn to offeree company shareholders' attention in the offer document or announcement; and
— whether the condition was included to take account of the particular nature of the business of the offeree company.[90]

Finally, the Code Committee held the view that the Panel should be more willing to permit the bidder to invoke a specific condition rather than relying on a general MAC clause.[91] Although such an approach preserves the Panel's exclusive right to determine whether the satisfaction or waiver of a condition is material enough to justify unilateral withdrawal, it recognises an element of subjectivity, as long as the bidder's views are clearly expressed and properly disclosed ex ante. In that, it seems more in keeping with the wording of rule 13.4 that seems to suggest such an element of subjectivity.[92]

V ALTERNATIVE GET OUTS

In view of the difficulties associated with invoking a material adverse change condition, and in cases that the bidder has not foreseen the adverse change by including a bespoke condition in its offer, it may be easier for the offeror to walk away by relying on three other conditions: the 'acceptance' condition, the 'competition clearance' condition or the 'approval by the acquiring shareholders' condition, where applicable.

An offeror who wishes to cause its offer to lapse is often able to do so by not relaxing the acceptance condition for less than 100 per cent of the

[88] The Panel on Takeovers and Mergers, PCP 2004/4 (n 4 above) 8.
[89] The Panel on Takeovers and Mergers, PCP 2004/4 (n 4 above) 9–10. See also The Panel on Takeovers and Mergers, RS2004/4 (n 30 above).
[90] The Panel on Takeovers and Mergers, PCP 2004/4 (n 4 above) 10.
[91] The Panel on Takeovers and Mergers, PCP 2004/4 (n 4 above) 10–11.
[92] See above.

target shares. In practice, the condition as to acceptances is usually drafted so as to require acceptances of 90 per cent of the shares to which the offer relates. It should be noted that this is only relevant in voluntary offers, since in mandatory offers the acceptance condition must be set to 50 per cent.[93] The reason for choosing 90 per cent is that when this level is reached, it is possible for the bidder to invoke the compulsory sale procedure contained in section 979 of the Companies Act 2006. The problem, however, lies in the fact that the more the bidder wishes for the target shareholders to decline the offer, the more likely it is that the latter will tender their shares due to the adverse change. In that sense, even a 90 per cent acceptance condition may not work. This is exactly what happened with WPP. One day after it posted its offer documents, the 11 September terrorist attacks occurred and Tempus's shareholders accepted the offer, reaching the 90 per cent level of acceptances by the first closing day.[94]

The bidder may be also able to rely on a competition clearance condition for which the materiality test does not apply.[95] However, the bidder must be aware of the fact that rule 13.4(b) expressly provides that the offeror is obliged

> to use all reasonable efforts to satisfy the conditions and pre-conditions to its offer and that, for example, the use by an offeror of a statutory/regulatory condition as a device to cause its offer to lapse in such a manner would be a breach of this obligation and the spirit of the Code.[96]

For example, the bidder is expected 'actively to pursue, in a timely manner, any application made to competition or other regulatory authorities'.[97]

In addition, an offer may be subject to the condition that it must be approved by the acquiring company's shareholders, according to the requirements of the Listing Rules in the case of class 1 transactions.[98] The invocation of a 'class 1 shareholder approval' condition is not subject, in practice, to the application of the materiality test of rule 13.4.[99] This means that, in cases where an adverse change occurs, but the materiality test is not met so as for the bidder to invoke the general MAC clause, and there are no relevant bespoke or negotiated conditions (for which the materiality test could be more easily satisfied),[100] the bidder itself may be able to cause the approval condition not to be satisfied, and subsequently, cause its offer to lapse. In fact, in such situations, it would probably be easier for

93 See above.
94 See Panel Statement 2001/15 (n 10 above).
95 See note 2 on r 13. See also above.
96 See also The Panel on Takeovers and Mergers, PCP 2004/4 (n 4 above) 27.
97 The Panel on Takeovers and Mergers, PCP 2004/4 (n 4 above) 27.
98 See ch 5 above.
99 See above.
100 See above.

the offeror to invoke the approval condition instead of invoking the material adverse change condition. The approval condition, as well as the competition clearance condition, can also be included in a firm intention announcement as acceptable pre-conditions to the posting of the offer.[101]

Invoking the approval condition would normally require the offeror's directors to refrain from recommending the offer to its shareholders. However, this could have a number of implications. As in the case of the invocation of a competition clearance condition, causing an offer to lapse in such way may constitute a breach of the bidder's obligations under the Takeover Code.[102] The relevant duty of offerors and their advisers under the Code was considered by the Panel in relation to the proposed offer by Wm Low and Co PLC for Budgens plc.[103] There, the Panel acknowledged the fact that directors who are inviting their shareholders to vote on the issue of whether or not to support an offer must give their advice in the light of their continuing fiduciary duty to the company, which means that, in the event of a fundamental change of circumstances, it may be necessary for them to change the view which they conscientiously held at the time of the announcement of the offer.[104]

The Panel continued that in its 1974 Annual Report it made clear that where resolutions from the acquiring shareholders are necessary the Panel does not take the view that the offeror's directors are obliged to recommend shareholders to vote in favour of the offer in all circumstances. This is in keeping with the law of fiduciary duties. As discussed in chapter seven above, in the *Rackham v Peek Foods* case, it was held that the offeror's directors do not breach a covenant to use best endeavours to procure the fulfilment of the shareholders' approval condition on an acquisition of shares where to fulfil it would mean giving bad advice.[105] Although the *Rackham v Peek Foods* case should not be taken as an authority that the acquirer's directors are never to be bound by a contract if it is not for the best interests of their shareholders, it is established that under the specific facts, namely, when there is a genuine change in circumstances and it is in the directors' genuine belief that proceeding with the offer is no longer in the best interests of their shareholders, they can change their recommendation.

Accordingly, it seems that in takeovers where the acquiring shareholders' approval is required under the Listing Rules,[106] adverse changes are only required to meet a lesser test, namely that completion of the offer is no longer in the best interests of the acquiring shareholders, and not the strict materiality test of note 2.

101 See above about pre-conditions.
102 See above.
103 Panel Statement 1989/14 (n 45 above).
104 Panel Statement 1989/14 (n 45 above).
105 *Rackham v Peek Foods* [1990] BCLC 895 (HC).
106 See ch 4 above.

However, the Panel emphasised that the bidder's directors must do all they can to avoid a situation arising where they may ultimately recommend their shareholders to vote against an offer which they have announced or posted. Therefore, the company directors and its advisers have to meet a high standard in fulfilling the obligation to exercise care, under rule 13.4.[107] It is also logical to expect that the acquirer's directors must ensure that they do not take any steps to prevent the condition becoming fulfilled. Accordingly, the acquirer must not fail to convene the meeting at which shareholders are to vote, or convene it at a date that is not consistent with the bid timetable.[108] This also derives from the general law of contract, where it is a general principle that when a contract is subject to the satisfaction of a condition a contracting party must not take active steps to prevent the conditions from being satisfied.[109]

Invoking the acceptance condition may prove even more difficult where the acquirer can contractually oblige certain shareholders to vote in favour of the offer. In that case, the Panel may require it to pursue its contractual right. Failure to do so, without the clearance of the Panel,[110] may also lead to an action being brought by the target's shareholders who have already accepted the offer, since a failure of the acquirer's management to exercise its contractual rights may be regarded as an attempt to prevent the occurrence of a certain condition.[111]

An additional shortcoming of the invocation of a class 1 approval condition is that the class 1 criteria are not under the control of the bidder. It may be possible, though, at least in theory, for the bidder to be afforded similar protection in cases where the approval of its shareholders is required under its articles of association. In such cases, any offer, irrespective of the Listing Rules requirements, will be subject to the approval of the acquiring shareholders and, thus, subject to a relevant condition. Scheduling the general meeting as late as possible within the offer timetable will provide the bidder with the option to withdraw its offer in cases of adverse changes, no matter how material these may be considered by the Panel.[112]

[107] Panel Statement 2001/15 (n 10 above).

[108] MA Weinberg and MV Blank, *Takeovers and Mergers*, 2nd edn (London, Sweet & Maxwell, 1989) 3190; Stedman, *Takeovers* (n 48 above) 306.

[109] *Mackay v Dick* (1881) 6 App Cas 251 (HL); *Bournemouth & Boscomble Athletic FC v Manchester United FC, The Times* (22 May 1980).Weinberg and Blank, *Takeovers and Mergers* (n 108 above) 3190; Stedman, *Takeovers* (n 48 above) 306.

[110] If clearance by the Panel is given, then the courts may take the view that the parties to the offer have contracted under a regulatory regime, which specifies what is allowed and what is not, and this regime will be seen as replacing the general law.

[111] See Weinberg and Blank, *Takeovers and Mergers* (n 108 above) 3190; Stedman, *Takeovers* (n 48 above) 306.

[112] See, however, above about General Principle 3.

VI CONCLUSION

The strict interpretation of the materiality test of rule 13.4 and especially the frustration analogy adopted by the Panel, which goes beyond the general law of frustration, left many practitioners wondering whether circumstances could ever arise that could permit the bidder to invoke any condition attached to its offer and justify unilateral withdrawal.[113] Some attacked it as being too strict and only attending to the interests of institutional shareholders.[114] The Executive subsequently undermined the frustration analogy. It insisted, though, on the qualitative characteristics of the requirements of the materiality and objectivity test imposed by the Panel, which were also subsequently upheld and extended in the case of pre-conditions by the Code Committee, and its proposals are reflected in the revised Rules.[115]

The position of the Panel seems to substantially expose the bidder to material adverse changes during the offer. First, the bidder can only withdraw its offer by invoking a relevant protective condition. In doing so, it cannot rely on a change which undermines, from the offeror's perspective, the rationale for having made the offer at the price and on the terms specified. The strict interpretation of 'material significance' in rule 13.4 also means that the bidder cannot effectively rely on standard MAC clauses. The bidder is also not able to make the posting of its offer subject to any MAC-related pre-conditions, apart from regulatory clearance/approval conditions. And even in such cases the exception seeks to ensure that the bidder is bound by its initial offer, its terms and its price. Although the Panel recognises the bidder's substantial exposure to MAC risk, it accepts it as a reasonable trade-off in favour of market certainty.

The only potential option that the Panel's approach provides to a bidder is the invocation of bespoke or negotiated MAC conditions. However, even in these cases the Panel retains the exclusive power to determine the materiality of the events that give rise to the invocation of the relevant conditions. The fact that the bidder ex ante specified what constitutes a significant event for its offer to lapse, or the fact that the conditions attached were also approved by the target's board, are only factors that the Panel will take into consideration. On top of that, drafting very specific clauses carries the risk of otherwise significant events escaping the protecting clauses attached to the offer, and carries the additional drawback of additional legal fees. Furthermore, acquiring the target's consent to negotiated MAC conditions will more likely result in a higher price being offered. Finally, the position of the Panel in relation to normal offer conditions also

[113] Birkett, 'Untying the Knot: Material adverse change clauses' (n 58 above).
[114] Birkett, 'Untying the Knot: Material adverse change clauses' (n 58 above).
[115] The Panel on Takeovers and Mergers, *Practice Statement No 5* (n 62 above).

exposes the bidder to unnecessary uncertainty. It seems that the Panel's purpose to prevent the creation of a false market as a result of a posted and subsequently withdrawn offer could equally be served by not allowing the bidder to post its offer on conditions that are not adequately defined and significant in the first place, rather than prohibiting it from invoking such conditions if the risk that it seeks to cover eventually materialises.

Other than relying on MAC clauses, some comfort could be provided to the bidder in cases where material adverse changes arise as a result of actions by the target's board, since any such attempts can be considered as actions frustrating the offer. Such actions not only require the target's shareholders' approval, but also permit the bidder not to proceed with the offer if it has not been posted yet.

In the face of the difficulties that the bidder may encounter when invoking an MAC condition, it may be more practical to try to invoke one of the acceptance or competition clearance or class 1 approval conditions. However, as seen above, the more the bidder wishes for the target shareholders to decline the offer, the more likely it is that the latter will tender their shares due to the adverse change.[116] In addition, the criteria for the application of conditions related to competition clearance or the class 1 approval are not under the control of the bidder. Hence, at least in theory, the only way that the bidder may be able to have a viable exit in any offer, irrespective of the materiality of the adverse change or whether it included a specific condition or not, is to alter its articles of association so as to require its shareholders' approval of the acquisition, and to schedule such a general meeting as late as possible within the offer timetable.

[116] See, eg the WPP example, Panel Statement 2001/15 (n 10 above).

10

Conclusion

FURTHER TO POPULAR belief that takeovers raise considerable concerns for the target shareholders—and hence takeover regulation mainly addresses such issues—this thesis has identified a number of risks faced by the acquiring company's shareholders, which, although they have received a little, fragmented, consideration in the relevant literature, have not been until now fully examined in their entirety.

The starting point for our enquiry has been that a substantial number of studies, irrespective of the 'window' period or the benchmark used, report that target shareholders earn, on average, significant returns, while the acquiring company's shareholders most commonly suffer losses or receive at best zero or insignificant returns. In the introduction to this book, it was suggested that those puzzling results could be explained in four ways:

— Takeovers are not value-maximising events for the acquirer and they are pursued for other reasons ('agency explanation');
— Takeovers are intended to maximise the value of the acquirer but most of the time the acquirer's managers tend to overpay ('business explanation');
— The acquiring company's shareholders can be adversely affected by the financial structure of the acquisition and the choice of the medium of payment ('financial explanation');
— Takeovers are intended to maximise the combined value of the two firms. However, due to reasons external to the acquirer and especially due to regulatory intervention, it is the target shareholders that receive the benefits of the acquisition ('regulatory explanation').

The analysis that followed showed that the risks identified support the above explanations. The identified risks have been categorised into two main groups: first, risks generated by managerial choices that materialise as acquisitions driven by managerial self-interest (agency explanation), or as overpayment as a result of inadequate due diligence (business explanation), or as dilution or high leverage due to the choice of the medium of payment (financial explanation); and secondly, regulatory or external risks, which fall outside the control sphere of the acquirer's management (regulatory explanation).

I MANAGERIAL DECISIONS IN TAKEOVERS AND THE ACQUIRING SHAREHOLDERS' PROTECTION

Corporate acquisitions, as more acute types of business decisions, were found to involve significant conflicts of interests for the acquiring company's shareholders. Agency problems between the target shareholders and their management have traditionally been addressed at a takeover regulation level, by assuming that the decision to accept an offer lies entirely in the hands of the target shareholders and that the target's board is not allowed to interfere with the shareholders' decision. No interference is achieved through the prohibition of defensive tactics. In contrast, the protection afforded to the acquiring company's shareholders mainly remains a subject of company law and of broader securities regulation for listed companies. This does not mean, though, that the City Code on Takeovers and Mergers ('the Takeover Code') completely overlooks agency problems in the acquiring company. When conflicts of interests are faced by the acquiring directors, rule 3.2 attempts to address the issue by imposing the requirement for competent independent advice on the offer and the communication of such advice to the acquiring company's shareholders. However, the Takeover Code does not go so far as to challenge the authority of the board to approve the transaction.

One reason for such a difference has been found to be the fact that the agency problems faced by the target shareholders represent 'final-period problems'. In contrast, the acquiring company's managers are still subject to the control of their beneficiaries and the control of the market after the acquisition. In addition, English law has followed a broader approach, encompassing disposals and acquisitions by listed companies that do not necessarily constitute a takeover under the Takeover Code. Hence, the class 1 approval requirement of the Listing Rules is based on the size of the transaction relative to the value of the acquiring company and thus, also covers disposals and acquisitions that do not necessarily result in control of the target being obtained. Had it not been for the UK Listing Authority's ('UKLA') Listing Rules, decision rights could have been recognised for the acquiring shareholders at a Takeover Code level. Even then, a rule would have still had some de minimis exemptions to avoid unnecessary regulatory intervention.

However, addressing conflicts of interests is not limited to the class 1 approval requirements. In addition, the acquiring shareholders were also found to be vulnerable to other risks, such as overpayment[1] and risks associated with the financial structure of the takeover, like, for example,

[1] Our analysis revealed that empirical studies support theories like hubris and 'winner's curse'.

high leverage in debt-financed acquisitions, and dilution in share-financed takeovers. Other mechanisms were also identified and it was suggested that any future developments should seek to enhance the effectiveness of judicial intervention, ensure increased shareholders' voice and make the bidder more susceptible to the market of corporate control:

(i) *Addressing the Inefficiencies of Capital Market Pricing*

The price function performed by capital markets can provide an important 'warning signal' against the announced offer and it is an underlying prerequisite for the operation of the market of corporate control. However, it has been argued that the market price function suffers from its own limitations, such as 'noise trading' (especially the operation of risk arbitrage funds), discounted prices, short-termism and information asymmetries.

All the above inefficiencies result in the market function occasionally being a problem for the acquiring shareholders (market volatility), rather than a solution. This is especially the case in share exchange offers, where the value of the bid is directly related to the market value of the bidder. Empirical studies indicate that share exchange offers are accompanied by more market discounts than cash offers. In that respect, regulatory intervention was found to be important, not only in relation to protecting the acquiring shareholders from abnormal market discounts that have nothing to do with the value of the deal proposed, but also in order to ensure the proper operation of the market of corporate control, which requires accurate pricing of the companies involved in a takeover.

(ii) *Ensuring High-quality Information*

High-quality information is an underlying assumption of the effective operation of the market. Disclosure requirements included in both the Takeover Code and the UKLA Rules (Listing, Prospectus, Disclosure and Transparency Rules) and provisions that seek to ensure a high standard of published information (especially pursuant to the implementation of Market Abuse and Transparency Directives) minimise market biases and help towards ensuring an accurate market valuation of the takeover offer. In addition, information provision is an underlying assumption of the effective operation of the class 1 approval requirements.

Increased disclosure requirements externalise the acquiring directors' duty of care, either by operating as a warning signal during the due diligence process, or by serving as an objective account of the directors' due care and diligence. In this context, and in the light of the ongoing debate regarding the need for a statutory liability regime for disclosures, the statutory liability regime for statements and omissions contained in prospectuses could also be a useful starting point.

Finally, it was found that controlling the quality of the information that the directors have to produce during a takeover could serve as a control mechanism over self-interested acquisitions. Accordingly, ex ante quality controls of published information and criminal sanctions, although designed to ensure the proper operation of financial markets, can also minimise the occurrence of value-decreasing or self-interested acquisitions. In this context, the statutory footing of the Takeover Panel provides certain advantages. However the minimum changes have been made to retain the regime in place prior to the implementation of the Directive. Providing the Panel with the power to fine for breaches of the Code, extending the Panel's power to provide financial redress in cases of breaches of takeover rules that relate to published information during a takeover, or introducing a restitution procedure for misstatements made in takeover documents (including defence documents) could also be helpful.

(iii) *Minimising 'Noise Trading'*

It has been suggested that to ensure that the acquirer's price accurately reflects the market's appreciation of the acquisition, noise trading should be minimised. Since risk arbitrage amounts for most of noise trading in takeovers, it has been argued that one way to address this issue is by limiting the operation of short-selling during takeovers. This could decrease market volatility and relieve the acquirer from some of the downward price pressures that it experiences once the offer is announced. Unfortunately, restrictive measures on short-selling are currently favoured neither by the regulator nor by market participants, and thus, it falls upon the institutional shareholders, when the acquirer's price is depressed, to control such an operation by not lending their shares for such purposes.

(iv) *Addressing Market Volatility in Share Exchange Offers*

The operation of some of the price stabilising rules (MAR 2), which already apply to initial public offerings for cash, could also be extended to cover share exchange offers, subject to the approval and monitoring of the Panel. Currently, the rules allow lead managers to support the price of new issues of equities and bonds—and some secondary offers—for a limited period after their issue, by buying them on the secondary market, and create a 'safe harbour', against the offences of market abuse and insider dealing. Of course, due to constrains imposed by European Law, such rules cannot constitute a statutory safe harbour against the offences of market abuse and insider dealing, but they may enjoy the same regime and status as the Takeover Code provisions.

(v) *Enhancing the Acquiring Directors' Standard of Care in Takeovers*

The statutory objectivisation of the duty of care permits the courts to utilise the strict standards of care that the Takeover Code requires from both executive and non-executive directors. This can provide a useful basis for an enhanced standard of review of the acquiring directors. On the basis of the Code's requirements, an enhanced duty of care can thus be formulated that collectively requires the entire board of the acquiring company to operate on a fully-informed basis—which may extend to seeking additional information—to continually monitor the acquisition process and to raise immediately any disagreement or disclose any concerns to the Panel. To that extent the Prospectus Rules' requirement that a director, in order to escape responsibility must, as soon as practicable, give reasonable public notice that the prospectus was published without his knowledge or consent, could also be helpful in the case of takeover documents.

(vi) *Enhancing the Role of Non-executive Directors*

Diligence requirements imposed on non-executive directors may also help to shed light on their role in takeovers, and provide a point of reference for the role in takeovers of the risk-management committees required by the Combined Code on Corporate Governance. In that respect, the standards of care embodied in the Takeover Code—which, due to their regulatory nature, can easily evolve to cover changes in practice—can be a useful tool not only for the judicial review of the transaction, but also for the implementation of effective corporate governance systems in takeovers.

(vii) *Building on the Role of Institutional Shareholders*

In the light of the excessive dispersion of UK public ownership and the documented passivity of private investors, the effectiveness of approval rights was found to rely heavily on institutional investors' activism. Clawbacks and limitations to the delegation of authorisation powers to directors are two areas where institutions have considerable influence. In addition, recent examples indicate that institutional shareholders can make the acquirer's management more susceptible to the market of corporate control. Although empirical studies provide very little evidence on the disciplinary role of the market of corporate control in self-interested or unsuccessful acquisitions in the United Kingdom, there are some high-profile examples where 'bad' acquirer's were eventually disciplined by the market, such as the acquisition of NatWest by the much smaller RBS, which can be mainly attributed to the role that institutions played in supporting the disciplinary takeover. In respect of class 1 transactions, the role of institutional shareholders could be further strengthened by requiring institutions to communicate their views to the rest of the shareholders. Section 1277 of the Companies Act 2006 is a first step in the right direction but it remains to be seen whether and how this power will be exercised. Whether mandatory voting is necessary is part of a more general debate that goes beyond the scope of the present work, and further research is necessary.

(viii) *Structuring the Right Remuneration Policy*

Share incentive schemes may provide the necessary incentives to the bidder's managers to avoid overbidding or value-decreasing diversifying acquisitions. However, there is a fine line between the convergence of interests and entrenchment. Accordingly, a share incentive scheme must take both those parameters into consideration. Recent developments at a statutory level and, more importantly, institutional intervention in the form of relevant guidelines, create a framework that can contribute to the formulation of an effective reward strategy in takeovers.

II REGULATORY INTERVENTION—THE ACQUIRING SHAREHOLDERS' INTERESTS

In cases of risks associated with decisions made by the bidder's management, any legal or regulatory responses could not logically do other than focus on monitoring and limiting managerial discretion. In other words, the shareholders' main concern is that either, when making such decisions, their managers meet high standards in discharging their duties, or that they themselves participate directly or indirectly in the decision-making process. In contrast, risks that fall outside the control sphere of the acquirer's management cannot be effectively addressed by such strategies. Any intervention must be made at a regulatory level and involves a considerable investigation of efficiency and policy issues. In making such policy choices, regulation must inevitably reconcile the interests of the shareholders of the target company, on the one hand, and those of the shareholders of the acquiring company, on the other hand.

Those interests do not necessarily always collide. It was found, for example, that a rule that regulates auctions not only permits the target shareholders to receive the best possible price for their shares, but also protects the bidder from more damaging implicit forms of auction. It has also been argued that horizontal equity rules not only protect minority interests in the target, but also ensure fair distribution of the takeover gains in the bidder. However, it has also been suggested that there are circumstances where takeover regulation imposes costs on the bidder and must make a trade-off between opposing interests. An example of such a situation is the Panel's treatment of MAC clauses, where the legitimate interests of the bidder in seeking protection under general law are superseded by the undesirability of an offer failing contrary to the reasonable expectations of the target shareholders and the market as a whole.

Neither the deprivation of the acquiring shareholders of gains that would result from putting pressure on the target shareholders or the market, nor the goal of high takeover frequency, were found to be sufficient to justify deviations from rules that seek to protect the market and the target shareholders. Similarly, it was suggested that regulation is not expected to normally intervene in the distribution of costs, risks, and benefits between the parties of a transaction. However, law and regulation are expected to intervene in cases where a party in a transaction—in this case the acquiring shareholders—is expected to systematically lose because of involuntary wealth transfers to the other party—in this case the target shareholders (involuntary distribution argument)—or in cases where the bidder's interests are supported by efficiency benefits for the market (efficiency argument). In such cases, regulation should address the interests of the acquiring company shareholders in a more direct and explicit way. For that, the following principles may be useful:

(i) *Achieving Finality in Auction Situations*

Regulation should ensure that auctions are not escalated to an unidentified period of time. This not only permits the bidder to determine in advance various costs that depend on the period for which the offer remains open, such as underwriting facilities, and protects the acquiring shareholders from negative market pressures during the period for which the offer remains open, but also protects the target from a prolonged period of siege. Furthermore, achieving the highest possible premium for the target shareholders should not be the only driving force in determining the method of resolving late auctions. On the contrary, such a method should also take into account other qualitative characteristics of the competitive offers so as to minimise the risk of overpayment. In that respect, the recent changes in the Takeover Code seem to head in the right direction.

(ii) *Protecting the Bidder against Free Riding by Rival Bidders*

Free riding by rival bidders on the identification efforts of the initial bidder affects not only the bidder, but also the market of corporate control, since it is the first bidder who initiates an auction, and consequently, the process of the assets' reallocation to a highest-value use. Therefore, it is necessary to provide the initial bidder with the right incentives. In that respect, regulation should permit the bidder to recoup some of its costs against the risk that it may lose the target in an auction. This can be achieved through permitting undetected stake-building or break fee agreements. Although restrictions should apply to ensure that competition is not deterred, further research should be done to determine whether the current levels of permitted undetected stake-building or break fees provide adequate protection for the initial bidder.

In the light of the new Companies Act, it might have been more appropriate for the break fee agreements to be entirely excluded from the statutory prohibition, since they represent a negotiated arrangement that benefits not only the bidder but also the target shareholders, through an increase in the offer price. This could allow the Panel to raise the current level of permitted break fees. At the same time, any abuse of break fee agreements in order to interfere with the target shareholders' decision can be effectively addressed by the neutrality rules of the Takeover Code and the law of fiduciary duties, as well as the relevant statutory duties imposed by the Companies Act 2006 itself.

On top of that and instead of a more liberal approach on break fees, a further implication derives from the wording of new section 172 of the CA 2006 as to whether the duty to promote the success of the company permits the target's board to provide a break fee when it knows that the bidder, for example, is expected to absorb or even dissolve, or asset-strip the company. It remains to be seen how this new wording is going to be interpreted by the courts, and it is worth exploring in the form of empirical studies how this new approach affects the attitude of the target's board attitude in committing to offers made and providing break fees.

(iii) *Protecting the Bidder against Free Riding by the Target Shareholders*

While there is no justification for pressurising target shareholders as a public policy to increase takeover occurrence, a level of coercion may be necessary in the form of freezing out the remaining shareholders, when the bidder needs to acquire 100 per cent of the target's shares in order for the acquisition synergies to materialise, and in order to discourage adverse incentives to the target's shareholders that may cause a value-adding offer to fail.

(iv) *Addressing Information Asymmetries*

Regulation should ensure the provision of equal information to less welcomed bidders in cases of auctions that involve an MBO or a 'white knight'. This not only permits the bidder to compete on equal terms, but also ensures the passing of the target's assets to their highest possible use, thus promoting allocative efficiency. Similarly, in the case of adverse changes, regulation should ensure that the target is required to disclose all necessary information that permits the bidder to meet the high burden of proof required by the Panel in invoking a protective condition of its offer. Otherwise, the bidder will in practice suffer the involuntary assumption of a risk that was differently allocated in the offer document or according to the Takeover Code.

(v) *Recognising the Importance of Partial Offers*

There may be cases where a partial offer makes more business sense for both the bidder and the target, such as in the case of business partnerships or where the bidder wants to retain a separate listing of the target. In the latter case, the remaining shareholders in the target also benefit, since they retain the protection of the market and the Listing Rules.

(vi) *Addressing Overpayment by Deviating from Horizontal Equality Rules*

While it is a strong argument that the highest price or the mandatory bid rules only apply if the bidder puts himself in such a position by engaging in extra-offer dealings, deviations should be allowed in cases of unusual market volatility, in cases of transfers of de jure control and in cases where the target's minority shareholding consents. In contrast, further strengthening the horizontal equality rules may make the posting of an offer unnecessarily burdensome, in exchange for only relatively small benefits for some of the target's shareholders. One such example is the mandatory share offer requirement. This seeks to ensure that all institutional shareholders are offered shares in the bidder on the same terms, but at the same time it imposes additional costs on the bidder. Overall, the impact of horizontal equality rules on the bidder is an area in which empirical research falls behind in the United Kingdom, when compared with US data. Additional research will shed more light on the effects that the strict equality rules of the Takeover Code have on acquisition returns and takeover frequency in the United Kingdom, as opposed to the more permissive and coercive approach of the Williams Act in the United States.

(vii) *Addressing Material Adverse Change ('MAC') Risk*

Regulation should ensure that the bidder can rely on specific conditions and pre-conditions to which the posting or the fulfilment of its offer is subject. The bidder should also be certain that it can invoke a condition attached to its offer. Hence, any materiality review of any of the conditions attached to the offer should be made before the offer is announced and not at the time that the bidder wishes to invoke the condition in question. This not only permits the bidder to know in advance the MAC risk that it will carry and thus assess the desirability of proceeding with the offer, but also serves no less the goal of the Panel to ensure that no false market will arise in the target's shares.

Overall, our analysis indicated that the Panel has a very protective approach, with its main mandates being the prohibition of the creation of a false market in relation to the takeover bid, and the protection of the reasonable expectations of the target shareholders that they will realise their investment at the highest possible price and on the best possible terms. These mandates proclaim the institutional heritage of the Takeover Code. However, the same mandates provide little help when it comes to addressing the acquiring shareholders' concerns. There are strong arguments that high-premium deals do not necessarily result in efficiency gains and that over-restrictive regulation may result in many otherwise efficient wealth transfers not taking place. The latter is something that even the Panel explicitly recognises. Similarly, false market concerns can be addressed on an 'act and explain' basis by ensuring prompt dissemination of high-quality specific information instead of relying on mandatory rules that prohibit or oblige.

In view of the above, one could argue that the issue of the acquiring shareholders' protection is part of a broader well-documented debate between a policy choice that facilitates acquisitions and transfers of controls, on the one hand, and a policy choice that promotes institutional and private investment in equity markets, on the other hand. The Panel seems to head in the latter direction. However, economic theory provides that the underlying mandate of any regulator who seeks to resolve a difference between two parties on issues that fall under its 'jurisdiction'—especially now that the Panel has a statutory footing and even more so when it operates as an independent judiciary—is to promote allocative efficiency, at a primary level, and to protect any of the parties involved against involuntary wealth transfers, at a secondary level. Those mandates operate over and regardless of any policy choices; and it is at this level that the acquiring shareholders' concerns identified herein were found to merit attention.

Bibliography

Articles and Books

Financial Times (27 January 2003) 'Observer in Davos' 20.

Business Week (1995) 'The Case against Mergers' 123.

Agrawal, A and Knoeber, CR (1996) 'Firm Performance and Mechanisms to Control Agency Problems between Managers and Shareholders' 31(3) *Journal of Financial and Quantitative Analysis* 377.

Agrawal, A, Jaffe, JF and Mandelker, GN (1992) 'The Post-Merger Performance of Acquiring Firms; a Re-Examination of an Anomaly' 47 *Journal of Finance* 1605.

Alcock, A (2003) '*Partco v Wragg*: Liability for Misrepresentation Affecting Secondary Market Dealings' (September) *Journal of Business Law* 515.

Amihud, Y and Lev, B (1981) 'Risk Reduction as a Managerial Motive for Conglomerate Mergers' 12 *Bell Journal of Economics* 605.

Asquith, P, Bruner, R and Mullins, D (1983) 'The Gains to Bidding Firms from Merger' 11 *Journal of Financial Economics* 121.

—— (1986) 'Equity Issues and Offering Dilution' *Journal of Financial Economics* 15.

—— (1987) *Merger Returns and the Form of Financing* (Boston, MA, Harvard Business School).

Ayres, I (1990) 'Analysing Stock Lock-Ups: Do Target Treasury Sales Foreclose or Facilitate Takeover Auctions?' 90 *Columbia Law Review* 682.

Bagnoli, M and Lipman, B (1988) 'Successful Takeovers without Exclusion' 1 *Review of Financial Studies* 89.

Bainbridge, SM (1990) 'Exclusive Merger Agreements and Lock-Ups in Negotiated Corporate Acquisitions' 75 *Minnesota Law Review* 239.

Baker, George P (1987) 'Incentives in Hierarchies: Promotions, Bonuses, and Monitoring' in *Harvard Business School Working Paper* (Boston, MA, Harvard Business School).

Banerjee, A and Owers, J (1992) 'Wealth Reduction in White Knight Bids' (Autumn 1992) *Financial Management* 48.

Baskin, BJ and Miranti, JPJ (1997) *A History of Corporate Finance*, 1st edn (New York, Cambridge University Press).

Baumol, W (1967) *Business Behavior, Value and Growth*, Rev edn (New York, Harcourt, Brace & World).

Beale, HG (ed) (1999) *Chitty on Contracts*, vol 1, 28th edn (London, Sweet & Maxwell).

Bebchuck, L (1982) 'The Case for Facilitating Competing Tender Offers' 95 *Harvard Law Review* 1028.

—— (1982) 'The Case for Facilitating Competing Tender Offers: A Reply and Extension' 35 *Stanford Law Review* 23.

Berger, PG and Ofek, E (1996) 'Bustup Takeovers of Value-Destroying Diversified Firms' 51(4) *The Journal of Finance* 1175.

Berle, AA and Means, GC (1968) *The Modern Corporation and Private Property*, Revised edn (New York, Harcourt, Brace & World Inc).

Bhagat, S, Shleifer, A and Vishny, R (1990) 'Hostile Takeovers in the 1980s: The Return to Corporate Specialization', *Brookings Papers on Economic Activity* 1.

Birkett, K (2002) 'Untying the Knot: Material adverse change clauses' XIII (March) *PLC* 17.

Black, BS (1989) 'Bidder Overpayment' 41 *Stanford Law Review* 597.

Boot, AWA (1992) 'Why Hang on Losers? Divestitures and Takeovers' 47(4) *The Journal of Finance* 1401.

Bradley, C (1990) 'Corporate Control: Markets and Rules' 53 *Modern Law Review* 170.

Bradley, M (1980) 'Inter-firm Tender Offers and the Market for Corporate Control' 35 *Journal of Business* 345.

Bradley, M, Desai, A and Kim, EH (1988) 'Synergistic Gains from Corporate Acquisitions and their Division between the Stockholders of Target and Acquiring Firms' 21 *Journal of Financial Economics* 3.

Brealey, RA and Myers, SC (1999) *Principles of Corporate Finance*, 6th edn (London, McGraw-Hill).

Button, M and Bolton, S (1997) *A Practitioner's Guide to the Stock Exchange Yellow Book* (London, City and Financial Publishing).

Byrd, J and Hickman, K (1992) 'Do Outside Directors Monitor Managers?: Evidence from Tender Offer Bids' 32 *Journal of Financial Economics* 195.

Carney, WJ (2000) *Mergers and Acquisitions: Cases and Materials*, 1st edn (New York, Foundation Press).

Caves, RE (1989) 'Mergers, Takeovers and Economic Efficiency' 7 *International Journal of Industrial Organization* 151.

Charnley, W and Breslin, B (2000) 21 'Break Fees: Financial Assistance and Directors' Duties' *The Company Lawyer 269*

Cheffins, B (1997) *Company Law: Theory, Structure, and Operation* (Oxford/New York, Oxford University Press).

Chowdhry, B and Nanda, V (1993) 'The Strategic Role of Debt in Takeover Contests' 48 *Journal of Finance* 731.

Coates, JC and Subramanian, G (2000) 'A Buy-Side Model of M&A Lockups: Theory and Evidence' 53 *Stanford Law Review* 307.

Coffee, JC (1984) 'Regulating the Market for Corporate Control: A Critical Assessment of The Tender Offer's Role in Corporate Governance' 84 *Columbia Law Review* 1145.

Coffee, JC, Lowenstein, L and Rose-Ackerman, S, (eds), *Knights Raiders & Targets: The Impact of the Hostile Takeover* (Oxford, Oxford University Press, 1988).

—— (1991) 'Liquidity Versus Control: The Institutional Investor as Corporate Monitor' 91 *Columbia Law Review* 1277.

Cornelli, F and Li, DD (1999) *Risk Arbitrage in Takeovers* (Philadelphia, PA, The Rodney L White Center for Financial Research).

Cornu, P and Isakov, D (2000) 'The Deterring Role of the Medium of Payment in Takeover Contests: Theory and Evidence from the UK' 6(4) *European Financial Management* 423.

Cosh, A (2001) 'The Long-Run Performance of Hostile Takeovers: UK Evidence', *ESRC Centre for Business Research, University of Cambridge Working Paper No 215.*

Cosh, A and Hughes, A (2001) 'Managerial Discretion and Takeover Performance', *ESRC Centre For Business Research, University of Cambridge Working Paper No 216.*
Cosh, A, Hughes, A and Singh, A (1980) 'The Causes and Effects of Mergers: An Empirical Investigation for the UK at the Microeconomic Level' in DC Mueller (ed), *The Determinants and Effects of Mergers,* (Cambridge, MA, Oelshlager, Gunn & Hain).
Cosh, A, Hughes, A, Lee, K and Singh, A (1989) 'Institutional Investment, Mergers and the Market for Corporate Control' 7(1) *International Journal of Industrial Organization* 73.
—— (1998) 'Takeovers, Institutional Investment and the Persistence of Profits' in I Begg and S Henry (eds), *Applied Economics and Public Policy* (Cambridge, Cambridge University Press).
Davies, PL (1994) 'Institutional Investors in the United Kingdom' in T Baums, RM Buxbaum and KJ Hopt (eds), *Institutional Investors and Corporate Governance* (Berlin, Walter de Gruyter & Co).
—— (1997) *Gower's Principles of Modern Company Law,* 6th edn (London, Sweet & Maxwell).
—— (2002) 'The Notion of Equality in European Takeovers' in J Payne (ed), *Takeovers in English and German Law* (Oxford, Hart Publishing).
Davies, PL and Hopt, KJ (2004) 'Control Transactions' in R Kraakman, P Davies, H Hansmann, G Hertig, KJ Hopt, H Kanda and EB Rock (eds), *The Anatomy of Corporate Law: A Comparative and Functional Approach* (Oxford, Oxford University Press).
Davis, G, Diekmann, K and Tinsley, C (1994) 'The Decline and Fall of the Conglomerate Firm in the 1980s: The Deinstitutionalization of an Organizational Form' 59(4) *American Sociological Review* 547.
Deakin, S and Slinger, G (1997) 'Hostile Takeovers, Corporate Law and the Theory of the Firm' in S Deakin and A Hughes (eds), *Enterprise and Community: New Directions in Corporate Governance* (Oxford, Blackwell Publishers).
Denis, DJ, Denis, DK and Sarin, A (1997) 'Agency Problems, Equity Ownership, and Corporate Diversification' 52 *Journal of Finance* 135.
Dent, GW (1986) 'Unprofitable Mergers: Toward a Market-Based Legal Response' 80 *Northwestern University Law Review* 777.
Dimson, E and Marsh, P (1986) 'Event Study Methodologies and the Size Effect' 17 *Journal of Financial Economics* 113.
Downes, J and Goodman, JE (1998) *Dictionary of Finance and Investment Terms,* 5th edn (New York, Barron's Educational Series).
Easterbrook, FH and Fischel, DR (1981) 'The Proper Role of a Target's Management in Responding to a Tender Offer' 94 *Harvard Law Review* 1161.
—— (1982) 'Symposium: Auctions and Sunk Costs in Tender Offers' 35 *Stanford Law Review* 1.
—— (1998) *The Economic Structure of Corporate Law,* 4th edn (Cambridge, Harvard University Press).
Eckbo, BE (1985) 'Mergers and the Market Concentration Doctrine: Evidence from the Capital Market' 58 *Journal of Business* 325.
Eckbo, BE, Giammarino, RM and Heinkel, RL (1990) 'Asymmetric Information and the Medium of Exchange in Takeovers: Theory and Tests' 3(4) *Review of Financial Studies* 651.

Faccio, M and Lasfer, M (1999) 'Managerial Ownership, Board Structure and Firm Value: The Uk Evidence', *City University Working Papers.*

Fama, EF and French, KR (1996) 'Multifactor Explanations of Asset Pricing Anomalies' 51 *Journal of Finance* 55.

Fama, EF and Jensen, MC (1983) 'Separation of Ownership and Control' 26 *Journal of Law and Economics* 235.

Ferran, E (1999) 'Creditors' Interests and "Core" Company Law' 20(10) *Company Lawyer* 314.

—— (1999) *Company Law and Corporate Finance* (New York, Oxford University Press).

—— (2004) 'Corporate Transactions and Financial Assistance: Shifting Policy Perceptions but Static Law' 63(1) *Cambridge Law Journal* 225.

Firth, M (1980) 'Takeovers, Shareholders' Return and the Theory of the Firm' (March) *Quarterly Journal of Economics* 225.

Fischel, DR (1978) 'Efficient Capital Market Theory, the Market of Corporate Control and the Regulation of Cash Tender Offers' 57 *Texas Law Review* 43.

Fishman, MJ (1988) 'A Theory of Preemptive Takeover Bidding' 19 *Rand Journal of Economics* 88.

—— (1989) 'Preemptive Bidding and the Role of the Medium of Exchange in Acquisitions' 44(1) *Journal of Finance* 41.

Franks, JR and Harris, RS (1989) 'Shareholder Wealth Effects of Corporate Takeovers: The UK Experience 1955–1985' 23 *Journal of Financial Economics* 81.

Franks, JR and Mayer, C (1996) 'Hostile Takeovers and the Correction of Managerial Failure' 40 *Journal of Financial Economics* 163.

Franks, JR, Harris, RS and Mayer, C (1988) 'Means of Payment in Takeovers: Results for the United Kingdom and the United States' in AJ Auerbach (ed), *Corporate Takeovers: Causes and Consequences* (Chicago/London, University of Chicago Press).

Furmston, M (2001) *Law of Contract*, 14th edn (London, Butterworths).

Galbraith, JK (1967) *The New Industrial State* (New York, Signet Books). .

Giammarino, RM and Heinkel, RL (1986) 'A Model of Dynamic Takeover Behavior' 41 *Journal of Finance* 465.

Gilson, RJ (1981) 'A Structural Approach to Corporations: The Case against Defensive Tactics in Tender Offers' 33 *Stanford Law Review* 819.

—— (1982) 'Seeking Competitive Bids Versus Pure Passivity in Tender Offer Defense' 35 *Stanford Law Review* 51.

Gilson, RJ and Black, BS (1995) *The Law and Finance of Corporate Acquisitions*, 2nd edn (Westbury, NY, The Foundation Press, Inc).

Goergen, M and Renneboog, L (2003) 'Shareholder Wealth Effects of European Domestic and Cross-Border Takeover Bids', *ECGI Working Paper Series in Finance, Working Paper No 08/2003.*

Goode, R (1995) *Commercial Law*, 2nd edn (London, Penguin Books).

Gordon, JN (1994) 'Institutions as Relational Investors: A New Look at Cumulative Voting' 94 *Columbia Law Review* 124.

Gordon, RA (1945) *Business Leadership in the Large Corporation* (Washington, DC, Brookings Institution)

Gregory, A (1997) 'An Examination of the Long Run Performance of UK Acquiring Firms' 24 *Journal of Business Finance and Accounting* 971.

Gregory, A, Matatko, J and Luther, L (1997) 'Ethical Unit Trust Financial Performance: Small Company Effects and Fund Size Effects' 24 *Journal of Business Finance and Accounting* 703.

Grossman, SJ and Hart, OD (1980) 'Takeover Bids, the Free-Rider Problem, and the Theory of the Corporation' 11(1) *The Bell Journal of Economics* 42.

Hackl, J and Testani, R (1988) 'Note, Second Generation State Takeover Statutes and Shareholder Wealth: An Empirical Study' 97 *Yale Law Journal* 1193.

Hansen, RG (1987) 'A Theory for the Choice of Exchange Medium in Mergers and Acquisitions' 60(1) *Journal of Business* 75.

Harris, M and Raviv, A (1988) 'Corporate Control Contests and Capital Structure' 20 *Journal of Financial Economics* 55.

Healy, PM, Palepu, KG and Ruback, RS (1992) 'Does Corporate Performance Improve after Mergers?' 31 *Journal of Financial Economics* 135.

Hechler, MP (1997) 'Towards a More Balanced Treatment of Bidder and Target Shareholders' 1997(2) and (3) *Columbia Business Law Review* 319.

Hermalin, BE and Weisbach, M (1988) 'The Determinants of Board Composition' 19 *RAND Journal of Economics* 589.

Hitt, MA, Harrison, JS and Ireland, RD (2001) *Mergers and Acquisitions, a Guide to Creating Value for Shareholders* (Oxford, Oxford University Press).

Holland, KM and Hodgkinson, L (1994) 'The Pre-Announcement Share Price Behaviour of UK Takeover Targets' 21 *Journal of Business Finance and Accounting* 467.

Huang, Y and Walking, RA (1987) 'Target Abnormal Returns Associated with Acquisition Announcements: Payment, Acquisition Form and Managerial Resistance' 19 *Journal of Financial Economics* 329.

Hubbard, RG and Palia, D (1995) 'Benefits of Control, Managerial Ownership, and Stock Returns of Acquiring Firms' 26(4) *RAND Journal of Economics* 782.

Ireland, P (1999) 'Company Law and the Myth of Shareholder Ownership' 62 *Modern Law Review* 32.

Ireland, P, Grigg-Spall, I and Kelly, D (1987) 'The Conceptual Foundations of Moden Company Law' 14(1) *Journal of Law and Society* 149.

Jarrell, G and Bradley, M (1980) 'The Economic Effects of Federal and State Regulations of Cash Tender Offers' 23 *Journal of Law and Economics* 371.

Jarrell, G, Brickley, J and Netter, J (1988) 'The Market for Corporate Control: The Empirical Evidence since 1980' 2 *Economic Perspectives* 49.

Jennings, R and Mazzeo, M (1991) 'Stock Price Movements around Acquisition Announcements and Management's Response' 64 *Journal of Business* 139.

Jensen, MC (1986) 'Agency Costs of Free Cash Flow, Corporate Finance and Takeovers', Papers and Proceedings of the Ninety-Eighth Annual Meeting of the American Economic Association 76(2) *American Economic Review*) 323.

—— (1988) 'The Takeover Controversy: Analysis and Evidence' in JC Coffee, L Lowenstein and S Rose-Ackerman (eds), *Knights Raiders & Targets: The Impact of the Hostile Takeover* (New York, Oxford University Press).

Jensen, MC and Meckling, WH (1976) 'Theory of the Firm: Managerial Behavior, Agency Costs and Ownership Structure' 3 *Journal of Financial Economics* 305.

Jensen, MC and Ruback, RS (1983) 'The Market for Corporate Control' 11 *Journal of Financial Economics* 5.

Kahan, M and Klausner, M (1996) 'Lockups and the Market of Corporate Control' 48 *Stanford Law Review* 1539.

Kaplan, S and Weisbach, M (1992) 'The Success of Acquisitions: Evidence from Divestitures' 47 *Journal of Finance* 107.

Karpoff, J and Malatesta, P 1989 'The Wealth Effects of Second Generation Takeover Legislation' 25 *Journal of Financial Economics* 291.

Kay, J and Silbestron, A (1995) 'Corporate Governance' in F Patfield (ed), *National Institute Economic Review* (London / The Hague / Boston, Kluwer Law International).

Kennedy, VA and Limmack, RJ (1996) 'Takeover Activity, CEO Turnover, and the Market for Corporate Control' 23(2) *Journal of Business Finance and Accounting* 267.

Khorana A. & Zenner M., (1998) 'Executive Compensation of Large Acquirors in the 1980s' 4 *Journal of Corporate Finance 209*

Kraakman, R (1988) 'Taking Discounts Seriously: The Implications of "Discounted" Share Prices as an Acquisition Motive' 88 *Columbia Law Review* 891.

Kumar, M (1984) *Growth, Acquisitions and Investment* (Cambridge, Cambridge University Press).

Lang, L, Stulz, R and Walking, RA (1989) 'Managerial Performance, Tobin's Q and the Gains from Successful Tender Offers' 24 *Journal of Financial Economics* 137.

Levive, P and Aaronovitch, S (1981) 'The Financial Characteristics of Firms and Theories of Merger Activity' 30 *Journal of Industrial Economics* 149.

Levy, H and Sarnat, M (1990) *Capital Investment and Financial Decisions* (London, Prentice Hall).

Lewellen, WG, Loderer, C and Rosenfield, A (1985) 'Merger Decisions and Executive Stock Ownership in Acquiring Firms' 7 *Journal of Accounting and Economics* 209.

Limmack, RJ (1991) 'Corporate Mergers and Shareholder Wealth Effects: 1977–1986' (Summer) *Accounting and Business Research* 239.

Lloyd, W, Hand, J and Modani, N (1987) 'The Effect of the Degree of Ownership Control on Firm Diversification, Market Value and Merger Activity' 15 *Journal of Business Research* 303.

Loderer, C and Martin, KJ (1990) 'Corporate Acquisitions by Listed Firms: The Experience of a Comprehensive Sample' (Winter) *Financial Management* 17.

Manne, H (1965) 'Mergers and the Market for Corporate Control' 73 *Journal of Political Economy* 110.

Maris, R (1964) *The Economic Theory of Managerial Capitalism* (London, Macmillan).

Maris, R and Mueller, DC (1980) 'The Corporation Competition and the Invisible Hand' 18 *Economic Literature* 32.

Martin, KJ (1996) 'The Method of Payment in Corporate Acquisitions, Investment Opportunities, and Management Ownership' 51 *Journal of Finance* 1227.

Martin, R (2004) 'Guinness Peat Group Partial Offer. Breaking the Mould' 15(4) *PLC* 10.

Mason, RH and Goudzwaard, M (1976) 'Performance of Conglomerate Firms: A Portfolio Approach.' 31 *Journal of Finance* 39.

Masulis, R and Korwar, AN (1986) 'Seasoned Equity Offerings: An Empirical Investigation' *Journal of Financial Economics* 15.

McConnell, J and Servaes, H (1990) 'Additional Evidence on Equity Ownership and Corporate Value' 27 *Journal of Financial Economics* 595.

McCormack, G (1997) 'Institutional Shareholders and the Promotion of Good Corporate Governance' in BA Rider (ed), *The Realm of Company Law*, London, Kluwer Law International).

Meeks, G (1977) *Disappointing Marriage: A Study of the Gains from Mergers* (Cambridge, Cambridge University Press).

Mikkelson, WH and Partch, MM (1986) 'The Valuation Effects of Security Offerings and the Issuance Process' *Journal of Financial Economics* 15.

Miles, D (1995) 'Testing for Short-Termism in the UK Stock Market' 103 *Economic Journal* 1379.

Mitchell, ML and Lehn, K (1990) 'Do Bad Bidders Become Good Targets?' 98(2) *Journal of Political Economy* 372.

Morck, R, Shleifer, A and Vishny, R (1990) 'Do Managerial Objectives Drive Bad Acquisitions' 45 *Journal of Finance* 31.

Murphy, K (1985) 'Corporate Performance and Managerial Remuneration: An Empirical Analysis' 7 *Journal of Accounting and Economics* 11.

Nolan, RC (1997) 'The Proper Purpose Doctrine and Company Directors' in BA Rider (ed), *The Realm of Company Law* (London, Kluwer Law International).

Palepu, KG (1986) 'Predicting Takeover Targets: A Methodological and Empirical Analysis' *Journal of Accounting and Economics* 8: 3.

Parkinson, JE (1993) *Corporate Power and Responsibility: Issues in the Theory of Company Law* (Oxford, Clarendon Press).

Pearson, C (2004) 'Practice Note: Break Fees', *www.practicallaw.com/a29103.*

P'ng, IPL (1987) 'Facilitation of Competing Bids and the Price of a Takeover Target' *Business Economics Working Paper No 87-10.*

Porter, M (1987) 'From Competitive Advantage to Corporate Strategy', *Harvard Business Review* 43.

Powell, R (1997) 'Modelling Takeover Likelihood' 24(7) and 24(8) *Journal of Business Finance and Accounting* 1009.

Rappaport, A and Sirower, ML (2001) 'Stock or Cash? The Trade-Offs for Buyers and Sellers in Mergers and Acquisitions' *Harvard Business Review on Mergers and Acquistions* (Boston, MA, Harvard Business School Press).

Ravenscraft, D and Scherer, FM (1987) *Mergers, Sell-Offs & Economic Efficiency* (Washington, DC Brookings Institution).

Romano, R (1987) 'The Political Economy of Takeover Statutes' 111 *Virginia Law Review* 111.

—— (1992) 'A Guide to Takeovers' in KJ Hopt and E Wymeersch (eds), *European Takeovers: Law and Practice* (London, Butterworths).

—— (1993) 'Public Pension Fund Activism in Corporate Governance Reconsidered' 93 *Columbia Law Review* 795.

Salter, M and Weinhold, W (1979) *Diversification through Acquisition* (New York, The Free Press, Macmillan, Inc).

Scanlon, K, Trifts, J and Pettway, R 1989 'Impacts of Relative Size and Industrial Relatedness on Returns to Shareholders of Acquiring Firms' 12 *Journal of Financial Research* 103.

Schipper, K and Thompson, R (1983) 'The Impact of Merger-Related Regulations on the Shareholders of Acquiring Firms.' 21 *Journal of Accounting Research* 184.

Schumann, L (1988) 'State Regulation of Takeovers and Shareholder Wealth: The Case of New York's 1985 Takeover Statutes' 19 *Rand Journal of Economics* 557.

Schwert, WG (1996) 'Markup Pricing in Mergers and Acquisitions' 41 *Journal of Financial Economics* 153.
Sealy, L (1989) 'Bona Fides and Proper Purposes in Corporate Decisions' 15 *Monash University Law Review* 265.
Sealy, L (1996) *Cases & Materials on Company Law*, 6th edn (London, Butterworths).
Servaes, H (1991) 'Tobin's Q and the Gains from Takeovers' 46 *Journal of Finance* 409.
Short, H and Keasey, K (1999) 'Managerial Ownership and the Performance of Firms: Evidence from the UK' 5 *Journal of Corporate Finance* 79.
Sicherman, N and Pettway, R (1987) 'Acquisitions of Divested Assets and Shareholders' Wealth' 42 *Journal of Finance* 1261.
Smiley, R (1975) 'The Effect of the Williams Amendment and Other Factors on Transaction Costs in Tender Offers' 3 *Industrial Organization Review* 138.
Smith, CW (1997) 'Raising Capital: Theory and Evidence' in JM Stern and DH Chew (eds), *The Revolution of Corporate Finance*, 3rd edn (Oxford, Blackwell Publishers).
Smith, P and Saigol, L (2003) 'Share Drop Cuts Morrison Offer to £2.2bn' *Financial Times* (1 February 2003).
Sneirson, JF (2002) 'Merger Agreements, Termination Fees, and the Contract-Corporate Tension.' *Columbia Business Law Review* 573.
Stallworthy, M (1991) 'Company Law: Negligence: Directors' and Financial Advisers' Representations—Statements Influencing Conduct of Bidder' 6(3) *Journal of International Banking Law* 50.
Stedman, G (1993) *Takeovers* (London, Longman).
Stulz, R (1988) 'Managerial Control of Voting Rights: Financial Policies and the Market for Corporate Control' 20 *Journal of Financial Economics* 25.
Sudarsanam, PS (1995) *The Essence of Mergers and Acquisitions* (London, Prentice Hall).
Sudarsanam, PS, Holl, P and Salami, A (1996) 'Shareholder Wealth Gains in Mergers: Effect of Synergy and Ownership Structure.' 23 *Journal of Business Finance and Accounting* 673.
Thomas, LG, (ed) *The Economics of Strategic Planning: Essays in Honor of Joel Dean* (Lexington MA, Lexington Books, 1997)
Travlos, NG (1987) 'Corporate Takeover Bids, Methods of Payment, and Bidding Firms' Stock Returns' 42(4) *Journal of Finance* 943.
Varaiya, N (1988) 'The "Winner's Curse" Hypothesis and Corporate Takeovers' 9(3) *Managerial and Decision Economics* 209.
Varaiya, N and Ferris, K (1987) 'Overpayment in Corporate Takeovers: The Winner's Curse' (May–June) *Financial Analysts' Journal* 64.
Wansley, JW, Lane, WR and Yang, HC (1987) 'Gains to Bidder Firms in Cash and Securities Transactions' 22 *The Financial Review* 403.
Watts, P (2005) 'Case Comment, Authority and Mismotivation 121 *Law Quarterly Review* 4.
Weinberg, MA and Blank, MV (1989) *Takeovers and Mergers*, 2nd edn (London, Sweet & Maxwell).
Welles, C (1981) 'Inside the Arbitrage Game' (August) *Institutional Investor* 41.
Weston, JF and Johnson, BA (1999) 'What It Takes for a Deal to Win Stock Market Approval' 34 *Mergers and Acquisitions* 43.

Weston, JF, Siu, JA and Johnson, BA (2001) *Takeovers, Restructuring & Corporate Governance*, 3rd edn (London, Prentice Hall).

Williamson, O (1981) 'The Modern Corporation: Origins, Evolution, Attributes' 19 *Journal of Economic Literature* 1537.

—— (1964) *The Economics of Discretionary Behavior: Managerial Objectives in a Theory of the Firm* (Prentice-Hall, Englewoods Cliffs, NJ).

—— (1970) *Corporate Control and Business Behavior: An Inquiry into the Effects of Organization Form on Enterprise Behavior* (New Jersey, Prentice-Hall).

Winkler, RL and Brooks, DG (1980) 'Competitive Bidding with Dependent Value Estimates' 28(3) *Operations Research* 603.

Wippell, M and Knighton, G (2004) 'Inducement Fees: A US Import Takes Root' 15(3) *PLC* 31.

You, V, Caves, RE, Smith, M and Henry, J (1986) 'Mergers and Bidders' Wealth: Managerial and Strategic Factors' in LG Thomas (ed), *The Economics of Strategic Planning: Essays in Honor of Joel Dean* (Lexington MA, Lexington Books).

Reports, Statements, Guidelines and Consultation Papers

Association of British Insurers (1995) *Directors' Power to allot shares.*

Association of British Iinsurers (1993) *Shareholders' Pre-emption Rights and Vendor Placings.*

Association of British Insurers (2002) *Executive Remuneration – Principles.*

Association of British Insurers (2002) *Guidelines for Share Incentive Schemes.*

Association of British Insurers (2002) *Guidelines for the Structure of Remuneration.*

Association of British Insurers (2006) *Executive Remuneration—ABI Guidelines on Policies and Practices.*

ABI, NAPF (2002) *Best Practice on Executive Contracts and Severance—a Joint Statement by the Association of British Insurers and the National Association of Pension Funds.*

Association of Unit Trusts and Investment Funds (2001) *Code of Good Practice; Institutional Investors and Corporate Governance.*

Bank Of England Quarterly Bulletin (1987) *Pre-Emption Rights* 545.

Cadbury Committee (1992) *The Financial Aspects of Corporate Governance (Report of the Cadbury Committee).*

CESR (2005) *Final Technical Advice on Possible Implementing Measures of the Transparency Directive.*

Financial Services Authority (2002) *FSA Discussion Paper 17: Short Selling.*

Financial Services Authority (2002) *Discussion Paper 14: Review of the Listing Regime.*

Financial Services Authority (2003) *Feedback on DP17.*

Financial Services Authority (2003) *FS14: Review of The listing Regime; Feedback on DP14.*

Institutional Shareholders' Committee (2002) *The Responsibilities of Institutional Shareholders and Agents—Statement of Principles*: 1.

Institutional Shareholders' Committee (2006) *The Responsibilities of Institutional Shareholders and Agents - Statement of Principles.*

Investment Management Association (2001) *The Terms for Discretionary Fund Management.*

Law Commission (1996) *Shareholder Remedies: A Consultation Paper.*

NAPF (2002) *A Modern Regulatory Framework for Company Law in Europe: A Consultative Document of the High Level Group of Company Law Experts: Response by the National Association of Pension Funds.*

NAPF (2006) *National Association of Pension Funds Corporate Governance Policy.*

The Company Law Review Steering Group (2001) *Modern Company Law for a Competitive Economy: Final Report.*

The Panel on Takeovers and Mergers (1974) *Panel Statement 1974/02.*

The Panel on Takeovers and Mergers (1974) *Panel Statement 1974/07.*

The Panel on Takeovers and Mergers (2001) PCP 3: *Consultation Paper Issued by the Code Committee of the Panel: Equality of Information to Competing Offerors. Revision Proposals Relating to Rule 20.2 of the Takeover Code.*

The Panel on takeovers and Mergers (2001) RS3: *Equality of Information to Competing Offerors: Statement by the Panel Following the External Consultation Process on PCP 3.*

The Panel on Takeovers and Mergers (2001) PCP 6. *Consultation Paper Issued by the Code Committee of the Panel on 16 October 2001: Purchases by the Offeror of Shares in the Offeree in Exchange for Securities. Revision Proposals Relating to Rule 11 of the Takeover Code.*

The Panel on Takeovers and Mergers (2002) PCP 10: *Consultation Paper Issued by the Code Committee of the Panel: Shareholder Activism and Acting in Concert; Revision Proposals Relating to Note 2 on Rule 9.1 of the Takeover Code.*

The Panel on Takeovers and Mergers (2002) PCP 11: *Consultation Paper Issued by the Code Committee of the Panel: Dual Listed Company Transactions and Frustrating Action. Revision Proposals Relating to the Definition of an Offer and Rule 21.2 of the Takeover Code.*

The Panel on Takeovers and Mergers (2002) RS11: *Dual Listed Company Transactions and Frustrating Action. Statement by the Code Committee of the Panel Following the External Consultation Process on PCP 11.*

The Panel on Takeovers and Mergers (2002) RS10: *Shareholder Activism and Acting in Concert. Statement by the Code Committee of the Panel Following the External Consultation Process on PCP 10.*

The Panel on Takeovers and Mergers (2003) PCP 7: *Consultation Paper Issued by the Code Committee of the Panel: Resolution of Competitive Situations. Revision Proposals Relating to Rules 31.6, 32 and 35 of the Takeover Code.*

The Panel on Takeovers and Mergers (2004) PCP 2004/2: *Consultation Paper: Possible Offer Announcements. Revision Proposals Relating to Rule 2.4 of the Takeover Code.*

The Panel on Takeovers and Mergers (2004) PCP 2004/1: *Consultation Paper: 'Put up or Shut up' and No Intention to Bid Statements. Revision Proposals Relating to Rules 2.4, 2.8 and 35.1 of the Takeover Code.*

The Panel on Takeovers and Mergers (2004) PCP 2004/4: *Consultation Paper Issued by the Code Committee of the Panel: Conditions and Pre-conditions. Revision Proposals Relating to Rules 2.4, 2.5, 2.7, 9.3, 13, 23, 24.6, 34, 35.1 and 38.3 of the Takeover Code.*

The Panel on Takeovers and Mergers (2004) *Practice Statement No 3: Rule 20.2—Controlled Auctions.*

The Panel on Takeovers and Mergers (20040 *Practice Statement No 4: Rule 21.2, Inducement Fees.*

The Panel on Takeovers and Mergers (2004) *Practice Statement No 5: Note 2 on Rule 13—Invocation of Conditions.*
The Panel on Takeovers and Mergers (2005) RS 2004/4: *Conditions and Pre-Conditions, Statement by the Code Committee of The Panel following the external consultation process on PCP 2004/4.*
The Panel on Takeovers and Mergers (2005) *Practice Statement No 10: Cash Offers Financed by the Issue of Offeror Securities.*
The Panel on Takeovers and Mergers (2005) *Practice Statement No 11: Working Capital Requirements in Cash and Securities Exchange Offers.*
The Panel on Takeovers and Mergers (2005) *Practice Statement No 15: Inducement Fees, Agreements between the Offeror and the Offeree Company etc.*
The Pre-emption Group (2006) *Displaying pre-emption rights—A statement of principles.*

Index